*This book is dedicated to my family: Elizabeth, Erin, Nana and Papa, Grandma and Grandpa. I love you all very much!*

# Contents at a Glance

# Contents

## Chapter 9: Web Applications ............................215

## Chapter 10: Web Services ............................247

## *Part 4: Mobile .NET*                            *271*

## Chapter 11: Mobile Web Services ......................273

## Chapter 12: The Mobile Internet Toolkit ...........303

## Chapter 13: Extending the MIT .........................339

# Foreword

MY FIRST INTERACTION WITH THE author occurred shortly before his speech at the Wireless DevCon 2000 conference in San Jose. He had been one of a select few authors for whom, months prior to its public unveiling, we had "sneak previewed" our new .NET technologies. His question to me was quite simple: "What do you have in .NET to help the mobile developer?"

As you will see for yourself in the remainder of this book, there is *a lot* in .NET to help developers—mobile and otherwise! By choosing the eXtensible Markup Language (XML) as our foundation in creating the .NET platform, we have harnessed the power of one of the most important and *open* industry standards in the world today. Visual Studio .NET uses this power to help developers of all ability levels create, deploy, and maintain applications that can interact with virtually any kind of remote client.

Specifically, there are three kinds of mobile software under .NET:

- Mobile Web Services

- Mobile Web Applications

- Mobile Device Applications

In this book, Derek Ferguson does an excellent job of explaining how to build, deploy, and utilize all three of these. By the time you are done reading, you should be able to invoke .NET Web Services from virtually any kind of mobile device. Similarly, you should be able to leverage my own team's technology—the Mobile Internet Toolkit—in creating Web applications for access by the most diverse suite of devices imaginable.

At the end of this book, we have allowed Derek to bring you some of the first coverage of our newest .NET technology for mobile developers: the .NET Compact Frameworks (.NETcf). .NETcf brings the power of .NET directly to devices in the form of two distinct profiles. One of these profiles is intended for use on "Talisker" devices, and the other is cross-platform.

By the time you have finished reading this book, I think you will agree that creating mobile software with .NET allows you to build applications that are many times more powerful than their predecessors. Thanks to this book, you will be able to see exactly how quick and easy creating mobile .NET software really can be!

*David Kurlander*
*Product Unit Manager*
*Microsoft Adaptive UI/Mobile Internet Toolkit Team*

# Acknowledgments

As I LOOK AT THE TWO PAGES of acknowledgments that I have accumulated over the last six months spent writing this book, I can only say, "What a long, strange trip it has been!" Thank you all for your efforts on my behalf—it is now time for my vacation!

### Microsoft-ies

Christopher Flores, Andres Sanabria, Mike D. Smith, Steven Lees, John Montgomery, David Kurlander, Rob Howard, Susan Chory, Petri Oksanen, Seth Demsy, Chris Stirrat, Oshomo Momoh, Kei Amos, Ivo Salmre, Craig Neable, and Nishan Jebanasam—jeesh, there sure are a lot of you folks, aren't there?

### Apress-ites

Gary Cornell for agreeing that my Mobile .NET seminars would make a good book.

Grace Wong, Karen Watterson, Ami Knox, Martin V. Minner, Tory McLearn, and Sofia Marchant for making my book good.

Stephanie Rodriguez for helping the world to realize that it is good.

### Open-Source Allies

Simon Fell of www.pocketsoap.com for speeding up his Beta 1.1 deadline especially for me. (The free book is in the mail, I swear!)

Everyone at Enhydra (www.enhydra.org) for creating kXML and kSOAP, and particularly Renaud Tognelli for creating the CashConv sample upon which much of my J2ME sample code in the Web Services sections are based.

### "The Publicity Department"

Stewart Quealy of Internet.com and Alton Finley of Camelot Communications for inviting me to the Wireless DevCon that started it all!

Neil Bauman of Geek Cruises (www.geekcruises.com) for trying to arrange Wireless Whirl 2003.

Jeremy Geelan for the invitation to Wireless Edge 2002.

Matthew Ferris of the Chicago Wireless Developers Users Group for hosting the very first post-authoring Mobile .NET presentation!

Ian Tang of the Software Productivity Institute in Vancouver, British Columbia, for inviting me to teach in one of the most wonderful places on Earth.

Ken Coar and Lars Eilebrecht of the ApacheCon organization for inviting me to speak at ApacheCon 2001 in Dublin, Ireland (one of the most wonderful places on Earth).

Taz Kuwano and Trisha Henshaw of Sun Microsystems for all your support at JavaOne 2001 this year (bet you didn't ever expect to see your names in a .NET book, did you?!).

Sara Faatz at Brinkster for going way above and beyond the call of duty in helping to promote my Mobile .NET articles.

### Magazines and Such

Michael Domingo of *Microsoft Certified Professional* magazine for printing the first excerpt from this book.

Robert Diamond and Gail Schultz of Sys-Con Media for printing the second and third excerpts from this book, respectively.

Steve Anglin of ONJava.com—any idea when my article is going to see the light of day?

### Expand Beyond Corp.

Ari Kaplan*, CEO, for envisioning a world where technology professionals are no longer chained to their desks.

Dr. Tal Schwartz, CFO, for convincing Ari that what he had envisioned was actually a whole new industry.

Stephanie Taddei** and Peter Kim in Technical Support for making sure that reality always exceeds even our most optimistic customers' expectations.

Rachel Greene, V.P. of Marketing, and Gayle Glickman*, Director of Public Relations for telling the world about our vision.

Dave Claussen and Matt Rosauer of Confirmative Technologies (www.confirmative.com) for making the initial dream into a reality.

Tom Emmons and John Bekas of Confirmative Technologies for continuing to build on Matt and Dave's foundation.

Lyle Wells*, Kevin Doyle, and Joe Redd in Sales for being pretty decent people to work with—as far as sales people go. :-)

Dr. Margaret LeClair, COO, and Maureen Gallagher, for doing all of the unpleasant jobs like accounting—ick!

Sundar Bandepalli, David Cesareo, and Tahir Chaudhry, a.k.a. "the new guys."

* Extra kudos for sneaking me down from my legitimate seats at the back of the Yes concert to a much better vantage point in the 10th row.

** Extra special mega-kudos for breaking up a lengthy technical session early so that I could get to go to the Yes concert in the first place.

### *Literary Allies*

Sandra Jun, my technical editor, for forcing me to actually make sense most of the time.

Chris Van Buren, my agent, for dealing with the business side of things so I can just focus on writing.

### *And Lastly, Musical Inspiration for This Book Courtesy of. . .*

Black Sabbath, Yes, Cake, Procol Harum, the Soggy Bottom Boys, Chef of the Future, Kansas, Jethro Tull, and (of course) Marillion.

*Part One*

# The .NET Devices

# CHAPTER 1

# Mobility and Microsoft

## And Where the Two Shall Meet . . .

IN THIS CHAPTER, YOU'LL BEGIN your journey towards the development of mobile applications using Microsoft's .NET technology. But before you begin, it seems reasonable to answer a few questions you may have about the history behind these technologies. This chapter constitutes a brief background on the evolution of both mobile technologies and Microsoft. By the time you are finished reading, you should understand why Microsoft's latest technology initiative, .NET, is a natural choice for the development of many mobile applications.

## A Brief History of Mobility

For as long as there have been computers, the tendency over time has been to pack more and more computing power into smaller and smaller devices. Similarly, the trend throughout the past century has been towards allowing people to stay connected in more and more ways and in increasingly remote situations.

Consider, for example, the progress that has been made in radio technology over the past 100 years. Originally, radios were large consoles that were no more mobile than the average armchair. The development of transistors allowed the creation of radios that could be carried in the palm of the hand. Nowadays, few people would be surprised, much less impressed, to see a radio built into a device the size of the average wristwatch.

In this section, you will learn a little about the evolution of connectivity devices that have been traditionally aimed at the business user. It is from this family of machines that the current rage in Internet devices has emerged. It is this family for which you will be learning to develop mobile .NET applications.

### Pagers

Pagers are in many ways the great-grandfathers of all mobile information devices. In their simplest form, they were originally conceived to be used in the following manner:

1. Person wishing to establish contact dials a specific telephone number.

2. Paging system answers the telephone.

3. Person wishing to establish contact enters a callback number and hangs up.

4. Paging system transmits callback number to pager.

5. Pager receives the callback number and alerts the pager owner to its presence.

6. Pager's owner finds a telephone and dials the callback number

All things considered, six steps seems like a lot of effort to go through simply to put two people in touch with one another. As you might imagine, this system was developed to account for a number of limitations in the underlying technology rather than for its innate convenience. Chief amongst these limitations were insufficient bandwidth and data formats.

## Communications Link

The wireless networks that service most pagers are typically limited to transmitting less than 10 kilobits per second (Kbps)of data. By way of comparison, the typical modem that is currently used to connect most personal computers to the Internet can send and receive data at up to 56 Kbps. This means that it would take more than five times as long to send data to a pager as to download the same information off the Internet using the typical dial-up modem.

 **NOTE** *The most common network system for pager communications in the United States is known as* Mobitex.

Besides the obvious slowness of this system, there is a potentially more serious limitation in its support for bidirectional communications. In short, most paging devices are only capable of receiving data—not transmitting it. This saves on both size and cost of the device because a radio transmitter does not need to be included in the body of the device, only a receiver. Figure 1-1 illustrates the one-way nature of data transmission for pagers.

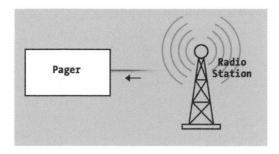

*Figure 1-1. Signal travelling from station to pager*

## Data Specifications

There are many kinds of information that one might want to send across a wireless network, a few examples of which are included here:

- Text

- Still images

- Sound

- Video

Of all of these, pagers have historically only supported the first item, text. There are a few reasons why this is so. To begin with, text is one of the easiest data types to render onto a display. In the Roman alphabet, for example, there are only 26 characters. This means that for each location on the device's screen, a maximum of 26 different symbols need to be capable of display. Given that the typical message may only consist of 10 to 20 words and that scrolling to read a message is completely acceptable, text is technologically simple.

Contrast this to the situation with images. Even a small image can be expected to have a size in excess of $100 \times 100$ pixels. This means a total of 10,000 distinct points on the display's device that need to be capable of generating output. Also, scrolling to see parts of an image is not nearly as acceptable as it is for text data.

## Cellular Phones

Cellular phones represented the first great breakthrough in true mobile information exchange, rather than merely distribution. For the first time, you could get in touch with someone no matter where they were or what they were doing. More importantly, that person could get back to you in an immediate fashion.

## Communications Link

The technological innovation that makes cellular communication possible is the use of so-called cell architecture. Under cell architecture, a single mobile device may be serviced by many different transmitter stations as it moves from point A to point B. This is important for several reasons:

- Building single (ground-based) transmitters large enough to service entire cities would be extremely expensive.

- Building single (ground-based) transmitters large enough to service areas larger than cities would be virtually impossible.

- Users may often cross the bounds between different transmitters while still communicating.

To resolve the third situation described in the preceding list, an intelligence cell-switching technology is required. This system is capable of detecting when a device is about to move out-of-range of the station by which it is currently being serviced and seamlessly switch it to the station for its new location without any loss in connectivity. Figure 1-2 illustrates this system in action.

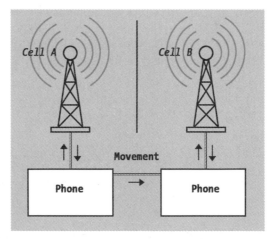

*Figure 1-2. Signal travelling from phone to different stations*

## Data Specifications

The networking infrastructure underlying most cellular networks is equally suited for transmitting either data or voice transmissions. Unfortunately, many carriers made assumptions early in their implementations that have since made it difficult for them to support anything other than voice communications.

The typical transmission rate for cellular networks is approximately 20 Kbps. To continue the comparison from the previous section, this means that cellular data transmissions can typically be expected to occur at about half the speed of the average dial-up modem connection.

## Coverage

More than any other system, the coverage afforded by cellular networks varies greatly from one wireless carrier to the next. This is due to cellular's reliance on small, ground-based cells—each serviced by its own transmission station. If you happen to be in an area that is not serviced by a station, then you will find yourself without cellular connectivity.

## Setup

The purchase and setup of cellular phones is an area in which the history of devices has taken two vastly different turns. One approach is used inside the United States. Another is used in Europe, most of Asia, and parts of Africa.

In the American approach, cellular devices are resold directly by the wireless carriers. These carriers program the phones for use with their own service before they are sold to consumers. The argument in favor of this approach is that it is easier for the consumers—everything is done for them by their carrier. Some arguments against this approach:

- It encourages the use of nonstandard hardware.

- It makes it harder to switch providers.

- It makes it harder to buy phones nonconventionally (via the Internet, for example).

An alternative to this approach relies on what is known as the SIM card widely used in Europe, Africa, and Asia. For more information on this, see "Setup" in the following section.

## Mobile Devices

The emergence of what people currently refer to as mobile devices can be seen as the culmination of the past two decades' work on mobile devices coupled with the explosive growth of the Internet phenomenon. A truly mobile device is clearly distinguishable from its mobile forebears in every respect.

### Communications Link

Bandwidth is a central focus for many of the current wireless carriers across the globe. It seems that the more data people have available to them, the more they want—and the faster they want it. Towards this end, a number of initiatives are underway.

A technology known as Richochet is the closest to availability at the time of writing. Under this system, data rates as high as 128 Kbps are possible. This is over twice as fast as the typical telephone modem connection to the Internet. It is, in fact, more comparable to the connection speeds attained via a two-channel ISDN connection, only without the wires!

 **NOTE**   *To show just how dynamic and ever-changing the world of wireless Internet is, Richochet has been completely abandoned in the United States since the preceding paragraph was written.  It proved to be entirely too costly to ever achieve mass appeal.*

### Data Specifications

As the wireless Internet increases in its popularity, more and more carriers are announcing a data-based service of some sort. In many cases, this has required the carriers to invest in some degree of re-architecting their existing networks. Whatever the case, the true mobile device is capable of sending and receiving data on equal levels, as shown in Figure 1-3.

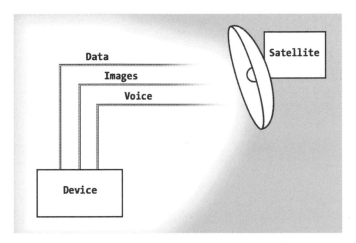

*Figure 1-3. All kinds of transmissions going in all directions*

As processing power becomes cheaper and smaller, the barriers to the types of data that can be rendered by devices will fall with it. At the time of writing, sufficient bandwidth exists in most areas to support the streaming of video directly to cell phones, for example. However, most cell phones currently lack the processing power to support this.

True mobile Internet devices must therefore feature greater processing power than is currently typical.

## Coverage

In addition to the original, ground-based cellular system that service mobile phones, there are also satellite-based systems now available. These systems offer significantly larger service areas and do not require the use of cellular-switching technologies. This system is in widespread use in Europe and is often known by the acronym GSM.

True mobile Internet devices will be usable in any place and under any circumstance (including on planes during takeoff and landing).

## Setup

In much of the rest of the world, phones are designed and constructed to make use of personal information that is prestored on chips called *SIM cards*. A single SIM card is sufficient to uniquely identify an individual and communicate billing information to whatever service is providing connectivity for a device.

This means that when a European buys a cell phone, he or she may do so off a store shelf. The person simply takes the SIM card out of the old cell phone, places it into the new one, and the phone is ready to go. The rest of us may only look on in wonder at the sophistication of this system!

True mobile Internet devices will be available for purchase off-the-shelf and immediately usable through some kind of mechanism, SIM card or otherwise.

## A Brief History of Microsoft

Now that you've learned a little about how we got to where we are in the development of mobile devices, it's time to go back in time again. The purpose for this regression is to trace the development of the other significant player in our story: Microsoft. Embraced by many, reviled by some, Microsoft has become the dominant trend-setting force in the personal computer arena.

If you want to develop software for the mass market, chances are good you are going to have to deal with Microsoft technologies at some point along the line. These technologies have evolved like the company itself, from the early days of DOS through to the most recent release of Microsoft Windows.

### The Dark Ages of DOS

In many ways, DOS is still the most popular operating system in the world. Beneath the surface of all the commercial versions of Windows prior to Windows Me lay the kernel of DOS. Its strength was its simplicity and, for this reason, it continues to be a favorite choice for many applications—such as games—that require every ounce of performance that a computer can provide.

When PC applications were still relatively simple (basic spreadsheet and word processing programs, for example), this foundation was sufficient. As the Internet came to prominence, however, users began demanding more out of their operating systems, such as true multitasking to prevent situations in which one ill-behaved application was capable of monopolizing a computer's CPU resources.

As application design became more complicated, even more serious limitations in DOS-based application architecture became evident. The most widely known of these is commonly referred to as DLL Hell. Simple, so-called flat DLLs are basically libraries of functions that can be shared amongst multiple applications. In order to use a function out of such a DLL, an application needs to know the offset address within the DLL at which a given function is located.

Figure 1-4 shows an application attempting to call the same function twice. First, the application calls the function in the original DLL. It then tries to call the same function in a newer version of the DLL.

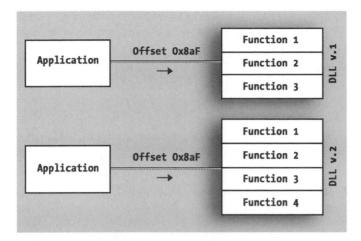

*Figure 1-4. Trying to use the wrong version of DLL*

As Figure 1-4 makes obvious, replacing a DLL with a newer version under the original DOS application architecture would usually cause older applications that used that DLL to break. The reason for this is that the offset locations of the functions would typically be changed in the newer versions. The applications, however, would continue trying to access the original—now incorrect—offset addresses.

## COM

The most significant advance in the history of Microsoft development is known by the rather unassuming acronym COM. As its name implies, COM is all about facilitating component development.

Component development differs from traditional development methodologies by attempting to envision systems as interoperating groups yet independently operating pieces. It is closely related to object-oriented analysis and design. If you can construct a system in this manner, you can realize a number of benefits:

- Easier troubleshooting and debugging via encapsulation

- Greater ability to buy off-the-shelf pieces of functionality

- Superior performance through load distribution

- Less chance of complete system failure

- Finer-grained control over security

COM was Microsoft's entry into the component standards war of the late 1990s. A competing standard with which you may be familiar is OMG's CORBA proposal. Unlike COM, CORBA was designed to operate on a number of different platforms. COM, however, has a number of advantages over CORBA and other standards.

## Code Interoperability

One of the main challenges addressed by COM is that of getting code written completely separately to work together seamlessly. It does this by defining a binary standard for how objects are packaged and how their methods are called. This means two things:

- A client application does not need to know the specific offset address of a method within a component in order to call it.

- A client application can be written in a completely different language from the component into which it wishes to call.

Figure 1-5 illustrates the method by which clients may call into components using COM methodology.

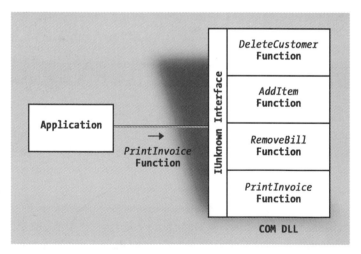

*Figure 1-5. Binary is binary is binary is binary . . .*

As you can see in Figure 1-5, a COM-stipulated interface is provided for resolving method calls by external clients into specific internal function references. Note that because everything is happening at a binary level, the choice of language for developing both the client and component is completely irrelevant.

## Location Independence

The COM standard goes on to specify a level of component interactivity that extends beyond even the system described in the preceding section. The Distributed COM standard, commonly known as DCOM, describes how COM clients and components running on completely different machines can interact across networks just as if they were operating on the same CPU. This is made possible by a network services layer provided for the application developer by the COM implementation.

In Figure 1-6, you see a client on machine A invoking the `explode` method on a component named "bomb." As far as the client application is concerned, this application is located on its own machine. It believes this because COM has provided a so-called proxy object for installation on the client machine. This proxy object accepts all the same function calls as the real component would. It does not, however, provide any implementations for these methods.

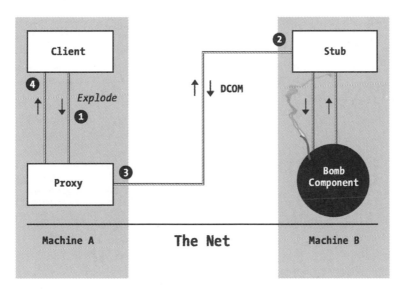

*Figure 1-6. The call remains the same*

What happens instead when a COM client calls into a proxy object is that this call is redirected across the network via DCOM. The machine that receives this call is the machine where the actual component is installed. On this machine, DCOM is constantly listening for connections by client machines that may want to use this component. When it receives a request, it immediately directs that request to the appropriate component.

When the component is finished executing the requested method, its return results are packaged up and sent back across the network as shown in Figure 1-6.

## COM+

When COM was originally released to the public, Microsoft said that there would never be a COM version 2. The reason for this, they claimed, was that COM by its very definition was a standard that would adapt as further improvements were needed, rather than being replaced. For this reason, it should come as no surprise that the next advance in Microsoft development retained the name "COM" in some manner.

COM+ represents a far less revolutionary leap in Microsoft development than COM did. In many ways, it is merely the bundling together of many Microsoft technologies that had already existed separately. Chief amongst these technologies were Microsoft Transaction Server (MTS) and Microsoft Message Queue Server (MSMQ).

## Publishing and Subscribing

COM solved the problem of client applications and server components needing to understand each other's inner workings. By reducing everything to binary messages sent across common interfaces, a general-purpose messaging interface between client applications and their components was created.

What about cases in which components want to announce events for consumption by multiple, possibly unknown, clients? This case was not very well accounted for by COM in its initial version. For this reason, COM+ introduces the concept of publishers and subscribers, as shown in Figure 1-7.

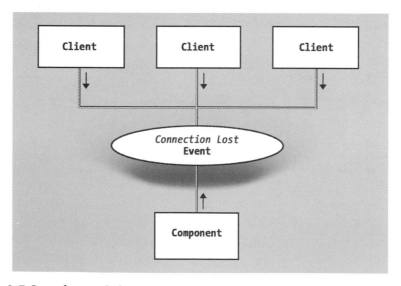

*Figure 1-7. Loosely coupled events*

As you can see in this figure, under COM+ a single component can choose to publish events for consumption by one or more external clients. These clients need not be known in advance or have any direct interaction with the components producing the events. This loose coupling between components and their clients is particularly efficient and fault resistant.

## Queued Components

The publish/subscribe model of COM+ elegantly addresses the problems associated with components needing to communicate blindly with one or more client applications. What about the opposite case, though? There are instances in which a client application wants to send a message to a component, but doesn't particularly care whether or not the message is received before it proceeds. For example, consider the following sequence of events:

1. A customer orders a new pair of mittens on an e-commerce Web site.

2. The e-commerce site checks the customers credit card.

3. The e-commerce site records the transaction in the database.

4. The e-commerce site thanks the customer and completes the transaction.

Of all of these steps, only Step 2 would be a case in which you might reasonably want your application to completely fail in the absence of a valid response. Ideally, you would not want to have to stop taking customer orders simply because your database had gone offline. This is exactly what would happen, however, in the case of a failure in Step 3, as shown in Figure 1-8.

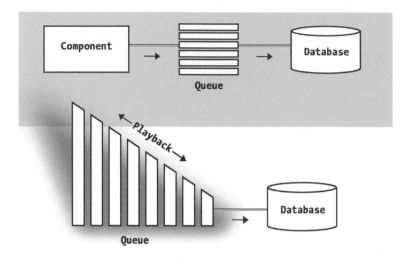

*Figure 1-8. Why COM+ is more reliable than COM*

COM+ introduced the idea of queued components, borrowed from MSMQ, that allows method invocations to components to be queued up in the case of failure. These queued method invocations can then be played back at a later point in time—when the component becomes available again. In the case of Figure 1-8, the calls begin queuing when the database goes offline. They are replayed later, when the database is available again.

## A Matter of Focus

COM and COM+ are both great technologies and well respected within the industry. As the Internet has developed into the dominant technological trend, however, it has become obvious that there are some fundamental limitations to how far this architecture can go. Amongst its limitations, two major ones stand out:

- A dependence on the Microsoft platform for client, server, and everything in between

- An inefficient use of networking bandwidth

As you'll see in the next section, Microsoft is moving aggressively to address these challenges with its latest technology initiative: .NET.

# Microsoft Meets the Brave, New, Interconnected World

At this point, you have attained a reasonably sound foundation in understanding the histories of both mobile data communications and Microsoft's development philosophy. So now you may be thinking, "How are these two related, and what does it mean to me?" In a word, the two are related by that which is (arguably) mankind's greatest single invention: the Internet.

## The Rise of the Internet

The rise of the Internet during the 1990s is a phenomenon that has few equals throughout history. The most obvious comparison might be the invention of the printing press. In both cases, previous barriers to the dissemination of information were quickly brought tumbling down. What distinguishes the Internet from previous information distribution technologies, however, is its inherently bidirectional nature.

In contrast to books—or even the pagers you learned about at the start of this chapter—the Internet facilitates the exchange of information, rather than merely its distribution. This is an idea very much in keeping with the origins of the Internet as a top-secret military project aimed at ensuring the delivery of mail even in the event of nuclear war.

### It Began as a Military Project . . .

Computers had been arranged into networks long before the advent of the Internet. The process was reasonably simple:

1. Determine which computers would be in your network.

2. Figure out the order (or topography) into which they should be arranged.

3. Run cables directly between them to match the established topography.

There were two problems with this approach. The first was what to do in the case where you couldn't possibly know ahead of time all of the computers that would want to connect to your network. In such a situation, it would be impossible to decide on a topography—or connection pattern—ahead of time.

A second, related question was how to build a network in such a way that the topography could change without interrupting communications. For example, if computer A is connected to computer C via computer B, how can one ensure than computer A and computer C will remain connected, even if computer B is removed from the network?

As you can see in Figure 1-9, the Internet's chief technical innovation was its solution to these two problems. Through intelligent routing technologies, the Internet is able to operate in a topology-independent way.

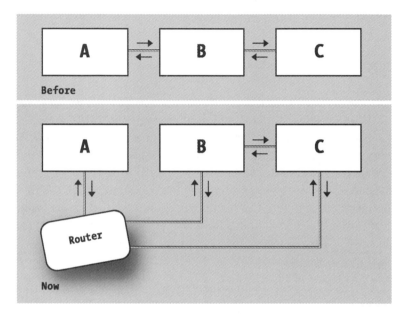

*Figure 1-9. Why even World War III won't get you out of paying taxes*

## . . . Became a College Craze . . .

In the 1970s it was proposed that all of the dollars sunk into military projects, such as the Internet, could be leveraged for the mutual advancement of science. Towards this end, access to large portions of the Internet's infrastructure was opened up to supercomputers running at some of the largest academic and research institutions in the United States. For the first time, scientists working separately across the nation were able to communicate with one another instantaneously.

This benefit soon found its way out of college labs and into the dormitories. Universities were gradually allowed to provide more and more of their students with Internet e-mail accounts that allowed them to also communicate instantaneously with each other. As colleges and universities in other countries linked their own networks up with the Internet in increasing numbers, it gradually became easy to send a message across the globe in the blink of an eye.

## ... And Ended Up a Commercial Success!

For every great invention, there is a great potential for making money. In the 1990s, commercial services in the United States were first allowed to begin reselling connectivity to the Internet. What followed was an explosion of interest in this medium for all sorts of purposes and uses. Overnight, it seemed that if something could be done at all, it could be done better and quicker via the Internet!

## Microsoft's First Response

By most accounts, Microsoft was initially blindsided by the emergence of the Internet. The initial release of Windows 3 didn't even feature direct support for TCP/IP—the fundamental protocol upon which all Internet communications depend!

The initial moves made by Microsoft in response to this phenomenon, then, may be excused for seeming somewhat half-baked in retrospect. Technologies such as the Internet Database Connector, which had been all but forgotten, soon evolved into more lasting tools, such as Active Server Pages.

### Client-side Technologies

The most important client-side Internet technology made by Microsoft is Internet Explorer. In the next chapter, you will learn about Internet Explorer in great detail. Besides being just another Web browser, Internet Explorer has been the focus of Microsoft's attempt to make Internet access a transparent activity when conducted from its Windows operating system.

In particular, the benefits afforded by Internet Explorer include the following:

- A high level of integration with the Windows interface

- Substantial developer programmability

- Excellent support for the incorporation of scripting in Internet content

- Full DHTML object model for dynamic restructuring of pages

- XML transmission, receipt, and manipulation support

In Chapter 3, you will learn about another client-side innovation that is key to Microsoft's Internet strategy, the Pocket PC. The Pocket PC is a PDA solution based on Microsoft's Windows CE operating system. Pocket PCs are similar to other PDAs, such as the Palm or Visor, but typically feature superior integration with Microsoft products and a fuller range of functionality (such as PCMCIA card support).

### Server-side Technologies

The focal point of Microsoft's Internet strategy on the server up to this point has been the Internet Information Server (IIS). Within the framework of IIS, there are typically several smaller, more specific server functionalities. These include the Web Publishing Service, the Simple Mail Transport Protocol Service, the Microsoft News Service, and a few others.

Of all of these, the Web Publishing Service is of most direct concern to aspiring mobile .NET developers. Before IIS, the standard in Internet applications was to create batches of static HTML pages loosely interconnected via the Common Gateway Interface (CGI). Using CGI, a server-side developer could write programs that were executed in response to form submissions and which then returned their data via standard output mechanisms.

There were, however, many obstacles to CGI programming. These included difficulties maintaining state between page requests and the high performance costs associated with spawning a completely new process for each new CGI script invocation. Microsoft answered both of these issues with the introduction of its Active Server Pages technology. Chapter 7 gives you a thorough foundation in understanding what Active Server Pages are all about, as they form the gateway to one of Microsoft's most important .NET innovations: ASP.NET.

## The Brave, New .NET World

Microsoft first publicly announced its .NET technology initiative at its Professional Developers Conference in May 2000. At first, details on this initiative were sketchy, and many pundits were therefore prompted to prematurely announce that .NET was nothing more than vaporware. As you will see in the next sections (and in the rest of this book), however, .NET is anything but vaporware!

### The Problem

There are myriad mobile devices out there. Over the course of the next five chapters, you will learn about the specifics of some of the more popular of these: Pocket PCs, PalmOS devices, J2ME devices, and so on. And as you learn more about each of these, please try to remain focused on the big picture: they all require a completely different approach to development!

As you can see in Figure 1-10, creating an application for WAP phones, Web browsers, and PalmOS devices has heretofore meant creating a different version of your application for each unique client platform. As the number of unique client platforms multiplies exponentially over the next decade, this approach will become quite impossible. So the question is, what alternative exists?

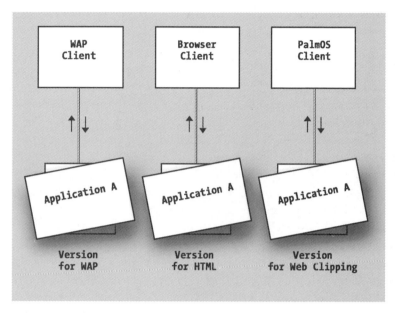

*Figure 1-10. For each device, a different approach*

## The Answer

Microsoft's .NET is about getting your applications into a situation where you can write them once and expect them to work with any client without significant customizations. Does this sound like Java at all to you? It should—but, as you'll see in the next section, there is a key difference!

## The Ideal

Java is Sun's technology for "write once, run anywhere." The theory is that when you're writing something in Java, you're not writing it for any device or computer in particular. Instead, you're writing it for something known as a *virtual machine*. Different virtual machine implementations exist for a wide variety of different platforms. Therefore, all you need to do in order to run the same Java application on a Mac, a Windows computer, and a Unix computer is install Java virtual machines (VMs) on each of them.

With .NET, however, you are writing your applications for Microsoft's own virtual machine, called the *Common Language Runtime* (CLR). The CLR runs on a Windows server—not the client devices themselves! As Figure 1-11 illustrates, it is the CLR's responsibility to adapt your application's output for consumption by different kinds of devices, rather than to run on the devices themselves.

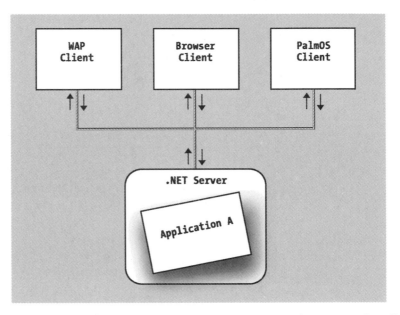

*Figure 1-11. .NET means "write once, adapt on the server, receive anywhere."*

 **NOTE** *In just the few months since these paragraphs were first written, three things have occurred that somewhat blur the picture painted in the preceding text. To begin with, Corel has announced plans to port the CLR to the FreeBSD operating system. Next, an open source project called Mono was launched to port the CLR to Linux. Finally, as you will learn in the final chapter of this book, Microsoft has developed the .NET Compact Framework—a subset of .NET that runs on a device, the Pocket PC, rather than a server.*

## The Reality

Of course, there are still business realities to be dealt with. As you will see in the next five chapters, where .NET is concerned, not all clients are created equal!

# CHAPTER 2

# Internet Explorer

## The Greatest Browser in the History of Humankind

Now it is time to turn our attention to what is perhaps the most pivotal piece of software in Microsoft's entire Internet initiative: Internet Explorer. What once began as a humble response to Netscape's market dominance has now grown into the cornerstone upon which much of Microsoft's software empire is built.

Before this chapter is finished, you will understand how Internet Explorer first came into being and how it has grown into such a potent force within the Microsoft world. We will explain how creating applications for Internet Explorer is less like creating traditional HTML pages and more like creating full-blown Windows applications. At the end of the chapter, a practical exercise will walk you through the creation of a fully functional Internet Explorer application.

## History

The history of Internet Explorer represents one of Microsoft's few come-from-behind victory tales. Apparently blindsided by the explosion of the Internet, Microsoft didn't even have a browser of its own until the relatively late Internet period of the mid-1990s. By that point, a clear market leader, Netscape, had already emerged from a decidedly non–Microsoft-controlled source.

### Starting from Behind

By the time Microsoft finally became clued in to the explosion of the Internet phenomenon, many of its chief competitors were already far ahead in terms of their product support. In the case of Unix, for example, TCP/IP (the protocol upon which the Internet is based) had been a part of most of the implementations of the OS since the early 1980s!

Specifically, Microsoft faced direct challenges to its dominance on two fronts: client and server. On the client front, the Web browser of choice was not a Microsoft invention, but a product known as Netscape Navigator. On the server front, the software of choice was rapidly becoming a product that wasn't even produced by a company, as such, but which was instead being compiled by a group of volunteers for free!

## Netscape

Netscape is the brainchild of Marc Andreessen. He envisioned it while he was working on a previous Internet browser, called Mosaic, at the Center for Supercomputing, University of Illinois. Netscape was, in many ways, the first of the "dot-com superstars," in that it generated a hugely successful IPO long before most people had even had the opportunity to use it!

What concerns us in this section, however, are the technologies that distinguished Netscape in the marketplace and allowed it to become the dominant browser before Internet Explorer. This technology took two main forms:

- Standards support

- Integration

### Standards Support

Netscape was one of the first commercial browsers. Before Netscape, browsers were largely academic and volunteer-created affairs. There was no pressing urgency before Netscape to create the absolutely greatest browsers possible. If a volunteer organization, for example, managed to produce a browser that was even almost as good as the competition, it would consider its efforts a victory for the free software movement.

Netscape, however, was subject to the business laws of profit and loss and so, for the first time, had to think of ways to ensure that its browser product would always be head-and-shoulders above the competition. Fortunately for Netscape, in the mid-1990s there were plenty of areas in browser technology that were left for improvement!

The first browsers only supported the rendering of HTML. HTML, in its earliest forms, allowed only for the statement of what should be put on a page—it gave the designer *no* control over how that content should appear. For a minority of technically focused users, this limitation was fine. After all, they were using Internet browsers to get serious work accomplished, and didn't really care what the rendered HTML looked like.

In order to be truly successful, however, Internet browsers had to emerge from the labs and become mass-market applications. The vast majority of end users deeply care about how things look. This interest in appearances lay behind the first several revisions to the HTML markup language. It is important that you remember this point, because the seeds of XML were sown during these revisions. And XML, as you will see later, forms the foundation of what .NET is all about.

As HTML evolved, a fierce competition arose amongst various browser manufacturers. Whose browser would support all of the nice formatting features enabled by the latest version of HTML? Early in the game, Netscape beat the competition time and time again.

What seemed to be the killing blow for its competitors, however, was when Netscape became the first commercial browser to host Java applets. Few people had even heard of Java before. Now, with the addition of applets to a Web page, it was suddenly possible to perform all kinds of sophisticated layout and data operations that had never been seen previously in a Web browser!

Clearly, Netscape won the first round of the browser wars by supporting new standards long before its competition.

### Integration

The other area in which Netscape clouted its competitors was in its ability to integrate with other applications. Early on, these integrations meant things as minor as being able to launch your default mail application whenever you clicked an e-mail link. These integrations required little or no additional coding on Netscape's part, merely a realization of the fact that browsers didn't exist in a vacuum. This realization later became a key part of Microsoft's own browser initiative, as you will see shortly.

After a while, Netscape introduced the idea of plug-in applications. Rather than integrating Netscape with applications already on your computer, you could buy (or download) components intended to extend the functionality of Netscape itself. For example, it was around this time that the idea of listening to music and watching videos over the Internet first came to prominence, thanks in part to the creation of Netscape plug-ins designed for this task.

The final level of integration came when Netscape began bundling a news and e-mail program along with its base browser package. This bundle, which eventually came to be known as Communicator, allowed users to perform many of the most common Internet tasks without ever leaving the Netscape application! Once again, Microsoft soon imitated this capability in its own browser.

### Apache

The other great gap in Microsoft's initial Internet strategy lay in the development of a server to go along with its client. The server that we now know as Internet Information Server was not even a glimmer in Bill Gates' eye when Apache first produced its completely free Web server for noncommercial use. Apache was not originally a bells-and-whistles Web server. It did, however, feature incredible reliability and support for CGI scripting.

## Reliability

Any operating system can only be as stable as the quality of the applications that are designed for it. One important feature of the Apache Web server is that it runs reliably on both Unix and Windows operating systems. Even to this day, simple Web sites that require little in the way of dynamic server-side content but which must remain functional on a 24×7 basis are typically found on Apache servers more than 50 percent of the time!

## CGI

The big coup in the early days of Web servers, however, was to have a server that offered support for the Common Gateway Interface (CGI) standard. Before CGI, Web sites were little more than collections of static HTML pages connected to one another by static links, as illustrated in Figure 2-1.

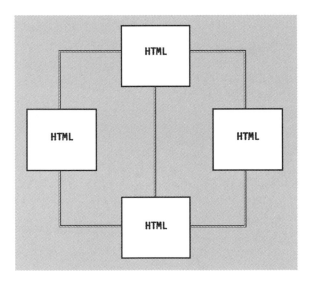

*Figure 2-1. Web sites before CGI*

Once CGI was introduced, however, for the first time it became possible to run scripts on the Web server in response to requests from Internet clients. The advent of CGI meant that programs could accept input from browsers across the Internet, generate responses, and return truly dynamic content for the first time. Figure 2-2 shows CGI in action.

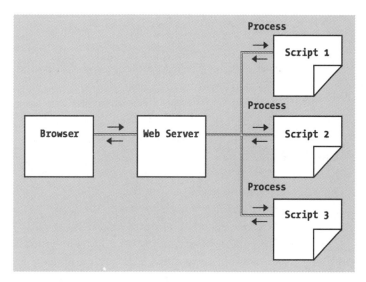

*Figure 2-2. Web sites after CGI*

Notice in Figure 2-2, however, that for every client making a request, there must be exactly one new CGI process spawned on the server. This seemingly harmless design limitation would be exploited brilliantly by Microsoft in the development of its Active Platform Internet strategy, which is the precursor to all of .NET.

## Victory through Activation

Whether through luck, brilliance, divine intervention, or all three, by the late 1990s the tide had turned decidedly in Microsoft's favor. Two things contributed to this stunning reversal of fortunes:

- Microsoft's ability to bundle its applications as part of the Windows operating system

- The increasing ability of Microsoft's products to do things that competing products couldn't

In the first case, litigation soon emerged to challenge the appropriateness of Microsoft's actions. The final outcome of this litigation has yet to be decided at the time of this writing, but the issues under debate are relatively far from the focus of this book.

The second point, however, is of crucial importance in understanding what .NET is all about. Microsoft managed to beat Netscape and achieve parity with Apache by offering a suite of features that were completely different from those provided by the competition. Microsoft named these technologies the Active Platform.

Some of the more popular of these technologies are summarized in Table 2-1.

*Table 2-1. The Active Technology Suite*

| TECHNOLOGY | DESCRIPTION |
| --- | --- |
| ActiveX controls | Microsoft's answer to Java applets. Technically just COM components intended for use with graphical control containers (such as application forms or Web pages). ActiveX controls differed significantly from Java applets in that they were based on native code and therefore able to do *many* more things on their host system than applets. |
| Active scripting | The ability to write code in simplified scripting languages for execution either on the client (within Internet Explorer) or on the server (under Active Server Pages). For more information on Active Server Pages, see Chapter 7. |
| Active Desktop | The ability to integrate browser-based content with the desktop of the Windows operating system. This might mean running an ActiveX control on your screen all the time or simply being able to enter a Web site URL in place of a regular filename. |
| Active Channels | Probably the least successful of Microsoft's Active technologies. Intended as a vehicle for server "push" that would allow Web users to keep abreast of changes in their favorite sites without having to constantly revisit them. |

## Along Comes .NET

As discussed in the previous section, Microsoft achieved its dominance in the browser wars by offering a suite of features and functionality that were unavailable under any of the competing platforms. For example, Netscape Navigator was the first commercial browser to feature integrated support for Java applets.

Microsoft added similar support to Internet Explorer and could have chosen to compete directly with Netscape in attempting to provide even *better* support for Java applets than the competition (faster execution, tighter security, and so forth).

Instead, Microsoft chose to enable Java applets run within Internet Explorer to directly interact with the operating system in ways that were completely different from what anyone else was doing at that time. .NET represents a similar shift in philosophies that proposes a radically different vision of software: software as a service.

As you will see later in this chapter when you begin working with SOAP (Simple Object Access Protocol), .NET is about repackaging application functionality as smaller, more easily interconnected Web services. By choosing XML as the basis for how these separate Web services interact with one another, Microsoft makes it possible for software on virtually any platform to tap into similar functionality on virtually any other platform.

**TIP** *If you are familiar with Microsoft's history on interoperability, you may be forgiven for looking upon the previous paragraph with some degree of skepticism. What can Microsoft possibly be up to with true interoperability? As you will see later on, .NET positions Microsoft to become the ultimate service provider, regardless of your choice of client. In a world that is rapidly becoming wireless, this is an essential move for the world's dominant software manufacturer.*

## Creating Applications

Creating applications for Internet Explorer is decidedly unlike creating traditional HTML-based static Web applications. In many ways, it is more comparable to creating full-blown Windows applications. In this section, we will describe the theoretical advances that make the Internet Explorer a development platform that is heads-and-shoulders above the competition.

Once we have sold you on the fact that Internet Explorer is a truly great development platform, we will assist you in procuring some tools to help you along your way. Some of these tools are free, some of them are not. In the case of the ones that are free, we will walk you through their download and installation.

### Fundamentals

Internet Explorer differs from competing browser applications in several ways. Earlier in this chapter, you learned that one of its oldest and most obvious differences is in its close integration with the Windows operating system. In recent times, however, two features have greatly outpaced this integration in terms of their direct impact on application development for Internet Explorer:

- DHTML

- XML

### DHTML

DHTML represents an important way for browser-based applications to compete with traditional Windows applications by reducing the amount of inter-action that is required with the Web server in order to perform useful work. As you will see at the end of this chapter when you create your own DHTML-based application, DHTML allows Internet Explorer to radically redesign the interface offered by its Web pages on-the-fly.

Internet Explorer's use of the Document Object Model (DOM) facilitates this redesign. DOM specifies a way of addressing every part of a Web page in terms of methods, properties, and events. This way, everything that a Web page's user does (such as clicking a button) can be "caught" as an event and responded to. Similarly, every item on a page (such as a picture) can be manipulated via code and altered in almost every way imaginable.

Recent versions of Internet Explorer have gone even a step further with the concept of DHTML. By introducing the concept of *behaviors*, Internet Explorer has made it possible for client-side developers to encapsulate their logic in discrete script-based components that are downloaded from the server on an as-needed basis. This design has numerous benefits, including intellectual property protection, improved performance, and superior documentation.

### XML

XML, in its simplest form, allows Internet Explorer to communicate with the Web server on a level that goes far deeper than simple presentation markup language. In a more expansive sense, however, XML lays at the foundation for Microsoft's entire .NET technology initiative. For this reason, it is essential that you under-stand the two key XML components of Internet Explorer: MSXML and XMLHTTP.

MSXML is Microsoft's XML parser. For more information on what an XML parser is and does, please refer to Appendix A. By using the version of MSXML that comes bundled with Internet Explorer 6, all of the XML-enabled applications on your computer are able to support all the latest XML standards and feature sets. For example, Internet Explorer's built-in ability to render XML documents using a default tree-control stylesheet is powered by its use of the MSXML parser component.

XMLHTTP is the component that allows Internet Explorer to communicate across the Internet using XML. By calling methods on the XMLHTTP component, you can post XML data to Active Server Page applications, for example, and receive XML responses back. These responses can drive DHTML update code in your client-side application, thus completely eliminating the need to include *any* HTML in your Web applications!

## Getting the Tools

Developing applications without tools would be difficult at best. If you stop to think about it, even the simplest development environments (such as creating C applications on a Unix computer) require the use of numerous tools between the initial conception and final execution of a development project. The following is a list of some common development tools:

- Editors

- Compilers

- Linkers

- Source control

- Diagramming packages

Of all of these tools, some would be essential on any project (such as a compiler), others would not. In this section, we introduce you to the tools that would be essential for creating any kind of serious Internet Explorer application. Some of them are free, others must be purchased.

### Internet Explorer 6

Internet Explorer is the focus of this chapter so, as you might imagine, you can't go very far without first obtaining it. The good news is, for all versions of Windows since 95, Internet Explorer comes included as a part of the operating system. The bad news is, the only Windows operating system that comes with the correct version of Internet Explorer (version 6) for our purposes is Windows XP.

*If you are using anything other than Internet Explorer 6, then you must upgrade now!* To get the newest version of Internet Explorer, point your current Internet browser (whether IE or Netscape or something else entirely) to

```
http://www.microsoft.com/ie
```

If you are using Internet Explorer, you should now see a screen similar to the one in Figure 2-3.

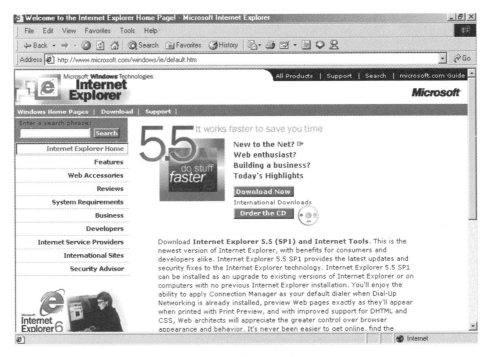

*Figure 2-3. Looking for new IE versions from within IE*

Internet Explorer sends a header identifying itself every time it visits a Web page. When you visit this Web page, Microsoft's Web site understands Internet Explorer's identification and asks itself whether or not this represents the latest version that is available. If it is, you get a page showing add-ons. If it is not, you get a page that strongly recommends upgrading to the latest browser.

**NOTE**   *At the time of this writing, it appears that the Microsoft Web site no longer supports visits from the first two versions of Internet Explorer (IE 1 and IE 2). If this is the only browser software that you have on your computer, you will need to find some other way of upgrading. Suggestions include installing the latest version of Visual Studio or Microsoft Office, both of which include more recent versions of Internet Explorer. Also, you might consider installing Netscape Navigator first, and then migrating to Internet Explorer.*

If you used Netscape to visit the Microsoft page for IE, then you should see a screen similar to the one in Figure 2-3, except that there is less likely to be any direct reference to your current version of Internet Explorer.

 **CAUTION**   *For the remainder of this book, it is absolutely essential that you use Internet Explorer 6 in order for most of the exercises to function properly. If you have not already upgraded to Internet Explorer 6 by following the preceding instructions, you must do so now!*

## Stuff for Purchase

In addition to the free stuff that you have just acquired, Microsoft offers for sale a number of products to facilitate the creation of Internet Explorer—enabled applications. One of these will be an absolute requirement for your continued development in this book. The other two are completely optional.

### Internet Information Server

Internet Information Server is Microsoft's entry into the great Web server debates. As you saw earlier in this chapter, Microsoft's chief technology innovation in IIS (as far as developers are concerned) was the Active Server platform. With the Active Server platform, developers can create powerful Internet applications that are extremely scalable using relatively simple scripting languages such as VBScript and JScript.

In order to get the most out of this book, you will need to be running some flavor of IIS on your computer. Fortunately, if you are running NT, Windows

2000, or Windows XP, IIS was included in the purchase price of your operating system. To see if IIS is already installed on your computer, perform the following procedure:

1. Choose Settings from the Windows Start menu.

2. Click Control Panel.

3. On NT, click Services. On 2000 and XP, click Administrative Tools first, and then click Services.

4. Towards the bottom of the list, look for World Wide Web Publishing Service. If you see it listed, make sure that it is started. (If it isn't, highlight the item and hit the Play button at the top of the window.)

If you couldn't find the appropriate service listed, then IIS is not yet installed on your machine. In order to install it, insert your Windows CD-ROM into your computer and choose the option Add/Remove Components. Progress through the dialog boxes until you are asked to choose components for addition. Make sure that the check box by the IIS option is selected and proceed through the rest of the dialog boxes. You will be prompted to restart your computer. Once you have done this, go back and verify that IIS is installed and running, using the preceding steps.

If you are running Windows 98, ME, or some other consumer flavor of Windows, then you will have to purchase your IIS functionality. The easiest way to do this is by getting yourself a copy of Microsoft FrontPage.

### FrontPage

FrontPage is Microsoft's tool for Web site design. It is not typically useful in the development of serious Web applications, but is more commonly used in the creation of cosmetically appealing personal and corporate identity Web sites.

 **TIP**  *In this book, as in much of business, the terms* Web design *and* Web development *are used noninterchangeably. Where "Web design" is specified, it refers to semiskilled creation of attractive Web pages. Where "Web development" is specified, we mean the highly skilled creation of Web applications involving the use of actual programming code. We don't want to sound elitist about this, but we are.*

The main value proposition to you as a developer is that if you are running a commercial version of Windows (such as 98 or ME), FrontPage is one of the easiest ways to get a flavor of IIS up-and-running on your machine. This flavor is known as Personal Web Server (PWS) and is, for most purposes, functionally equivalent to IIS.

### Visual InterDev

Visual InterDev is a real developer's tool. As part of Visual Studio 6, you can use this tool to create, modify, and otherwise hack server-side script running on IIS to your heart's content. In Visual Studio .NET, the functionality behind Visual InterDev has been merged into the overall functionality of VB .NET and the rest of Visual Studio .NET. As a stand-alone product, then, it has ceased to exist.

If you are a Visual InterDev fan, however, do not despair. You will *love* what has become of the tool in Visual Studio .NET, we absolutely guarantee!

## Setting Up Internet Explorer

Now that you have acquired the tools to help you build your applications, it is time to put them to good use! In this section, we will walk you through the installation of the most important tool in this chapter: Internet Explorer.

### Installation

The installation of Internet Explorer onto a Windows computer should be a relative no-brainer for most people. As such, we won't insult your intelligence by including detailed instructions for it here. However, you should be aware of the Active Installation of the setup file.

In keeping with the "Active" naming scheme for all technologies introduced by Microsoft during the late 1990s, the installer for Internet Explorer is known as an Active Installer. What this means is that when you download the setup file for IE from Microsoft's Web site, you might be quite surprised by the relatively small size of the file. On our computer, for example, the latest version of Internet Explorer clocked in at just 500K. What happened?

Well, when you download IE from Microsoft's Web site, what you are really downloading is a program that will ask you about the specific features you would like to install. This program will then expect to reconnect to the Internet and download additional components, depending upon your responses. These components will constitute the vast majority of your Internet Explorer downloading time.

It is important that you realize this ahead of time so that you don't download the installer, disconnect from the Internet, and then expect to run the installer on your way home from work on the train. Unless you have an Internet connection on the train, this isn't going to work!

## Testing

Now that you have installed all of the software that you will need for creating your Internet Explorer applications, you would probably like to know whether or not the software is working properly. Picky, aren't you? Here are some simple tests for all of the tools installed so far.

### Internet Explorer's XML Capabilities

The purpose of this test is to verify that Internet Explorer is up-and-running and integrating properly with the XML components installed previously. To begin with, you should open Internet Explorer and try to visit your favorite Web site. If you can't do this, then you will immediately know that something is wrong with Internet Explorer.

Assuming that this little test worked properly, you should choose About Internet Explorer from the pull-down Help menu. On the screen that pops up, please verify that you are running the latest version of Internet Explorer (or at least the one that you thought you had downloaded). If not, try restarting your computer to make sure that the installation takes effect.

And now for some code. The final test is to make sure that XML is functioning properly in Internet Explorer. Enter the code from Listing 2-1 and save it with the filename sample.xml. If you are already familiar with XML, feel free to create your own example instead of the one we have provided. If you have no idea what XML is, we encourage you to read Appendix A at this point for some useful background information.

*Listing 2-1. A Simple XML File*

```
<?xml version='1.0' ?>
<pocketdba>
    <staff>
        <name>
            <first>Ari</first>
            <middle>D</middle>
            <last>Kaplan</last>
        </name>
```

```
        <title>Founder</title>
    </staff>
    <staff>
        <name>
            <first>Derek</first>
            <middle/>
            <last>Ferguson</last>
        </name>
        <title>Chief Technology Evangelist</title>
    </staff>
</pocketdba>
```

If you now open this file under Internet Explorer, you should see a tree-style rendering similar to the one shown in Figure 2-4. Verify that you are able to expand and collapse the nodes properly. If so, you can be sure that Internet Explorer is now properly using XML.

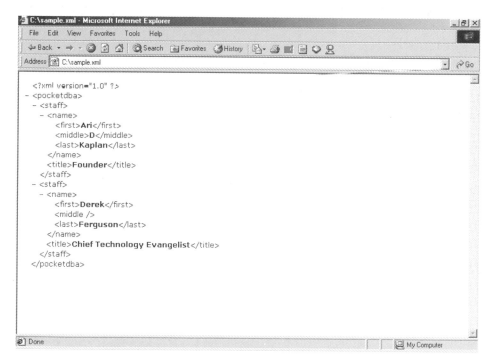

*Figure 2-4. Internet Explorer rendering XML*

## Exercise

The purpose of this and the next several chapters is to teach you enough about each of our target platforms to enable you to do the following:

- Know the capabilities of each target platform.

- Understand how to creating very simple applications on your own.

- Find the information you need to go even further with your applications.

Towards this end, we will be concluding each of these chapters with a brief exercise. In these exercises, we will walk you step-by-step through the creation of a simple application targeted at the platform about which the chapter is written. You won't be an expert by the time you have finished an exercise, but you will know enough to be dangerous!

## Writing the Server

At this point in the book, we have yet to touch upon any truly .NET material. The intention in these few chapters is, instead, to teach you a little bit about each of the client devices at which your .NET applications may be targeted. Still, it is necessary for us to build *some* server logic in each of these exercises in order to have something with which our client may communicate.

## Code Overview

The server that we will create in this exercise consists of a single Active Server Page. This page will accept whatever XML is transmitted by our Internet Explorer client script, and then echo it back.

### The Code

Listing 2-2 shows the code for the sample ASP page.

*Listing 2-2: The ASP Server*

```
<%
    Response.ContentType = "text/xml"
```

```
%>

<?xml version="1.0"?>

<%
    Set doc = Server.CreateObject("Microsoft.XMLDOM")
    doc.load (Request)
    Response.Write (doc.xml)
%>
```

### The Walk-Through

The code for this server is devastatingly simple. It begins by preparing to send an XML response by setting the MIME type correctly, and then sending a processing instruction that sets the version appropriately (to 1.0). The remainder of the code simply instantiates an instance of the Microsoft XML parser, populates it with whatever was received from the client, and then bounces it right back to the client.

## Trying It Out

To verify that the server is functioning properly, follow these steps:

1. Open a simple text editor such as Notepad.

2. Enter the code from Listing 2-2 earlier.

3. Save the code with the filename echo.asp in the main directory of IIS (for example, \inetpub\wwwroot).

4. Open a browser and go to http://localhost/echo.asp.

5. Verify that the error you receive looks exactly like Figure 2-5.

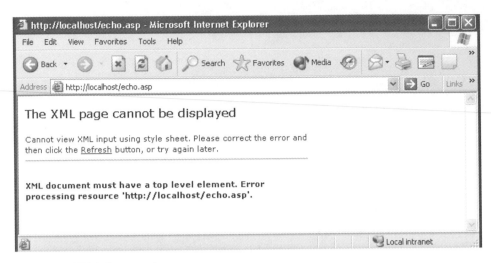

*Figure 2-5. This is a good error.*

If you are able to follow all of the preceding steps without generating any errors, then the chances are excellent that your server is fully functional!

## Writing the Client

In order to show off Internet Explorer's special capabilities as a mobile Internet client, you need do only two things:

- Manipulate some XML

- Change your page's layout dynamically

## Code Overview

The client in the following section accomplishes both of the preceding goals. It manipulates XML by both sending and receiving it on the Internet. It changes the page's layout dynamically by writing whatever response it receives from the server directly into a reserved portion of the page's user interface.

### The Code

Listing 2-3 shows the code for the DHTML client.

*Listing 2-3: The DHTML client*

```
<html>
    <head>
    <script language="jscript">
        function sendit()
        {
            oXMLHTTP = new ActiveXObject("microsoft.xmlhttp");
            oXMLHTTP.Open("POST", "http://localhost/echo.asp",
false);

            oXMLHTTP.send ("<?xml version=\"1.0\" encoding=\"UTF-8\" " +
"standalone=\"no\"?><SOAP-ENV:Envelope " +
"SOAP-ENV:encodingStyle=\"http://schemas.xmlsoap.org/soap/encoding/\" " +
"xmlns:SOAP-ENV=\"http://schemas.xmlsoap.org/soap/envelope/\">" +
"<SOAP-ENV:Body><m:Add " +
"xmlns:m=\"http://tempuri.org/message/\"><A>1</A><B>2</B>" +
"</m:Add></SOAP-ENV:Body></SOAP-ENV:Envelope>");
            var objXML = oXMLHTTP.responseXML;
            echo.innerText = objXML.xml;
        }
</script>
</head>

<body>
<input type="button" id="go" onclick="sendit()" value="Send XML">
<p>
Echo:
<div id="echo"></div>
</body>
</html>
```

### The Walk-Through

The first bit of code to notice in Listing 2-3 is the onclick attribute on the page's
only button. This stipulates that, when clicked, the button will invoke the sendit
function. This function is located in the HEAD element at the top
of the page.

The sendit function begins by creating an instance of the Microsoft XML-
HTTP component. It then uses this component to send a predefined batch of
XML across the Internet to the ASP server created in the previous section.

At this point, the `sendit` function blocks while it waits for a response from the server. Once the response arrives, it stuffs it into the blank portion of the browser screen that has been reserved for this purpose by the `div` tag at the end of Listing 2-3.

### Trying It Out

Seeing all of the code from this exercise in action should be quite easy, assuming you have both Internet Explorer and Internet Information Server running on your computer. Simply save the code from Listing 2-3 into a standard HTML file using your favorite text editor, and then open that file using Internet Explorer. When you click the button, there should be a short pause, and then a mass of XML should appear at the bottom of the page.

## Final Thoughts

This chapter has served as a brief introduction to the Internet Explorer Web application. It is important that you understand how very different Internet Explorer is from all of the other Web browsers out on the market. At the center of this difference is Microsoft's wish that Internet Explorer should constitute a full platform in and of itself for the development of full-featured Windows applications.

The experience you've had in this chapter with XML is just a foretaste of the work that you will be doing later in this book. XML is an essential part of Microsoft's .NET strategy, and will be key to creating top-quality applications on the widest possible variety of wireless devices.

# CHAPTER 3

# Pocket PCs

## Microsoft's Palm Pilot Killer?

THE POCKET PC HAS TRULY taken the world of portable digital assistants (PDAs) by storm over the last year. For many of the more popular models, devices are now in such short supply that customers often must wait several weeks just to purchase one! So with this in mind, you might be wondering what all of the fuss is about.

In this chapter, we will discuss how the Pocket PC has come to challenge the dominance of Palm OS in the handheld PDA market by being a vastly different kind of device. Exactly what those differences are and how you can leverage them to create your own Pocket PC applications will be explained in the exercise later in this chapter.

## Background

You might think of Pocket PCs as being Microsoft's answer to the Palm OS–powered line of PDAs. The capabilities of the average Pocket PC, however, go far beyond the limits of most Palm OS–based devices. In this section, we explain what Pocket PCs are, how they came into being, and where they are headed.

### History

The story of how Pocket PCs have come to be the current rage in portable computing is an interesting one. In many ways, it is the story of Microsoft winning by doing everything wrong. This is a story that has repeated itself numerous times in the development of the modern PDA.

#### How Palm OS Got the Better of Microsoft

The majority of PDAs in use today are based on the Palm OS operating system (http://www.palmos.com). For this reason, we have devoted an entire chapter of this book (Chapter 5) to showing you how to develop applications for them. It may surprise you, however, to realize that this technology evolved with virtually no involvement from Microsoft.

### Building on the Bones of Newton

There were many attempts at designing successful PDAs before the Palm Pilot, such as Apple's Newton (`http://home.rmi.net/~rbruce/`). The key mistake that all of them made was that they attempted to do too much. For example, most of them tried to actually interpret human handwriting. This was a bad idea for several reasons:

- Complexity of the software required

- Resource-intensive nature of running this kind of software

- Vast differences in the way that different people write

Another foolish thing that many early PDAs tried to add was the ability to connect to local area networks. This capability required building both hardware and software into devices to allow them to understand sophisticated protocols like Ethernet. This practice resulted in old PDAs being significantly bigger and more expensive than the Palm Pilot would ultimately be.

### Keep It Simple, Stupid!

The brilliance of the Palm OS, then, lay in its utter simplicity. Rather than try to understand human handwriting, for instance, the Palm OS devices require their users to learn a special, stylized kind of writing known as Graffiti. For more information on Graffiti, please see Chapter 5.

The lesson is that, in order to beat the competition, Palm did the wrong thing according to the common marketing wisdom of the time. Palm offered fewer features. In doing so, however, Palm managed to produce a PDA that was smaller, cheaper, and (best of all) almost completely reliable.

## The Empire Strikes Back

Things change, however. And, as you might have guessed, Microsoft was not about to sit back and allow Palm's ownership of a key piece of technology real estate go unchallenged. In order to compete, Microsoft has attempted to seize upon changes in technology and business since the original creation of the Palm OS.

### *A Whole Computer, Right in Your Pocket*

As many have already observed, technology gets cheaper, faster, and smaller every year. In practical terms, this means what was completely impossible ten years ago is very often commonplace nowadays. For example, when many of us were children, VCRs were either nonexistent or extremely expensive. Nowadays, almost everyone has one—if not several!

So, the folks at Microsoft pondered, what sorts of things were impossible when Palm OS was first being developed that have since become commonplace? They were able to think of several things fairly quickly:

- Color displays

- Easy application development

- External accessory integration

- Communications connectivity

- Faster processors

- Additional memory

As you can see, this adds up to quite a list of improvements!

 **TIP** *You don't need to have a Pocket PC in order to have a color display anymore. One of Palm's most successful competitors, which also uses the Palm OS operating system, is the Visor PDA. This PDA comes in color and is quite popular at the time of writing.*

As you will learn in the remainder of this chapter, application development for Pocket PCs is also much easier than for Palm OS. Whereas under Palm OS you would have to craft most custom applications in a low-level language like C, with Pocket PCs you can typically use a much friendlier language like eMbedded Visual Basic.

### *And It Integrates with Office!*

The real coup in Microsoft's battle against Palm OS, however, came when Microsoft was finally able to produce PDA-size versions of some of its most popular Office applications. Up to this point, a recurring complaint among Palm OS users had been, "How can I take my e-mail with me?" Or, "How can I work on this Word document while I am away from my computer?" With the introduction of Office for Pocket PCs, these questions were quickly answered: buy a Pocket PC!

Currently, users can use Outlook on their Pocket PCs to send and receive e-mails. They can also use Word on their Pocket PC to create documents completely compatible with the copy of Word running on their "real" desktop PCs. They can even update spreadsheets with their expenses on their Pocket PCs while they are on the road, and then update these to their real computers when they get back home.

## What Are Pocket PCs Made Of?

So, now that we've convinced you that Pocket PCs are the proverbial "all that and a bag of chips," you are probably wondering what exactly these devices are. As technical people, when we see a new gizmo, we aren't just interested in what it can do. We want to know *how* it is doing it.

### Hardware Is Half the Battle

The first advance in Pocket PCs over their Palm OS competitors lies in their hardware. The incredible increase in computing hardware power and decrease in cost over the last decade have given Microsoft a lot of new technology with which to play around. For the Pocket PCs, Microsoft has elected to use some of the best stuff that is out there, both for the devices and their accessories.

 **TIP** *Within the category of "best stuff out there," flashable ROMs fall high on our list. If you are still in the market for your own Pocket PC, by all means make sure to get one with a flashable ROM. This allows you to upgrade your operating system without having to purchase a new device.*

#### About the Devices Themselves

The first thing to understand about Pocket PCs is that, like Palm OS devices, they are made by a wide variety of vendors. For this reason, there is no single hardware profile that completely describes all Pocket PCs. However, a quick comparison of some of the features of the more popular Pocket PC models will give you a good idea of what is typical for them in terms of hardware.

*Table 3-1. Comparing Pocket PC Hardware*

| PROCESSOR SPEED | MEMORY | DISPLAY | BATTERY | SOUND | PROCESSOR TYPE |
|---|---|---|---|---|---|
| 133 MHz | 32MB | 240×320 color | 8 hours | Play/Record | ARM |
| 206 MHz | 32MB | 240×320 color | 8 hours | Play/Record | MIPS |
| 131 MHz | 16MB | 240×320 b&w | 6 hours | Play | SH3 |

As you can tell from Table 3-1, processors on Pocket PCs range in speed from 131 MHz up to 206 MHz. Bear in mind that these are speeds that would have been impressive for ordinary desktop computers just a few years ago! Nowadays, these processors are inexpensive enough to make it into state-of-the-art PDAs, however. Technology marches on!

In terms of memory, you can also find technology comparable to older PCs. 32MB is considered high end, whereas 16MB is normal. The displays are all the same size, 240×320, but some are color and some are not.

**CAUTION** *When designing applications for use with Pocket PCs, always remember that support for color is not a required part of the specification!*

Battery life varies widely from one model to the next and depends entirely on what tasks are being performed on a given Pocket PC. Obviously, simple word processing is far less battery intensive than running several accessories, such as modems.

### Getting Connected

Pocket PCs have a bewildering assortment of accessories. There are several reasons for Microsoft's success in getting such a huge number of vendors to create hardware accessories for its new PDA platform:

- Immediate popularity of the platform

- Platform's close links to the Windows operating system

- Pocket PCs' use of standard PC card interfaces

Of all of these, the last is probably the most important. By making the hardware specification for Pocket PCs extremely close to that of desktop computers, Microsoft has managed to greatly decrease the amount that it costs a company to develop an accessory for the Pocket PC. The reason for this is that once the accessory is designed, with very little additional effort it can be retrofitted for use with standard desktop PCs running Windows.

Of all the interesting accessories, however, probably none are as important to this discussion as the add-on modems and network cards. These are the pieces of hardware that allow Pocket PCs to connect to the Internet and thus become the kind of wireless clients for which you will be writing your .NET applications.

There are three principal kinds of connectivity for Pocket PCs:

- Land-line modems

- Network cards

- Wireless modems

Land-line modems are probably the least interesting way to connect a Pocket PC to the Internet. These are just your typical dial-up modems, which leverage the Pocket PCs closeness to a regular PC to make a standard dial-up connection to the Internet. This means that a cable must be run from the telephone jack to a stand-alone modem, which then connects to the RS-232 port on your Pocket PC. This is illustrated in Figure 3-1.

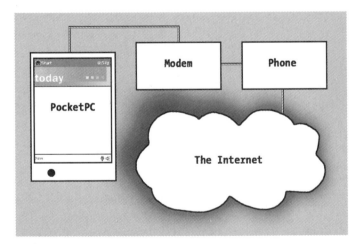

*Figure 3-1. Connecting a Pocket PC with a regular modem*

A significantly more interesting though equally primitive way to connect a Pocket PC modem to the Internet is via the use of a network card (see Figure 3-2). This approach is more comparable to that taken by desktop computers using DSL than anything else. Once again, a line must be run from the wall to a modem (typically a DSL or cable modem), which then connects to the Pocket PC. In this case, however, the Pocket PC must have a special card in its expansion slot that is capable of accepting an Ethernet connection.

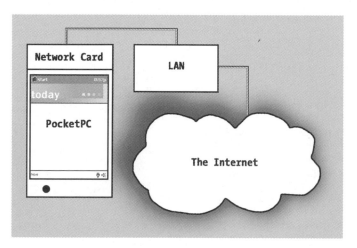

*Figure 3-2. Connecting a Pocket PC with a network card*

 **TIP** *If you are connecting to an ISP that uses all open standards for its service, you should have no problem using your Pocket PC to surf the Internet. If, on the other hand, you want to use a service with a proprietary interface, such as AOL, you may be in for difficulties. In general, the only way that connections like this can work is via software specially created by the service for specific platforms (iMac, Windows, and so on). As of the time of writing, neither AOL nor MSN officially support connections from Pocket PC.*

The final way of connecting to the Internet with a Pocket PC is to use a wireless modem. These modems are produced by a wide variety of hardware manufacturers, but perhaps one of the best known is Novatel. This company produces modems, named Minstrels, specifically for handheld devices. A Minstrel modem connects to a Pocket PC like an expansion card, except that it typically winds up encasing it, in addition to sliding into it.

When the Pocket PC informs the modem that it wishes to make an Internet connection, the Minstrel modem uses a specific Internet service targeted at wireless devices. This allows the device to get the maximum bandwidth "for its buck," because the networking is specially adapted for use on the wireless Internet. Figure 3-3 illustrates a typical connection using a wireless modem.

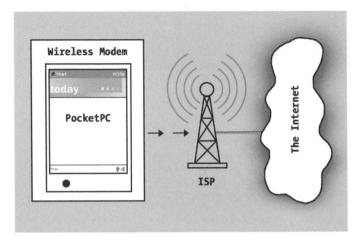

*Figure 3-3. Connecting a Pocket PC with a wireless modem*

## Software Is the Other Half

So far, we have told you quite a bit about all the hardware that goes into making a wireless Pocket PC Internet device. However, we haven't really said much about the software that makes it all work. Fortunately, if you have already had experience creating software for the Windows operating system, then you have already fought a good deal of the battle!

### Meet Windows CE

Pocket PCs by definition must run a specific subset of the Windows CE operating system. This subset is known as the Pocket PC operating system. It is the one thing that all Pocket PCs have in common—regardless of their manufacturer.

**TIP**   *Microsoft has never officially stated what CE stands for, but the speculation is that it was originally intended to mean* consumer electronics.

**NOTE**    *The Windows CE operating system is in its third version at the time of writing, with a fourth edition on its way. The first version of Windows CE was released to little fanfare a few years ago, as the current buzz about devices and mobile computing was still in its infancy. The first Pocket PCs ran a subset of Windows CE 2, about the time the mobile Internet craze really began to take off. However, Pocket PCs running Windows CE 2 have some serious restrictions compared to those running Windows CE 3 and later, as discussed later.*

Windows CE is a special flavor of the Windows operating system that is intended for use with embedded systems. What is an embedded system? It can be thought of as just about anything that runs software *other* than a computer. For example, the new generation of cable TV boxes that provide program listings and a high degree of interactivity typically contain some embedded systems.

Microsoft created Windows CE for use with cable boxes, automobiles, satellites, and a whole range of other devices—long before the rage in wireless Internet was upon us. Once this trend became apparent, it seemed logical to Microsoft to make Windows CE the basis for its own entry into the PDA wars.

There is something special about creating embedded operating systems, however. Recall that we said Pocket PCs feature a wide variety of hardware. Well, how can Microsoft know which hardware to use as a target for its operating system then? Some hardware is very powerful, and could use many features (like an army tank). Other hardware is very minimal and needs as much functionality in as little space as possible (like a cable TV box).

### Creating Your Own OS with Platform Builder

With Windows CE, Microsoft allows different hardware vendors to customize the operating system appropriately for its devices. For example, Table 3-2 shows the (hypothetical) choices that the creator of a killer robot might make in comparison to someone designing a new Internet toaster.

*Table 3-2. Choosing (Make Believe) Bits of Windows CE*

| FEATURE | KILLER ROBOT | INTERNET TOASTER |
| --- | --- | --- |
| Voice control | Yes | Yes |
| Laser targeting | Yes | No |
| Marmalade dispensing monitor | No | Yes |
| TCP/IP | Yes | Yes |
| International support | No | No |

As you can see from our (admittedly fanciful) example, although there are a total of five make-believe components in this operating system, either operating system will include only two or three. When you consider that there are hundreds of pieces in Windows CE, you will understand where this kind of a la carte approach to OS creation can be particularly efficient.

**NOTE** *One of the most important parts of the Pocket PC specification is, in fact, the list of Windows CE components that must be included in a Pocket PC's OS. This is why you will often hear people say that a certain device runs the Pocket PC operating system. This is a bit of a misnomer. In actuality, it runs Windows CE—but it runs the specific combination of Windows CE components that are required in order to be called a Pocket PC.*

The application that is used to create new Windows CE–based operating systems is known as the Microsoft Platform Builder. If you had not read this section, you might be confused when looking at the documentation for Pocket PCs on Microsoft's Web site. So, let's make this perfectly clear: *You do not need Microsoft Platform Builder in order to create Pocket PC applications!*

The only case in which you need Microsoft Platform Builder is if you are looking to release your own variation on the Windows CE operating system. Insofar as this is completely beyond the scope of this book, we will not discuss it here at any length.

## What Does the Future Hold?

This more or less brings us to the end of our discussion about what Pocket PCs are. It is important, however, that you also have a sense of where Pocket PCs stand in relationship to other technologies, and in which direction their technology will likely evolve in a few years.

### Better Hardware

The one constant in computing technology over the last 30 years has been that, given time, everything will become faster, smaller, and less expensive. This will hold true for Pocket PCs, too.

### *More Powerful Devices*

Given decreases in cost and increases in performance, it is almost certain that tomorrow's Pocket PCs will be much more powerful than today's devices. The real question is whether they will be smaller and cheaper.

The question of size has to do with features and end-user requirements. The size of the screen, for example, is an end-user requirement that cannot be reduced through technology. People simply will not want to work on screens that are much smaller than the ones that they have now.

Another thing that will make smaller Pocket PCs unlikely in the future is the continued demand to incorporate additional performance and features. True, the 300 MHz chip of tomorrow may only be half the size of today's 300 MHz chip. By tomorrow, however, people may very well be demanding 600 MHz chips—which are liable to be the same size, if not larger.

So far as cost is concerned, the rapid reduction in computer hardware price is one of the reasons that the Pocket PC succeeded at all. Recall that before the Pocket PC, Palm OS had first made its inroads into the market by offering a reduced feature set at a more affordable price. If Pocket PCs are to remain successful, they will need to remain competitively priced.

### *Better Accessories*

The quality of accessories available for Pocket PCs is also likely to improve over time. Some of the devices that are just now coming to market include the following:

- Full-size keyboards

- Infrared (I/R) ports

- Microdrives

- Code wands

If these devices are coming to market less than two years after the introduction of the Pocket PC, imagine what will be available two years from now!

## Better Software

And here's where you come in! In order for Pocket PCs to really take off, they need killer apps. The great thing about working for wireless devices is that all of the great killer apps haven't already been written and patented by someone else.

For example, PocketDBA Systems was able to create an application for managing Oracle databases that would've been swamped with competitors if we had created it for a standard PC.

### *More Off-the-Shelf Solutions*

Whether you're a software creator or consumer, more off-the-shelf solutions is good news for you. From the standpoint of the consumer, the advantage is obvious—more selection and better prices.

The same trend will benefit you as an application designer, too. Whereas today you are limited to using Microsoft's own tools (plus those of a couple of competitors) for the creation of Pocket PC applications, for example, in the future there may be several other off-the-shelf development environments available.

Similarly, today there is a very small pool of components available for use in creating new Pocket PC software. As the platform grows in popularity and seniority, this pool should increase nicely. The more components you can buy rather than build, the quicker your solutions will be done and the more profitable they will be!

### *And, You Guessed It, .NET Integration!*

When laying out the outline for this book, we chose to cover Pocket PCs immediately after Internet Explorer for a very good reason. Both of these platforms represent the targets that have received the official Microsoft "blessing" for .NET development. This means that over time Microsoft will be bringing more and more technologies to market that are intended specifically to help these platforms interoperate with .NET.

**TIP**   *In the next chapter, you will learn about WAP and i-Mode phones, which are best described as tolerated by .NET. In the subsequent chapters, you will learn about two platforms, Palm OS and J2ME, which can perhaps be described as foreign to .NET. So, you should think of the first several chapters in this book as moving from most-accepted to least-accepted platform by the .NET technology initiative.*

The single most important .NET technology for Pocket PCs is the .NET Compact Frameworks—commonly referred to as .NETcf. Chapter 15 of this book is dedicated specifically to discussing .NETcf and explaining how you can use it to create .NET applications for the Pocket PC, among other devices.

Creating an application for the Pocket PC is probably the easiest exercise that you will undertake in this book. So get ready to enjoy yourself!

## eMbedded Visual Tools

The eMbedded Visual Tools (eVT) offered by Microsoft are arguably some of the most straight-forward development tools available for any kind of embedded development on any platform. Using some of the tools, it is possible to create an application and test it within a matter of minutes right from your own desktop—without even having to own a Pocket PC!

### Languages Included with eVT

Two different languages make up the eMbedded Visual Tools. Both of them are derivatives of languages found in Microsoft's development suite for the standard Windows operating system, Visual Studio.

#### eMbedded Visual Basic

The first of the two languages referred to in the previous paragraph, eMbedded Visual Basic (eVB), is a subset of the standard Visual Basic 6 development environment. Programmers familiar with this language should be able to quickly get up and running when it comes to creating applications for Pocket PCs. Because a knowledge of Visual Basic is one of the assumptions we have made about you in this book, we will be taking a much closer look at this environment later in this chapter.

#### eMbedded Visual C++

The other language offered by the eMbedded Visual Tools is eMbedded Visual C++ (eVC++). Like its bigger brother in Visual Studio, it is considered a more flexible yet much more complicated language than Visual Basic.

There is a key difference between developing for Pocket PC using eMbedded Visual C++ and using eMbedded Visual Basic. If you develop an application in eMbedded Visual Basic, it is processor independent. However, if you develop an application in eMbedded Visual C++, it is not.

This means that if you build a program using eMbedded Visual C++, you are not building it for Pocket PCs in general. Instead, you must build it for a specific processor (or set of processors)—and this limits it to certain models of

Pocket PC. For writing code with the greatest range of use, rely on eMbedded Visual Basic.

## And They Give You Some Emulators, Too

The embedded programming languages would represent excellent tools if these were the only things that came included in eMbedded Visual Tools. But wait, there's more.

### *We're Interested in the Pocket PC Emulator*

In addition to the languages, there are several SDKs included in the eMbedded Visual Tools. One of these SDKs is the Microsoft Windows Platform SDK for the Pocket PC. In the next section, we will show you how to install this—as it is essential for creating Pocket PC applications.

One of the most important things that is included in this package is the Pocket PC emulator. The Pocket PC emulator allows you to test your Pocket PC applications directly on your own desktop computer, as shown in Figure 3-4.

*Figure 3-4. The Pocket PC emulator*

The Pocket PC emulator includes all of the Microsoft-distributed software that comes as a part of the standard Pocket PC distribution. This includes Pocket Internet Explorer, which is an important part of developing wireless applications for the Pocket PC.

### Pocket Internet Explorer

In this book, we will most often show you how to create mobile applications that feature both a client section and a server section. However, sometimes you will just want to create a server-side Web page for consumption by Pocket PCs. In these cases, you will have to deal with Pocket Internet Explorer.

Pocket Internet Explorer can be thought of as a reduced version of the "regular" Internet Explorer to which you were introduced in the previous chapter. The current version of Pocket IE (version 3), which is available on all Pocket PCs running Windows CE 3, is quite good. All the major features of HTML 3.2 are available and supported.

The version of Pocket IE (version 2) that shipped on older Pocket PCs running Windows CE 2.12 is quite unlike the full version of Internet Explorer. Pocket Internet Explorer 2 had a number of limitations:

- No client-side scripting

- No client-side binary controls or applets

- Limited graphics format support

- No frames

- No SSL

- No cookies

As you can probably tell from this list, developing Web pages for use with Pocket Internet Explorer 2 was a lot like creating Web pages in 1995. Add to this the fact that the overwhelming majority of Pocket PCs now in use are running version 3 of Windows CE, and you quickly realize why we will be focusing exclusively on Pocket IE 3 and higher in this book.

## A Crash Course in eVB

If you already know Visual Basic, then you already know 90 percent of what you need to get started developing applications for the Pocket PC.

### This Isn't the Same as "Regular" Visual Basic

Like Pocket Internet Explorer's relationship to the full Internet Explorer, eMbedded Visual Basic is essentially a limited version of Visual Studio's Visual Basic. Besides creating applications for the Pocket PC, there is really nothing that can be done with eMbedded Visual Basic that can't be done with standard Visual Basic.

#### Resources Are Limited

The first great limiting factor in creating applications with eVB is that the resources available to you on a Pocket PC are not nearly the same as on a standard desktop machine. One obvious example is the limit on battery life available on Pocket PCs. However, from a developer's standpoint, the limited storage on these devices is of much more pressing concern.

As one example of limited storage, consider the situation if the amount of free memory on a Pocket PC should run low. This is a situation that rarely presents itself on a desktop computer, where the OS will begin swapping memory pages out to hard disk long before physical RAM is completely exhausted. However, on most Pocket PCs, there is no disk storage upon which swapping may be performed.

What will happen in this case is that applications, including the ones you write, may be suspended to conserve available RAM. As other applications are closed, the suspended applications may be restored. Otherwise, if the situation becomes critical, they may actually be terminated—possibly without the opportunity to save their data.

Another limitation on storage is described in the section "The Language Isn't Exactly the Same, Either" later in this chapter.

#### You Can't Create All the Same Projects

The full version of Visual Basic that comes with Visual Studio allows you to create a dizzying array of projects. As Table 3-3 indicates, only a small handful of these are possible under eVB.

*Table 3-3. Project Variety under eVB? Forget about It!*

| PROJECT TYPE | VISUAL BASIC FOR VISUAL STUDIO | eVB | eVC++ |
|---|---|---|---|
| Standard EXE | Yes | Yes | Yes |
| ActiveX component | Yes | No | Yes |
| ActiveX control | Yes | No | Yes |
| ActiveX document | Yes | No | No |
| Add-in | Yes | No | No |
| Data project | Yes | No | No |
| DHTML application | Yes | No | No |
| IIS application | Yes | No | No |

So, as Table 3-3 illustrates, you have a *very* limited project selection under eVB that is only slightly better under eVC++. Specifically, by using eVB instead of eVC++, you lose the ability to create COM components under Windows CE.

 **CAUTION**  *If you want to create a custom driver for some reason, you will not be able to do this using eVB, either. As a general rule, anything that is low level and requires dealing with the hardware at its own level is impossible under eVB.*

### You Don't Have Access to All the Same Libraries

The final thing that you might find limiting about the eVB environment is that you don't have access to any of the libraries and supporting components with which you may be familiar from "regular" Visual Basic. The reason that you don't find the same controls and libraries available to you under Windows CE as under Windows is that they really are two completely different operating systems. The Windows operating system is closely tied to the Intel (sometimes Alpha) processors and PC-style hardware. Creating an operating system for embedded devices, which may feature literally hundreds of different processor types, requires creating a completely different architecture.

Along with this new architecture comes the need for the creation of completely new controls and components. Existing ones simply won't work with Windows CE. It would be like trying to run Solaris software on a Mac computer (assuming it isn't Java).

## The Language Isn't Exactly the Same, Either

As if having lost your plentiful resources and components wasn't bad enough, you will also have to compensate for certain shortcomings in the eVB language.

### You Can't Access the Entire API

In case you have never worked with them before, the Windows APIs are the low-level functions and procedures upon which the operating system is actually built. By calling directly into the APIs from your applications, it has always been possible to expand their functionality and allow them to do things which would be otherwise impossible from Visual Basic.

The same principal holds true under the Windows CE operating system. Although all of the APIs are different internally, their names and parameter lists are generally the same as or very similar to APIs in the Windows operating system. For this reason, the ability to call APIs under Windows CE to sidestep limitations in eVB is very appealing.

Unfortunately, it is not possible to call directly into Windows CE APIs from eVB. If you want to do this, you will have to write your client applications in eMbedded Visual C++.

### You Don't Have as Rich a File Structure

Another limitation on storage in Pocket PCs involves their primitive file systems. On a desktop computer, you might be quite familiar with creating directory structures that are often several levels deep. Take a look at this example:

```
C:\Program Files\PocketDBA\Tomcat\Bin\Startup.bat
```

In this example, the script Startup.bat is located in a directory structure that is four levels deep. This is not possible on current Pocket PCs. The Pocket PC storage system only supports a file structure that is a single level deep. For example:

```
\AccountsPayable
```

## Getting Started

In this section, we will finally get started creating Pocket PC applications. As you will soon see, the tight integration of the Pocket PC with the rest of Microsoft's product line makes for one of the easiest application creation procedures of all the devices we will discuss in this book.

### Installing the Right Software

In order to build Pocket PC–compliant software, you must first install the software Microsoft produces specifically for this task. The first piece of this software is eMbedded Visual Basic. The second is the Pocket PC SDK.

 **NOTE** *Those of you with MSDN Universal subscriptions should be able to find the Microsoft eMbedded Visual Tools included among your regular monthly software shipments. If you do not have an MSDN Universal subscription, a set of CDs containing these tools may be ordered directly from Microsoft for only the cost of shipping. The URL (current as of the time of writing) to place these orders is* http://www.microsoft.com/windows/embedded/ce/tools/emvt30order.asp.

#### First, Install eVB

It is important to note that each step in this section builds upon the foundation laid by the previous step. *Please do not try to skip around.* If you do, you will find that the process does not work as intended. Instead, follow each step through carefully from beginning to end!

To install eMbedded Visual Basic, follow these steps:

1. Insert the CD containing eMbedded Visual Tools.

2. At this point, the Installation Wizard should automatically start. If it doesn't, follow these steps.

     a.   Right-click your CD's icon.

     b.   Choose Explore from the pop-up context menu.

     c.   Double-click the icon labeled Setup.

3. Click Next.

4. Accept the license agreement.

5. Enter your product number and user information.

6. Deselect Windows CE Platform SDK (H/PC Pro) and Windows CE Platform SDK (Palm-size PC 1.2).

7. Choose a location on your hard disk for the installation.

8. Choose eMbedded Visual Basic (eVB) on the next screen.

9. When prompted to do so, change CDs.

### Next, Install the Pocket PC Emulator

Once the installer prompts you to insert the second CD, you will be ready to begin installing the Pocket PC emulator. The Pocket PC emulator is just one component of the complete Pocket PC SDK that you elected to install in the previous procedure. To complete this procedure, follow these steps:

1. After changing CDs, the Pocket PC SDK Installation Wizard should appear.

2. Click Next.

3. Accept the licensing agreement.

4. If asked, choose to install the application for all users.

5. Choose a location on your hard disk for the installation, and then click Next.

6. Choose the Complete installation option, and then click Next.

7. Click Install.

This installation can be fairly lengthy, owing to the large number of files that must be copied from the CD to your local hard disk. A progress bar should keep you informed as to how the installation is proceeding.

## Testing Your Installations

At this point, you are all set to create and execute your first Pocket PC application.

### *Creating an Application in eVB*

On the Windows Start menu, you should now find a program group labeled Microsoft eMbedded Visual Tools. Under this group, you may now select eMbedded Visual Basic to open the eVB designer. It should look like Figure 3-5.

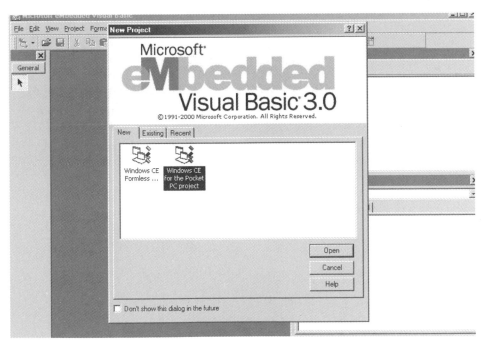

*Figure 3-5. Welcome to eMbedded Visual Basic*

At this point, you are being given the option to create two different kinds of projects:

- Windows CE Formless project

- Windows CE for the Pocket PC project

Choose the latter of these two to begin. If you are familiar with Visual Basic, you will easily recognize the screen that now presents itself. On the toolbox at the left of the screen, double-click the Command Button icon to add a single command button to the screen. Use the Property Editor on the lower-right of the screen to change this button's caption to Press Me. When you are done, it should look like Figure 3-6.

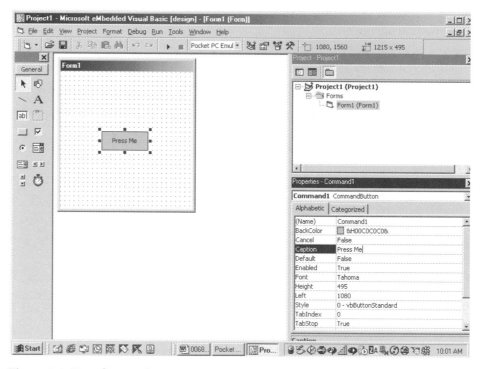

*Figure 3-6. Your first Pocket PC project*

Double-clicking the command button that you have just added to the form should now take you into code-editing mode. Specifically, you should find yourself within the Click event for this button. Change the code to look as follows:

```
Private Sub Command1_Click()

  MsgBox "Hello World!"

End Sub
```

Once you have made these changes, close the code-editing window. You are now ready to test your application.

### *Viewing the Application in the Emulator*

Very little in the world of embedded development is as easy as creating and testing code using eMbedded Visual Basic. To test your code, simply find the Debug button on the eVB action bar. This is the icon that looks like a little Play button, located directly beneath the Tools menu. If you are familiar with the full version of Visual Basic, this is the same button as the Run button.

If you press this button now, a number of things will happen:

- You will see a message on the screen that reads "Connecting to the remote device."

- You will see a message on the screen that reads "Registering" followed by the programmatic identifier of your new project.

- The Pocket PC emulator will display itself, with your new application already running.

Go ahead and click the button labeled Press Me. It should pop up a message box similar to the one shown in Figure 3-7.

*Figure 3-7. See how easy it is?*

You have to admit, this makes for a very painless development cycle! To close your application, click OK in the upper-right corner of the message box. Next, click OK in the upper-right corner of the application itself. You may close the emulator at this point.

# Internet Links

For the latest information, nothing can beat the Internet. With this in mind, here is a list of Pocket PC Web sites that you may find useful for further research:

- http://www.pocketpc.com

- http://www.pocketgamer.org

- http://www.pocketpcpassion.com

- http://www.pocketpchelp.com

- http://www.pocketpcthoughts.com

- http://windowsce.kensai.com/faq

*Part Two*

# The "Other" Devices

# CHAPTER 4
# Mobile Phones
## This Is NOT Your Father's Cell Phone

AT THIS POINT, YOU HAVE seen a number of devices that can be used to surf the wireless Web. In some ways, one of the most promising devices to hit the streets in recent years isn't really new, but has been around for almost a decade: the mobile phone, or so-called cell phone.

What makes the new generation of mobile phones so different from their forebears is their capacity to receive and transmit data, rather than just voice. In this chapter, we will look at a bit of the hardware behind these devices. However, our real focus (as you should probably have guessed) will be on the development of applications to work with them.

## Foundations of the Smart Phone

The world of mobile phones is rapidly dividing itself into two camps. The first camp comprises all the older, non–Internet-enabled phones, which we will call mobile phones or cell phones in the context of this discussion. The newer, Internet-enabled models, however, we will refer to as *smart phones*.

The "smart phone" label implies a number of different functionalities beyond the mere making and receiving of calls that we use our phones for. Amongst these functions are the following:

- Contact management

- Enhanced telephony (call waiting, voice mail, and so on)

- Data transmission

- Data reception

- Phone-to-phone infrared

- Alphanumeric input capabilities

- Built-in games and utilities

As you can see, the expected suite of functions for true smart phones is much greater than for the older mobile phones with which we are all familiar. So, how did all of this evolve out of the modest functionality that was first embodied by cell phones?

## History of Internet Phones

In order to understand the origins of the modern smart phone, you must first understand the evolution of the languages upon which they run. Originally, the only language for cell phones was known as the Handheld Device Markup Language (HDML). Nowadays, enhancements have changed this language into what is commonly known as WML—the Wireless Markup Language. Also, in Japan, NTT DoCoMo has offered a very successful service known as i-Mode, which is based upon the cHTML (compact HTML) language.

In this section, we will confine ourselves to giving you a brief overview of how HDML came into existence and how it laid the foundation for WML. We'll show you some of the fundamental points about mobile phone hardware that often prove to be limiting factors in the creation of new smart phone technologies. Finally, we'll explain how all of this fits into .NET—so that you can be motivated to learn everything else that awaits you in the chapter!

### What Was HDML?

HDML was a subset of the HTML language first introduced by Unwired Planet. Early on, people attempting to bring the Internet to cell phones realized that they had several limitations not present on more traditional Internet connections. Many of these limitations are discussed in detail later in the section "The Hardware of Internet Phones," but here are some of the important ones:

- Slowness

- Limited memory

- Limited screen space

HDML addressed a number of these issues for the first time for mobile devices.

### *It Was Derived from HTML*

HTML, as you already know, is the markup language used to describe pages on the World Wide Web. For example, a standard Web page might include HTML similar to that shown in Listing 4-1.

*Listing 4-1. A Typical HTML Page*

```
<html>
    <head>
        <title>Our Sample Page</title>
    </head>
    <body>
        Well, isn't this nice?<br>
        Click <a href="forward.html">here</a> to go to the next page<br>
        Click <a href="back.html">here</a> to go the the previous page<br>
    </body>
</html>
```

This code will create a very simple Web page in the receiver's browser. At the top, there will be a title reading "Our Sample Page." In the body, there will be a sentence reading "Well, isn't this nice?" and two hyperlinks. One of these will take the reader to a page called forward.html. The other will take the reader to a page called back.html.

However, consider the difficulty of rendering even this simple page on a small telephone display. To begin on a screen with only four rows of display size, the title, welcome message, and two hyperlinks will consume all available screen space. This would leave no room for the display of the soft buttons that would be used to actually navigate to any of the links.

Furthermore, the text on each of these lines is so wide that it would require wrapping onto multiple lines. This would easily consume much more than the limited screen space that is available.

### *But It Was Improved*

The approach taken by HDML, which would later be incorporated into WML, was to arrange data in the form of multiple "cards" within a single page. By downloading multiple screens of data at once, the expenses associated with round-trips back to the server were reduced. Figure 4-1 illustrates this concept.

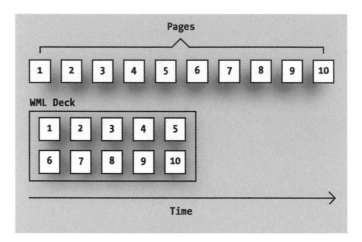

*Figure 4-1. HDML cards reducing bandwidth*

As you can see in the illustration, to download ten separate pages of information would take almost twice as long as to download the same ten pages as separate cards within a single HDML page. This architecture proved very successful for HDML, and numerous mobile phone vendors in the United States quickly became interested in adding HDML support to their devices.

In the section on WML later in this chapter, we will show you how this technology also addresses the issues of presentation when data is too large for the display.

## What Was Wrong with HDML?

So, if HDML was such a great idea, then why isn't it around anymore? As of the time of writing, it is still used quite a bit in the United States. HDML has proven to be quite a scalable and reliable technology for delivering Internet content onto mobile phones.

Even so, there were many areas in which it could be improved. The desire to improve upon an already good product led to the development of WML—the Wireless Markup Language. The two areas that are most targeted for improvement then are the manner in which standards are introduced into the language, and its focus on presentation as opposed to content.

### It Started Out with a Single Vendor

HDML started out as the vision of a single software vendor, Unwired Planet. In the current Internet economy, multivendor alliances and standards-making bodies are the order of the day. So, for version 2 of its HDML language, Unwired

Planet (which became Phone.com somewhere around this time) made sure to enlist the cooperation of several technology vendors in the design of its language. This laid the groundwork for what would ultimately become WML.

### *It Was All About Presentation*

The other area in which HDML took a lot of flack initially was in its lack of foundation in XML. In other words, around the time that HDML was being put together, the XML standard was just emerging. Early adopters of the XML standard felt that it was obviously destined to completely replace HTML as the standard for content on the World Wide Web.

"Why then," they reasoned, "would anyone built a new standard for mobile devices that is based on HTML?" If HTML was going to be made obsolete, then why not base the mobile language on XML, which was clearly the better technology going forward.

Well, history has shown that HTML has *not* been rendered completely irrelevant by the introduction of XML. Nevertheless, the designers of HDML felt that there was some truth to what these critics had to say.

For this reason, as you will see in the next section, WML was crafted to be more like XML and less like HTML. This allows the language to focus more on the information to be conveyed, and less on the presentation of that information.

## The Hardware of Internet Phones

Because you are a developer, the chances are good that you are not terribly interested in the details of the hardware underlying mobile devices. True, these are the devices that will be running your code, but that doesn't mean that you have to understand all of their internals, does it? Of course not!

On the other hand, there are some significant differences between the hardware that runs your average cell phone and the hardware on your laptop or desktop computer. If you wrote a massively complicated program for a modern Pentium computer, you wouldn't expect it to run properly on a 20-year-old Apple home computer, would you?

For this reason, it is important that you be aware of the limitations inherent in most cell phone hardware.

### They're Slow

Mobile phones are slow. A good part of the battle in creating true smart phones, in fact, is simply to increase the speed of the devices. The slowness typically manifests itself in two ways:

- Slow connections

- Slow processors

Of the two of these, you might be surprised to learn that slow processors are actually often considered to be the more formidable of the two problems, from a technical standpoint.

### *Slow Connections*

The connections currently offered by cell phones are pretty slow in comparison to the Internet connections that most of us are used to having on our desktops. The mobile phone that I own, for example, features a data transfer rate of just 9 Kbps. The more expensive model that was just released has 14.4 Kbps connectivity. These are data transfer rates that haven't been impressive since the late 1980s, if memory serves!

Fortunately, if you are in Europe, hope is on the horizon. Countries on this continent have been moving quickly to auction off and roll out portions of the high-speed wireless spectrum. This portion of bandwidth will allow Internet access from cell phones that will (finally) rival what most of us are used to on our desktops.

Unfortunately, in the United States the decision has been made to skip this generation of phones. The plan is to catch up with other countries by pushing for "the next big thing" now. Exactly what form this next big thing will take is not yet clear. In the meantime, those of us in the U.S. are simply out of luck where high-speed connections from our phones are concerned.

### *Slow Processors*

So, if those of us in the United States are going to be stuck with slow connections for the next few years, how can slow connections *possibly* be the worse problem? There are two primary reasons.

On one hand, the amount of data that can be shown on a mobile phone's screen at once is relatively small. For this reason, the amount of data to be transferred is equally small. In a roundabout way this means that the slowness of the typical mobile phone's connection is not felt as much as it would be if complete, fancy HTML Web pages were attempting to be viewed instead of small, HDML (or WML/cHTML) pages.

The other reason that slow processors are more of a problem is that a big part of the dilemma here is a financial one. Fast processors are expensive. This will probably always be true because as technology advances, so does the definition of what is fast. Ten years ago, a 40 MHz processor was considered fast, and it was therefore very expensive. Today, such processors are considered extremely slow—the fact that they are also cheap is therefore irrelevant.

What it boils down to is this: mobile phones aren't likely to be as powerful as desktop computers until people are willing to pay comparable amounts for them. People aren't likely to be willing to spend $1000 on a cell phone—no matter *what* it can do—at any point in the near future. Therefore, mobile phones will remain low-powered technology for quite some time.

## They Have Limited Resources

Besides being generally slow devices, mobile phones lack many of the resources that desktop computer users take for granted.

### *Limited Memory*

Whereas the typical desktop computer's memory is measured in megabytes, the average memory of cell phones is measured in kilobytes. In other words, you typically only have 1/1000th as much memory in a cell phone as you would on an Internet-enabled desktop computer. For this reason, any solution that attempts to deliver Internet content onto a mobile phone must be very space efficient.

As you will see in the section "Fundamentals of WAP" later in this chapter, many WAP servers address this problem by precompiling the code that they send to the mobile phones. This means that comments in the raw WML code, for example, need not be held in a device's memory while it finishes the job of interpreting and executing the instructions.

### *Limited Electrical Power*

The final limitation, which should be familiar to all of us who have ever owned a mobile phone, is that mobile phones do not have a limitless supply of electrical power. Great strides have been made in recent years to increase the amount of so-called standby time that cellular phones can stay turned on when they are actually in use. This allows the modern mobile phone to wait for long periods (often as long as multiple weeks) to receive a call.

Unfortunately, this ability to exist in standby mode for weeks at a time does not help you at all when you are connected to the Internet. For all intents and purposes, a connection to the Internet from modern mobile phones is the same thing as a telephone call. If you can expect one hour of talk time on a single battery with your current phone, then you should expect about the same amount of Internet connectivity.

## What Does the Future Hold?

The future for cellular phones is very bright indeed. As more and more functionality is added to the devices, they are almost certain to become even more popular than they already are. There are three future trends that most directly affect you as a potential wireless developer, however:

- .NET's support for Internet access by mobile phones

- The continued success of i-Mode

- The success or failure of WAP

### .NET Will Support the Smart Phone

If the question were simply whether .NET will support Internet access via mobile phone, then the answer could be as simple as yes. However, there is a great deal of vagueness associated with a question like this. To begin with, what does it really mean for any technology to support the use of another technology? Technically, Windows supports the execution of software written for Unix—provided that you are willing to first translate it all into Windows code.

Clearly, stupid questions make for stupid answers. Let us refine our question then to be, "How (if at all) will .NET support Internet access via mobile phone?" The answer to this is much clearer. First, a key piece of .NET called the Mobile Internet Toolkit will directly interoperate with both the WAP and cHTML protocols. Secondly, Microsoft's own entry into the mobile phone wars—the Stinger phone—will support the use of WAP (in addition to standard HTML). Finally, XSLISAPI can support both WAP and cHTML (among many other things).

**NOTE** *As you will learn in Chapter 15, the Windows CE Profile of the .NET Compact Frameworks will be an integral part of almost all Windows CE 4 devices (Stinger phones, Pocket PC 4, and so on) Also, the cross-platform profile of .NETcf is targeted for availability on many non-Microsoft mobile phones. What all of this means is that very shortly you will be able to run your .NET-based code on a wide range of devices—mobile phones included!*

### *The Mobile Internet Toolkit Supports WAP and i-Mode*

In Chapters 12 through 14, you will learn a great deal about the Mobile Internet Toolkit, because it is one of the most important parts of .NET. From the standpoint of an aspiring wireless developer, it is arguably the most important part. We don't want to get too ahead of ourselves at this point by delving into the details of what the Mobile Internet Toolkit is and what it can do. Suffice it to say that through its use, a single piece of code on a .NET server can be accessed and used by Internet Explorer, a Pocket PC, a WAP phone, or an i-Mode phone without alteration!

### *The Stinger Phone Supports WAP*

The Stinger phone is Microsoft's proposed mobile phone model for use with the wireless Internet. It is similar to many of the most advanced WAP-enabled cell phones that are currently on the market. However, it has a few features that are particularly surprising:

- A standard POP/IMAP e-mail client

- Support for HTML

- Support for WAP

- Software updates right over the Internet

- Close integration with other Microsoft applications (such as Exchange)

- Windows CE 4 with .NET Compact Frameworks support

- Color screens

Since the Stinger phones support WAP and HTML, they are completely compatible with .NET (which uses both of these protocols).

### *XSLISAPI Supports Many Things (WAP and cHTML among Them)*

In Chapter 11, you will learn how to use XSLISAPI to invoke what are known as Web Services from WAP and i-Mode. We don't want to get too ahead of ourselves, but here is what it does in a nutshell. You put a single XML file on your server someplace where IIS can serve it up as a Web page. When a request comes in from any browser or device, XSLISAPI catches the request and determines what kind of a device it is coming from. If the request is from a standard browser,

XSLISAPI instructs IIS to send back HTML. If the request is from a mobile phone, WML or cHTML can be returned. And so on and so forth.

---

 **NOTE** *If you are at all familiar with Java 2 Enterprise Edition (J2EE), then this is very similar to the functionality offered in that arena by Apache's Cocoon software. For more information, please visit* `http://xml.apache.org`.

---

## Succeeding in Wireless with NTT DoCoMo

If you'd like proof that success is still possible for the wireless Internet, even as the global IT recession appears to be picking up its pace, then pay a visit to this URL: `http://www.nttdocomo.com/i/i_m_scr.html`.

As of the time of writing, the total number of subscribers to NTT DoCoMo's i-Mode service is close to 26 million. Considering that this service is only available in the relatively small country of Japan, this number is even more astounding. In Japan, the total number of users connecting to the Internet via handhelds has now exceeding those connecting via traditional PCs!

So, what do you need to know as a developer in order to cash in on this enormous market for wireless applications? cHTML is essential, and a knowledge of Japanese wouldn't hurt.

### The Easy One: cHTML

The good news about cHTML is it's just like HTML, only limited. If you browse to the URL `http://www.nttdocomo.com/i/tag/index.html`, you will find that almost all of the tags listed are familiar to you. The trick to creating cHTML Web sites is to simply avoid those features of HTML that are not supported. For example, you will notice on the site that the <BODY> tag is listed as accepting no parameters. This is in contrast to the way that the tag is used on many Web pages:

```
<BODY BGCOLOR="white">
```

In this example, the BGCOLOR parameter is being used to set the page's background color to white. On early i-Mode phones, the BGCOLOR parameter would be completely ignored. On the newer phones, support for this parameter has been added.

For a list of all the latest cHTML tags and their use, go to the following URL: `http://www.nttdocomo.com/i/tag/lineup.html`.

**NOTE** *The particularly observant among you may have noticed by this point that none of the URLs cited previously are written in Japanese. You may be disappointed to learn, however, that these sites represent the exception rather than the rule where i-Mode sites are concerned.*

### The Hard One: Japanese

As you might have guessed, teaching Japanese is just a little beyond the scope of this book. If you *really* want to create and market a successful i-Mode application, however, you will have to avail yourself of the services of someone (or some organization) that completely understands both the language and culture.

The technical reason, as you will see shortly, is that virtually all of the tools and documentation associated with i-Mode and cHTML are written in Japanese. If you are really desperate, you can try putting online docs through AltaVista's Babel Fish translator, which is at the following URL: `http://babelfish.altavista.com`.

Unfortunately, we've only had limited success in using this tool with Japanese. For one thing, machine-based translation is still only about 50 percent accurate at best. For another thing, this does nothing to help translate images or screens on the emulator that we will show you later in this chapter.

### So, Is WAP Any Good?

Now that we have spent several pages selling you on the benefits of Internet access via mobile phone, it may surprise you that we are questioning its value. To be perfectly blunt, you may have to write applications for mobile phones today *even if* everyone decides to abandon this technology tomorrow (or to do it a completely different way). The simple reason for this is that at the moment, almost everyone else is doing it—and you don't want to be left behind on the technology curve as a developer.

### It Has Limited Functionality

In many ways, this is the perfect spot at which to alert you to the shortcomings of mobile phone Internet technology circa 2001. Since you are just about to begin looking at the actual nuts and bolts of WAP, this is a good point at which to engage in some judicious "expectations management."

To begin with, there are no features in WAP for specifying the exact placement of objects upon the display. Instead, WML (the markup language of WAP) tends to specify more *what* should be on a given card, and then lets the individual device determine the most appropriate way to do the rendering.

Also, when you first start using WAP applications, you may feel that the data input mechanism leaves something to be desired. For example, just trying to enter the name Derek Ferguson into an application would probably require in the neighborhood of 30 key presses. Considering that the name in question is only 14 characters long, this may not seem terribly efficient.

Finally, there is a tendency in WAP applications to have to do a lot of paging back and forth between multiple cards. Some might argue that the "card and deck" architecture of WML encourages this kind of application design.

### But the Technology Is Still in Its Early Days!

All of these criticisms are fair in a general sort of way, but there is one thing that you must bear in mind: mobile phones are only just now being adapted for serious use with the wireless Internet. Although WML doesn't let you do much in the way of fancy presentation formatting, given the current size, lack of resolution, and lack of colors on most cell phone displays, chances are that the devices can do a much better job of formatting themselves than any application developer could.

Data input is indeed a chore under WAP. On the other hand, considering that most mobile phones only possess a nine-button numeric keypad with which to do any kind of input, this is hardly the fault of WAP. Instead, WAP has proposed a solution to a problem that other vendors have simply avoided altogether.

## Creating Applications

Now that you have learned everything that there is to know about how the Internet came to be on people's mobile phones at this point in time, wouldn't it be nice to know how to create applications for them? We will begin a look at exactly this topic in this section. By the time you reach the end of this section, you will have gathered all of the right tools, installed them, and tested them. But first, you need to understand what we hope to build with them.

### Fundamentals of WAP

In the previous section, you learned that Internet content delivered to mobile phones really began with a markup language from Unwired Planet called HDML. This language is still in widespread use across the United States. However, it is rapidly being eclipsed by a newer markup language known as WML.

## The Wireless Markup Language

Wireless Markup Language (WML) is the markup language component of WAP. You might think of WML as being to WAP what HTML is to HTTP. That is to say, WAP is the overall protocol (or more appropriately suite of protocols) and WML is the format of the actual messages that are sent back and forth across those protocols.

Along with WMLScript, WML is one of the things with which you absolutely must become comfortable in order to create applications for mobile phones.

### *How Is WML Architected?*

WML can be thought of as the XML-oriented successor to HDML. Like HDML, pages are organized as a series of cards—with each card corresponding more-or-less to a single screen's worth of data. Listing 4-2 shows an example of a simple WML page.

*Listing 4-2. Your First Glimpse of WML*

```
<?xml version="1.0"?>
<!DOCTYPE wml PUBLIC "-//WAPFORUM//DTD WML 1.1//EN"
    "http://www.wapforum.org/DTD/wm1_1.1.xml">

<wml>
    <card id="one" title="Hello World">
      <p>
          Hello World, what do you think of this?
      </p>
    </card>
</wml>
```

 **CAUTION**  *If you are not already comfortable with XML, then you should take a break now to familiarize yourself with its syntax and usage before continuing. See Appendix A for an introduction to XML. All WML is in fact a kind of XML. So, if you try to proceed here without first understanding XML, you are going to have serious problems. You have been warned!*

As you can see, the entire document begins with a declaration that it will contain XML. Good WML is always well-formed XML. As such, all the other bits of this document subscribe to the rules that you would expect for an XML document. For example, the paragraph tag <p>, which would usually be used by itself in standard HTML, is in this document paired up with a matching </p> tag. This meets the requirement of well-formed XML, which stipulates that every tag have a matching closing tag.

### How Is WML Constructed?

To quote Steve Martin, "The thing about the French is, they have a different word for everything!" The situation with WML is similar—there is a different tag for everything. Fortunately, knowing a few key points will take you a good part of the way. For the rest, we provide links to numerous Web sites where you can learn more.

To begin with, you should understand the <card> tag. A card corresponds more-or-less to a single screen's worth of data in your WAP application. As you can see in Listing 4-2, cards have id and title parameters. The id parameter is what you will use to programmatically refer to a given card (often to navigate to it, for example). The title parameter, on the other hand, is often displayed by the device as a label for the entire card.

The paragraph tag is also very important to understand. All text on a WML card must be a part of some paragraph. If we had simply had the text "Hello world, what do you think of this?" in Listing 4-2 without the paragraph tag, it would generate an error as soon as we loaded it onto a device.

Table 4-1 shows some other commonly used tags.

*Table 4-1. A Brief Sampling of Common WML Tags*

| TAG | EXAMPLE | PURPOSE |
| --- | --- | --- |
| <br/> | Make</br>this</br>four</br>lines | To cause a linebreak to occur on the display, rather than wrapping |
| <do> | <do type="prev"> | To assign a function to one of your device's command buttons |
| <img> | <img src="hi.wbmp"> | To insert an image onto the card |
| <go> | <go href="#second"> | To navigate to a different card or page |
| <onevent> | <onevent type="ontimer"> | To enclose WML intended for rendering upon the occurrence of some event |
| <timer> | <timer value="30"/> | To cause an ontimer event to happen after the specified number of seconds |

In the exercise at the end of this chapter, you will see much more thorough examples of all of these tags in action. For now, you should take away from Table 4-1 a general idea of the kinds of things that are possible using WML. For more information regarding WML, please refer to the following Web sites:

- `http://www.w3schools.com`

- `http://www.wapforum.org`

- `http://www.allnetdevices.com`

## Client-Side Scripting for WAP

The "other half" of WAP, as far as application developers are concerned, is WMLScript. Using WMLScript, you can create the same kind of client-side scripts that you might write using VBScript for an Internet Explorer application (as in Chapter 2).

### What Is WMLScript?

WMLScript is a kind of client-side scripting that is adapted for use with mobile information devices in general and WAP-compliant devices in particular. WMLScript is a derivative of ECMAScript, which is itself the "standardized" form of JavaScript. You might recall that this is one of the two scripting languages supported for use with Internet Explorer (the other being VBScript).

There are three key benefits to having the ability to create client-side scripts for WAP devices:

- Telephony features

- Client-side data validation

- Client-side presentation generation

Of all of these, the first is probably the most WAP specific. As part of the ongoing development of the WAP specification, the vendors involved are keen to make the standard even more mobile-phone centered (as opposed to mobile-device centered). In order to do this, they have to create an architecture in WAP that is even more in tune with the fact that these are, at the gut level, telephones and are therefore capable of doing a lot of phone-specific things.

In the future, for example, it should be possible to write WAP applications that tell a phone to dial a specific telephone number. You also might write an application that knows how to retrieve and automatically organize voice mail. The code that you use to do this will be written in WMLScript.

Client-side data validation is another key reason to use WMLScript. Recall that the data links offered by mobile phones are painfully slow—averaging between 10 and 15 Kbps in the United States. The more work you can do on the client without talking to the server, the quicker and more responsive your application. If you can avoid going back to the server to figure out if a given user's input makes sense, then you are going to save considerable time and bandwidth.

As a final example of what you might do with WMLScript, suppose you wanted to generate a pie chart of some information. As one approach, you might actually send the pie chart graphic across the data link. If the graphic is large, this might take a while. You might instead opt to just send the set of data points (which are much smaller) and generate the graphic on the client using WMLScript.

### How Do You Write WMLScript?

Since WMLScript is a derivative of ECMAScript, myriad Web sites exist out there that can give you a pretty good idea of how to write code in WMLScript. There are, however, a few caveats that bear mentioning.

Let's begin by looking at an example of calling a WMLScript function, shown in Listing 4-3.

*Listing 4-3. Calling a WMLScript Function*

```
<a href="debt.wmls#collect('Jerry', 'Smith')">
   Send Vito after Jerry Smith
</a>
```

Notice first that this snippet is referring to a file that is actually stored on the server. To be as completely bandwidth-sensitive as possible, WAP only downloads WMLScript functions as they are needed. This way, you may create a single WMLScript file that serves as a collection for multiple functions. If this file grows to be very large, you needn't worry about the entire thing being downloaded just to access one or two functions—WAP will only take the functions it needs!

After the filename comes a pound sign (#) and the name of the specific function. In this case, the function is named collect and takes some unfortunate soul's first and last names as parameters.

Another point is that, unlike ECMAScript, WMLScript does not support the concept of object data types. Instead, data in WMLScript may be one of five types:

- String

- Float

- Boolean

- Integer

- Invalid

Although there are no objects in WMLScript, there is such a thing as a library. A *library* contains commonly used functionality that is prewritten and supplied to you by the vendor of your specific device. The functions in a given library are called using a very object-like syntax. For example, in order to refresh a screen display, one might issue the following call from WMLScript:

```
WMLBrowser.refresh();
```

For further information about WMLScript, you may consult the following excellent online resource:
`http://www.wirelessdevnet.com/channels/wap/training/wmlscript.html`.

## Getting the Tools

At this point, you should have a fairly good idea both of what is possible using WAP on a modern mobile phone *and* of how WML and WMLScript might be used together to make it happen. At this point, the only thing standing between you and development in WML is your lack of tools.

### What Can You Get for Free? Emulators!

Fortunately, you don't need to go out and buy any kind of fancy development environment—there is plenty of stuff available for free. You don't even need to go out and buy a phone!

#### *WAP*

Begin by getting a WAP emulator that will allow you to test your WML pages without even having to have a phone. Once this emulator is up and running, it will look like the image in Figure 4-2.

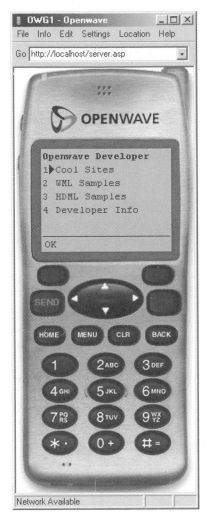

*Figure 4-2. WAP emulator*

The WAP emulator that we have in mind is one of the first and the best. The reason for this may be that it comes from the company that developed HDML in the first place—Openwave.

 **TIP** *No, you aren't going crazy. The company was called Unwired Planet when it developed HDML. It then changed its name to Phone.com around the time that WAP started being developed. Recently, the company merged with Software.com and became Openwave. Hey, the company can call itself whatever it likes so long as its tools work, right?*

The Openwave WAP emulator is known as the UP.Simulator and comes bundled as part of Openwave's UP.SDK software package. Using just the software in the UP.SDK, you should have everything that you need to create powerful WAP applications. In order to get this software, follow these steps:

1.  Browse to `http://developer.phone.com`.

2.  Click Download SDK.

3.  Click the link to the most recent version of the SDK available.

4.  Agree to the Export Declaration.

5.  Save the file to your local hard disk.

### *i-Mode*

Choosing an i-Mode emulator is very easy for English-speaking people. You just search through all of the Japanese-language ones until you find one that is available in English. You then thank your lucky stars and download it immediately, before it disappears.

Fortunately for you, we have done much of the legwork already. In order to get your very own i-Mode emulator, follow this procedure to download the Pixo Microbrowser:

1.  Browse to `http://www.modezilla.com`.

2.  Click Tools.

3.  Click the Mobile Page Viewers and Emulators link.

4.  Choose the Pixo Microbrowser.

5.  Fill out the form and click Download Now.

6.  Save the file to your local hard disk.

## What Do You Have to Pay For?

There are a couple of tools associated with serving up cell phone content from Windows that are not free. The first of these is called a *gateway*. A gateway in this context is the piece of software that is responsible for translating standard Internet content, such as WML or cHTML, into an electronic form that can be understood by cellular stations and vice versa. If you are operating your own cellular carrier service, you will have to invest tens of thousands of dollars in this software. Otherwise, you may safely ignore it. We mention it here more to familiarize you with the terminology than anything else.

The other piece of software that you will need is Internet Information Server. If you have been following along with this book from start to finish, you will already have taken the steps required to get IIS set up and operational on your computer. If not, please go back to Chapter 2 to learn how to get, install, and configure IIS.

## Let's Get Started Talking to Phones!

Well, we're finally at that most exciting part of the chapter—the hands-on bit! Since we're sure you're impatient to dig right in, we'll get started right now.

### Installing the Right Software

Getting set up to develop phone-based applications is as simple as installing both of the software packages that we instructed you to download in the previous section: the UP.SDK and the Pixo Microbrowser.

#### Installing the UP.SDK

The UP.SDK package comes as a standard Windows installer executable. So, to install it, simply find its icon and double-click it. You will see a number of progress bars while it unpacks itself for installation. Walk through the dialog boxes with which you are presented (making careful note of the bit about publishing screenshots, in case you want to verify that we've followed all of the rules in putting together this book). Agree to everything, and the software will soon be installed and ready for use.

#### Installing the Pixo Microbrowser

The Pixo Microbrowser is also packaged in a Windows installer. To get it set up and running on your computer, simply find its icon and double-click it.

Follow the instructions in all of the dialog boxes, and you should be ready to run this emulator.

## Testing Your Installations

Now that you've got UP.SDK and the Pixo Microbrowser up-and-running on your system, the next step is to verify that they are both operating properly.

### *Creating, Serving Up, and Viewing a WML Page*

Begin by creating a simple WML page. To do this, simply create a text file named chapter4.wml and enter the text shown earlier in Listing 4-2.

In order to set up your system to *really* serve WAP applications, you will need to configure IIS a little. This setup will essentially consist of telling IIS about the various filename extensions that are associated with WAP applications. This will allow IIS to set its MIME types properly whenever it has to work with WAP content.

Here is an example of the steps you need to take to configure WAP support under MIME for Windows 2000:

1. Open the Windows Control Panel.

2. Choose Administrative Tools.

3. Open the Internet Services Manager.

4. In the left-hand navigation tree, right-click the icon for your computer and choose Properties from the pop-up context menu. For Windows NT, we had to insert the MIME types in the Default Web site properties under the My Computer icon in order for the extensions to work.

5. In the frame labeled Computer MIME Map, click Edit.

6. For each of the rows in Table 4-2, click New Type and fill in the suggested extension and content type.

7. Close all of the open dialog boxes by clicking OK to save your changes.

*Table 4-2. Common WML MIME Types*

| EXTENSION | MIME TYPE |
| --- | --- |
| .wml | text/vnd.wap.wml |
| .wmlc | application/vnd.wap.wmlc |
| .wmls | text/vnd.wap.wmlscript |
| .wmlsc | application/vnd.wap.wmlscriptc |
| .wbmp | image/vnd.wap.wbmp |

**NOTE**    *Under IIS 4, you will have to insert the MIME types shown in Table 4-2 in the Default Web site properties under the My Computer icon in the Internet Services Manager.*

At this point, you should be ready to view the code you have created in the browser from the UP.SDK. To do so, simply open the UP.Simulator option in the UP.SDK program group on the Windows Start menu. You should see two windows open on your display. The one in which you are most interested is the one shown earlier in Figure 4-2.

Notice that at the top of this window there is a text area labeled Go. In this area, you may now type the URL of the page created in the previous section. For example, if you saved the page to c:\inetpub\wwwroot, then you might simply type:

```
http://localhost/chapter4.wml
```

Once you type this and hit return, you should see the text from your page displayed in the screen of the emulator. Congratulations, you have just entered, published, and received your first WAP application!

**CAUTION**    *For some reason or another, the UP.Simulator program does not always refresh itself when the Reload command is issued (F9 in this release). For this reason, do not be surprised if changes in your code are not always immediately obvious to the browser. If you ever have doubts, simply hit Clear Cache (F12) in the Edit menu, and then go back to the URL and press Enter.*

### *Creating, Serving Up, and Viewing a cHTML Page*

If you already know HTML, then creating cHTML is easy beyond words. Just think of cHTML as HTML with numerous limitations. As you are creating, keep checking the tags you are using against the list of acceptable cHTML tags, the URL for which was given earlier in this chapter.

To test the i-Mode emulator, create a text file containing the code shown in Listing 4-4 and save it to any location where IIS can serve it up. No changes to your MIME types or other configurations are needed!

*Listing 4-4. Your First cHTML Page*

```
<HTML>
    <HEAD>
        <TITLE>Your first cHTML Page</TITLE>
    </HEAD>
    <BODY>
Could it really be this simple
    </BODY>
</HTML>
```

Once you have entered this code, you can fire-up the i-Mode emulator by selecting the Pixo Internet Microbrowser from the Windows Start menu. Select Options, select Open URL, and then enter the URL for your file. The page should appear in the display presently. Piece of cake, right?

<hr>

## Exercise

By this point, we think you will agree that i-Mode applications are decidedly much easier to create than WAP-based software. For this reason, in this final section of the chapter, we will demonstrate the creation of a simple WAP application that will return dynamic WML to your client.

## Writing the Server

The application we have in mind is quite simple. Provided with a short string by the client, the server will return the number of characters in that string. For example, if the string passed in by the client was "HELLO WORLD," then the application would return "11".

## Code Overview

For simplicity's sake, the application will be written in Active Server Pages.

### The Code

Listing 4-5 shows the code for the WAP server application.

*Listing 4-5. The WAP Server Application*

```
<%
    response.contenttype = "text/vnd.wap.wml"
%>
<?xml version="1.0"?>
<!DOCTYPE wml PUBLIC "-//WAPFORUM//DTD WML 1.2//EN"
"http://www.wapforum.org/DTD/wml12.dtd">

<wml>
    <card>
        <p>The length is. . .
<%
    response.write len(request("string"))
%>
        </p>
    </card>
</wml>
```

### The Walk-Through

The first important thing to notice about this code is that it has to set its own MIME type. All Active Server Page applications share the same extension, .asp. For this reason, the extension MIME map that you set up for WAP in the previous section does you no good here. Instead, you must use the ContentType property of the intrinsic ASP response object.

After this, the code switches back to static markup while the XML heading is produced. The bulk of the only card on the page is also static.

The one dynamic bit in the code is the line that reads

```
response.write len(request("string"))
```

This grabs hold of the parameter passed in from the client known as "string". It gets the length of this in bytes using the len function, and then returns this value to the client using the write method of the intrinsic response object.

# Writing the Client

Unlike some of the devices we have looked at so far (Internet Explorer and Pocket PCs, for example), it is highly unusual to have a stand-alone application running on a WAP client. Instead, the assumption is that the server will deliver a "deck" of cards to the WAP client, and the client will display as many cards as it can before returning to the server for additional processing. This is in line with the severe hardware limitations of most WAP devices.

## Code Overview

For this reason, the client code for the WAP application will really be just another WAP page. This page will create the form that will be submitted back to the ASP server application.

### The Code

Listing 4-6 shows the code for the WAP client application.

*Listing 4-6. The WAP Client Application*

```
<?xml version="1.0"?>
<!DOCTYPE wml PUBLIC "-//WAPFORUM//DTD WML 1.2//EN"
"http://www.wapforum.org/DTD/wml12.dtd">

<wml>
    <card>
        <p>
            Give me the string:
            <input name="string"/><br/>
            <anchor>
                <go method="post" href="http://localhost/server.asp">
                    <postfield name="string" value="$(string)"/>
                </go>
            </anchor>
        </p>
    </card>
</wml>
```

### The Walk-Through

The first tag that you haven't seen before is the <input> tag. In WML, data entered into an <input> tag winds up filling in a local variable that exists on *only* the WAP device. In order to send this to the server then, you must use a second tag, <postfield>. The <postfield> tag in this example essentially says, "Post a field back to the server named "string" and populate this field with the contents of the local variable named "string"." Without this line, your <input> field value would never go back to the server.

Notice that the <postfield> tag is surrounded by a <go> tag that points back to the server application. This <go> tag is further surrounded by an <anchor> tag that makes this entire section clickable.

## Trying It Out

WML applications share at least one thing in common with HTML applications—they are extremely easy to test.

### Building

The build phase of a typical WML application usually consists of entering its text, dropping it into a directory that can be served up by a standard Web server, and then browsing to it with a WAP emulator. This is approximately the same procedure that you will follow in this section.

1.  Save the code from Listing 4-5 into a file called server.asp (put this file in a location where IIS can serve it up).

2.  Save the code from Listing 4-6 into a file called client.wml (put this file in a location where IIS can serve it up).

3.  Open the UP.Simulator application.

4.  Enter the URL for your client.wml file and press Enter.

### Execution

If you are able to enter a string and successfully get back the number of characters in your string, congratulations—you have just written, compiled, and tested your first complete WAP application!

## Final Thoughts

We've only just scratched the surface of what is possible using cHTML and WAP in this chapter. There are many other resources out there for free that can take you even further along the path of developing for cell phones—and we have referred you to several of these.

Our intention in this chapter, rather than making you an i-Mode or WAP guru, was simply to introduce you to Internet development on modern mobile phones. When we get to the sections on .NET later in this book, you will understand the full importance of this—as WAP and cHTML are two of the platforms *specifically* targeted for support by .NET!

# CHAPTER 5

# Palm OS

## The Two-Ton Gorilla of the PDA World

AT THE TIME OF WRITING, Palm OS–based personal digital assistants (PDAs) still constitute better than 75 percent of the PDA market. This is a remarkable achievement for a device that many people openly mocked when it first came to market. At this point in time, it is obvious that the very reasons these people initially mocked the Palm OS wound up being the device's true secret to success.

In this chapter, we will explain exactly what has allowed the Palm OS platform to be as successful as it has been up to this point. We will then explain both of the principal native Palm OS technologies for creating mobile applications: the Palm OS C SDK and Web Clipping.

## Background

Before the Palm produced the Palm OS, many other corporations tried their hand at manufacturing the ultimate PDA. In their bids to outdo the competition, these organizations added more and more features to their products. Examples of these included the following:

- Built-in disk drives

- Infrared ports

- Network cards

- Handwriting recognition

The problem with adding all of these features is that, at the time, they were all quite costly. Furthermore, the technology required to make these devices small enough to be portable was still quite unreliable. Most people balked at the idea of paying extra for something that didn't work nearly as well as their PCs! Where Palm made its breakthrough was by selling a cheap, more reliable device that cut out all of the unnecessary frills just described. People flocked to buy Palm OS handhelds in droves, and it still remains the most popular PDA platform to this day.

## Meet the Palm

Before you can start programming for the Palm OS, you need to know a bit about how these devices operate.

### Hardware Is Half the Battle

The traditional Palm OS device features a monochrome display, although color models such as the Handspring Visor are rapidly becoming more popular. 8MB of memory is considered the maximum for current models, which in comparison to the 16MB to 64MB of memory available on most Pocket PCs is not much at all.

Older Palm OS devices connected to the Internet via add-on modem hardware. There are two main disadvantages to this approach. The first disadvantage is that when attached, these modems approximately double the size of the devices. The other problem is that these modems often have to dial up and log in to a third-party Internet service to access the Internet, just like regular telephone modems.

A newer technology, used on Palm VIIs, is to actually build a radio into the device itself. Although this makes the device a little larger, it is still small in comparison to the older Palms with attachable modems. On the other hand, the maximum speed achievable with these built-in radios is approximately 9.6 Kbps, as opposed to the 28.8 Kbps speeds attainable by some of the attachable modems.

### Software Is the Other Side of the Coin

In many ways the development of Graffiti, as the Palm writing system is known, was one of the great technological leaps forward that brought the Palm popularity. Although learning to write on the Palm is a little difficult at first, it gives much greater reliability in the long run. For this reason, people almost always seem to prefer this technology over attempts at true handwriting recognition.

There are four main applications that are built into every Palm OS:

- Calendar

- Contact manager

- To-do list

- Memo pad

Besides these standards, modern Palm OS devices have added two extremely important Internet applications. The first of these is iMessenger, the Palm OS e-mail client. One important thing to know about this is it can only be used with your Palm's special e-mail account—not the regular e-mail account that you may have with your local ISP. The other important thing to realize is that sending e-mails to Palm devices is often the only way to deliver information to them in an asynchronous fashion.

 **CAUTION**  *Even in this case, the user must still take some action in order to receive a notification. Specifically, he or she must connect to the Internet (however the user's device enables this), start iMessenger, and request delivery of unread mail. As of the time of writing, there is no way to truly send asynchronous message notifications (like beeper pages) to Palm OS devices.*

The other Palm OS Internet application, Clipper, is of central interest to us in this chapter. Clipper is the special Web browser built for use on Palm OS devices. Like iMessenger, however, it is not designed for use with ordinary Web sites. Instead, in order to work with Palm OS devices, a Web author must create special Web Clipping applications for deployment directly onto the devices themselves. At the end of this chapter, we will walk you through the construction of an advanced Web Clipping application from scratch.

## Looking into the Future

At this point, you may be wondering, "Where is the Palm OS platform headed, and how does it relate to learning .NET?" This section is for you, my friend!

### Fighting the Pocket PC

In just a little over one year of life, the Pocket PC has managed to ship over 1,000,000 units. Just one year and six months ago, this feat would have been unthinkable in a PDA universe completely under Palm's domination. As you read in Chapter 3, the secret weapon at the heart of Microsoft's challenge to the Palm OS market was its close integration with standard Windows applications.

In order to thrive as a PDA platform, then, one of the first challenges that Palm will undoubtedly try to overcome in the immediate future is its ability to interoperate with a wide variety of third-party software. One example of this is Palm's embracing of the J2ME standard that you will learn about in the next chapter. By allowing Java code to run on the Palm OS platform, Palm opens its handheld devices up to a world of new software and software developers.

Actively seeking new content developers is yet another way in which Palm may attempt to increase its device's interoperability. The long awaited release of Quicken for Palm OS may be seen as a signal of future software releases to come.

Finally, in order to compete with Pocket PCs, Palm OS devices must gain and remain upon the forefront of wireless connectivity. This may mean abandoning the Web Clipping architecture, which is fast becoming obsolete in the face of more demanding wireless application users. At the very least, it will require the providers of connectivity to Palm OS devices (such as Palm.Net and Omnisky) to continue to upgrade their networks to constantly provide the fastest possible Internet connections.

## Where Does .NET Fit In?

"What does all of this have to do with .NET?" we hear you asking. The best answer in this case is also the shortest: Microsoft's mobile .NET technologies do not directly support the use of Palm OS–based devices. Is reading this chapter simply a waste of your time then? Hardly!

As we have already mentioned in this chapter, Palm OS devices currently command better than 75 percent of the PDA market. This makes them the single most popular kind of PDA currently on the market. Do you really want to turn your back on such a significant marketshare? Not if you value the effort involved in your own development!

Part of the beauty of .NET is that it is largely based upon XML and XML-derived standards, such as SOAP and WSDL (which are discussed in greater detail in Chapter 10). For this reason, most devices—not just the ones specifically supported by Microsoft—may be used with .NET technologies. For the remainder of this book, Palm OS devices will serve as our primary example of devices that are not supported by Microsoft, yet are extremely popular.

## Creating Applications

The Palm OS environment is by far one of the most user-friendly operating systems on the planet. And yet, through careful application design and development, it can be harnessed for some truly impressive purposes. For example, using a Palm OS device, you could play a game of chess one moment

(http://www.nonvi.com) and administer your Oracle databases the next
(http://www.pocketdba.com).

It should come as little surprise then that a variety of methodologies and
technologies exist to facilitate the creation of Palm OS applications.

## Clipping the Web

At the most abstract level, simple Web Clipping applications allow Internet-
enabled Palms to surf a small subset of the World Wide Web.

### How It Works

In order to understand Web Clipping on Palm OS–powered devices, you must
understand two things. To begin with, when Palm OS devices browse the
Internet using Web Clipping, they use an architecture that is specially designed
to compensate for the low bandwidth and poor reliability of their connections.
Also, the content that they are able to receive and correctly interpret is not the
same as that included in most modern Web pages.

#### About the Architecture

As mentioned in the preceding text, the architecture used by the Web Clipping
system is not as simple as merely connecting a Palm OS–powered device directly
to the Web sites that it wants to browse. Instead, a system involving the use of
special, intermediate servers called Web Clipping Proxy (WCP) servers is used.
This system is illustrated in Figure 5-1.

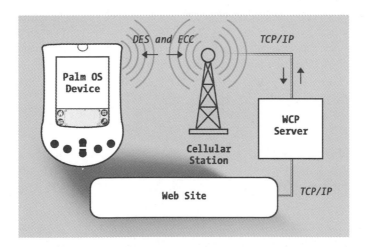

*Figure 5-1. The Web Clipping process*

As you can see, the process begins with the Palm OS device sending a radio signal out via either its built-in radio or an add-on modem. While this signal is in transit across the airwaves, it is protected by DES encryption. DES is a rather old encryption methodology that is fairly well respected in the industry. The important thing to realize is that even if someone should have the hardware needed in order to intercept your signal in the airwaves (very unlikely), that someone would also have to break the encryption in order to use it.

The signal eventually reaches the wireless receiving station for the device's service provider. Which station this is depends upon two things:

- The location of the device

- The device owner's choice of service provider

In any event, once the signal has been received, it is the job of the service provider to convert the signal into proper TCP/IP packets for use on the Internet. Once this translation has taken place, these TCP/IP packets are forwarded to the WPC servers. The transmission between the receiving stations and the proxy servers is typically encrypted using SSL, and is therefore also extremely secure.

The WPC servers are intended to act as the Palm user's representatives in any and all exchanges with the target Web sites. This job typically consists of three functions:

- Submitting requests to the specified Web sites

- Stripping unsupported content out of the Web sites' responses

- Compressing the remaining content for travel back across the airwaves

At this point, the entire process reverses itself. The WCP server sends its stripped, compressed content back to the service provider's wireless stations for transmission back to the Palm OS device. All of the same encryption protection is afforded on the journey back as it was on the way to the Web site.

### *Features Missing from Web Clipping HTML*

As you might have noticed in the preceding section, one of the most important things that the Web Clipping Proxy servers do is to strip unsupported content out of target Web sites. Since we firmly believe in giving you the bad news first, this seems like a good point at which to tell you what bits of HTML are *not* supported by Web Clipping.

To begin with, Clipper (as the Palm OS browser is known) expects any links within a page to come in the form of simple anchor tags, as shown in this example:

```
<a href="http://www.pocketdba.com">The PocketDBA Home Page</a>
```

This requirement makes the use of image maps impossible. For this reason, any image maps that are included in your Web pages will either be converted to standard images by Clipper or (more likely) completely removed.

Unlike Internet Explorer, Clipper is not equipped to interpret scripts and binaries that are downloaded onto the Palm client. For this reason, the use of VBScript or ECMAScript (a.k.a. JavaScript) on Web pages will be completely ignored. Similarly, any kind of Java applets or ActiveX controls will be completely ignored.

Some of the formatting offered by standard HTML 3.2 is also unsupported. This is a function of the Clipper requirement to operate well in the reduced screen space available on Palm OS devices. One example of an unsupported display feature is the use of frames. Frames are commonly used on the Web to aid in navigation by adding a so-called menu bar to the display that remains constant—even as other parts of the screen change.

Another unsupported display feature is the ability to nest HTML tables one within another. Tables are commonly used in this manner when frames are not available, so this is an unfortunate thing to have missing. On the other hand, you are free to use non-nested tables in your pages.

The final remaining feature that is not supported by Clipper is the use of cookies. This issue can be an absolute killer for large-scale Web applications. For example, if you want to create a site that requires users to log in before use, you will have to be particularly clever in your design. If your site uses cookies to remember from one page to the next whether or not a given user has already logged in, it simply will not work with Clipper. Users will be prompted to log in on every page, because the cookies identifying them will get lost after each visit.

### And Now, We'll Give You the Good News

The good news is there are also some features supported by Clipper that are otherwise unknown in the world of HTML. Some of these are merely nifty, whereas others are downright exciting—assuming you're a tech geek, of course.

The first thing you should know is that Web Clipping applications tend to be partnerships between client-side HTML and images and server-side HTML and images. This means that you could theoretically build a Web Clipping application that existed 100 percent on the Palm OS device and never has to call out for additional content across the Internet. Figure 5-2 compares this kind of application to a more traditional Web site.

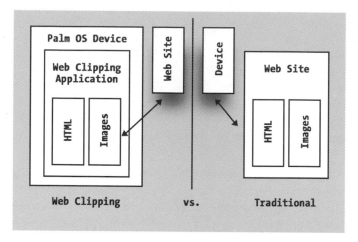

*Figure 5-2. Web Clipping applications vs. traditional Web sites*

The most minor application of this technology is to use a special META tag to reference client-side images from your HTML pages. These pages may either be located on the client or the server. Take a look at this example:

```
<meta name="LocalIcon" content="diskspace.gif">
```

This command tells Clipper to load an image named diskspace.gif from the local application rather than from whatever server upon which the page might be located. This improves the display of pages on Clipper by reducing the amount of time required to load images.

Another way in which Clipper improves the display of pages is by allowing Web site designers to specify portions of their pages that should *not* be displayed by Clipper. This way, a single page may be used both for Clipper and for "regular" Web browsers. However, if there is content on this page—such as an image map—that shouldn't be sent to Clipper, the Web designer can instruct Clipper to skip that content by enclosing it in the following tag pair:

```
<smallscreenignore></smallscreenignore>
```

One of the most promising functions for mobile computing is the delivery of location-sensitive data to users. For example, there is a Web Clipping application available from Starbucks that can tell a Palm OS user where the nearest Starbucks is without ever asking where the user is. How does it do this? Through the use of the special value %ZIPCODE. If you embedded this value in your page, the Web Clipping Proxy server will substitute the zip code of the Palm OS user.

Another special value that you may choose to embed in your Web pages is %DEVICEID. Many (but *not* all) Palm devices have unique hardware identifier numbers hard-coded within them. By using this code in your pages, you can access a device's unique identifier. This might be useful in a high-security situation in which you want to limit access to specific Palm devices in *addition* to password security.

**CAUTION**   *Remember that there are two problems with using* %DEVICEID *as the only security for your systems. The first problem is that the device might get stolen. In this case, the right device could be used to give the wrong person access to your information. Furthermore, not all Palm devices have IDs.*

The final cool addition that we will discuss here—although not the last cool addition available—is the ability to link to "real" Palm applications directly from Web Clipping pages. For example, by including the following link in your page, you could allow a user to start the built-in calculator application directly from your Web page:

```
<A HREF="PALM:CALC.APPL">Start the Calculator</A>
```

## Trying It Out

In this section, we will give you a brief taste of creating Web Clipping applications.

### Getting the Tools

Before you start doing any serious development for the Palm OS platform, you should have some capability for testing those applications. You may already own a Palm OS device, such as a Palm VIIx (our personal choice), in which case you are in good shape. If you don't own a Palm OS device, however, simply downloading the Palm OS emulator off the Web is a much more affordable choice.

The single most popular Palm OS emulator on the market is known as POSE, which stands for (appropriately enough) Palm OS Emulator. To get the emulator, follow these steps:

1.   Browse to `http://www.palmos.com`.

2.   Hover over Developers on the left-hand navigation bar.

3.   Choose Tools from the pop-up context menu.

4. Scroll down to the section labeled Development Essentials.

5. Click Palm OS Emulator.

6. Scroll down to the section labeled Download the Emulator.

7. Follow the link to the Emulator Application for Windows (ignore the Emulator Skins link for now).

8. Download the file onto your local hard disk.

---

 **TIP** *At the time of writing, Palm has just announced that it will split its business into two separate companies. One of these companies will focus upon development of the Palm OS operating system. The other will focus on development of hardware that runs the Palm OS operating system. It is not clear at this point which company will get to keep the name, but you may need to adjust the URLs in this chapter accordingly!*

---

When this process is complete, you will have an emulator for Palm OS on your computer. You need only unzip it to get started. We will use this emulator throughout the rest of this book, so make sure you unzip it to a location where you can keep it around for a while (not on your desktop, for instance).

However, if you actually try running the emulator at this point (by double-clicking the icon labeled Emulator and clicking New to start a new emulator session), you will notice that it prompts you, as shown in Figure 5-3.

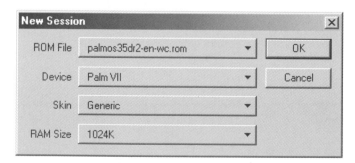

*Figure 5-3. Starting a new emulator session*

**TIP** *In some versions of the emulator, you may get an error message about needing certain skins in order to function properly. This message is safe to ignore, as skins simply allow the emulator to imitate the specific appearance of various Palm OS devices (Palm VII, Handspring Visor, and so on). Simply click OK, and you will be allowed to continue.*

Notice that at the top of this dialog box, you are prompted for a ROM file. The way it works is this: the Palm emulator imitates the hardware of the Palm itself. For example, the CPU's functionality is handled by the emulator. The operating system itself, Palm OS, is stored on ROM chips within the regular PDA, however. It is therefore also packaged in different files. You *must* download the ROM images in order to use the emulator effectively!

Unfortunately, the ROM images for most current Palm devices contain strong encryption that is carefully protected by the U.S. government. In order to get these ROMs, then, you must join the Palm OS developers' alliance by following these steps:

1. Browse to `http://www.PalmOS.com/alliance/join`.

2. Enter your e-mail address where specified and click Join Now.

3. Fill out the survey and click Continue.

4. Fill out the Profile form and click Submit Profile.

5. Wait to receive an e-mail from Palm with your new password. (This can take up to 48 hours!)

6. Browse to `http://www.PalmOS.com/alliance/resources`.

7. Enter your e-mail and new password, and then click Enter.

8. Click the ROM Images Clipwrap Area link.

9. Accept the licensing agreement.

10. Follow the links to the 3.5 versions of the Palm OS ROMs.

11. Click the little Windows icon to download the ROMs (the smiling faces are for Macs).

**TIP**   *Even after you get your password for the Palm OS Developers' Pavilion, it may take a few more hours before the ROM Images Clickwrap Area link appears for you on the Palm OS Web site.*

At this point, you have gotten everything you need to use the emulator. However, what about the Web Clipping content in particular? There's little or no point in being able to emulate a device if you don't have any content for it or tools with which to create content. We'll show you how get both of those things now.

The set of tools for creating Web Clipping applications, or Palm Query Applications (PQAs) as they are known in the trade, is called the PQA Builder tools. It is available off the same Developer Essentials page that you visited earlier in this section. Simply browse back to that page and scroll down to the section labeled Web Clipping and Wireless Tools. Follow the links and make sure to download the Windows version of the tools.

In the next section, you will download a prebuilt Web Clipping application off the Internet and test your emulator by running it.

### *Testing, Testing, Testing*

You are now just about ready to begin. Unzip the ROMs you just downloaded to an appropriate place on your local disk and use the dialog box shown earlier in Figure 5-3 to tell the emulator where to find them. Choose the most recent model of Palm device (VII should be fine for your purposes). Also, use the Generic skin with the most memory available.

**CAUTION**   *If you cannot find the Palm VII ROM among the ones you downloaded, then you most likely did not download the ROMs for version 3.5 of the Palm OS operating system. In this case, you should go back to the previous section and reexecute the steps that describe how to download the appropriate ROMs.*

Once you click OK, you should see a welcome message on the emulator screen, followed by the main configuration menu, as shown in Figure 5-4.

*Figure 5-4. Welcome to POSE!*

Choose Wireless from the drop-down menu in the upper-right corner. This will take you to a screen labeled iMessenger that contains a single IP. This IP is *extremely* important, because under Web Clipping all traffic to and from the Palm OS device must travel across the Internet via a special Web Clipping Proxy server. This was discussed earlier and illustrated in Figure 5-1.

The IP being shown is the IP of the Web Clipping Proxy server that will be used by this device. If this IP is not set correctly, Web Clipping applications will not work on this device! Unfortunately, the appropriate IP to use here changes frequently. So, to get the most recent IP recommendation, browse to http://www.palmos.com/dev/tech/webclipping/status.html.

Once you know the current IP of the Web Clipping Proxy server, enter it into POSE and click Applications (one of the four round buttons at the bottom of the device) to go to the main screen of applications.

If you've never used a Palm OS device before, feel free to play around here. Don't worry about hurting anything. In a worst-case scenario, you can always just restart the emulator to undo any damage.

When you are feeling fairly comfortable with the more general aspects of the interface, you are ready to try out your first Web clipping application. The Web

Clipping application with which we are most familiar, and therefore the one we will use for demonstration purposes, is the PocketDBA Web Clipping demo. You may download this from http://www.pocketdba.com.

Simply go to the Demo page, fill out the form at the bottom, and then click Submit to have the PQA sent to you via e-mail. When the e-mail arrives, it will contain two files, as described by Table 5-1.

*Table 5-1. PocketDBA Files*

| FILENAME | DESCRIPTION |
| --- | --- |
| pdba.pqa | The Web Clipping application file |
| PocketDBA.PRC | The native C launcher application |

Save both of these attachments to your local hard disk and right-click in the margin of the Palm OS emulator. You should see a pop-up context menu that includes the option Install Application/Database. Select this option.

Choose Other from the pop-up list of recent files and you will be presented with a file dialog box. Select both of the files that you received in the e-mail, and they will both be installed on your emulator. In a few seconds, the logo for PocketDBA should be clearly visible. Click it to begin the demonstration.

**NOTE** *If the icon doesn't appear after several seconds, use the screen menu in the upper-right corner to switch to the Main program group, and then switch back to All. This will cause the icon list to refresh itself and display PocketDBA properly.*

**TIP** *There seems to be some weird bug in certain versions of the emulator ROMs that causes Web Clipping icons to not be displayed after loading. If you find that this is happening to you, first verify that you are using a Palm OS 3.5 ROM. If you verify this and continue to experience problems, try emulating a different Palm OS 3.5 device.*

The first thing that you will get is a warning that the Parameters file can't be found. This is normal on first use, so just ignore it.

The idea behind the application is to facilitate the wireless administration of Oracle databases. In this case, since it is just a demo, you will only be able to administer the database running at PocketDBA headquarters. Since knowledge of Oracle administration isn't assumed for this book, try the following:

1. Click the icon labeled Conn. This will show you all of the current connections to the database.

2. Notice the little black dot swirling at the top of the screen. This means that Web Clipping is accessing the Internet.

3. If you get a login screen at this point, congratulations—you've correctly configured your Palm OS emulator for Web Clipping!

4. Click Submit to go ahead and log in.

5. Notice the Web Clipping access again and, voila!—you have all the connections currently on the database.

## Delving into the Internals

Digging down into the deepest layers of the operating system, a C-based software development kit (SDK) allows the creation of virtually any kind of application imaginable.

### How It Works

The C-based interface to Palm OS is, by far, the most complicated of all the ways to create Palm OS software. Since almost everything involving wireless can be done using Web Clipping, we won't discuss this at great length. It is important, however, for you to understand the limited instances in which C-based coding can be useful.

To begin with, the world of C-based code on Palm OS revolves around the idea of numerous manager libraries that are provided for you as a part of the operating system's SDK. These managers are always a part of any Palm OS operating system, but in order to access them from your own C code, you have to download and install the SDK. We will discuss this in more detail later in the section "Trying It Out."

Table 5-2 briefly describes some of the most important managers that are part of the SDK.

*Table 5-2. Important SDK Managers*

| NAME | PURPOSE |
| --- | --- |
| UI | Works with user interface elements |
| Memory | Manipulates chunks of memory |
| Databases | Creates, modifies, and deletes permanent storage |
| System | Creates various Palm OS functions, such as alarms |
| Serial | Allows communication via serial port |
| Beaming | Allows communication via infrared port |
| Network | Allows communication via TCP/IP stack |
| Internet | Provides special communications library for Palm VII–style hardware |

These managers act rather like the Win32 API, with which you may be familiar. They are all essentially collections of low-level functions that may be called from your code to perform various operations on the Palm device.

The other thing that you should know about C-based Palm OS software is that almost all of these programs have an event-driven structure. What this means is that, after a short startup function, almost all of these programs segue into an infinite loop that lasts for the entirety of the program's lifespan. All this loop does, as shown in Figure 5-5, is respond to external events.

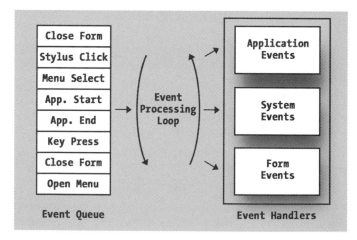

*Figure 5-5. A typical Palm OS application's structure*

### *Why You Won't See Us Using C*

In general, many developers find the use of the C SDK for Palm OS to be a little too much effort for too little return. Developers see the C and C++ languages as being harder to use than other languages based upon the following criteria:

- Direct memory management

- Cryptic syntax

- Lack of robustness

The first of these, direct memory management, refers to the requirement in C that memory (such as the memory required to contain a string or number) be explicitly allocated by the application developer. This is in contrast to languages such as Visual Basic or Java, where the application developer would simply request the declaration of a string or integer variable.

Furthermore, the deallocation and cleaning up of these memory allocations once they are no longer needed is completely the job of the developer. Unlike Java, there is no garbage collector to automatically free memory when it is no longer in use.

Memory that is never returned to general circulation once it is no longer in use may, over time, create a so-called memory leak in an application. These errors can be extremely difficult to track down, as an application can often run for quite a long time before the effects build to a point where an application becomes unusable and crashes.

This lack of robustness in the C language is another common complaint among high-level application developers. Besides the memory leaks caused by memory that isn't cleaned up, there is an even more common error caused by memory that is insufficient in size for the task required. An example of this would be trying to store a 100-byte string in a 32-byte chunk of memory. A more robust platform might simply disallow or truncate the string. In C, the usual outcome of such an attempt is a complete application (and possibly device) crash.

### *It Is Good in Small Doses, However*

Now that we have sold you on the fact that C is a horrible, horrible programming language, you may be wondering why anyone would ever use it. The simplest answer is there are just some things that you can't do without it. PocketDBA is a great example of this.

As you might have noticed in the last section, before you were able to access a list of current connections on the database, you were asked to log in to the server. Now suppose that after logging in, you worked for a few minutes to resolve a problem with a downed database server and then realized that you needed some vital information that was stored in the Memo application on your Palm. So, you click into the Memo application, get the data, and then return to PocketDBA.

If PocketDBA were simply a Web Clipping application, at this point you would have to log in to the system again. This would also be true if you accidentally turned off your Palm, or if the Palm froze up for some reason. Typically, people don't like having to log into their applications multiple times, so this is obviously inadequate.

What C allowed us to do in constructing PocketDBA was to build a launcher application around our Web Clipping code. This means that state information, such as your unique session identifier, can be persisted by the C-based code in a way that can survive interruptions in the Web Clipping application.

## Trying It Out

As we have said many times, C-based Palm OS code will not be a focal point of this book in any way, shape, or form. In wireless terms, everything we will be doing can be accomplished straight from Web Clipping. Still, as you progress in developing your applications, you may eventually want to branch out into the C SDK on your own. For that reason, we provide the information in this section.

### Getting the Tools

The C SDK and a compatible C compiler are really the only tools that you need in order to create C applications for Palm OS. There is, however, one 2000-pound gorilla in this arena that nicely integrates both of these components. On top of this, it provides an excellent WYSIWYG editor for the creation of UI components. It is called CodeWarrior.

The full version of CodeWarrior is for-cost software. However, a limited version of this software, called CodeWarrior Lite, is available for free, and you can download it from the Palm OS Web site. To get and install this software, follow these steps:

1. Browse to `http://www.PalmOS.com/dev/tech/tools/cw`.

2. Scroll slowly down the page, looking carefully for the section labeled CodeWarrior for Palm OS R7 Demo.

3. Click the link to Windows.

4. Save the file downloaded to your machine to an appropriate location on your local disk.

5. Once the file has finished downloading, double-click it to run the installer.

6. Follow the installer's prompts to complete the installation.

### *Testing, Testing, Testing*

Once the CodeWarrior installer has finished, you should be able to start the IDE right from the Windows Start menu. It should be a part of its own CodeWarrior Lite program group. Once it starts, your screen should resemble what is shown in Figure 5-6.

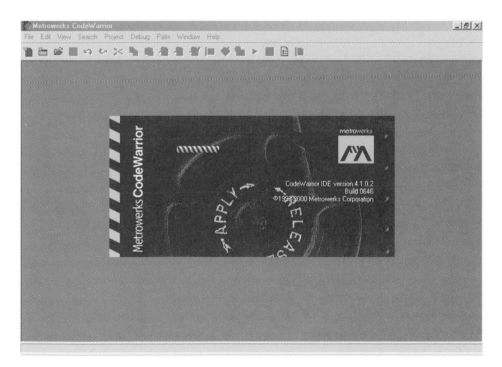

*Figure 5-6. CodeWarrior Lite*

In order to see how this works, run one of the samples that play a game known as SubHunt. In order to get to this sample, simply navigate to \Program Files\MetroWerks\CodeWarrior Lite\CodeWarrior Examples\Palm OS 3.5 SDK Examples\SubHunt. If you installed the software to a different location, you may have to search around a little. Once you find it, double-click the SubHunt project file (the one with the .mcp extension) to begin.

This will leave you with a Project Window for SubHunt, as shown in Figure 5-7. To build the project into an executable, click the icon that looks like a little hand on top of a diamond. After a short period of active work, you should see that a PRC file has been built and is ready for execution in the emulator.

In order to get the emulator setup to work with CodeWarrior, you must first perform a few additional steps:

1. Choose Preferences from the Edit menu.

2. At the bottom of the IDE Preference Panel, click Palm Connection Settings.

3. Under Palm Connection Settings, verify that the target is the Palm OS emulator.

4. Next to the blank labeled Emulator, click the Choose button.

5. Navigate through your file system to the location where you installed the Palm OS emulator.

6. Double-click the icon for the file emulator.exe to tell CodeWarrior where to find your Palm OS emulator's executable.

7. Click OK to exit the IDE Preference dialog boxes.

8. Choose Enabled Debugger under the Project menu (if this option isn't available, then the debugger is already enabled).

9. Under the Palm menu, choose Launch emulator.

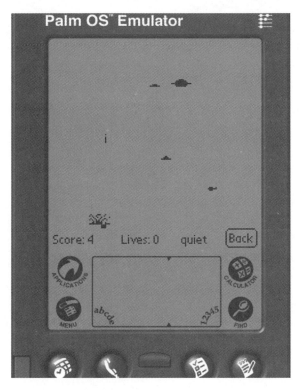

*Figure 5-7. The SubHunt project window*

At this point, the Palm OS emulator should appear, and you are now ready to play SubHunt.

From the Project menu at the top of the screen, choose Debug. This will download the code to your emulator and actually kick off the process of running the sample application. Immediately after it begins, however, it will pause on the first line of code. This procedure, called PilotMain, is the starting point for every Palm OS application. Simply click the little green arrow icon (which displays the word "Run" when you hover the cursor over it) to continue.

Now you should be able to play a full game of SubHunt against the computer right on your Palm emulator. Isn't technology great?

---

**TIP**   *Two hours after writing the preceding text, we now realize how addictive SubHunt can be. A brief overview of the controls: the phone and tasks buttons at the bottom of the emulator drop bombs off the left- and right-hand sides of the ship, respectively. The calendar and memo buttons cause the ship to move left and right, respectively.*

---

In this exercise, you will be creating a Web Clipping application that uses ASP and COM on the server side to kick off a batch file. The same Web Clipping application could be used to retrieve whatever output was generated by a previous run of the application.

## Writing the Server

Running batch files on the server requires three distinct pieces of code:

- An ASP script to receive the Web Clipping request

- A COM component to kick off the batch

- A batch file to target

Fortunately, none of these are very complicated at all.

### Code Overview

Under pre-.NET Active Server Pages, you are restricted to using a small subset of the Visual Basic programming language known as VBScript. Because VBScript is incapable of spawning an OS process (such as a shell script) on its own, you need to create a COM component to provide assistance with this task.

***The Code***

Listing 5-1 shows the code for the ASP script, and Listing 5-2 shows the code for the COM component.

*Listing 5-1. The ASP Script*

```
<html>
  <head>
    <title>Batch File Response</title>
    <meta name="PalmComputingPlatform" content="true">
    <meta name="PalmLauncherRevision" content="1.0">
  </head>
  <body>
```

```
<%
Set obj = Server.CreateObject("ClipExample.ClipShell")

if request("action") = "run" then
    obj.run("c:\" & request("filename"))
    Response.Write "Run request sent!"
else
    rspns = obj.read("c:\" & request("filename"))
    Response.Write server.htmlencode(rspns)
end if

%>

    </body>
</html>
```

*Listing 5-2. The COM Component*

```
Public Sub run(filename As Variant)

    Shell filename, vbHide

End Sub

Public Function read(filename As Variant) As Variant

    On Error GoTo Oops

    Open filename For Input As #1

    Do Until EOF(1)

        DoEvents
        Line Input #1, strBuffer

        strBetter = Replace(strBuffer, Chr(13), "<br>")
        strBetter = Replace(strBetter, Chr(10), "<br>")

        read = read & strBetter

    Loop
```

```
    Close #1

    Exit Function

Oops:

    read = "*** NO OUTPUT AVAILABLE ***"

End Function
```

And finally, the code for the batch file that you will be attempting to execute:

```
net start smtpsvc 1> c:\emailon.txt 2> c:\emailon.bad
```

### *The Walk-Through*

In order to use the code as reproduced here, you must first change a setting on your server machine. Under the Windows Control Panel, open the Services for your server. Find the Service named IIS Admin Services and right-click it to view its properties. On the tab marked Login, you must make sure that the box labeled Allow service to interact with desktop is checked. If you fail to do this, you will not be able to start and stop services from Active Server Pages.

Once this is taken care of, you are ready to begin. Listing 5-1 represents an Active Server Page script that should be saved beneath your Web directory structure. Notice the presence of the two <meta> tags for the benefit of Web Clipping clients. When a connection is made to this page, it will first instantiate an instance of the COM component developed in Listing 5-2. Then, depending upon the specific request received, it will ask this component to either execute a given batch file or read-in the contents of a given text file. In the latter case, the contents will be formatted as HTML and returned to the client.

As you can see in Listing 5-2, the COM component is able to run this batch script via use of Visual Basic's Shell keyword. It is relatively straightforward, but returns immediately without waiting for the script to finish running. For this reason, you need to provide a second method on the component that may be used later to collect whatever output there is. The read method accomplishes this simply by reading every line of a text file, replacing the CR/LFs with HTML break tags (<br>), and returning a concatenated string.

And finally, there is the single-line batch file that you will target with this application. It simply starts the SMTP service on the server. Furthermore, it pipes its standard output to one text file and its standard error output to a different file. These are the files that you will later interrogate in order to find out whether or not your service-starting attempts have succeeded or failed.

*Trying It Out*

In order to try this code out, you don't even need to use a Palm OS emulator, much less a Palm OS device. First, you must use VB6 to create and compile a COM component from Listing 5-2 called `ClipExample.ClipShell` (in this book, we assume a level of familiarity with Visual Studio 6 that should render explaining this process unnecessary). Once you have done this, simply copy the code shown in Listing 5-1 to a location on your Web server and hit it with any ordinary Web browser (such as Internet Explorer). You should see a screen very much like the one shown in Figure 5-8.

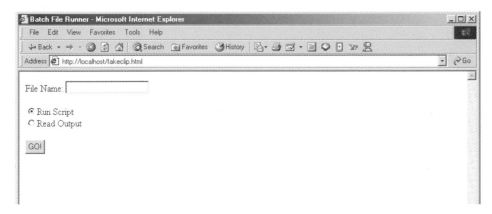

*Figure 5-8. The power to run any shell script!*

First, you should enter the name and full path to the batch file you created, select Run Script, and click GO! After a few moments, you should see a message informing you that the request has been sent. At this point, you can go back, enter the path c:\emailon.txt, choose Read Output, and click GO! If all has gone well, you should see some text that indicates the service was started successfully.

## Writing the Client

The client, like most Web Clipping applications, is just a collection of HTML.

## Code Overview

The code for this application is even simpler than most PQAs, because it doesn't include any images and is only a single file in length.

### The Code

Listing 5-3 shows the code for the Web Clipping client.

*Listing 5-3. The Web Clipping Client*

```html
<html>
  <head>
    <title>Batch File Runner</title>
    <meta name="PalmComputingPlatform" content="true">
    <meta name="PalmLauncherRevision" content="1.0">
  </head>
  <body>
    <form method="post" action="INSERT-URL-FOR-YOUR-SCRIPT-HERE">
    File Name: <input type="text" name="filename"><br><br>
    <input type="radio" name="action" value="run" checked>Run Script<br>
    <input type="radio" name="action" value="read">Read Output<br><br>
    <input type="submit" value="GO!">
  </body>
</html>
```

### The Walk-Through

If you tested this file in the previous section using a standard Web browser, then you should already have it in your possession. In this case, you only need to create a Web Clipping application out of it. For details on how to do this, read on!

## *Trying It Out*

In order to turn Listing 5-3 into a Web Clipping application, first open the text editor of your choice (Notepad, for example). Next, enter all of the code from Listing 5-3, making sure to replace INSERT-URL-FOR-YOUR-SCRIPT-HERE with the URL of the Active Server Page you created in the previous section. Finally, save your text file with the extension .html.

At this point, the only thing left to do is build your client code into a working PQA file, load it onto the Palm OS emulator, and try it out!

### *Building*

In order to build the application, you must use the Web Clipping Application Builder tool that you downloaded previously. Simply follow these steps:

1. Open the Web Clipping Application Builder.

2. Choose Open Index from the File menu.

3. Select the file created in Listing 5-3 and click Open.

4. Choose Build PQA from the File menu.

5. Select a name and location for your application and click Build.

Once the PQA file has been built, load it into your emulator the same way that you loaded PocketDBA earlier in this chapter.

### *Execution*

At this point, you should have a new icon on your Palm display that looks like a solid black diamond. The label beneath this diamond will be the same as the name you chose for the file. Click this icon to bring up a page that looks like the one in Figure 5-9.

*Figure 5-9. Your first Web Clipping application!*

You can follow the same steps here as you did when testing the application with a regular Web browser. If for some reason you get no response when attempting to check the regular output, check c:\emailon.bad instead. This is where errors are regularly accumulated.

## Final Thoughts

In this chapter, you learned about one of the most popular mobile Internet devices on the market today: the Palm OS handheld device. By acquainting yourself with the particulars of this platform, you will be able to address a majority of the wireless PDA market.

In the next chapter, we will show you the final type of device that you should know about when creating wireless applications. In many ways, this device is the antithesis of .NET, as it represents the mobile portion of the Java platform. On the other hand, the ability of .NET to serve up content even to J2ME devices is perhaps the strongest argument in favor of the flexibility of the .NET platform.

CHAPTER 6

# J2ME Clients

## Write Once, Run on Any
## Java-Powered Device

WITH THIS CHAPTER, WE TURN our attention to the world of Java-powered devices. Those of you who have any familiarity with the recent history of events in the technology world may be aware of a certain legal dispute arising between Microsoft and Sun over Java. For this reason, any coverage of Java in a Microsoft-centric book such as this may be surprising. It is important, therefore, that you understand that .NET's ability to interact with Java devices represents perhaps the best proof of this new technology's superior flexibility.

## History

Before looking at the technologies underlying J2ME devices, it seems reasonable to give a brief historical overview of the development of these technologies. In this section, you will learn a bit about J2ME's parent technology: Java. Specifically, we will show you where Java came from and how the J2ME flavor of Java compares to other versions of the technology.

The section concludes with a look at the often adversarial relationship between Microsoft and Java.

### Java

Java was developed by Sun Microsystems in 1991 as part of a project named Green. Its main focus is on abstracting software development to a level at which the specifics of the underlying hardware become as close to irrelevant as possible.

In many ways, you can think of Java as just another third-generation language. In this scheme, it would fall directly in the middle of the following progression:

1.  Binary

2.  Assembler

3.  Low-level languages

4.  End-user–oriented languages

5.  "Natural" languages

What separates Java from other third-generation languages, however, is that it also embodies an entire technology for making applications created with it platform independent.

## Platform Independence

What does it mean to be platform independent? Sun has often summarized its vision for Java's platform independence as "write once, run anywhere." What this means is that, ideally, a single piece of Java code should be able to run on any machine where Java is available without modification.

As shown in Figure 6-1, a single piece of code written in Java is able to run on a Mac OS, Unix, or Windows system without alteration. The reason for this is the Java code is not compiled into a form that is in any way machine specific. This means that, unlike normal compilers, the Java compiler does not produce instructions that are aimed at specific operating systems or CPUs.

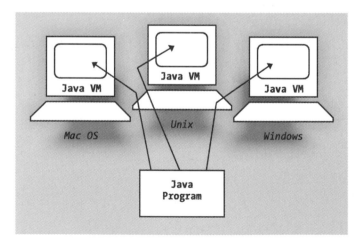

*Figure 6-1. Java code operating on multiple platforms*

Instead, when you compile a Java application, it creates a special kind of code known as *bytecode*. Although some hardware out there exists that is capable of directly running Java bytecode, this is not where the "magic" lies. Instead, the magic of Java lies in the Java Virtual Machine implementations, which are capable of running bytecode.

### Applications Written for Virtual Machine

In this book, you have already worked with several virtual machines, possibly without even realizing it. For example, the Pocket PC emulator that you operated in Chapter 3 was a kind of virtual machine. It performed all the functions that you would expect of an actual Pocket PC, but it didn't involve any actual hardware. Instead, it was a piece of software that knew how to use the hardware and operating system already on your computer to imitate the functionings of another computing device.

This is also a good description of the Java Virtual Machine (JVM). The JVM is a kind of emulator that uses the operating system and hardware of whatever computer it runs on to imitate the functioning of a machine that can read and execute Java bytecode. The only wrinkle is, with Java, the JVM existed long before any hardware that was capable of directly executing bytecode. And, for its main value proposition, it is the JVM—not the hardware it imitates—that is the real focus of interest in Java.

The reason for this is JVMs now exist for virtually every popular computing platform: from mainframes to Macs to Windows. By writing an application in Java, therefore, you are creating an application which can usually, in line with Sun's claim, run anywhere.

### Virtual Machine Specifications Are Public Knowledge

If the inner workings of the Java Virtual Machine (JVM) were a mystery to the outside world, much of the promise of Java would be lost. Under these circumstances, the only JVM implementation we'd likely see would be those offered by Sun itself. If the past history of other technology vendors is any indicator, this would probably mean the following:

- JVMs running on Sun systems (hardware or software) would typically function a little better than those running on other systems.

- Implementations of the JVM for non-Sun systems would typically lag a little behind those for Sun systems.

- Less popular systems would rarely, if ever, receive JVM implementations.

Fortunately, the specifications for building a virtual machine capable of executing the Java bytecode are public knowledge. This addresses each of the preceding points by allowing vendors well versed in the peculiarities of their own platforms to build their own JVMs. Because these vendors are the ones building JVMs for other platforms, there is no discernible bias in favor of Sun-based systems. Furthermore, platforms that once teetered on the edge of obsolescence (such as mainframe computers) have in many cases been rescued by the development of JVMs for their peculiar combinations of hardware and operating systems.

This openness has been a powerful force for the proliferation of the Java system itself as well. Had the functionality of the virtual machine been kept strictly to the world of Sun and its affiliates, much of the appeal of the system would have vanished. What makes Java appealing is the truly ubiquitous nature of its implementation.

## Low Resource Requirements

Besides the platform independence benefits of Java, there are numerous performance benefits to be derived from using bytecode technology. As you will learn later in this book, Microsoft itself has leveraged many of these same advantages in constructing its own virtual machine for .NET: the Common Language Runtime (CLR).

### Bytecode Requires Fewer Bytes

The use of bytecode to convey computer instructions winds up, in general, requiring fewer bytes than would be required to convey the same instructions using actual machine language. As shown in Figure 6-2, one reason for this is bytecodes are typically a richer means for communicating instructions than simple CPU instructions.

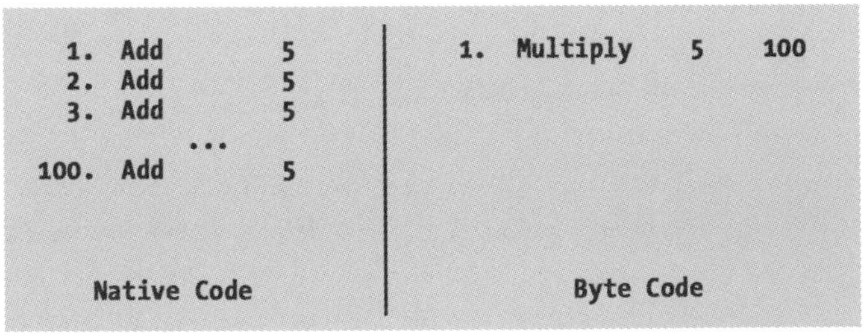

```
   1.  Add        5          1.  Multiply   5   100
   2.  Add        5
   3.  Add        5
              ...
 100.  Add        5


       Native Code                   Byte Code
```

*Figure 6-2. Bytecode vs. machine language*

As you can see in Figure 6-2, whereas it would take 100 add operations in machine language to tell a CPU to multiply a number 100 times, it only takes a single multiply bytecode. In reality, the Java Virtual Machine (JVM) will now have to translate the bytecode into machine language and will therefore wind up having to generate the same 100 instructions anyhow. So, how did this help?

It is an enormous help whenever active code needs to be sent across a network connection. This is most clearly illustrated in the difference between applets and ActiveX controls downloaded off the Web and run in browsers. ActiveX controls need to use machine-specific instructions and are therefore typically hundred of times the size of Java applets designed to do exactly the same thing.

This means it takes less bandwidth to transfer bytecode across a network, less space to store it on disk, and fewer bytes to hold it in memory.

### *Virtual Machine Is Optimized*

There is yet another reason why bytecode tends to be less of a resource hog than equivalent machine code. Languages that compile to machine language typically result in greater developer control over the specifics of application infrastructure. For example, in the C programming language, applications routinely manage their own allocation and cleanup of memory.

In the hands of a truly gifted developer, this can sometimes prove beneficial to performance. Resource allocation can be delayed until the last possible moment and reclaimed at the earliest possible opportunity. Unfortunately, most developers are not that truly gifted.

For the rest of us, systems designed to automate the minutiae of the internal resource usage of our applications are probably a much better bet. Virtual machines represent exactly such a system. Since all bytecode must be translated into equivalent machine language before execution, a virtual machine can avail itself of the opportunity presented by this process to ensure that the machine language generated is absolutely the most optimal for its purposes with respect to resource usage.

## J2ME

Java 2 Micro Edition (J2ME) is the flavor of Java technology that is intended for execution on small devices. In many ways, this makes it the Java equivalent of Microsoft's own .NET Compact Frameworks (.NETcf) technology.

In this section, you will learn a little about the other flavors of Java. This way you will be able to recognize what makes J2ME special and therefore the focus of our brief study of Java. Once you understand this, we can begin talking about what makes J2ME actually function and do useful work.

## Compared to Other Editions

Probably the easiest way to come to grips with the nature of J2ME is to compare it to the other two dominant flavors, or versions, of Java currently in use, which are listed here:

- Java 2, Standard Edition (J2SE)

- Java 2, Enterprise Edition (J2EE)

### J2SE

The Standard Edition of Java represents what might be called "classic Java." In terms of its functionality, it is very similar to the original Java programming language that was first released by Sun. There are two main tools associated with it: the Java Development Kit and the Java Runtime Environment.

The Java Development Kit (JDK) includes a compiler (javac) and the standard libraries needed in order to develop and compile Java software. Using the Java Development Kit, a developer should be able to create most any standalone Java application. Because the JDK also includes a Java Runtime Environment (JRE), a developer should also be able to test his or her work.

The Java Runtime Environment is just a nicely packaged JVM that comes with the runtime libraries needed in order to run Java software.

### J2EE

J2EE is best thought of as an addition to the functionalities available under J2SE, as depicted by Figure 6-3. Whereas J2SE is essentially a programming language bundled along with the whole concept of the Java Virtual Machine, J2EE goes much further. The crux of J2EE's technical benefits lies in the realm of Internet-enabled software and component software.

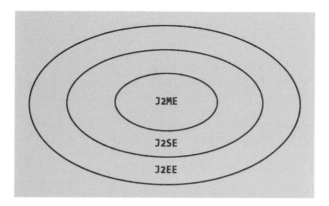

*Figure 6-3. J2SE vs. J2EE*

J2EE introduces a number of new technologies to assist with creating collaborative applications. For Internet applications, servlets and Java Server Pages (an ASP-inspired superset of servlet functionality) are both a part of J2EE. For component software, Enterprise Java Beans (EJBs) amount to Sun's answer to COM and DCOM componentry.

## Configurations

The primary level of organization for the J2ME is the configuration. In many ways, this name is too confusing, as it doesn't represent a way of configuring a device, but rather a particular collection—or configuration—of Java componentry intended to run on a certain broad category of devices.

Configurations are typically designed and implemented directly by Sun.

## Profiles

Profiles represent a more specific implementation of the base features found in any given configuration. For example, the same Connected, Limited Device Configuration (CLDC) implementation may be shared by two different devices. One of these may support the concept of data entry via a stylus (as supported by most Palm OS–powered devices), whereas the other requires the use of a keyboard. As Figure 6-4 shows, since the CLDC only talks about input at an abstract level, it doesn't care about the specific mechanism.

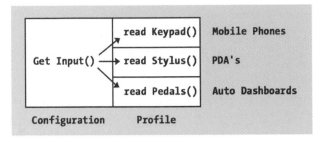

*Figure 6-4. Configurations vs. profiles*

Profiles, on the other hand, care about the specifics of the device. It is the profile that must specify concrete routines to handle such events as keystrokes (in the case of keyboard input) and so-called pen down events (in the case of style input). This concept extends beyond specific input mechanisms, however, and embraces anything concrete that might differ from the design of one group of devices to the next.

For this reason, profiles are most often developed and implemented by groups of device vendors working in collaboration with Sun.

## Microsoft's Angle

Microsoft has been described as hating Java, though the truth of this statement is difficult to determine. Officially, Microsoft's position on Java boils down to the following statement: they support the language, but not the platform. The significance of this is explained in the following section.

### Platform Independence = Lowest Common Denominator

The standard party line from Microsoft is that true platform independence is a pipe dream. The ideal of writing a single set of code and then being able to run it on any computer or device without modification is simply not likely to succeed. And, even if you could do it, why would you want to?

The obstacles to achieving Java's vision of platform independence include the following:

- Differences in hardware

- Differences in operating system

In the first case, it seems fairly obvious that different hardware platforms have different capabilities. In order to support different hardware, therefore, Java tends to aim for the lowest common denominator. Rather than requiring millions of colors, obscure input devices, and tons of memory, Java strives to operate on the most bare bones of hardware architectures imaginable.

Operating systems are similar in the variety of feature sets that they do and do not support. For example, some are capable of starting and stopping with little or no load time. Others, such as Windows 2000, must be properly shut down in order to avoid data corruption. Java's answer to these differences, once again, is to choose *not* to support special functionality on operating systems that can perform cold starts in favor of continued compatibility with those that can't support this.

## Agree with the Language, not the Platform

So, it is clear to see that Microsoft does not agree with Sun's vision of "write once, run anywhere." If this is the case, then, can we deduce that Microsoft has had absolutely no involvement in the Java world whatsoever? Not at all.

Microsoft was among the first software companies in the world to license Java for inclusion in its Windows operating system. Java was released, after all, in the early days of the browser wars between Netscape and Internet Explorer. If Netscape had been allowed to become the only browser capable of serving up Java applets, then Microsoft's eventual dominance in this market may never have come to pass.

But Microsoft's involvement in Java went beyond merely including it as a standard part of Windows. Soon, Microsoft extended the functionality of Java to incorporate some native Windows functionality. This extended functionality was made accessible via Microsoft's Java SDK, the IDE for which soon came to be known as J++.

The main idea behind J++ was that code written in the Java programming language could be compiled into native Windows code. This code could then be accessed from other components that may or may not be Java based. For example, a Java applet running on a Web page could potentially use Java's Remote Method Invocation (RMI) protocol to run methods on a COM component on the server. Figure 6-5 shows this in action.

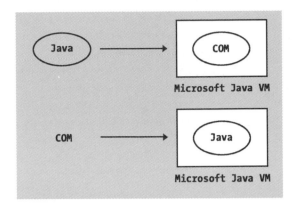

*Figure 6-5. ActiveX and Java*

Unfortunately, this unholy marriage of so-called platform-neutral Java code with native Windows functionality ran afoul of Sun and soon resulted in a lawsuit. Unlike other Internet standards, Java is not an open standard—meaning that it is not standardized and maintained by a vendor-neutral committee. Instead, Sun retains ownership over Java and all of its associated copyrights, which gave Sun the ability to tell Microsoft to stop using the name Java for what it was doing.

**TIP**   *This legal hassle is one of the key reasons behind the creation of Microsoft's new C# language.*

## Creating Applications

Now that you understand the origins of J2ME, it is time to dig in and finally begin creating applications with this technology! In order to do this, you must know three things:

- The fundamental architecture of J2ME

- Where to get J2ME and associated tools

- How to use your tools to develop, test, and deploy code

In this section, we explain the J2ME architecture fundamentals, where to find the tools you need, and how to use those tools.

## Fundamentals

Before you can build on any platform, you must first acquaint yourself with the fundamental architecture of that platform. For example, someone wanting to create Windows applications using Microsoft's Visual Basic technology must first have an idea of what forms and controls are. The J2ME world has a similar number of buzzwords and elements with which you must familiarize yourself.

## Configurations

There are two main configurations of J2ME as of the time of writing. The first of these is called the Connected Device Configuration (CDC). The other is called the Connected, Limited Device Configuration (CLDC).

### CDC

Of the two configurations currently in existence, the CDC is the more powerful. This is to say it is targeted at devices that have more "horsepower," and is therefore able to incorporate more of the standard Java functionality.

The virtual machine that runs as a part of this configuration is known as the CVM, or C Virtual Machine. This means that, unlike other virtual machines that are typically written in Java, this virtual machine is written in the C programming language.

The CDC's requirements are aimed primarily at next-generation devices, which are expected to be considerably more powerful than those currently in widespread use. For this reason, there are not a wide variety of devices available that currently support the CDC.

### CLDC

In contrast to the lack of current industry support for the CDC, there are numerous device manufacturers that have either already shipped products supporting CLDC or announced such shipments in the near future. One of the key factors in this strong level of early support is the enormous popularity of the Java technology. Another is the very light hardware and performance requirements for CLDC-compatible devices. Table 6-1 compares the requirements of the CDC and CLDC configurations.

*Table 6-1. Comparing CDC and CLDC Requirements*

| REQUIREMENT | CDC | CLDC |
|---|---|---|
| CPU | 32-bit | Anything |
| Memory | >= 2MB | 160KB–512KB |
| Connection | Yes | Yes |
| Power | Stable | Limited |
| UI | Yes | Yes |
| Java | Full | Partial |

Within the CLDC, there is a special virtual machine known as the K Virtual Machine (KVM). Of all three virtual machines discussed so far (JVM, CVM, and KVM), KVM has by far the smallest memory footprint. This relates to one of the two stories behind how it came by its name: its memory requirements are measured in KB instead of MB.

**NOTE**  *The other story is that, since the letter K comes after the little J in the alphabet, this is intended to be the virtual machine that comes after the JVM.*

Also within the CLDC you will find implementations for a small subset of the standard Java 2 functionality. These classes form a completely different codebase from the actual Java 2 Standard Edition (J2SE) classes. They are bundled into four packages:

- java.io

- java.lang

- java.util

- javax.microedition.io

The first three of these packages embody analogs to J2SE functionality, and their use should be fairly obvious to you if you have already worked with Java. The classes in the final package, however, are unique to J2ME and are, of course, the most interesting. It is within this package that the base classes supporting networking connectivity may be found. However, the implementation of specific protocols (HTTP or FTP, for example) are left to the designers of specific profiles.

## Profiles

At the time of writing, there are just two profiles in wide circulation. The first of these is called the Foundation profile, and the second is called the Mobile Information Device Profile (MIDP).

### Foundation Profile

The Foundation profile is intended for use with CDC, which you read about earlier in this chapter. As such, it embodies the rather large set of features that are expected to be available in future, more high-powered Internet devices. Although hardly comprehensive, Table 6-2 shows a comparison of the differences in feature sets offered by the Foundation profile and its smaller cousin, the MIDP.

*Table 6-2. Comparing Foundation and MIDP Profiles*

| PACKAGE | CDC | CLDC |
|---|---|---|
| java.io | Yes | No |
| java.lang | Yes | Yes |
| java.lang.ref | Yes | No |
| java.lang.reflect | Yes | No |
| java.lang.math | Yes | No |
| java.net | Yes | No |
| java.security.* | Yes | No |
| java.text | Yes | No |
| java.util | Yes | Yes |
| java.util.jar | Yes | No |
| java.util.zip | Yes | No |
| javax.microedition.io | Yes | Yes |
| javax.microedition.rms | No | Yes |
| javax.microedition.midlet | No | Yes |
| javax.microedition.icdui | No | Yes |

What you should take away from this table is the fact that much more of standard Java's functionality is exposed by the Foundation profile than the MIDP profile. Nevertheless, like the CDC with which it is associated, it is currently far less implemented than its competitor, MIDP. For this reason, we will be focusing exclusively on the MIDP for the remainder of the book.

### MIDP

The MIDP is intended for use with the current generation of relatively low-powered mobile Internet devices. It became the first J2ME profile in the world to be rolled out at a national level, thanks to the efforts of NTT DoCoMo in Japan. Furthermore, it is the first profile to be used in cellular phones within the United States as a result of Motorola and Nextel's efforts.

In the remainder of this chapter, you will learn how to download and install the MIDP so that you can get started building some mobile J2ME applications!

## Getting the Tools

In this section, you will learn how to obtain and install some J2ME-related tools. Some of these tools, such as the JDK, are absolute necessities. Others, such as the VisualAge IDE, are simply options for making your life (potentially) a little easier.

Similarly, some of these tools are freely available for download off the Internet. In these cases, we will show you where to look and what to do once you've downloaded the tools. In other cases, you are actually going to have to make a purchase if you like what we describe. Unfortunately, we can't help you there!

### Sun Stuff

The first items that you need to get your hands on are the tools produced by Sun itself.

#### The Java Development Kit

You won't get very far creating Java applications of any variety without the Java Development Kit. The Java Development Kit is to Java what Microsoft's Visual Studio is to Visual Basic or Visual C++. It contains all of the essential Java run-time libraries as well as a compiler to turn your simple text files full of Java source code into fully functional Java bytecode.

In order to get and install the JDK, follow this procedure:

1. Navigate to `http://java.sun.com`.

2.  Click Products and APIs.

3.  Choose Java 2 SDK, Standard Edition from the Product Shortcuts list.

4.  Click Microsoft Windows.

5.  Scroll to the bottom of the page and click Continue.

6.  Accept the licensing agreement.

7.  Choose your download location and click its button in order to download the self-extracting executable.

8.  Run the executable setup program you just downloaded to install the JDK on your computer.

**NOTE**   *You should also add the Java executable subdirectory (bin) to the PATH environment variable for your development system. For instructions on how to do this, see the Windows Help system.*

### Wireless Toolkit

By far, the most useful software that you can possibly obtain for creating J2ME applications for the wireless Internet is Sun's Wireless Toolkit. The Wireless Toolkit brings together a number of tools needed to create J2ME applications, including the MIDP.

As if this weren't enough, Sun has bundled a primitive IDE into the toolkit to make it a little easier for you to package and deploy your MIDP software in the form of so-called MIDlet suites. And, finally, for those of you who haven't seen quite enough emulators yet, there is an excellent emulation tool included in the Wireless Toolkit that allows you to test your MIDlets against a wide variety of different J2ME-compliant devices without having to go out and buy any or all of those devices.

To download the Wireless Toolkit, follow these steps:

1.  Navigate to `http://java.sun.com/j2me`.

2.  Find the section entitled Related Downloads.

3.  Click the J2ME Wireless Toolkit link.

4. Click Continue.

5. Agree to the licensing agreement.

6. Download the software.

 **CAUTION** *It is absolutely essential that the JDK be installed on your machine before the Wireless Toolkit is!*

## IDEs

As time goes by, more and more IDEs will support the new J2ME flavor of Java. For the time being, there are two IDEs that are clearly leaders in the field. If you think that you might be interested in augmenting your development efforts with a little bit of automated assistance, then you might want to check out one or both of the products described in the following sections. Otherwise, if you are itching to get started developing, skip to the section "Getting Started" a little later in this chapter.

### CodeWarrior for Java

CodeWarrior is a product from a company called Metroworks. If you are an avid Mac OS, Palm OS, or games developer, chances are good that you are already familiar with this company. It has made producing compilers and other development tools its main business for a long time now. On the platforms cited, it has long been the dominant player.

Metroworks' J2ME-enabled product is called CodeWarrior for Java. It specifically supports the CLDC/MIDP combination that we will be using for the remainder of this book. Furthermore, it is available for MacOS as well as for Windows. For more information, visit http://www.metroworks.com.

### VisualAge Micro Edition

VisualAge is from IBM. Ever heard of that company? IBM's entry into the realm of portal Java is a product called VisualAge Micro Edition. This makes it one of a family of Java IDEs from IBM, all of which are called VisualAge. In terms of popularity, this family of IDEs is almost always listed among the top five IDEs most popular with Java developers whenever polls are taken on the topic.

Unfortunately, IBM has decided to create its own configurations and embedded virtual machine (called the J9 virtual machine) for this product. This means the product is not officially compliant with Sun's J2ME standards, and therefore will not work with the CLDC or the MIDP profile.

## Getting Started

At this point, we are finally ready to turn our attention to the topic that is nearest and dearest to most developers' hearts: coding. If you have purchased a J2ME-compliant IDE for this purpose, then now is the time to fire it up. In this section, we will show you how to compile a simple J2ME MIDlet that you can either run in an emulator on your computer or install on a real device for further testing.

The application developed in this section will not, however, be a true mobile application, insofar as it will not encompass any wireless networking access. For this, you will just have to wait until the next section, "Installing the Wireless Toolkit."

### Installing the Wireless Toolkit

The installation of the Wireless Toolkit includes a fancy Windows installer that will automatically create the right directories and files for you. Simply run the program file downloaded previously, named j2me_wireless_toolkit-1_0_1-fcs.exe.

**TIP** *Since the Wireless Toolkit's filename includes its current version number, the exact name of the file may change by the time you read this.*

You should accept the licensing agreement and accept all the defaults unless you have a good reason to do differently (such as lack of storage space). This is to increase your chances of out-of-the-box integration with other J2ME tools as much as possible.

**CAUTION** *At one point, you will be prompted whether you want to do an integrated or stand-alone installation. Whether or not you have Forte for Java, you should choose the option Stand Alone for the purposes of this discussion. All future examples in this book will be done in stand-alone mode, so it will be easier for you to follow along this way. After you're done reading this book, you can always reinstall the Wireless Toolkit in integrated mode for further exploration.*

The whole installation should take about 10MB and, assuming you followed the defaults, result in the creation of a folder named C:\J2MEWTK. More interesting, however, are the entries that should have been added to your Windows Start menu under J2ME Wireless Toolkit 1.0.1:

- Documentation: Excellent documentation for the MIDP APIs.

- KtoolBar: A tool to help automate the compilation and testing of your MIDP applications.

- Preferences: A tool for setting up your development and testing environment.

- Remove J2ME Wireless Toolkit 1.0.1: Use this to remove the Wireless Toolkit (perhaps to reinstall it in integrated mode when you're done with this book).

- Run MIDP Application: Here's how to test MIDP applications without actually having to own a MIDP device!

Once you have these options on your Start menu, you can test your installation to verify that you are ready to begin creating your own MIDP applications!

## Testing

In this section, you will learn how to compile, pre-verify, package, and run your own MIDP applications. In doing this, you will also be testing to make sure that your installation of MIDP is fully functional.

### *Compiling*

We will begin by compiling the standard Hello World MIDlet that comes as part of the MIDP bundle.

1. In your midp-fcs directory, navigate to the src\example subdirectory.

2. Open HelloMIDlet.java in your Java IDE of choice (or in Notepad).

3. Briefly familiarize yourself with the code, referring to the MIDP documentation in your Windows Start menu if you have any questions.

4. In your midp-fcs directory, navigate to the classes subdirectory.

5. Make a subdirectory named test.

6. Type the following command:

```
javac -d test ..\src\example\HelloMIDlet.java
```

> **TIP** *If Windows complains about not knowing where to find any of the files in this section, you may wish to add the JDK executables directory to your PATH environment variable. This is usually the bin subdirectory beneath wherever you installed the JDK. For example, "\jdk1.3\bin" is a very common Windows location for the JDK executables directory.*

7. Navigate to the test subdirectory created in Step 5 and verify the presence of HelloMIDlet.class.

You have now successfully compiled your first MIDP application!

> **TIP** *To keep your class files as small as possible, add the switch -g:none to the command line shown in Step 6.*

### Pre-verifying

Included with the Wireless Toolkit that you have now installed is a J2ME pre-verifier. The purpose of this tool is to go through your class files and do as much work in advance as is possible. This advance work takes some burden off the KVM, which will be running on the device itself. Pre-verification is an essential part of creating J2ME applications!

To pre-verify your Hello World MIDlet, follow these steps:

1. In your midp-fcs directory, navigate to the classes subdirectory.

2. Type the following command:

```
\j2mewtk\bin\preverify test
```

This should be sufficient to pre-verify your new MIDlet.

### *Packaging*

At this point, only one thing stands between your MIDlet and actually seeing it run: packaging. MIDlets like to be bundled together into archives known as MIDlet suites. A full discussion of MIDlet suites is beyond the scope of this book, but you should be able to pick up fairly easily on how to create simple suites by following along with the example here.

To create a MIDlet suite for your Hello World MIDlet, follow these steps:

1. In your midp-fcs directory, navigate to the classes\test subdirectory.

2. Use your favorite text editor to create a file named hello.jad.

3. Put the text from Listing 6-1 into this file.

4. Save and close the file.

5. Use the following command to bundle your MIDlet into an archive:

```
jar cf hello.jar HelloMIDlet.class
```

6. Verify the existence of both hello.jad and hello.jar in this directory.

At this point, you have created both a Java Archive (hello.jar) to contain your MIDlet and a Java Archive Descriptor (hello.jad) to tell your J2ME device (or emulator) about your MIDlet suite.

*Listing 6-1. Your hello.jad File*

```
MIDlet-1: HelloWorld,, HelloMIDlet
MIDlet-Description: Sun's Hello World MIDlet
MIDlet-Jar-URL: hello.jar
MIDlet-Name: HelloWorld
MIDlet-Version: 1.0.0
MicroEdition-Configuration: CLDC-1.0
MicroEdition-Profile: MIDP-1.0
```

The most important line in your JAD file is the one labeled MIDlet-Jar-URL. This is the line that will tell your device where it can find the JAR file. In this case, because we haven't prepended any protocol or directory information to the archive's filename, it will simply look in the same directory as the JAD file on the local computer. In other cases, it would be possible to direct the device to any location on the Internet!

### Running

Testing J2ME applications would be very difficult without emulation. You would have to own at least one actual J2ME device just to know whether or not your code even did what you wanted it to do! If you wanted to make sure it worked on more than just that device, you would also need to buy at least one of every other device upon which you wished to test.

Fortunately, the Wireless Toolkit includes an excellent emulator that allows you to test your applications on a wide variety of J2ME devices. Let's begin by seeing your new Hello World MIDlet in action:

1. On the Windows Start menu, open Programs.

2. Navigate to the J2ME Wireless Toolkit 1.0.1 group.

3. Select Run MIDP Application.

 **NOTE** *On some Windows machines, this option may not work. In these cases, you may try a workaround by navigating directly to your J2MEWTK directory under the command prompt interface. From there, go into the bin subdirectory and execute RunMidlet.bat. This should either run or, if it fails, give you a much better idea of the reason for the failure.*

4. When the emulator begins running, it will pop up a dialog box asking for the JAD file that it should use.

5. Navigate to the hello.jad file you created in the previous section and click Run.

6. You should see a screen much like the one in Figure 6-6. This is a list of all the MIDlets contained in the suite that has been loaded.

7. In this case, HelloWorld is the only option. Click in the middle of the device's directional button to select it.

8. At this point, you should see something like Figure 6-7.

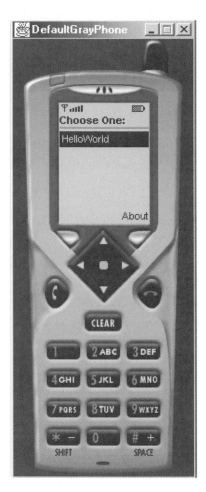

*Figure 6-6. Choosing the right MIDlet from your suite*

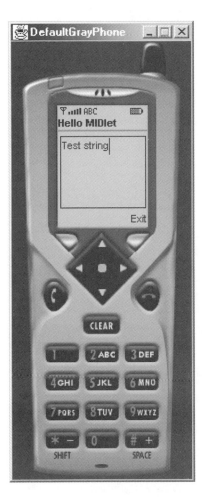

*Figure 6-7. Congratulations! Your first MIDlet suite!*

| Exercise |
| --- |

Almost all application development involves the same series of steps:

1.  Design

2.  Develop

3.  Test

4.  Repeat Steps 1 through 3 as often as required

5.  Deploy

When developing mobile applications, it can often be a challenge to negotiate your way smoothly through all of these steps. Developing for the J2ME flavor of Java is no exception.

In this section, we will undertake the design, development, testing, and deployment of a simple client/server using J2ME. It is hoped that, by carefully following this example, you will be able to get a good start on the creation of your own J2ME applications.

## Writing the Server

The server part of the example application will look up a Social Security number in a database and return the name of the employee associated with that number. As always, the server-side part of the system will be provided by a simple Active Server Pages application.

### Code Overview

As with previous chapters, the server for this exercise has been constructed using Microsoft's pre-.NET Active Server Pages technology.

***The Code***

Listing 6-2 shows the code for a simple ASP server.

*Listing 6-2. A Simple ASP Server*

```
<%
    Option Explicit

    Dim cn
    Dim rst
    Dim ssno

    cn.provider = "MSDASQL"
    cn.open "customers", "sa", ""

    ssno = Request.QueryString("ssno")

    rst.open "select name from customers where ssno = '" & ssno & "'", cn

    if rst.eof then
        response.write "No such customer!"
    else
        response.write rst.fields(0)
    end if

    rst.close
    cn.close
%>
```

### The Walk-Through

The code for this simple ASP server begins by declaring a few variables: cn and rst to hold our database object references, and ssno to hold the Social Security number that will be passed by the client.

After this, the script opens a connection to an instance of SQL Server known as customers using the Microsoft OLE DB Provider for SQL Server (MSDASQL).

After storing the Social Security number from the client into the variable ssno, the script sends a query to the database to ask about the full name associated with this number. If any data is returned, it is sent back to the J2ME client. If there is no such Social Security number in the database, an error message to this effect is returned instead.

**NOTE**   *It is important to note the absence of HTML in the data being returned to the J2ME client. The client is so simple that it will not interpret any markup, but instead expects to receive its answer in simple text format.*

The script finishes by closing all connections to the database.

### Trying It Out

To test this script, you can simply call it with a URL such as the following:

```
http://localhost/j2me.asp?ssno=475-22-2341
```

If you can set up a data source similar to the one shown being used by the script, you should get back a simple customer name in response. Alternatively, for learning purposes, you could opt to replace all of the data access code shown in the example with some static response.

## Writing the Client

The client portion will send a Social Security number to the server for further processing.

### Code Overview

At this point, you have successfully created your first J2ME application and had the satisfaction of seeing it run on your own device (or an emulation thereof). However, as you might have noticed, the application you created was in no way, shape, or form wireless. True, it was capable of running on a device that was not connected to anything else via wires, but doesn't it take more than that to be a true mobile application?

In this section, you are going to add the stuff that makes mobile applications truly interesting: network access. In its simplest form, the CLDC specification outlines a number of primitive classes for supporting mobile network functionality. For doing truly useful work, however, you must tap the MIDP for some protocol support.

### The Code

Listing 6-3 shows the code for the J2ME client.

*Listing 6-3. The J2ME Client*

```java
import javax.microedition.midlet.*;
import javax.microedition.io.*;
import javax.microedition.lcdui.*;

import java.io.InputStream;
import java.lang.String;

public class client extends MIDlet implements CommandListener
{
    private Command cmdQuit  = new Command("Quit", Command.EXIT, 2);
    private Display display;

    public client()
    {
        display = Display.getDisplay(this);
    }


    public void startApp()
    {
        makeContact();
    }

    private void makeContact()
    {
        StringBuffer b = new StringBuffer();
        HttpConnection c = null;
        TextBox t = null;

        try
        {
            long len = 0 ;
            int ch = 0;
            String strURL = "http://localhost/j2me.asp?ssno=343-81-6278";

            c = (HttpConnection)Connector.open(strURL);
            InputStream is = c.openInputStream();
```

```
            len =c.getLength() ;

            for (int i =0 ; i < len ; i++ )
            {
                if ((ch = is.read()) != -1)
                {
                    if (ch <= ' ') ch = ' ';
                    b.append((char) ch);
                }
            }

            is.close();
            c.close();

            t = new TextBox("Microsoft Speaks!", b.toString(), b.length(), 0);
        }
        catch (Exception e)
        {
            System.out.println(e.toString());
        }

        t.addCommand(cmdQuit);
        display.setCurrent(t);
    }

    public void pauseApp()
    {
    }

    public void destroyApp(boolean unconditional)
    {
    }

    public void commandAction(Command c, Displayable s)
    {
        if (c == cmdQuit)
        {
            destroyApp(false);
            notifyDestroyed();
        }
    }
}
```

*The Walk-Through*

The sample client begins by importing three important MIDP packages. The first of these, midlet.*, encompasses base functionality. You would typically find this imported into any useful MIDlet application. The second, io.*, contains base classes for MIDP-specific input/output processing. Finally, lcdui.* is for the creation of graphical user interfaces under the MID profile.

The next point of interest are the two static variables declared within the client class. The first of these, cmdQuit, will be used to place a command button on the screen to let users terminate the application when they are finished. The second is a reference to a display area. The constructor for this application performs the vital task of associating this variable with the current application's display area.

The startApp() function is the main point of entry for this application. It immediately passes to the makeContact() function. You might wonder why the useful work done by the application wasn't put directly into startApp(). The reason for this is that the startApp() function also kicks off a number of timing and maintenance threads. It is best to return as quickly as possible from startApp() in order to let these threads get up and running and reduce the risk of creating an application that potentially hangs the entire device.

Before we delve into makeContact(), let's look at the rest of the program—which is extremely obvious. The empty functions, pauseApp() and destroyApp(), are there simply because the MIDP specification requires them in any MIDlet. If you had any special tasks to perform whenever your appli-cation was paused or terminated (such as resource reclamation), this would be where such work would get done.

The final no-brainer in the code listing is the commandAction() function. This function gets called whenever a command button is pressed on your applica-tion. In this case, the function listens for the cmdQuit button to be pressed, at which point it terminates the MIDlet. Since this is the only button in the applica-tion, no further logic is required.

This leaves us with just the makeContact() function. And this is where the real work of the program gets done. To begin with, you should know that there are three classes that provide the base functionality associated with making wireless networking connections under J2ME:

- StreamConnection

- ContentConnection

- HTTPConnection

As you progress from the first of these classes to the last, you get more specific functionality and less abstraction. Since this is an application that will talk to a Web site, in this example we show you the most functional and "out-of-the-box" of these classes for the application: HTTPConnection.

In the try block of the code, a connection is opened to the ASP server—which for the purposes of this example is assumed to be running on the same box and named j2me.asp. Feel free to modify this code as necessary. Next, you find out how much data has been returned (in bytes) and begin retrieving characters from the InputStream that has been associated with the connection.

Once the end of available data is reached, the connection to the Web site is closed. Next, a text box pops up containing the message that was returned by the server script. The code concludes by making the Quit button available so that users may terminate the application at their discretion.

## Trying It Out

To try this code out for yourself, follow the steps in the next sections.

### Building

1. Enter all of the code from Listing 6-2, given earlier, and save it in \inetpub\wwwroot with the filename j2me.asp.

2. In your midp-fcs directory, navigate to the classes subdirectory.

3. Make one subdirectory named j2meclient and another named almostdone.

4. Enter all of the code from Listing 6-3, given earlier, and save it in your new j2meclient subdirectory under the filename client.java.

5. From the classes subdirectory of midp-fcs, enter the following commands:

```
javac j2meclient\client.java
\j2mewtk\bin\preverify -d almostdone j2meclient
```

6. Navigate to the almostdone subdirectory and verify the presence of a file named client.class.

7. Enter the following command:

```
jar cf client.jar client.class
```

8. Find the exact size (in bytes) of your new client.jar file using the DIR command.

9. Enter all of the text from Listing 6-4 and save it as client.jad. Be sure to substitute the number of bytes in your own JAR file for the number shown in the MIDlet-Jar-Size line in the listing that follows.

*Listing 6-4. Your New JAD File*

```
MIDlet-1: client,, client
MIDlet-Description: Sample MS Client
MIDlet-Info-URL: http://www.eviloscar.com/
MIDlet-Jar-Size: 1626
MIDlet-Jar-URL: client.jar
MIDlet-Name: client
MIDlet-Vendor: APress LP
MIDlet-Version: 1.0.0
MicroEdition-Configuration: CLDC-1.0
MicroEdition-Profile: MIDP-1.0
```

At this point, you should be all set to test your first J2ME client application with a Microsoft server backend!

### Execution

To execute your new MIDlet, do the following:

1. Select Run MIDP Application from your Windows Start menu.

2. Navigate to client.jad and click Run.

3. Press the center of the emulator's directional control to begin running the client application.

Soon, you should see output on your screen like that shown in Figure 6-8.

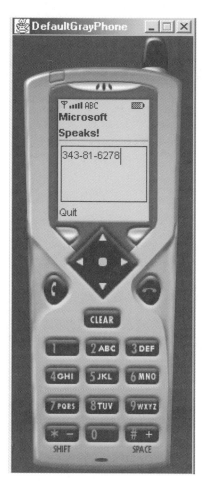

*Figure 6-8. The sweet taste of J2ME success!*

## Final Thoughts

In this section, we have rushed you through the creation of a simple J2ME client. Our intention was not to make you experts in J2ME. The title of this book is, after all, *Mobile .NET!* Instead, we hoped to show you enough to get you started and to light the fires of your interest if, indeed, it seems to you that J2ME may suit your purposes.

You may have noticed that the Social Security number was hard-coded into the client we created. If you are interested in learning more about J2ME, we suggest you use the MIDP documentation included with the Wireless Toolkit to add the ability to the client to accept different Social Security numbers dynamically from the user.

In researching further, there are two additional resources you may want to consult. The first of these is Bill Day's J2ME archives at `http://www.billday.com/j2me/index.html`. The other is *Wireless Java*, from Apress.

# CHAPTER 7

# Bringing It All Together, Part One

## The Second Most Important Chapter in the Book

WE HOPE THE TITLE OF this chapter will have suggested to you a certain vital importance in your continued reading. By now, you have invested six chapters' worth of reading to learning about all of the most popular wireless platforms currently on the market. So, you might be wondering when you'll actually be able to begin writing mobile applications.

This chapter will get you started. We are going to show you how, using pre-.NET Microsoft technologies, you could build a wireless application that will do the following:

- Accept a NASDAQ stock symbol.

- Verify that this symbol consists of exactly four letters, numerals, or underscores.

- Store this symbol into a session state for use by another page.

- Request a quote on the stock's current price from another Web site.

- Scrape the required data from the other site's HTML.

- Format the data appropriately for return to the client device.

In this chapter, we are setting the stage for our discussion of .NET, which will consume the remainder of this book. The idea is when you are done doing multidevice development the pre-.NET way, you will completely understand the need for a better way to do things. This is what we will teach you in the second half of this book.

## Writing the Server

In this section, we will construct the server-side part of the stock quote application. This part should by itself suffice for use by standard Web browsers (such as Internet Explorer), Pocket PCs, and WAP phones.

## *Targeting Internet Explorer*

As you recall from previous chapters, Internet Explorer is considered the ultimate client when dealing with most Microsoft Internet technologies. For this reason, we will begin by constructing an application that is capable of working with this browser.

### *The Code*

Enter the code in Listing 7-1 and save it under the filename stockreq.asp in a location where IIS can serve it up to connecting devices and browsers. One example of such a location might be c:\inetpub\wwwroot.

*Listing 7-1. The ASP Request Receiver Script*

```
<HTML>
  <HEAD>
    <SCRIPT LANGUAGE="JavaScript">
      function validate()
      {
          var sym = document.forms[0].symbol.value;
          var exp = /[ABCDEFGHIJKLMNOPQRSTUVWXYZ]{4}/;

          if (!(sym.length == 4))
          {
                      alert("Wrong number of characters!");
                      return false;
          }

          if (!(sym.toUpperCase().match(exp)))
          {
                  alert("Invalid characters!");
                  return false;
          }
      }
```

```
    </SCRIPT>

    <TITLE>Stock Quote Request</TITLE>
  </HEAD>
  <BODY>
<%
   if request("symbol") = "" then
%>

    <FORM ACTION="stockreq.asp" METHOD="POST">
      Stock symbol:
      <INPUT NAME="symbol" TYPE="TEXT" ID="symbol">
      <p>
      <INPUT TYPE="SUBMIT" onClick="return validate()" VALUE="Get Quote">
    </FORM>

<%
    else

      session("symbol") = request("symbol")
      response.redirect "stockrsp.asp"

    end if
%>
  </BODY>

</HTML>
```

The second piece of code that you will need in order to construct the server application is a custom COM component. The easiest way to create this component is to follow these steps:

1. Open the Visual Basic 6 IDE.

2. If you aren't immediately presented with the New Project dialog box, get it for yourself by choosing New Project from the File menu.

3. Double-click ActiveX DLL.

4. Enter the code shown in Listing 7-2.

5. Select your new project in the Project Explorer tree.

6. Change your project's name to NoDotNet.

7.  Select your new class module in the Project Explorer tree.

8.  Change your class module's name to Scraper.

9.  Right-click your new project in the Project Explorer tree and select Add a New Form from the pop-up context menu.

10. Change your new form's name to frmTalker.

11. Select Components from the Project menu.

12. Put a check-mark next to Microsoft Internet Transfer Controls and click OK.

13. Double-click the globe-and-computer icon that just appeared in your Components toolbox to add it to your new form.

14. Select Make NoDotNet.dll from the File menu.

At this point, you may close Visual Basic. You may also choose to save your project to avoid reentry work if you need to modify it later on.

*Listing 7-2. The COM Component*

```
Public Function getHTML(symbol As Variant) As Variant

    Dim strURL as String

    strURL = "http://finance.lycos.com/home/stocks/quotes.asp?symbols="
    getHTML = frmTalker.Inet1.OpenURL(strURL & symbol)

End Function
```

Enter the code in Listing 7-3 and save it as stockrsp.asp in the same location where you previously saved the code in Listing 7-1.

*Listing 7-3. The ASP Responder Script*

```
<%

    Set obj = Server.CreateObject("NoDotNet.Scraper")

    rsp = obj.getHTML(session("symbol"))
```

```
    a = instr(rsp, "Last Sale")

    if a = 0 then
        response.write "Error getting stock quote!"
    else
        b = instr(a, rsp, "<b>")
        c = instr(b, rsp, "</b>")

        response.write mid(rsp, b + 3, (c - b) - 3)
    end if
%>
```

## The Walk-Through

Use of this application begins when a client first points its browser at the file named stockreq.asp. IIS interprets the dynamic bit of code at the top of this file and realizes that the form field named symbol is blank in the data that is being submitted to it. This means one of two things:

- This is the first time the browser has hit this page.

- The user left the field blank when he or she submitted the page.

In either case, it is appropriate at this point for the script to display the form that will request the user's preferred stock symbol. This is exactly what a large portion of the static HTML in this file does.

When the user clicks the button labeled Get Quote, the request does not immediately go to the server. Instead, the JavaScript function named validate() executes. This is done because you entered its name in the onClick attribute of the submit button's HTML. The code for this function is towards the top of Listing 7-1 in the <HEAD> portion of the static HTML.

You may not be a JavaScript expert, and such expertise will neither be required nor imparted by the remainder of this book. So, for simplicity's sake, simply realize that this code performs three functions *on the client* whenever the Get Quote button is pressed:

- Verifies that there are exactly four characters in the stock symbol

- Verifies that all of the characters in the stock symbol are letters (A to Z)

- If both of the preceding items are verified successfully, the form is submitted. Otherwise, an error message is displayed.

When the form is submitted, the data goes straight back to the stockreq.asp script. At this point, the code realizes that the symbol field has been filled in and (at the bottom of Listing 7-1) stuffs it into the `Session` object for further processing. This further processing is accomplished via a redirection of the client to stockrsp.asp.

The code for stockrsp.asp is shown in Listing 7-3 in the previous section. It is essentially an HTTP wrapper for the business conducted by the `NoDotCom.Scraper` COM component that we show in Listing 7-2. The first thing that stockrsp.asp does, in fact, is instantiate an instance of our custom COM component. The second thing that it does is take the stock symbol out of the `Session` object in which it was packaged and pass it to the `getHTML` function of our COM component.

In Listing 7-2, you can see what happens inside the `getHTML` function. The `OpenURL` method of Microsoft's Internet Transfer Control is used to contact remote Web sites and return the HTML they produce. In this case, the publicly available Quote.com Web site is contacted and the HTML report that it returns for a stock symbol is used as the return value for our own `getHTML` function.

At this point, control returns to stockrsp.asp, which should be left with a bunch of HTML stuffed into its variable named rsp. The code searches the contents of this variable for the substring `Last Sale`. This is some static content on Quote.com's results pages that we feel we can rely upon to accurately calculate the position of a stock's price. The remainder of this page calculates the exact offset to the stock price's location with the HTML and returns it to the browser.

Earlier in this chapter, we said that we hoped you would find this exercise extremely tedious to complete. If you have been following along with the discussion so far, a number of thoughts might occur to you at this point:

- This application takes eight steps just to get a simple stock price—this can't be good for performance.

- Similarly, this system combines five independent applications—how good can this be for reliability?

- What happens if Quote.com changes or moves the phrase "Last Sale?" The entire system crashes, that's what!

- There are some serious threading issues with using the Microsoft Internet Transfer control in this fashion. What if this application gets 100 simultaneous requests?

So, are we insane for having done it this way? Not at all. This is the exact same architecture behind many a similar system running under pre-.NET technologies today. As you might guess, the flaws just described are some of the most important problems addressed by the arrival of .NET.

As bad as these problems are, however, you ain't seen nothin' until we start making this application work with multiple client devices!

## Targeting the Pocket PC and i-Mode

Now that you have seen the application in use with Internet Explorer, we will take a step into the world of Wireless Internet access.

Let's begin by seeing why any changes are needed at all. Do this:

1.  Start the Pocket PC emulator that you installed in Chapter 3 (eMbedded VB).

2.  Select Internet Explorer from the Pocket PC's Start menu.

3.  If the address bar is not visible at the top of the emulator's screen, choose Address Bar from the View menu at the bottom.

4.  Enter the same address you used to access stockreq.asp from the desktop version of Internet Explorer in the previous section.

5.  Click Go.

6.  Enter a string of garbage for your stock symbol. Make sure it includes numerals and is longer or shorter than four characters.

7.  Click Get Quote. You should find yourself redirected to a completely blank stockrsp.asp page.

Well, this isn't good at all, is it? The first page didn't verify your input before submitting it. If you attempt the same thing using the Pixo Microbrowser i-Mode emulator, you will find that it doesn't verify your input, either.

On the Pocket PC emulator, the second page won't generate an error message, either. In fact, it won't appear to generate anything at all. What the heck is the problem here?

## The Code

The first code listing we present in this section, Listing 7-4, is an adaptation of Listing 7-1 shown earlier. It features a single block of code modified to ensure compatibility with Pocket PC and i-Mode devices.

*Listing 7-4. The Code for stockreq.asp, with Added Support for Pocket PCs*

```
<HTML>
  <HEAD>
    <SCRIPT LANGUAGE="JavaScript">
      function validate()
      {
          var sym = document.forms[0].symbol.value;
          var exp = /[ABCDEFGHIJKLMNOPQRSTUVWXYZ]{4}/;

          if (!(sym.length == 4))
          {
              alert("Wrong number of characters!");
              return false;
          }

          if (!(sym.toUpperCase().match(exp)))
          {
              alert("Invalid characters!");
              return false;
          }

      }
    </SCRIPT>

    <TITLE>Stock Quote Request</TITLE>
  </HEAD>

  <BODY>

<%

    if request("symbol") = "" then

%>

    <FORM ACTION="stockreq.asp" METHOD="POST">
      Stock symbol: <INPUT NAME="symbol" TYPE="TEXT" ID="symbol">
      <p>
      <INPUT TYPE="SUBMIT" onClick="return validate()" VALUE="Get Quote">
    </FORM>

<%
```

```
        else

            '********************
            '* MOD #1: For JavaScript-challenged devices
            '********************

            symb = request("symbol")

            if len(symb) <> 4 then
               response.write "Wrong number of characters!</body></html>"
               response.end
            end if

            for i = 1 to 4
              if ucase(mid(symb, i, 1)) < "A" or ucase(mid(symb, i, 1)) > "Z" then
                  response.write "Invalid characters!</body></html>"
                  response.end
               end if
            next

            session("symbol") = symb

            '*********************
            '* MOD #1: Ends
            '*********************

        response.redirect "stockrsp.asp"

      end if

%>

  </BODY>
</HTML>
```

The second code segment, shown in Listing 7-5, is an adaptation of Listing 7-3 for added Pocket PC support.

*Listing 7-5. Internet Explorer on Pocket PCs Is Mighty Picky about HTML!*

```
<html>
   <head>
      <title>Your Quote, Sir</title>
   </head>
   <body>
<%

   Dim obj
   Dim rsp

   Set obj = Server.CreateObject("NoDotNet.Scraper")

   rsp = obj.getHTML(session("symbol"))

   a = instr(rsp, "Last Sale")

   if a = 0 then
      response.write "Error getting stock quote!"
   else
      b = instr(a, rsp, "<b>")
      c = instr(b, rsp, "</b>")

      response.write mid(rsp, b + 3, (c - b) - 3)
   end if
%>
   </body>
</html>
```

## The Walk-Through

Let's start at the end and work our way backwards, because the modifications to Listing 7-5 are much simpler than the ones made to Listing 7-4. In short, in Listing 7-5, we simply packaged our system's final output as a proper HTML/cHTML document.

If you compare Listing 7-5 to Listing 7-3, you will see that the original script featured markup of any kind. The desktop version of Internet Explorer is forgiving enough to accept this and display a valid page, anyhow. The Pocket PC version of Internet Explorer and most i-Mode emulators are not nearly as flexible. This is the reason why you were getting completely blank pages in response to the requests you issued via the emulators.

In Listing 7-4, we clearly denoted our modifications with the label MOD #1. We begin by saving the contents of the Request field, symbol, into the local variable symb.

**TIP** *This is good programming practice whenever you plan on working extensively with a value that is stored in an intrinsic ASP object. The reason for this is it is much less performance-intensive to work with a local variable than to work with an object's methods and properties.*

Once we have stored our submitted stock symbol in a local variable, we feel free to manipulate it as we see fit. In this case, we perform exactly the same validations using server-side VBScript that would have been performed by JavaScript on a "regular" Internet browser, such as Internet Explorer.

The reason for this is that the version of Internet Explorer that comes with the Pocket PC emulator does not support client-side scripting. This is an accurate simulation of older Pocket PCs that were, as you learned in Chapter 3, based on Windows CE 2 and featured no support for client-side script validation. This is why no client-side validation was taking place when you submitted your pages from the emulator; your scripts were simply ignored.

**TIP** *More recent Pocket PCs (Windows CE 3 and above) do, indeed, feature support for JavaScript. For instructions on adding JavaScript support to the Pocket PC emulator, see Knowledge Base article Q296904 at* http://support.microsoft.com.

At this point, you should try accessing the preceding code with your Pocket PC and i-Mode emulators to verify that you receive a response in both cases. You should also go back and verify that your scripts still work with Internet Explorer. Of course, we have tested them ourselves, but we want you to get a full sense for how tedious creating multiplatform wireless applications was before .NET!

## Targeting Palm OS

If we were to proceed strictly by chapter order, at this point we would show you how to adapt the application for use with WAP phones. However, as it turns out, the modifications needed in order to add WAP support are fairly extensive. For this reason, we have decided instead to proceed in order from least to most complicated. Following this ordering, Palm OS is our next target for support.

## The Code

As you learned in Chapter 5, the current approach to accessing the wireless Internet from Palm OS devices is known as Web Clipping. Because of Web Clipping, for the first time in this exercise you will need to install some special software on the client in order for the application to work properly.

This special software, the Web Clipping application (or PQA, as it is known), will be taken mostly from the existing code for stockreq.asp. The complete source listing for this PQA file will be given and explained in the section "Writing the Clients" later in this chapter.

For now, however, there is one change that you must make to the copy of stockreq.asp that will execute on the server. You must change the line that reads

```
response.redirect "stockrsp.asp"
```

to instead read

```
server.transfer "stockrsp.asp"
```

The reason for this is explained in the walk-through that follows this section. In the meantime, please examine the changes in Listing 7-6 that are required to stockrsp.asp.

*Listing 7-6. Server-Side Modifications Required for Web Clipping Support*

```
<html>
   <head>
      <!--
      '********************
      '* MOD #2: For Web Clipping devices
      '********************
      -->
      <meta name="PalmComputingPlatform" content="true">
      <meta name="PalmLauncherRevision" content="1.0">
        <!--
        '********************
        '* MOD #2: Ends
        '********************
```

```
    -->

      <title>Your Quote, Sir</title>
    </head>
    <body>
<%

  Dim obj
  Dim rsp

  Set obj = Server.CreateObject("NoDotNet.Scraper")

  rsp = obj.getHTML(session("symbol"))

  a = instr(rsp, "Last Sale")

  if a = 0 then
     response.write "Error getting stock quote!"
  else
     b = instr(a, rsp, "<b>")
     c = instr(b, rsp, "</b>")

     response.write mid(rsp, b + 3, (c - b) - 3)
  end if
%>
    </body>
</html>
```

## The Walk-Through

The first question that needs to be answered is, "Why is Server.Transfer now being used in stockreq.asp instead of Response.Redirect?" The answer can be summarized in one word: cookies. As we mentioned in Chapter 5, Web Clipping strips out any cookie content from traffic as it travels from the server to the client and vice versa. Without cookies, the example application will not work in its previous form.

You're probably thinking, "But I don't see cookies being used anywhere in this application!" Although this application isn't *directly* using cookies, ASP is using one very important cookie to keep things running properly behind the scenes. This cookie is known as the Session Identifier, and is used to uniquely identify a client each time it browses to a page within the same ASP application.

This cookie lives for the lifetime of a given client's session and is, therefore, the basis upon which the intrinsic `Session` object operates. Without support for cookies, the stock symbol that we store in the `Session` object is no longer available by the time the client is redirected to the stockrsp.asp page. This would cause the page to generate an error.

In this application, we are able to work around the issue simply by calling `Server.Transfer` instead of `Response.Redirect`. We are able to do this only because our use of session state in this application is extremely basic. In larger, more complicated applications, this lack of cookies becomes an *enormous* problem.

As a quick case study in developer suffering, one of the developers (who shall go nameless) responsible for prototyping PocketDBA (an application that allows wireless database administration from Palm OS devices) did not realize this limitation until his first public demonstration. In this case, the application server he had been using for development had been capable of working around Web Clipping's lack of cookie support.

 **NOTE** *This is a blatant hint about one .NET feature that you can expect to learn about in the second half of the book. Remember this question: "What can .NET do for me where cookie-less devices are concerned?"*

Unfortunately, the application server used for the demonstration demanded support for cookies from any device that connected to it. The demonstration failed miserably, the developer cried, and now you're learning from his mistakes. Well, someone should.

The modification to stockrsp.asp is more trivial in nature. Recall from Chapter 5 that Web Clipping devices expect to see two <meta> tags in the HEAD section of any HTML document they encounter. These <meta> tags are simply a developer's way of telling a Web Clipping device, "It's OK to download this page, I designed it with you in mind." If you add these lines, a Web Clipping device will at least *try* to interpret your page. If you don't, the device will reject them without even looking at them!

Getting frustrated yet? Don't worry. As Yoda says, "You will. . . *you will!*"

## Targeting J2ME

Now that we've arrived at J2ME, we are actually going to add support for what is probably the absolutely *least* supported of all client devices. From your perspective as a developer, the important thing to remember about J2ME is this: *Its rendering capabilities are the most primitive of all the devices we examine in this book.*

## The code

Listing 7-7 shows the server-side modifications for J2ME support.

*Listing 7-7. The stockrsp.asp Code Modifications for J2ME Devices*

```
<%
    '********************
    '* MOD #3: For J2ME Devices
    '********************
    if request.servervariables("HTTP_USER_AGENT") <> "PDBAJ2ME" then
%>

<html>
    <head>
    <!--
        '********************
        '* MOD #2: For Web Clipping devices
        '********************
    -->

    <meta name="PalmComputingPlatform" content="true">
    <meta name="PalmLauncherRevision" content="1.0">

    <!--

'********************
'* MOD #2: Ends
'********************
-->

    <title>Your Quote, Sir</title>

</head>
<body>
<%
    else
        session("symbol") = request("symbol")
    end if

'********************
'* MOD #3: Ends
'********************
```

```
Dim obj
Dim rsp

Set obj = Server.CreateObject("NoDotNet.Scraper")

rsp = obj.getHTML(session("symbol"))

a = instr(rsp, "Last Sale")

if a = 0 then
   response.write "Error getting stock quote!"
else
   b = instr(a, rsp, "<b>")
   c = instr(b, rsp, "</b>")

   response.write mid(rsp, b + 3, (c - b) - 3)
end if
%>
   </body>
</html>
```

## The Walk-Through

Like Palm OS devices, J2ME devices feature no built-in support for cookies (although a particularly enterprising developer could certainly write custom code to implement them). Unlike Palm OS devices, however, J2ME devices do not feature any built-in capabilities for rendering HTML markup either. Since they have no built-in browser component, the programmer is *completely* responsible for interpreting any data received from the server and displaying it as information to the end user.

Given the simplicity of our raw HTTP connection to the server, we have elected to completely bypass the HTTP POST operation to stockreq.asp. Instead, we will perform an HTTP GET operation directly to stockrsp.asp.

At the top of Listing 7-7, we have added code to recognize our custom J2ME client. In general, under pre-.NET Active Server Pages, you identify different kinds of clients by the strings they send into the HTTP_USER_AGENT parameter of the ServerVariables collection on the Request object. As you will see in the section "The J2ME Client," PDBAJ2ME is just something that we made up!

If the server code recognizes the client as being our custom J2ME code, it skips all of the initial formatting HTML and <meta> tags. It then copies the stock symbol that is being passed by the J2ME client to the Session object. It has to do this here because the stockreq.asp script that would ordinarily perform this function has been bypassed.

The script completes by returning the answer, in which you are interested, and a couple of closing HTML tags, in which you are not interested. It will be left up to the client to clean away the unwanted HTML closing tags.

 **TIP**   *In Chapter 13, we use Microsoft's Mobile Internet Toolkit to create a special device adapter that knows how to serve up pure XML to J2ME devices.*

## Targeting WAP

The end of our server-side application development for this exercise is in sight. The code has gotten pretty ugly by this point, but it is about to get a whole lot worse. The WAP phones are probably the least compatible with pre-.NET Microsoft technologies. They require an entirely different kind of markup called Wireless Markup Language (WML). Furthermore, they have a strange blend of capabilities where client-side scripting, form submissions, and cookies are concerned. For more information, consult Chapter 4.

### The Code

Listing 7-8 shows the final version of the server code, and Listing 7-9 displays the WML needed for the application.

*Listing 7-8. The stockrsp.asp Code, Final Edition*

```
<%
'*******************
'* MOD #4: For WAP Devices
'*******************
    if instr(request.servervariables("HTTP_USER_AGENT"), "UP") > 0 then
        response.contenttype = "text/vnd.wap.wml"
%>
<?xml version="1.0"?>
<!DOCTYPE wml PUBLIC "-//WAPFORUM//DTD WML 1.1//EN"
"http://www.wapforum.org/DTD/wml1_1.1.xml">
<wml>
    <card id="main" title="Your Stock Quote">
        <p>
<%
    end if
```

```
'*********************
'* MODS #3 & #4: For J2ME & WAP Devices
'*********************
if request.servervariables("HTTP_USER_AGENT") <> "PDBAJ2ME" and & _
    instr(request.servervariables("HTTP_USER_AGENT"), "UP") = 0 then
%>
<html>
    <head>
    <!--
    '*********************
    '* MOD #2: For Web Clipping devices
    '*********************

    -->

    <meta name="PalmComputingPlatform" content="true">
    <meta name="PalmLauncherRevision" content="1.0">

<!--

    '*********************
'* MOD #2: Ends
'*********************

-->

    <title>Your Quote, Sir</title>

</head>
<body>
<%
    else
        session("symbol") = request("symbol")
    end if

'*********************
'* MODS #3 & #4: Ends
'*********************

Dim obj
Dim rsp

Set obj = Server.CreateObject("NoDotNet.Scraper")

rsp = obj.getHTML(session("symbol"))
```

```
a = instr(rsp, "Last Sale")


if a = 0 then
    response.write "Error getting stock quote!"
else
        b = instr(a, rsp, "<b>")
    c = instr(b, rsp, "</b>")

    response.write mid(rsp, b + 3, (c - b) - 3)
end if


'********************
'* MOD #5: For WAP Devices
'********************


if instr(request.servervariables("HTTP_USER_AGENT"), "UP") > 0 then
%>
</p>
</card>
</wml>
<%
    else
%>
    </body>
</html>
<%
end if
'********************
'* MOD #5: Ends
'********************
%>
```

*Listing 7-9. The stockreq.wml Code*

```
<?xml version="1.0"?>
<!DOCTYPE wml PUBLIC "-//WAPFORUM//DTD WML 1.1//EN"
"http://www.wapforum.org/DTD/wml1_1.1.xml">
<wml>
    <card id="main" title="Your Stock Symbol">
        <p>
            Symbol: <input name="symbol"/>
          <do type="accept" label="Lookup">
             <go method="get" href="http://localhost/stockrsp.asp">
               <postfield name="symbol" value="$(symbol)"/>
```

179

```
        </go>
      </do>
      </p>
    </card>
</wml>
```

### The Walk-Through

Listing 7-8 shows an additional modification to the stockrsp.asp script. This modification is intended to change the MIME type that will be output if the target device is a WAP phone. The reason for this is that WAP phones, unlike all of the other devices we have examined, expect their output to come in the form of WML—not HTML.

Rather than even trying to add to stockrsp.asp the WML needed in order to create the request form on the client, we have decided to split it out into a separate file. This is the file that is first requested by the phone in order to begin a stock price quoting transaction. You can see the code for it in Listing 7-9 earlier.

The form consists of a single field named Symbol. The code in the go section creates the WML equivalent of a Submit button. In WML, you must explicitly tell the button to submit the value entered into the Symbol field via use of the <postfield> tag.

## Writing the Clients

In the previous section, we showed you how to write approximately 80 percent of the code that you need in order to create a multiple-target mobile application using pre-.NET technologies. The remaining 20 percent of the code exists, not on the server, but on the clients themselves. What Palm OS and J2ME devices share in common is that both kinds of devices require some kind of client-side code in order to effectively interoperate with Microsoft servers.

### The Palm OS Client

The code in the next section should be saved to a file named index.html. It may then be built into a Web Clipping application (PQA file) via use of the Web Clipping Builder application that was described in detail in Chapter 5.

#### The Code

The client-side code for Palm OS is shown in Listing 7-10.

*Listing 7-10. The Palm Query Application Code*

```html
<HTML>
  <HEAD>
    <!--
    '*********************
    '* MOD #2: For Web Clipping devices
    '*********************
    -->
    <meta name="PalmComputingPlatform" content="true">
    <meta name="PalmLauncherRevision" content="1.0">
    <!--
    '*********************
    '* MOD #2: Ends
    '*********************
    -->

    <SCRIPT LANGUAGE="JavaScript">
      function validate()
      {
          var sym - document.forms[0].symbol.value;
          var exp = /[ABCDEFGHIJKLMNOPQRSTUVWXYZ]{4}/;

          if (!(sym.length == 4))
          {
             alert("Wrong number of characters!");
             return false;
          }

          if (!(sym.toUpperCase().match(exp)))
          {
                 alert("Invalid characters!");
                 return false;
          }

      }
    </SCRIPT>

    <TITLE>Stock Quote Request</TITLE>
  </HEAD>

  <BODY>
    <!--
```

```
'*********************
'* MOD #2: For Web Clipping devices
'*********************
-->

<FORM ACTION="http://www.pocketdba.com/stockreq.asp" METHOD="POST">
<!--
'*********************
'* MOD #2: Ends
'*********************
-->

  Stock symbol: <INPUT NAME="symbol" TYPE="TEXT" ID="symbol">
  <p>
  <INPUT TYPE="SUBMIT" onClick="return validate()" VALUE="Get Quote">
  </FORM>

  </BODY>
</HTML>
```

### The Walk-Through

As with all Web Clipping HTML, Listing 7-10 begins with two <meta>tags that
mark the remainder of the content as having been designed for use with Palm
OS devices. This gives the Palm OS client the go-ahead to expend its time and
energy (and its owner's connect fees) downloading the rest of the file.

The other modification consists of pinning down the name of the server
to an actual, physical machine—rather than simply localhost. This is required
because of Web Clipping's peculiar 100 percent proxied architecture, as
described in Chapter 5.

## The J2ME Client

J2ME clients *always* require client-side code in order to effectively interact with
servers across the mobile Internet.

### The Code

Listing 7-11 shows the client-side code to access the server application from
J2ME clients.

*Listing 7-11. The Stock Quotation MIDlet*

```java
import java.io.*;

import javax.microedition.io.*;
import javax.microedition.midlet.*;
import javax.microedition.lcdui.*;

public class PDBAstock extends MIDlet implements CommandListener
{

    private Display dsp;
    private Command cmdExit, cmdLookup;
    private TextBox txtSymbol;

    public PDBAstock()
    {
        cmdExit = new Command("Exit", Command.EXIT, 0);
        cmdLookup = new Command("Lookup", Command.SCREEN, 0);

        txtSymbol = new TextBox("Stock Symbol", "", 32, 0);
        txtSymbol.addCommand(cmdExit);
        txtSymbol.addCommand(cmdLookup);
        txtSymbol.setCommandListener(this);
    }

    public void startApp()
    {
        dsp = Display.getDisplay(this);
        dsp.setCurrent(txtSymbol);
    }

    public void pauseApp()
    {
    }

    public void destroyApp(boolean unconditional)
    {
    }

    public void commandAction(Command c, Displayable s)
    {
        if (c == cmdExit)
```

```
{
    destroyApp(false);
    notifyDestroyed();
}
else if (c == cmdLookup)
{
    String quote = "", strURL = "http://localhost/stockrsp.asp?symbol=";
    InputStream in = null;
    OutputStream out = null;

    byte[] bf = new byte[512];
    int index = 0;

    try
    {
        HttpConnection cn = (HttpConnection)Connector.open(strURL +
        txtSymbol.getString());
        cn.setRequestProperty("User-Agent", "PDBAJ2ME");
        out = cn.openOutputStream();
        out.flush();

        in = cn.openInputStream();

        int i;

        while ((i = in.read()) != -1)
          {
            if (i == 60)
                break;

            bf[index++] = (byte) i;
            quote = new String(bf, 0, index);
        }

    }
    catch (Exception e)
    {
        System.out.println(e);
    }

    Alert answer = new Alert("Your Quote", quote, null, null);
    answer.setTimeout(Alert.FOREVER);
    dsp.setCurrent(answer, txtSymbol);
```

```
        }
    }
}
```

## The Walk-Through

Here, for the first time since the beginning of the chapter, you are presented with an entirely new bit of code. Expertise in Java is not expected in this book. However, a little familiarity with the language is required in order to follow along with a broad description of the preceding code.

To begin with the easiest methods, pauseApp() and destroyApp() are both completely empty. The reason they are included is that they are required by the definition of the MIDlet abstract class. In order to make this class concrete, therefore, some implementation must be provided for both of these methods—even if they are completely blank.

The constructor PDBAstock() creates the various GUI components and places them onto the main screen of the application. The startApp() method then simply requests that the prepopulated screen be drawn on the device's display.

At this point, the user may manipulate the GUI without further response from the application until one of the buttons is clicked, at which time the commandAction() method is called. In the simplest case, if the button clicked is the Exit button, the commandAction() method will request that the application be terminated.

On the other hand, if the Lookup button has been pressed, a network connection to the stockrsp.asp script is opened. This connection uses the HTTP GET methodology to send the symbol of the stock across to the server-side script. It then waits for a response from the server. The response is parsed for the appropriate answer, which is then displayed in a modal alert.

## Final Thoughts

Well, by this point, we hope you are convinced that creating multiclient mobile applications using pre-.NET technology is indeed possible. You should also be equally convinced that, as more and more different devices are added to the mix, this becomes a progressively more daunting task. Clearly, a better approach is sorely needed.

In the remainder of this book, you will see how .NET fits this bill perfectly.

*Part Three*

# The .NET Server

## CHAPTER 8

# Meet .NET

## Getting to Know Your New Best Friend

WITH THIS CHAPTER, WE BEGIN the third part of our five-part journey towards creating mobile applications using Microsoft's .NET technologies. At this point, we have finished looking at a broad enough sampling of mobile devices to clearly understand the diverse nature of this audience. The second half of this book, therefore, will be dedicated to understanding how .NET can help you cope with these differences.

## What Is All the Fuss About?

Chances are excellent that you had heard something about Microsoft's .NET initiative before you first saw this book. .NET represents Microsoft's desire to fundamentally change the rules of creating software for the Windows platform. In this section, we will not only explain the fundamentals of this change to you, but also try to explain *why* we feel Microsoft is doing this.

### Motivating the Change

In some ways, .NET is more of a response to industry changes than it is a change in and of itself. As you have seen thus far in the book, many, many different mobile devices are available on the market today. Taken individually, none of the devices represent particularly challenging platforms for the creation of new software. In combination, however, they form a complex web of variations that can be difficult, if not impossible, to target with a single application.

In Chapter 7, we combined many of the techniques you had been learning previously in the book into a single, multiclient ASP application. As you no doubt noticed during the completion of that chapter, targeting multiple clients with single Active Server Page scripts can be very, very tedious indeed.

## One Solution Rejected

One proposal on how this situation might be resolved is Sun's J2ME technology. Using J2ME, all different kinds of devices could agree to run Java. Presumably, these Java-powered devices would then connect to servers running Java Application Servers (JASs). Because Java is by and large platform independent, these JASs could potentially be running on anything from an Apple iMac to a Unix workstation.

The main problem with this approach is that it requires a lowest common denominator approach to software development. The only capabilities of any device that pure Java can ever access are those capabilities that it shares in common with ever other device. This results in a consistent "dumbing down" of applications that are created for the Java platform.

**TIP**   *For more information about Microsoft's plans for Java on the .NET platform, see Microsoft's JUMP to .NET home page at* http://msdn.microsoft.com/visualj/jump/.

## Dealing with Devices the .NET Way

For the reason sited in the preceding text, Microsoft has proposed an alternative solution to the problem of having numerous differences among different client devices. In the .NET solution, a single .NET-based server takes responsibility for adapting to the special needs of the different clients connecting to it.

At a minimum, this might mean adjusting to the minor differences in HTML supported by different Web browsers. We discuss this in some detail in Chapter 9. Taken a step further, however, properly equipped .NET servers are capable of sending completely different markup to different devices without any special programming on the part of application developers! We cover this in Chapters 12 through 14.

A third kind of .NET software is made possible by the .NET Compact Frameworks. This technology, known as .NETcf, is introduced in Chapter 15 and allows the execution of .NET code on actual devices—such as Pocket PCs and Stinger phones.

## The Common Language Runtime

The Common Language Runtime (CLR) is an environment provided by .NET for the execution of code that is compiled to bytecode, rather than to native machine instructions. In this sense, it is quite similar to Java, which leverages bytecode to produce platform-independent software.

**TIP** *As of the time of writing, CLR environments are only available for Windows-powered platforms. Microsoft has also announced that it will work with Corel to produce a version of the Common Language Interpreter(CLI) for the FreeBSD operating system.*

One advantage to .NET's use of the CLR is that code written in any .NET language may be freely mixed and matched with code written in any other .NET language. For example, a GUI interface written in C# .NET would have no problem calling subroutines written in Visual Basic.NET.

## What about the Real World?

Bytecode is all good and well as an abstract theoretical concept, but many people worry about the practicality of running software that never results in the creation of actual machine instructions. Well, to begin with, this perception is actually a bit mistaken. Bytecode is, in fact, ultimately converted to machine language before execution. The only difference is that the translation happens at runtime, rather than in an earlier compilation process.

So, how does this affect performance? Admittedly, there is some overhead associated with compiling to machine language at runtime rather than in a previous step. However, this overhead is more than compensated for by the fact that .NET's bytecode is uniquely optimized for execution on the Windows platform.

Security under .NET is also much improved over previous security models offered by the Windows operating system. For example, .NET offers the ability to assign code access permissions at the method level, rather than the component level. This means, for example, that if you were designing a banking application, you would not be forced to split bank account operations between two components: one for supervisors, and one for tellers.

Instead, you could create a single component named BankAccount and grant access to some of its methods to supervisors only, and make the rest accessible to everyone. This is much more in accordance with the principals of proper object-oriented design (OOD).

## The .NET Framework SDK

The functionality packaged within the .NET Framework SDK comprises .NET's "other half." The .NET Framework comprises a series of classes meant to provide the application developer with a variety of prebuilt functionality. In all cases, these classes may be added as-is to applications built under .NET for immediate use as components. In many cases, these classes may be inherited for the creation of entirely new classes.

One obvious benefit to the existence of the .NET Framework SDK is the decrease in the amount of custom code that application developers must write for themselves. This saves developers time. It may also save money for those who must employ application developers.

A less obvious benefit to the .NET Framework is that it provides a more standardized way to solve common application development problems. For example, searching for the existence of one complex string pattern within another might have been accomplished in any number of ways using pre-.NET Microsoft code. The .NET Framework, however, provides a series of classes that implement regular expression searches and matching.

By using these classes, the developer saves time. Any developers later inheriting the maintenance and upkeep of this code would be able to understand it much more quickly. This is true because the regular expression functionalities of .NET are well documented and standardized. The same would not be true of any pre-.NET custom approaches to solving this problem.

**TIP**    *After you have installed Visual Studio .NET in the next section, you may review the complete list of Framework classes by selecting Documentation under the Microsoft .NET Framework SDK option on the Windows Start menu. Some of the more important classes—many of which we will be using in the remainder of this book—include* System.Data, System.Net, System.Web, System.Windows.Forms, *and* System.XML.

# Installing .NET

Now that you have a basic understanding of what .NET can do for you as a developer, you are probably curious about how you can try it out for yourself. In this section, we will tell you what you need in order to complete all of the .NET exercises for the rest of this book. Furthermore, we will tell you where you can get this stuff and how to install it on your computer once you've gotten it!

## System Requirements

For your ease of understanding, we have divided the .NET system requirements into two sections: "Hardware" and "Software."

## Hardware

.NET is officially described as "Microsoft's Web Services platform." Implied in this description is the existence of both a server and one or more clients at all times. For this reason, it is important that you understand the hardware requirements for .NET clients as well as servers.

### *Client Requirements*

For simplicity's sake, we will divide every potential .NET client in the world into three groups:

- *Blessed:* A Microsoft-endorsed client for the .NET platform

- *Supported:* A client for which out-of-the-box .NET code is available

- *Cursed:* You want .NET support here? Do it yourself! (We'll show you how later in this book.)

Table 8-1 organizes all of the clients we have seen so far (plus a few new ones) into these categories.

*Table 8-1. Classification of Clients*

| CLIENT DEVICE NAME | BLESSED | SUPPORTED | CURSED |
| --- | --- | --- | --- |
| Internet Explorer | Yes | No | No |
| Netscape | No | Yes | No |
| Pocket PC | Yes | No | No |
| WAP | No | Yes | No |
| Palm OS | No | No | Yes |
| i-Mode | No | Yes | No |
| J2ME | No | No | Yes |

Of all the preceding clients, the ones that are most important to know fall into the blessed and the supported categories. If you keep good tabs on the current members of these lists, you can usually safely assume that any other client you hear about is in the cursed category.

### Server Requirements

Microsoft describes the hardware requirements for a .NET server as shown in Table 8-2.

*Table 8-2. The Hardware Requirements for a .NET Server*

| HARDWARE DESCRIPTION | MINIMUM | RECOMMENDED |
| --- | --- | --- |
| CPU type | Pentium II class | Pentium III class |
| CPU speed | 450 MHz | 600 MHz |
| Memory | 96 MB | 256MB |
| Disk space | 3GB | 500MB on system drive, 2.5GB elsewhere |
| CD-ROM | Yes | Yes |
| Display | VGA | SVGA |

All of the exercises in this book were completed on a Dell Inspiron 8000 laptop with an 850 MHz processor and 256MB of RAM. (Aren't you jealous?)

## Software

In Public Beta 2 of .NET, the support for different operating systems on the server is fairly minimal. Fortunately, its requirements for additional software installations are equally minor.

### Operating Systems

As of Public Beta 2, there are only three operating systems currently supported by .NET:

- Windows 2000

- Windows XP Professional

- Windows NT 4 Server

All of the examples in this book were completed using the Beta 2 of Windows XP Professional.

**CAUTION** *Microsoft claims that with this release you can probably install .NET onto an existing machine. Those of us who have heard this before during Beta 1 are not inclined to try this again until the final release. If you are using this book with anything short of the final release of .NET, we strongly recommend that you install .NET only onto a completely clean operating system. Yes, this means backing your entire computer up, wiping it out with a fresh OS installation, installing .NET, testing it, and only then putting everything back.*

The relatively short list of supported operating systems in no way, shape, or form compromises .NET's ability to work with an almost limitless range of client devices.

### Applications

There is only one piece of software that you should have up and running on your system before installing .NET. This is Microsoft's Internet Information Server (IIS). IIS is included on the CDs for all three of the operating systems currently supported by .NET. To install it under Windows XP, for example, follow this procedure:

1. Open the Windows Start menu.

2. Click Control Panel.

3. Double-click Add/Remove Programs.

4. Click Add/Remove Windows Components.

5. Place a check in the check box next to Internet Information Server.

6. Click Next.

## The Getting Your Hands on It

The way that .NET is currently made available to the public as of the time of writing is quite different from the way in which it will ultimately be distributed by Microsoft.

## The Way Things Are

As of the time of writing, the single best package for .NET is Beta 2 of Visual Studio .NET. By installing this application on your computer, you will not only be getting the Visual Studio, but also the complete set of .NET Framework classes. There are a few ways to obtain Beta 2 of Visual Studio .NET:

- Order the CD from Microsoft.

- Download the software (MSDN Universal subscribers only).

- Get the CD for free (MSDN Universal subscribers only).

- Bum it off a friend (our favorite).

To check for the latest availability when you read this, go to the following URL: http://www.msdn.microsoft.com/vstudio/nextgen/beta.asp.

## The Way Things Shall Be

Ultimately, the .NET Framework classes will be bundled as a part of Microsoft Windows .NET Server (the successor to Microsoft Windows 2000 Server). This would, theoretically, allow the deployment of .NET applications onto this server without the installation of any further software.

For those of us who wish to do .NET application development, however, purchasing Visual Studio .NET will be required. Although this software is free while still in beta, it won't stay this way for long.

**TIP** *If there is any way to convince your current employer to spend $2000, a Universal subscription to the Microsoft Developers Network (MSDN) is really a must-have for any serious Microsoft developer. For the cost of approximately $2000, you get full copies of everything developer-related that Microsoft produces (including Visual Studio, Microsoft Office, and all the Microsoft operating systems) for one full year. The only catch is that these are licensed for development purposes only.*

## Installing Visual Studio .NET

Fortunately, installing Visual Studio .NET is one of the simpler tasks that you complete in this book. Assuming that you have it on CD, the installation can typically be summarized in the following steps:

1.  Clean *all non–operating system software* off your computer.

2.  Insert the CD.

3.  Follow the instructions in the dialog boxes that appear.

4.  Restart your computer.

5.  Begin using .NET.

Of all of these steps, cleaning off your computer is probably the single most important factor in determining whether or not your installation attempt will succeed. The current beta claims that it can be installed properly, provided only that previous versions of .NET have been removed. However, for purposes of this book, we strongly recommend installing Beta 2 only onto completely fresh installations of the Windows operating system.

Once you have cleaned off your computer, you are ready to insert the first Visual Studio CD into your computer. For the time being, skip the CD labeled "Windows Components upgrade." Once the CD is inserted, it automatically starts and presents you with a series of dialog boxes that will guide you through the installation of Visual Studio .NET.

 **NOTE**   *The "Windows Components upgrade" CD will be requested at some point in these dialog boxes, if it is required. If it is never requested, then you didn't need it!*

When you have finished the installation, it is probably wise to restart your computer. Although the installer may inform you that this is not required, it can still be a good idea. If nothing else, this gives your system a chance to start IIS and install any files that may have been accidentally locked by running applications during the .NET installation.

## Installing the Tutorials

In order to complete the exercises with SQL Server towards the end of this book, you must install the .NET tutorials onto your development machine. Included with these tutorials is a single-user version of SQL Server and some sample databases that we will use heavily later on.

 **CAUTION** *It is vitally important that you complete these steps. If you do not install MSDE and the sample databases onto your development machine, you will not be able to complete the exercises at the end of many of this book's chapters!*

In order to get the tutorials set up and running on your machine, do the following:

1. Choose the Microsoft .NET Framework SDK from the Windows Start menu.

2. Click Samples and QuickStart Tutorials from the submenu.

3. Follow the instructions on this page to first install MSDE, and then the sample SQL Server databases.

4. Once this is done, restart your computer.

5. Go back to Samples and QuickStart Tutorials on the Windows Start menu.

6. Choose QuickStart tutorials.

7. Follow the hyperlink to start the ASP.NET QuickStart Tutorial.

8. Click Server Side Data Access on the left side of the page.

9. Follow the hyperlink to run the VB DataGrid1.aspx example.

10. If you now get a grid full of data on your screen, everything is working perfectly!

## Testing Your New .NET

In this section, you will test your new Visual Studio .NET installation by creating a simple Hello World application using Visual C# .NET.

Follow these steps:

1. Open Microsoft Visual Studio.NET 7.0 from the Windows Start menu.

2. Click Microsoft Visual Studio.NET 7.0.

3. In the main Visual Studio.NET window, click New Project.

4. In the New Project dialog box, click Visual C# Projects.

5. Click Windows Application in the New Visual C# Projects dialog box.

6. Enter the name **HelloCSharpWorld** in the Project Name field and click OK.

7. Double-click a button to add it to the default form.

8. Once the button is on the form, double-click it there to open its code view.

9. In the button1_click event, enter the following line of code:

```
System.Windows.Forms.MessageBox.Show("Hello World");
```

10. Choose Start from the Debug menu at the top of the screen.

11. Click Button1.

At this point, the screen should look like Figure 8-1.

*Figure 8-1. Hello World application in C#*

## A Closer Look at Visual Studio .NET

Visual Studio .NET is the successor to Microsoft's last release of Visual Studio, Visual Studio 6. For this release, Microsoft has made sweeping changes to Visual Studio, as listed here:

- Visual InterDev has been abolished.

- A new language, C#, has been added.

- C++ has been altered to support the CLR.

- Web-based content creation has been added to all languages.

- The Visual Basic language has been completely overhauled.

So, as you can see, our friends in Redmond have been up to quite a bit lately! Since this is a lot of ground to cover, we will go one language at a time.

### C# .NET

In some ways, C# is the easiest language for which to give a nutshell overview. This is because C# is a brand new language, and therefore has not yet had time to accumulate the baggage that comes along with both of the other languages supported by VS .NET.

## From Where Did C# Come?

The history of C# is closely intertwined with the history of Java and, in particular, with Microsoft's reaction to Java.

When Java first came to prominence in the mid-1990s, it was initially seen as a technology that allowed you to add interactive content to Web pages. Given HTML's minimal support for interactivity at that point in time, Java was embraced by virtually everyone when it was first unveiled. This included Microsoft, who quickly licensed the technology from Sun.

Unfortunately, legal disputes quickly arose between Sun and Microsoft. At the end of the legal battle, Microsoft was forced to stop distributing Java with its Windows XP operating system.

## Evaluating C#

The purpose of this section is not to teach you to program in C#. That would be well beyond the scope of this book, much less this chapter.

 **TIP**  *For an excellent introduction to programming in C#, we recommend Eric Gunnerson's book* A Programmer's Introduction to C#.

Instead, in the sections that follow, we will guide you through a brief comparison of each language's good and bad points. This way, you can at least decide whether or not any language that you might not already know is even worth learning.

### The Good News

The best news about C# is that its syntax is amazingly close to that of Java. Given Java's current reputation as one of the best-designed languages currently on the market, this is certainly a point in C#'s favor.

To illustrate the similarity between C# and Java, let's look at the C# code contained in Listing 8-1.

*Listing 8-1. Non-GUI Hello World in C#*

```
using System;

class HelloWorld
{
    static void Main()
    {
        Console.WriteLine("Hello World!");
    }
}
```

In this listing, the use of the keyword using on the very first line is almost identical to how one might use the keyword imports in the Java programming language. It is a way to signal that a given class or set of classes should be loaded by the CLR (or, in the case of Java, the VM), as it will be used in the remained of the code.

The way that a class is declared in this listing via the keyword class is identical to what would be used in Java, except for the absence of an access modifier (such as public) in this listing. Similarly, the absence of an access modifier and parameters is the only thing distinguishing the signature of the main method in this listing from one that might appear in any Java application.

### The Bad News

The bad news about C# might easily be guessed—it is new. Being new, there are two things about it that should concern you:

- Reliability

- Life expectancy

Reliability is a concern with any new technology, because it has not yet had the chance to become battle tested, as it were. As C# is gradually rolled out into more and more production-quality applications, it seems inevitable that issues will be discovered with its basic functionality. This is not so much a flaw in C# as it is simply the nature of software design and development. Given a few years of public availability, C# has exactly the same likelihood of advancing to the point of mission-critical reliability that Java has over the last five years.

Life expectancy is a particularly hard thing to gauge in this case. What you should be concerned about is the possibility that this language will fail to achieve any kind of widespread acceptance. If this happens, it is just entirely possible that Microsoft would abandon this language altogether. If you've invested heavily in creating a lot of C# code at this point, you will be faced with a choice between performing a major migration and using a discontinued Microsoft technology. Neither of these alternatives is very appealing.

## C++ .NET

C was probably the first attempt at a universal, so-called platform-independent computer language. By standardizing the syntax of the language, it was assumed that all that people would have to do to reuse C code on multiple platforms was recompile it for each platform. Unfortunately, circumventing the vast differences among computing platforms turned out to require much more than this simple approach.

Nevertheless, C grew into something of a lingua franca for serious computing during the 1970s. By the 1980s, it was easily the dominant player in advanced computing applications. However, the specter of object-oriented computing was on the horizon, with languages such as SmallTalk threatening to usurp C's dominance if action was not taken.

The action that was ultimately taken was an overhaul of the language that resulted in producing two competing standards: C++ and Objective C. Whereas Objective C failed to catch on, C++ succeeded admirably. For this reason, C++ .NET stands as the .NET language that can claim the long lineage and history.

It should come as no surprise that the single biggest point in Visual C++ .NET's favor is its compatibility with C++ and, by extension, C. The amount of preexisting code that utilizes these languages is enormous. Similarly, the printed documentation and Internet references available for assistance are, perhaps, without equal.

On the other hand, if you have never used C/C++ before, you should be aware that it is *not* an easy language to learn. The "pure" varieties of these languages both often require the direct access and allocation of system memory. This can be an extremely dangerous process—quite likely to crash an entire computer system in the hands of an inexperienced developer.

The .NET version of C++ spares you from some of this danger through the use of .NET's own memory management schemes. However, the syntax associated with this process is very .NET-specific and nonstandard. So, if standardization is the driving force behind your choice of Visual Studio C++ .NET, please guess again!

## Visual Basic .NET

By most estimates, Visual Basic is the single most popular programming language in the world. This estimate includes the numerous Visual Basic application developers who produce full-blown programs written in the Visual Basic programming language. Beyond this number, however, are the scores of nondevelopers who use the language without realizing it on an almost daily basis to produce what are known as macros for the Microsoft Office suite of productivity applications.

## From Where Did VB Come?

BASIC began life at Dartmouth University as the Beginners All-purpose Symbolic Instruction Language. It represented a true revolution in computing thought at that point in time because, before BASIC, programming languages seldom targeted a general audience. Instead, specialized languages like FORTRAN (for the scientific community) and COBOL (for business users) each targeted different segments of the population.

BASIC listed amongst its design goals simplicity of use and operation. Looking back, it is easy to see that it succeeded in this aspiration beyond its designers' wildest dreams. By the early 1990s, nondevelopers had used the BASIC programming language to create applications for almost every conceivable purpose.

Like C before it, however, a challenge arose that needed to be surmounted in order for BASIC to survive. In this case, the challenge was the growing dominance of GUI interfaces, such as the Windows operating system. The BASIC language relied upon primitive, console-based approaches to input/output—so how could it continue to exist in this brave, new graphical world?

## Evaluating VB

The answer to this question was given by Microsoft with the release of the Visual Basic operating system. With Visual Basic, Microsoft managed to deliver a true one-two punch for the benefit of developers everywhere:

- The BASIC language was saved via the addition of vast, new GUI capabilities.

- The Windows operating system was given arguably the easiest methodology for creating software applications in the entire world of GUI-based OSs.

The latter point was of special benefit to Microsoft itself. By keeping Windows an environment for which it was easy to develop programs, Microsoft ensured a constant supply of new software for its operating system. This supply of software has proven key to ensuring Windows' dominance in the operating system market.

In contrast to the obvious benefit of simplicity, VB has had one glaring drawback historically: a lack of robust functionality. One example of this is the inability of Visual Basic to directly manipulate memory in the manner of C or C++. Another example would be the less-than-complete implementation of object-oriented programming that the language has had—until .NET!

## Exercise

For the remainder of this book, we will be reusing the stock quote application exercise that we first introduced in Chapter 7. The idea is that over the course of the rest of the book, we will gradually create more-and-more sophisticated, "100 percent pure .NET" versions of the application. We will demonstrate how these .NET versions are so striking in their improvement over the non-.NET version that you will be forever convinced of .NET's supremacy.

## Writing the Server

At this point, we haven't really discussed anything about the mobile aspects of .NET. So, in this section, we will focus on rewriting the stock quote server in a way that capitalizes on two improvements in .NET infrastructure:

- Web page screen scraping

- Networking infrastructure

### The Code

Listing 8-2 shows the code for the Listener, and Listing 8-3 shows the code for the server console.

*Listing 8-2. The Listener*

```
Imports System
Imports System.IO.Stream
Imports System.Net
Imports System.Net.Sockets
Imports System.Text
Imports System.Text.RegularExpressions
Imports System.Threading
```

```
Public Class Listener

    Public Sub run()

        Dim tcpl As TcpListener = New TcpListener(1973)
        Dim enc As ASCIIEncoding = New ASCIIEncoding()
        Dim app As Application

        tcpl.Start()

        Do Until False

            Dim sckt As Socket = tcpl.AcceptSocket()
            Dim btChar(0) As Byte

            Dim strSymbol As String = ""
            Dim strResponse As String = ""

            sckt.Receive(btChar, 1, 0)

            Do Until (btChar(0) = 13)
                app.DoEvents()
                strSymbol = strSymbol & enc.GetString(btChar)
                sckt.Receive(btChar, 1, 0)
            Loop

            Dim hwreq As HttpWebRequest
            Dim hwres As HttpWebResponse
            Dim inStream As System.IO.Stream

            hwreq = CType(WebRequest.Create("http://finance.lycos.com/"  & _
            "home/stocks/quotes.asp?symbols=" & strSymbol), HttpWebRequest)
            hwres = CType(hwreq.GetResponse(), HttpWebResponse)
            inStream = hwres.GetResponseStream()

            Try
                Do While True
                    strResponse = strResponse & Chr(inStream.ReadByte())
                Loop
            Catch e As Exception
            End Try
```

```
        inStream.Close()

        Dim rgExp As Regex
        Dim m As Match
        Dim btPrice As Byte()

        m = rgExp.Match(strResponse, "\d+\.\d+", RegexOptions.Singleline)

        If m.Success Then
            btPrice = enc.GetBytes(m.Value())
        Else
            btPrice = enc.GetBytes("0.00")
        End If

        sckt.Send(btPrice, btPrice.Length, SocketFlags.None)

    Loop

  End Sub

End Class
```

*Listing 8-3. The Server's Console*

```
Imports System
Imports System.Threading

Public Class Form1
    Inherits System.Windows.Forms.Form

    Private Sub btnStart_Click(ByVal sender As System.Object, _
        ByVal e As System.EventArgs) Handles btnStart.Click

        Dim lsnr As Listener = New Listener()
        Dim tsLsnr As ThreadStart = New ThreadStart(AddressOf lsnr.run)
        Dim thrLsnr As Thread = New Thread(tsLsnr)
        Dim app As Application

        lblStatus.Text = "Starting server"

        thrLsnr.Start()
```

```
            Do While Not (thrLsnr.IsAlive)
                app.DoEvents()
            Loop

            lblStatus.Text = "Server started"

        End Sub
End Class
```

## The Walk-Through

To create the server application, follow these steps:

1. Start a new instance of Visual Studio .NET.

2. Click New Project.

3. Select Visual Basic Projects.

4. Choose Windows Application.

5. Enter Ch8StockServer for the name of the application and click OK.

6. In the Solution Explorer, right-click the icon for Ch8StockServer.

7. Choose Add and then Add Class from the pop-up context menu.

8. Name your file Listener.vb and then click OK.

9. Modify the code as needed to make it match Listing 8-2.

10. In the Solution Explorer, double-click the icon for Form1.vb.

11. Add a label to the default form. Name it lblStatus and clear its Text property.

12. Add a button to the default form. Name it btnStart and change its Text property to Start Server.

13. Verify that your form looks similar to Figure 8-2, and then choose Save All from the File menu.

14. Double-click the btnStart button to view its associated code. Modify the listing as needed to make it match Listing 8-3.

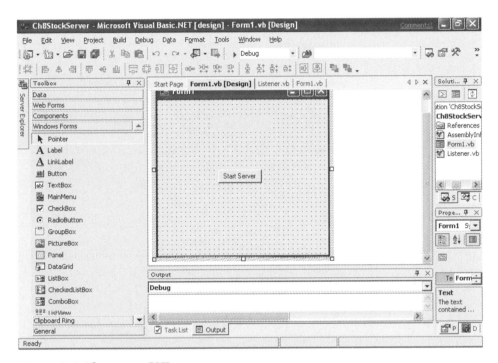

*Figure 8-2. The server GUI*

Let's begin by discussing the code in Listing 8-3. This code is responsible simply for taking the user's request to start up the server. This request is made by pushing the only button located on the only form in the application. When this is done, the code in Listing 8-3 uses a feature new to Visual Basic .NET—multiple threading—to create a Listener component that will run on its own thread. The code in this procedure then spins until the new thread has been started, at which point this procedure ends.

**NOTE** *Because the examples in this section are all in Visual Basic .NET, improvements due to .NET will be cited as improvements in the language. This is, in fact, an understatement, since these improvements are by and large features available to any .NET-enabled language.*

The Listener component, as shown in Listing 8-2, is still running, however. Specifically, it is the code in the run() method of this component that continues to run on another thread. This code begins by instantiating a TCPListener class. This class gives you a ready-made way to create Internet server applications directly from Visual Basic. Networking functionality like this is completely new to Visual Basic .NET.

The Listener thread blocks after creating a single instance of the Listener class; it is waiting for a client to make a connection on port 1973. Once such a connection is made, the Listener enters a loop, reading in characters from the client one at a time until it encounters ASCII character 13. This is the character that we have chosen to signal end of input for the primitive stock quoting protocol.

The next step is to pass the symbol received from the client over to the Web site Quote.com to find out what the last purchase price for this stock was. This is accomplished via the HttpWebRequest and HttpWebResponse classes, which are also new to Visual Basic .NET. The complete text of the response from Quote.com is stuffed into a string variable known as strResponse.

At this point, you have to parse the raw HTML for the price, which is the only bit that is of interest in this case. Visual Basic .NET has added regular expression parsing, similar to languages such as Perl. This allows you to use the following language construct to search for the first pattern matching one group of digits, followed by a period, followed by another group of digits:

```
m = rgExp.Match(strResponse, "\d+\.\d+", RegexOptions.Singleline)
```

The matching portion of text is stuffed into the Match object m. This object offers a success variable that allows you to find out whether or not the preceding parsing was successful. If so, the price is returned to the client. If not, we apologize to it.

# Writing the Client

In this section, we will show you how to write a GUI .NET client for use with our GUI .NET server!

## The Code

Listing 8-4 shows the code for the Windows .NET stock quote client application.

*Listing 8-4. The Windows .NET Client Application*

```
Imports System.IO
Imports System.Text
Imports System.Net.Sockets

Public Class Form1
    Inherits System.Windows.Forms.Form

    Private Sub btnSubmit_Click(ByVal sender As System.Object, _
      ByVal e As System.EventArgs) Handles btnSubmit.Click

        Dim app As Application
        Dim enc As ASCIIEncoding = New ASCIIEncoding()
        Dim btOut As Byte() = enc.GetBytes(txtSymbol.text & Chr(13))
        Dim btIn As Byte

        Dim client As TcpClient = New TcpClient("localhost", 1973)
        Dim theStream As Stream = client.GetStream()

        lblQuote.Text = ""
        app.DoEvents()

        theStream.Write(btOut, 0, btOut.Length)
        theStream.Flush()

        Try
            Do Until False
                btIn = theStream.ReadByte()
                lblQuote.Text = lblQuote.Text & Chr(btIn)
```

```
            Loop
        Catch problem As Exception
        End Try

        client.Close()

        txtSymbol.Text = ""

    End Sub
End Class
```

## The Walk-Through

To create the client application, follow this procedure:

1.  Start a new instance of Visual Studio .NET.

2.  Click New Project.

3.  Select "Visual Basic Projects".

4.  Choose Windows Application.

5.  Enter Ch8StockClient for the name of the application and click OK.

6.  Add a label to the default form. Name it lblQuote and clear its Text property.

7.  Add a textbox to the default form. Name it txtSymbol and clear its Text property.

8.  Add a button to the default form. Name it btnSubmit and change its Text property to Get Quote.

9.  Verify that your form looks similar to Figure 8-3, and then choose Save All from the File menu.

10. Double-click the btnSubmit button to view its associated code. Modify the listing as needed to make it match Listing 8-4.

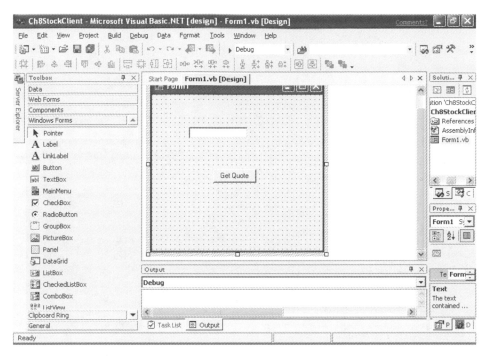

*Figure 8-3. The client GUI*

The client expects a stock symbol to be entered into the text field by the user before he or she clicks the Submit button. Assuming that this is the case, the client will convert the stock symbol string into a byte array when the button is pressed. It then uses the networking functionality newly added to Visual Basic .NET to open a connection to the stock server application. The stock symbol's bytes are sent across this connection.

The application then spins, waiting for a response, which it stuffs into the form's only label object. Note the use of a Java-like try/catch block. In this case, we are leveraging the fact that an error will be generated the first time that the application tries to read from the server's input stream without any input actually ready to be read. This allows you to code the input loop as infinite (do until false) and simply rely upon the error generation to get you out of it at the appropriate point.

**CAUTION** *There are probably much better ways to get out of a loop than this. More than anything else, we've coded it this way in the example to showcase Visual Basic .NET's new* try-catch *facility.*

## Final Thoughts

In this chapter, we have transitioned from examining various mobile devices to looking at .NET. We hope you now have a clear idea of what .NET is and how it differs (in theory, at least) from previous programming paradigms.

In the next chapter, we will begin focusing on the suite of .NET technologies that are specifically targeted at programming for the Internet. This will take you one step closer to the ultimate goal of programming for the *mobile* Internet with .NET.

# CHAPTER 9

# Web Applications

## This Is NOT Your Father's ASP

YOU HAVE NOW HAD YOUR first taste of developing with .NET. However, as you may have noticed, none of our .NET code in the previous chapter really applied to wireless devices as such. In order to begin developing for wireless devices, you must first make the leap into Internet development with .NET. The most common form of Internet application under .NET is the Web application.

## ASP.NET

Web applications are one of the three main kinds of Internet systems you can construct using Microsoft's new .NET technology.

**NOTE**   *One of the other kinds, Web Services, will be discussed in great detail over the course of the next two chapters. The final variety, Mobile Device Applications, are enabled by the .NET Compact Frameworks and are described in Chapters 15 and 16 at the end of this book.*

ASP.NET represents the next generation of Microsoft's popular Active Server Pages technology. We used Active Server Pages (ASPs, for short) in Chapter 7 to construct the first version of the stock quote application. Compared to the CGI scripts that came before it, we hope you will agree that ASP represents an enormous improvement in terms of ease of development and quality of finished product.

Even so, Microsoft realized (particularly after the release of Java Server Pages) that ASP could be improved upon. Towards this end, the company has bundled several improvements to ASP into the .NET technology initiative. These improvements occur mainly in the areas of development, performance, and security.

## Enhancing Development

Microsoft has enhanced the development of Active Server Pages by integrating them with two of its most important new technologies. One of these is, of course, .NET itself. The other, which has existed separately for long enough to warrant individual consideration, is Visual Studio.

### .NET Integration

The first, probably most shocking, benefit to integrating ASP with .NET is that developers are now able to use full language syntax in their Web applications, rather than just scripting subsets. For example, whereas developers used to be limited to VBScript, they may now use the full Visual Basic .NET programming language. Similarly, they may elect to develop Web applications using C# .NET or even C++ .NET!

IIS recognizes ASP.NET scripts by the extension .aspx. Any Web file ending with this extension will be assumed to be an ASP.NET script and an attempt at interpreting it as such will be made. This allows ASP.NET to coexist peacefully with installations of ASP on the same machine.

Of course, access to the Frameworks classes is another key benefit to ASP.NET integration with .NET. Most of the classes in the System.Web hierarchy are designed specifically for easing the development of Web applications. Table 9-1 briefly describes some of these classes.

*Table 9-1. Important Web Application Frameworks Classes*

| CLASS NAMESPACE | DESCRIPTION |
|---|---|
| System.Web.Caching | Facilitates the caching of Web application output |
| System.Web.Configuration | Governs the configuration of Web applications |
| System.Web.Mail | Helps to send e-mail messages directly from Web applications |
| System.Web.Security | Allows for fine-grained control over access to Web applications |
| System.Web.SessionState | Provides access to the state data maintained by Web applications |

*Table 9-1. Important Web Application Frameworks Classes (continued)*

| CLASS NAMESPACE | DESCRIPTION |
| --- | --- |
| System.Web.UI | Fundamental classes for the creation of your own Web controls |
| System.Web.UI.HtmlControls | Refers to the analogs controls described later in this chapter |
| System.Web.UI.WebControls | Refers to the rich controls described later in this chapter |

The final great advantage to integration with .NET is the ability for Web applications to support the same rich event-based execution model offered previously only by Windows applications. As you will see later in this chapter, buttons and other GUI elements in .NET Web applications can now raise events (such as the click event). These events may be responded to either by client-side or server-side code, depending upon the capabilities of the target device. .NET largely masks the implementation details involved in these operations.

## Visual Studio Integration

The ability to create Web applications using the drag-and-drop interface of Visual Studio is a real benefit to integration under .NET.

 **TIP** *If you have ever used Visual InterDev under previous versions of Visual Studio, then you may find some of Visual Studio .NET's features quite familiar. For this version of Visual Studio, the Web-centric abilities of Visual InterDev have been absorbed into the functionality offered by the other products in Visual Studio.*

Previous generations of ASP coders have had to place HTML controls on their Web forms through such primitive tools as the Windows Notepad. As you will see a little later in this chapter, there are many more controls now available for your ASP.NET applications. Furthermore, using these controls can be as simple as double-clicking their image in the Visual Studio toolbox and setting some properties in the Property Editor.

Also, for the first time, debugging Web applications can be accomplished on a true end-to-end basis. By this, we mean that it is now possible to use with

ASP.NET code almost all of the same debugging tools with which you might be familiar from "full" programming languages such as Visual Basic. This includes line-by-line stepping through of applications, often even right into the code of server-side components!

**TIP** *For more information on debugging ASP applications, we highly recommend the book* Debugging ASP, *written by Derek Ferguson (me!) and published by Osborne/McGraw-Hill.*

## Enhancing Performance

Another area of Web development that has benefited from the introduction of .NET is performance.

### State Maintenance

One of the most important changes to Web applications under .NET is the way that state data is maintained on a session-by-session basis. Session-level state data, in case you aren't familiar with it, is the data maintained by a Web site about each of its individual users. For example, the virtual shopping cart in which you accumulate products at an e-commerce Web site before checking out would be an example of your session data on that site.

By way of contrast, application-level session data would be shared in common by all the users of a given site. The total number of visitors to a given page at a certain point in time might be one example of application-level data maintained by a site.

Of the two levels of state data, it was session-level data that proved to be a real problem for high-performance Web sites under standard Active Server Pages. The way that traditional ASP applications maintained state was by assigning each client a unique identifier number. The clients were given these numbers as cookies, which they obediently sent back to the server every time they requested a new page.

This allowed the server to store all of the session data itself. The client's identifier number was used as an index into this server-side database of session data. Once the client's data was located in the database, it could be used in whatever manner the ASP script saw fit.

### The Problem

Unfortunately, there were two situations that proved problematic for ASP:

- When the amount of session data was not trivial

- When multiple Web servers were being used in tandem to form a cluster

In the first case, application performance suffered because the amount of data being stored on the server quickly became too great a load. Web servers should focus on serving Web content—not storing and retrieving large quantities of data. It is for this purpose that we have database servers.

The latter case is even more difficult to resolve. High-traffic Web sites often organize several, identically configured computers into arrangements known as *clusters*. A given cluster of computers appears to the outside world as a single entity—for example, www.pocketdba.com. Behind the scenes, however, whenever a request for this address is made, some kind of technology (hardware or software) is employed to redirect to a single computer within the cluster. Exactly which computer this is cannot usually be known in advance and may vary from one request to the next.

This is a problem because a given client could store session data on one machine, and then be handed to a completely different machine on its next request. This new machine would have no knowledge of the client and might even prompt the client to log in again. Various workarounds for this were possible under ASP, but none of them were completely satisfactory.

### The Solution

Under ASP.NET, session state may be sent back and forth between the server and the client at each page request. This solves both of the problems outlined in the previous section.

In the first case, the fact that the session data resides permanently on the client means that the burden of storage is lifted from the server. The only time that the server needs to manipulate the session data is between the receipt of a request from a client and the time that a response is issued. In comparison to the arrangement before .NET, this is a trivial amount of time.

The problem of clustered servers is also rectified by this approach. Since the client is responsible for maintaining its own state, it may present this data to each machine in a cluster, as required. It is therefore unnecessary for any machine in a cluster to have previous knowledge of a given client.

**NOTE** *Of course, .NET takes steps to protect its session state data while in transit. To begin with, the state data is compressed to prevent lengthy page loads. Also, the data is signed, so it cannot be modified by the client without detection by the server!*

## Output Caching

.NET has also added superior capabilities for the caching of server page output. In the past, ASP developers have had two choices:

- Cache their scripts' output

- Don't cache their scripts' output

This was a very difficult choice to make. If one elected to cache ASP output, he or she often found that changes in the scripts didn't take effect as quickly as required. A modification to make an ASP script output an urgent warning message, for example, might not actually appear for several hours. Everything was dependent upon how long it took IIS to sense that a given script had changed.

**CAUTION** *Of course, it was always possible to restart IIS. But this was a drastic price to pay just to make some ASP script alterations!*

On the other hand, running high-traffic ASP applications without any caching at all could result in seriously diminished performance. Even the most static scripts, for example, would have to be interpreted from scratch every time that they were requested.

For ASP.NET, Microsoft has given developers many more choices than the two shown previously. In brief, the choices now are as follows:

- Don't cache your scripts' output

- Cache the scripts' complete output

- Cache by parameters

- Cache by language

- Cache by user agent

- Cache only portions of your pages

- Set up custom caching

Covering all of these is beyond the scope of this book. For more information, consult the documentation included with .NET Frameworks.

To give you an idea of what this improvement can do for you, however, consider the option to cache by parameters. Using this option, you can tell ASP.NET that the output generated by the request

```
http://www.pocketdba.com/nearest-store.asp?city=chicago
```

is different from the output for

```
http://www.pocketdba.com/nearest-store.asp?city=topeka
```

In this case, ASP.NET would cache a different copy of the nearest store.asp script's output for every unique parameter that is passed in for `city`. This would give you the finest degree of control over page differences, while reducing the amount of processing needed to the bare minimum.


## Enhancing Security

In the previous chapter, we briefly discussed the fact that security under .NET can be much finer grained than previous approaches under Windows. For example, different users could be limited to accessing different methods on a single component, rather than simply being allowed or denied access to components in their entirety. Where Internet applications are concerned, Microsoft has done an equally good job of improving the flexibility of its security model.


### The Way Things Were

Under pre-.NET Internet Information Server, Web administrators had three primary choices for securing their applications over the Internet:

- Basic authentication

- Integrated Windows security

- Digital certificates

Unfortunately, there were problems associated with each of these choices. In the case of basic authentication, the glaring flaw is that passwords are transmitted across the network in clear text. This means that anyone who happened to be sniffing packets between the client and server could easily intercept and reuse any passwords that were entered while they were sniffing.

Integrated Windows security solved this problem, but only at the expense of platform independence. As the name implies, in order to use Windows security, the client (as well as the server) must both be running the Windows operating system. Furthermore, the client must be Internet Explorer.

Digital certificates are a true Internet standard. Unfortunately, they can be both difficult and expensive to set up. They require the installation of a so-called Certificate Authority certificate on the client, as well as on the server.

## The Brave, New World

For .NET, Microsoft has made two important additions to the authentication options listed previously:

- Passport authentication

- Custom forms-based authentication

### Passport

Passport is a new Microsoft technology initiative, and probably one of the most consumer-oriented of all the .NET pieces being rolled out. Passport is intended to address the problem of password proliferation currently being encountered by many avid Internet users.

You may have experienced this problem yourself: every time you go to a new Web site, it requires a new password. On one hand, you really shouldn't use the same password for multiple sites. From a security standpoint, this could easily enable the operators of a site to use whatever password you give them to try accessing other sites under your name.

On the other hand, even if you *wanted* to use the same password for every site you visited, you probably couldn't. Every site has different criteria for defining acceptable passwords. Sometimes your password needs to be at least eight characters—sometimes it can be no more than six. Sometimes it has to include at least one number, other times it has to be all letters.

Users that sign up with Microsoft's Passport service will be able to use a single username/password combination to get into all of its sites. The idea is that the users will log into Passport, and then Passport will take care of authenticating them into all of its other sites.

In order for a site to work with Passport, however, it has to use Passport authentication. This is one of the key features new to authentication under ASP.NET.

---

 **NOTE** *For more information on passport authentication, go to* `http://www.passport.com`.

---

### Custom Forms-Based Authentication

Of course, using the Passport service requires additional fees: both from the end-user and the Web site. For those of us who are cheap or unwilling to give Microsoft access to our user data, there is still another new authentication option available under .NET. This is termed the *custom forms-based authentication* (CFBA) solution and exists to facilitate the creation of the standard, HTML-based log-in forms with which we are all already familiar. This won't do anything to stop the proliferation of new passwords, but it will make your job as a developer easier.

Using the CFBA, you may define a certain page in your application as the login page. This page will be expected to authenticate users using some methodology customized to your application—it can be anything you like. The end result, however, needs to be informing .NET as to whether the login attempt should be accepted or rejected.

.NET uses this knowledge to either set a cookie for the user or refer the user back to your page for another authentication attempt. If .NET ever senses a client attempting to access to your application that does *not* have this cookie set, it will automatically redirect the client to your custom authentication page for further action.

## Installation

In the last chapter, we showed you how to install Visual Studio .NET on your development computer. In a perfect world, this would suffice to get you up and running for creating .NET applications.

In fact, if your development intentions are relatively simple, this very easily could be enough. However, in this book, we want to show you how to use some of the more exciting bits of .NET. And for this, you are going to need some additional bits of free software.

For the Beta 2 release of .NET, some of the more high-end ASP.NET features discussed in preceding sections haven't yet been integrated into the main .NET product. Also, there is some additional support for Internet Explorer only that will probably never be integrated into the main product.

### ASP.NET Premium Edition

The Premium Edition of ASP.NET adds support for the following:

- Output caching

- High traffic loads

- Round-trip session states

To download this edition of ASP.NET, visit the following URL: `http://www.msdn.microsoft.com/downloads/default.asp?url=/downloads/sample.asp?url=/MSDN-FILES/027/001/659/msdncompositedoc.xml&frame=true`.
If you click Download on this Web page, you will be sent a file named simply setup.exe. Save this to any location you choose.
Once the file has been saved, close any running applications and double-click the file's icon to start running it. The setup program will ask you where you would like to install the software. Choose any location you like and continue. Accept the licensing agreement, and then follow all the defaults until the installation has finished.
Restart your computer to make sure that the Premium features for ASP.NET take effect.

### IE Web Controls

The IE Web Controls are an especially exciting bit of ASP.NET's functionality. The concept is thoroughly explained in the next section on Web Forms but, in a nutshell, these controls are intended to add special support for Internet Explorer to .NET.
You can begin experimenting with the controls by downloading them from `http://msdn.microsoft.com/downloads/samples/internet/asp_dot_net_servercontrols/webcontrols/default.asp`. The download should result in a single file named WebControls.msi.

**NOTE** *The file may just be named WebControls on your Windows display—as the .msi extension is hidden on most modern implementations of Windows.*

Follow these steps to get the IE Web Controls installed on your development machine:

1. Double-click the WebControls icon.

2. Click Next to advance past the initial splash screen.

3. Using the Windows explorer interface, locate the aspnet-client subdirectory beneath Inetpub\wwwroot in your main Web site.

4. Right-click the aspnet-client folder's icon and choose Properties from the pop-up context menu.

5. Choose the Security tab.

6. Verify that the username under which you are currently logged in has full control over this directory.

7. Close out of this dialog box and return to the setup application.

8. Click Next to proceed past the security warning screen.

9. Allow the progress bars to run to completion, and then click Finished to close the application.

At this point, the IE Web Controls are installed on your computer, but Visual Studio .NET doesn't know anything about them. Follow this procedure to add the new controls to Visual Studio .NET's toolbox:

1. Start the Visual Studio .NET IDE.

2. Click New Project (ASP.NET Web Application).

3. Name your new project AddTheIEControls and click OK.

4. Right-click any of the controls in the toolbox and choose Customize Toolbox from the pop-up context menu.

5. Select the tab labeled .NET Framework Components.

6. Click Browse.

7. Navigate to \Program Files\Microsoft Web Controls 0.6.

8. Double-click Microsoft.Web.UI.WebControls.dll.

9. Place a check mark next to each of the highlighted new controls, and then click OK to exit the dialog box.

10. Close Visual Studio, and then click Yes when a confirmation box appears asking you if you want to save your changes.

11. Reopen Visual Studio and choose to open the AddTheIEControls project.

12. Scroll down in the Web Forms area of the toolbox to reveal the four new controls: Multipage, TabStrip, Toolbar, and TreeView.

**TIP** *Don't forget, if you can't find the Web Forms tab, you can always right-click in the toolbar and select Show all tabs!*

## Netscape

Of all the software that you need to add to follow the examples in this chapter, Netscape is probably the best known. This is evidenced by the fact that you can probably already guess the URL where it can be downloaded, but we will give it to you anyhow, just to be safe: http://www.netscape.com. Click the Download link, and then choose Netscape Browsers.

**CAUTION** *Netscape offers a suite of Internet tools bundled together as Netscape Communicator. This is complete overkill for our purposes. Instead, simply choose the smallest, least obtrusive Netscape browser possible.*

Downloading the appropriate application should give you a file named N6Setup. Double-click this file to begin installation. You probably noticed that the download was very quick. The reason for this speed is now made apparent as the application begins downloading the *rest* of the Netscape browser to your system. Simply follow the instructions in the dialog boxes, accepting all defaults, until the Netscape browser has been installed on your system.

## Web Forms

In order to learn about Web Forms, we will be adding some of the most common Web controls to a single application throughout the next section. In order to follow along, you should use the Visual Studio .NET IDE at this point to create a Web application named Chapter9Controls. This project may be hosted on any Web space available to you, including the copy of IIS that should be running on your development machine.

## Analogs

*Analogs* refer to the class of .NET controls that look and feel exactly like the simple HTML controls that came before them.

### Pure HTML

In the case of pure HTML .NET controls, the similarity to regular HTML extends all the way to the limited functionality of the controls themselves. In general, when you add pure HTML controls to .NET Web Forms, you are leveraging the Visual Studio IDE strictly as a Web design tool. Its benefits to you as a developer are almost nonexistent.

To play around with an HTML control, open the Chapter9Controls project you created at the start of this section. Now, choose the HTML tab from the toolbox on the left of the IDE. Double-click the control labeled Button to add it to the default form. Now, try double-clicking the button that you've added to your form. You may have been expecting a code view to open; instead you should see a dialog box like the one in Figure 9-1.

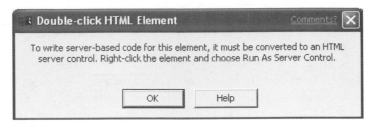

*Figure 9-1. This is just a dumb old HTML control.*

To further drive home the message of this dialog box, start your application by clicking the Run icon on the IDE's menu bar. Once Internet Explorer has opened, try clicking your button. Notice that nothing happens. In order to get any functionality out of an HTML button, you have to add code to it yourself.

Close Internet Explorer to stop the demonstration. Remove the HTML button by selecting it on the form in the IDE and pressing the Delete key on your keyboard.

### Reaping Server-Side Benefits

By simply adding the attribute RUNAT=SERVER to the markup for most HTML controls, you can deliver to them many of the benefits of .NET. To demonstrate this, we will now add a server-side HTML button to the form where we previously had a "pure" HTML button.

Begin by adding a "pure" text field control to the form. Next, change to the Web Forms section of the IDE toolbar. Double-click the control labeled Button to add it to your form. Double-click the control labeled TextBox to add a textbox to your form.

Now, try double-clicking the button that has been added to the form. Rather than the failure message that you saw in the previous section, you now get a code view. From this view, you can write code to respond to a button event on a Web Form just as you would on a regular Windows form.

Add the following line of code to your new button's click event:

```
TextBox1.Text = Val(TextBox1.Text) + 1
```

Now run the application. You should see something like what is shown in Figure 9-2.

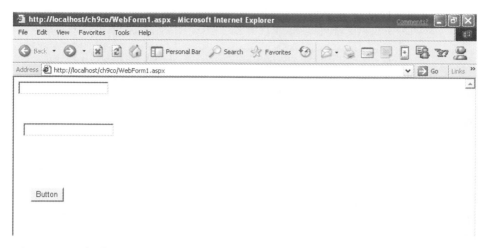

*Figure 9-2. The beauty of server-side controls*

If you click the button, you will notice that the value 1 appears in the textbox on top. If you click it again, it will increment to 2. This will continue with every press of the button—thanks to the code you put in the server-side `click` event for this button.

Now, if you enter a value in the other text field and click the button, you will notice that it disappears. It disappears like this because its state is not being maintained by the .NET server. It is, after all, a pure HTML control—and not under .NET's authority.

To change this, close Internet Explorer. Double-click the Web Form's icon in the Project Explorer to return to the GUI-builder view. Right-click the nonserver text field and choose the Run at server option from the pop-up context menu. Next, restart the application.

Anything that you type in this field will now be maintained from one click of the button to the next. In the case of your new .NET text field, this effect is quite easy to achieve. When you changed it to server management, .NET simply moved the field from outside the HTML form to inside of it and added the server-side logic needed in order to retrieve its latest value.

## Validators

Some server-side logic requires knowledge of which, if any, fields on a given form have changed since they were last sent to the browser. With your application still running, choose Source from the View menu in Internet Explorer. At some point in the source code, you should see a line very much like the one below:

```
<input type="hidden" name="__VIEWSTATE" value="dDw5MjAzMzYzOTc7Oz4=" />
```

This is your session state, also known as your online shopping cart. The previous values of every field on your form are compressed and signed and stuffed into this field every time that .NET needs to generate a form for you to view. This allows .NET to instantly recognize if any of the fields on your form have changed, and to take appropriate action.

Validators are one of the most important control-level beneficiaries of this kind of technology.

### Single-Purpose Validation

Before I came to work at PocketDBA as Chief Technology Evangelist, I worked as Head of Development for one of the big Internet service providers here in Chicago. A mind-numbing percent of my job entailed creating (or supervising the creation of) forms to facilitate signing up new subscribers.

One of the first rules you learn when designing a lot of these kinds of forms is that people rarely have the slightest idea what they're doing. So, what you wind up doing is devoting a lot of code to verifying that the data entered by your potential customers makes business sense. In .NET parlance, this is called *validation*.

.NET offers a number of Validator controls for use out-of-the-box to save you the time and trouble of writing many validation routines by hand. To see one of these in action, let's say that from now on the text field that we have been typing in must *not* ever be left blank when the form is submitted. To implement this, follow these steps:

1. Double-click the RequiredFieldValidator control to add it to your form.

2. For the ErrorMessage property, enter **What the heck?**

3. From the ControlToValidate property drop-down list, choose Text1 (which should be the name of your second text field, assuming that you haven't changed anything).

If you run your application again at this point, you will notice that the Validator control is not visible on your form's output. Leave your text field blank and click the button. The text "What the heck?" should now become visible on your display, as shown in Figure 9-3.

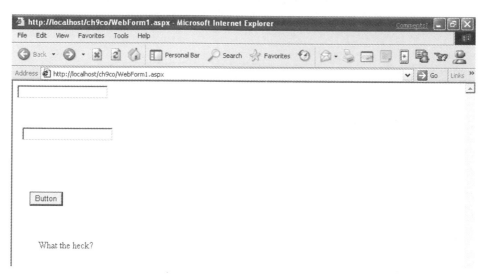

*Figure 9-3. Form validation made easy*

Something that may surprise you even more than this is the fact that no round-trip to the server was required in order to provide this validation. In order to see why, view the source for this page under Internet Explorer. If you look carefully, you will see gobs of JavaScript scattered throughout the page.

What has happened is that .NET has sensed that you were using Internet Explorer. Internet Explorer is JavaScript-enabled, so client-side validation was performed. If .NET had sensed that you were using a JavaScript-challenged browser, it would have performed a server-side validation instead. An example of this will be shown when using the Palm OS client in the exercise at the end of this chapter.

In the meantime, Table 9-2 summarizes some of the other important validators provided by .NET.

*Table 9-2. Important Single-Purpose Validator Controls*

| CONTROL NAME | PURPOSE |
| --- | --- |
| CompareValidator | Makes sure than the Validator control's value relates to the value of some other control in a certain, predetermined way (for example, the customer's age must always be greater than the years he or she has been married) |
| RangeValidator | Ensures that the validated control's value falls within a given range (for example, the applicant's age must be greater than 17 and less than 115) |
| RegularExpressionValidator | Validates that the specified control matches a certain pattern (for example, the lead's telephone number must be in the form ###-###-####) |

## Multipurpose Validation

There are two validation controls not mentioned in the preceding section. The first of these is the CustomValidator. The CustomValidator control provides little more than a framework for the construction of your own validation control. This, of course, makes it by far the most flexible of all the validators available under .NET. It also, however, makes it by far the most difficult to use. For more information, consult the documentation.

The final validator is the ValidationSummary control. This allows you to create a single message that summarizes the problems associated with all the other validators on a page. One possible use for this control is to add a pop-up error message to your page. This may be accomplished by setting the ValidationSummary control's ShowMessageBox property to True.

## Showing Off

The controls we've shown you so far have been pretty impressive. But now it is time to really show off. Some of the controls that .NET makes available are just downright nifty! (And we're not too ashamed of showing our nerd level by saying so!)

## Rich Controls

To see a rich control in action, first remove all of the other controls that have already been added to your form. Double-click the Calendar control in the Web Forms section of the toolbox. Next, drag-and-drop a Label control onto some empty part of the form. Double-click the calendar to open a code view and enter the following code into the calendar's SelectionChanged event:

```
Label1.Text = Calendar1.SelectedDate
```

Now run the application. You should see a page like the one in Figure 9-4.

 **CAUTION**   *You may also have to remove the line of code that reads* TextBox1.Text = Val(TextBox1.Text) + 1.

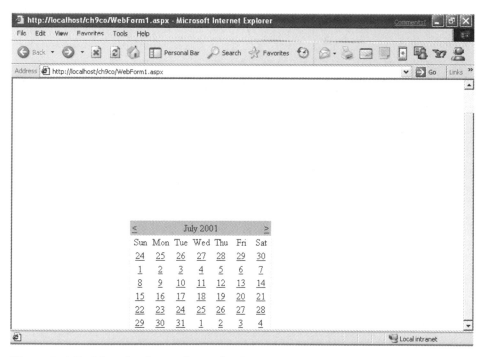

*Figure 9-4. Is this calendar cool, or what?*

If you select any date on the calendar at this point, you will see that the `Label` control is automatically populated with that date. To draw a calendar, enable its navigation, and retrieve its value like this using pre-.NET technologies would have required hour upon hour of custom programming. Once finished, it is doubtful that you would have anywhere near as nice an end product.

 **NOTE** *We first saw this control in a special sneak-preview at Redmond for a group of fellow technology gurus—long before the name ".NET" had been invented. At that point, no one believed that it was really a platform-independent HTML creation that we were looking at. If you have any doubt, examine the page's source under Internet Explorer. Better yet, get some Microsoft-hating Java fanatic to open up your test page under Netscape on Linux, so they can have a good cry.*

## IE Web Controls

Earlier in this chapter, you downloaded a new piece of software called IE Web Controls and installed the controls into the toolbox of your Visual Studio .NET IDE. At that point, you were promised a fuller explanation later in the chapter. The time has now come to explain to you the purpose of this software.

As mentioned previously in this chapter, Web controls under .NET have the ability to compensate for shortcomings in their clients by downgrading the level of functionality that they provide. If a given client doesn't support client-side scripting, for example, some controls can move processing onto the server to compensate.

Along a similar line, but in the completely opposite direction, some .NET controls have the ability to *capitalize* upon the unique *strengths* of their clients. This most often (though not always) happens when the client happens to be a Microsoft product. The IE Web Controls are intended to capitalize upon the unique ability of Internet Explorer to execute downloaded binary controls called *behaviors*.

The best way to explain is probably with a demonstration so, for this example, we will reuse the `AddTheIEControls` project that we began earlier in this chapter. To start, simply open the `AddTheIEControls` project in Visual Studio .NET IDE. Next, follow these steps:

1.  Scroll down on the toolbox under Web Forms until the TreeView component is visible.

2.  Double-click TreeView to add it to the default form.

3. Click Nodes in the Property Pane, and then click the ellipses ( . . . ) icon that becomes visible.

4. Click Add Root.

5. Under the node's properties, change Text to read Hello.

6. Click Add Child.

7. Select the new child node in the tree hierarchy view.

8. Under the new node's properties, change Text to read World.

9. Click OK to close the Property Builder.

10. Choose Start from the Debug menu.

At this point, Internet Explorer starts and opens your new Web application, as shown in Figure 9-5. Notice that you can freely expand and contract its single node without any server-side communication whatsoever. This is possible because the component being displayed on your screen is actually a Windows binary control—not HTML.

*Figure 9-5. The beauty of .NET's adaptability*

At this point, copy the URL being accessed by Internet Explorer to your clipboard. Open Netscape Navigator and paste this URL into the address bar to open it here. Notice that an equally usable tree control is displayed. However, this one requires a round-trip to the server whenever any kind of interaction is required, because the control is actually HTML rather than a true Windows control.

**CAUTION**   *If you try to use these controls on anything other than a Windows server implementation (such as NT Server or .NET Server), you may get an error involving too many concurrent connections to IIS. We hope this is a bug that will be resolved before the final release of .NET.*

Using these controls can be a great way to convince the stalwart anti-Microsoft users at your organization to at least get a Windows computer in addition to their platform of preference. If you have a guideline at your organization that all new applications have to be platform independent, this will fit the bill. It will, however, also pay a premium in added usability to anyone who uses Windows.

## Data Binding

The last bit of ASP.NET controls that we will look at are the ones associated with data. Data access under .NET is completely different from data access under pre-.NET Microsoft technologies. To cover the topic in its entirety would take us off on quite a tangent in this book. For further reading, we highly recommend *Programming VB.NET: A Guide for Experienced Programmers*, by Gary Cornell and Jonathan Morrison.

### *ADO.NET*

Before .NET the technology of choice for accessing data on Microsoft platforms was known as *Active Data Objects*, or ADO for short. The basis of ADO was COM. Not surprisingly, a new approach is required for data access under .NET. This approach has been dubbed ADO.NET.

Under ADO.NET, all data access is divided into two categories. The first category is for accessing data under the SQL Server family of databases (from the Developer's Edition all the way up to the Enterprise Edition). The second category is for everything else. Remember, ADO.NET was developed by Microsoft, just like almost every other technology mentioned in this book.

Fortunately for us, the naming schemes between both of these categories are quite consistent. They both revolve around the objects described in Table 9-3.

*Table 9-3: The ADO.NET Objects*

| OBJECT NAME | PURPOSE | SQL SERVER EXAMPLE |
|---|---|---|
| Connection | Connects to a .NET Managed Provider data source | SQLConnection |
| Command | Requests actions from the data source | SQLCommand |
| DataAdapter | Creates commands appropriate for the performance of useful work | SQLDataAdapter |
| DataView | Presents data in different ways, depending on need | DataAdapter |

Notice that the entries in this table proceed from most to least data-source specific. Indeed, all data sources under .NET share the use of the same DataView class.

### The Datagrid

The Datagrid control is the all-star control for showcasing ADO.NET functionality under .NET Web applications. Fortunately, Visual Studio .NET even includes a wizard interface to save you the trouble of having to program a data grid for demonstration purposes. Simply follow this procedure:

1. Open a new instance of the Visual Studio .NET IDE.

2. Click New Project.

3. Enter the name DataGridExample in the Project Name field and click OK.

4. Right-click the DataGridExample icon in the Solution Explorer window.

5. Choose Add and then choose Add Web Form from the pop-up context menu.

6. Click the Data Form Wizard icon and click Open.

7. Click Next.

8. Enter the name dsOrders for your new dataset and click Next.

9. Click New Connection.

10. Select the NetSDK database that you installed in the previous chapter, enter the username sa, and select the Northwind database before clicking OK.

11. Click Next.

12. Add the Employees and EmployeeTerritories tables and click Next.

13. Enter the relationship information in the Create a relationship between tables window, shown in Figure 9-6. Click the right arrow to save the relationship, and then click Next.

14. Click Finish.

15. Right-click the icon for DataWebForm1.aspx in the Solution Explorer window.

16. Click Set as Startup Page.

**NOTE** *The NETSDK database referred to in the preceding steps was created during the installation of the QuickStart Tutorials in the previous chapter. If installed, it should have a name of the form "machinename\NETSDK." If you don't see such a database, go back to Chapter 8 and follow the instructions there to install the QuickStart Tutorials.*

**Data Form Wizard**                                                    Comments?

**Create a relationship between tables**
The wizard will use the relationships to generate code that keeps the
tables synchronized as you work with them.

Relationships are based on common keys between tables. Name your new relation,
choose the parent and child tables and key fields, and then add it to the relations list
using the arrow button.

Name:                                                          Relations:

exRel

Parent table:            Child table:                 >

Employees  ▼             EmployeeTerritories  ▼

Keys:                                            ✕

EmployeeID  ▼            EmployeeID  ▼

            ▼                        ▼

            ▼                        ▼

            Cancel       < Back      Next >       Finish

*Figure 9-6. Data access made easy*

If you run the application at this point, you will see a single button labeled
Load. Click this button. The fruits of your labor now come into view: a completely populated grid view of your employee data with no custom coding
required. To find out details about the associated territories of any of these
employees, click Show Details next to the employee's row.

**NOTE**    *A couple of things should be pointed out here. First,
the rows in the Master view are further apart than they
should be due to the lengthy entries in each row's Notes column. Secondly, the details (visible at the very bottom of the
page) are not as easily understood as they could be, due to the fact that
the wizard only allows two tables to exist in a single relationship.*

At this point, we are finally ready to adapt the stock quoting application for use with .NET and a couple of wireless devices.

## Writing the Server

In order to create the Web application version of the stock quoting client, complete these steps:

1. Use the Visual Studio .NET IDE to create a new ASP.NET Web application project.

2. To the default Web Form, add the following controls, but do not change their names from the defaults assigned by Visual Studio: a text box, a label, a button, and a `RegularExpressionValidator` control.

3. Clear the label's Text property.

4. Change the `RegularExpressionValidator` text to Invalid stock symbol!

5. Change the button's text to Get Quote.

6. Change the validator's `ControlToValidate` property to TextBox1.

7. Change the validator's `ValidationExpression` to

`[a-zA-Z]{4}`

At this point, your form should look similar to Figure 9-7.

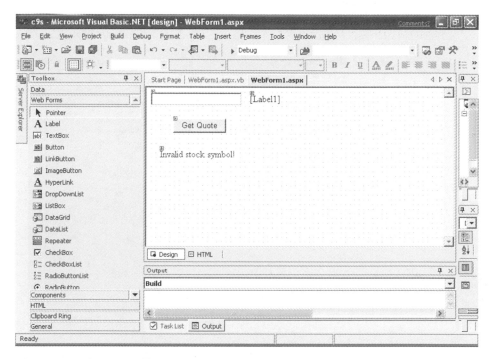

*Figure 9-7. The server GUI*

## The Code

Once you have built and saved your server's GUI, modify its code listing to look like the code shown in Listing 9-1.

*Listing 9-1. The Web Application Stock Quote Server*

```
Imports System.Net
Imports System.Text.RegularExpressions

Public Class WebForm1
    Inherits System.Web.UI.Page
    Protected WithEvents TextBox1 As System.Web.UI.WebControls.TextBox
    Protected WithEvents Label1 As System.Web.UI.WebControls.Label
    Protected WithEvents RegularExpressionValidator1 As _
  System.Web.UI.WebControls.RegularExpressionValidator
    Protected WithEvents Button1 As System.Web.UI.WebControls.Button
```

```
        Private Sub Page_Load(ByVal sender As System.Object,_
        ByVal e As System.EventArgs) Handles _MyBase.Load
            'Put user code to initialize the page here
        End Sub

        Private Sub Button1_Click(ByVal sender As System.Object,_
        ByVal e As System.EventArgs) Handles _Button1.Click

            If Page.IsValid Then

                Dim hwreq As HttpWebRequest
                Dim hwres As HttpWebResponse
                Dim inStream As System.IO.Stream
                Dim strResponse As String

                hwreq = CType(WebRequest.Create
                ("http://finance.lycos.com/home/"&_
                "stocks/quotes.asp?symbols=" & _
                TextBox1.Text), HttpWebRequest
                hwres = CType(hwreq.GetResponse(), HttpWebResponse)
                inStream = hwres.GetResponseStream()

                Try
                    Do While True
                        strResponse = strResponse & Chr(inStream.ReadByte())
                    Loop
                Catch ex As Exception
                End Try

                inStream.Close()

                Dim rgExp As Regex
                Dim m As Match
                Dim btPrice As Byte()

                m = rgExp.Match(strResponse, "\d+\.\d+", RegexOptions.Singleline)

                If m.Success Then
                    Label1.Text = " ... is trading at " & m.Value()
                Else
                    Label1.Text = " ... cannot be found!"
```

```
        End If

    Else

        Label1.Text = ""

    End If

End Sub
End Class
```

## The Walk-Through

Possibly the quickest way to understand this application is to zero in on the differences between it and the server application created in the exercise at the end of the previous chapter. Unlike the previous server, this server has about half of all its networking taken care of for it by Internet Information Server. For this reason, it doesn't need to import the fancy stream, threading, and socket libraries that were used by the previous server implementation.

All of the really exciting code for this application executes when the user clicks the Get Quote button. The first thing you probably notice is a new construction, `Page.IsValid`. We will discuss this in depth in the next section, "Writing the Client." For right now, assume that this test always succeeds.

The code at this point is virtually identical to that shown in the previous chapter. The only difference occurs after Quote.com has returned the current price of a stock. Rather than converting the price to a byte array and sending it back to the client via a socket-level interface, this code simply places the answer into the `Label` control.

### Internet Explorer

To test-drive the server under Internet Explorer, simply click the Run button on the Visual Studio toolbar. You should see a Web page with a text field and a Submit button. Enter some garbage in the text box that is anything other than exactly four letters. When you click the Submit button, you should see the validation error message pop up in the display.

This is an example of .NET sensing that your client (Internet Explorer) supports JavaScript and, therefore, uses client-side script to validate your data entry. In this case, the regular expression you entered requires that all stock symbols be a pattern of exactly four upper- or lowercase letters.

If you now change this into a stock symbol matching these criteria, you should be able to click the Submit button and get a price quote.

### Pocket PC

The first wireless client to be targeted by code in the preceding section, the Pocket PC, is an ideal platform for interoperation with .NET—owing to its existence completely within the Microsoft sphere of influence. With Internet Explorer still open, copy the URL from the address bar and enter it into the Pocket Internet Explorer address bar in the Pocket PC emulator. You should see a screen similar to the one displayed in Internet Explorer, only smaller. If you enter an invalid stock symbol and click Submit, you will notice that the request goes through to the server.

The reason for this is that .NET believes the Pocket Internet Explorer is incapable of using JavaScript, which was true with earlier versions of the browser. Fortunately, .NET compensates for this by performing the validation on the server. This kind of compensation is very important to understanding what .NET is all about.

**NOTE** *Our use of* Page.IsValid *is important at this point. Although .NET will automatically perform server-side validation in cases such as this, it will not automatically prevent processing of other activities on the server if an error should arise. For this reason, you must test for* Page.IsValid *yourself. In the case of the example application, the stock lookup is performed only if this is true. If not, the label's text is cleared out completely.*

## Writing the Client

In this section, we will create a Palm OS–based client application that will also work with the stock quoting server.

### The Code

Listing 9-2 shows the code for the Palm OS client and Listing 9-3 shows the HTML code for the GUI.

*Listing 9-2. The Web Application Stock Quoting Palm OS Client*

```html
<html>
    <head>
        <title>Stock Quote Client</title>
            <meta name="PalmComputingPlatform" contents="true">
            <meta name="PalmLauncherRevision" contents="1.0">
    </head>

    <body>
        <center>Welcome to the .NET Stock Quote Client!<p>
            Click <a href="http://www.pocketdba.com/c9s/WebForm1.aspx">
            here</a> to proceed!
        </center>
    </body>
</html>
```

*Listing 9-3. The HTML for the GUI*

```html
<meta name="GENERATOR" content="Microsoft Visual Studio.NET 7.0">
<meta name="CODE_LANGUAGE" content="Visual Basic 7.0">
<meta name="vs_defaultClientScript" content="JavaScript">
<meta name="vs_targetSchema" content="http://schemas.microsoft.com/
intellisense/ie5">
<meta name="PalmComputingPlatform" contents="true">
<meta name="PalmLauncherRevision" contents="1.0">
```

## The Walk-Through

In order to use this code, you must first change the URL to reference the location where your own code is stored. In the case of the preceding text, change www.pocketdba.com to reference your own server (remember we mentioned in Chapter 5 that localhost will not work!), and change c9s to whatever you named your server project under Visual Studio.

 **TIP** *You can get a good start on building this URL by copying it directly from Internet Explorer's address bar during a test run.*

You may recall from Chapter 5 that all Web Clipping clients expect the presence of two <meta>tags in any content that they receive. Looking at the Visual Studio .NET interface, it may not be immediately obvious where these tags should be added. With your Web Form's GUI interface visible, look at the bottom of its window. You should see two buttons, one labeled Design and the other labeled HTML.

If you click the HTML button, you will go into an HTML-based view of your application's user interface. You should see a number of META tags already in this code. Simply add the two required by Web Clipping, so that this section of the code matches Listing 9-3.

Once you have modified Listings 9-1, 9-2, and 9-3 accordingly, load the code from Listing 9-2 into the Web Query Builder and turn it into a PQA. Install this PQA onto your Palm OS device or emulator and start it up. You will be given a single link that will take you to the first page of your application. Try entering both valid and invalid stock symbols, and you will see that everything works as it should. Nifty!

## Final Thoughts

Three clients, WAP phones, i-Mode phones, and J2ME devices, have been excluded from the exercise in this chapter. The reason for this is that none of these devices are capable of rendering HTML on its own. Thus far in our discussions, different kinds of HTML are all that we have learned to serve up to these devices.

In the next chapter, however, you will learn how XML can enable communication with an even wider variety of devices. The methodology for this communication will be the much-hyped Web Service.

# CHAPTER 10

# Web Services

## So This Is What .NET Is All About?

It took about a year after .NET's initial release to get a single-sentence description of .NET that people could remember. In the end, that sentence wound up being ".NET is Microsoft's platform for Web Services."

So, what is this, apart from marketing-speak? Well, at its best, it is a profound new recognition of how the Internet has revolutionized the way that software applications can be assembled. Web Services offer some very attractive benefits:

- Quicker, easier software development

- Much more powerful applications

- More reliable business revenue streams

If these benefits sound appealing to you, then read on.

## The Limits of Web Applications

This book is based loosely on a presentation about wireless .NET that I have given on several occasions. Of all the parts of this presentation, the one that I'm about to share with you now is the most gratifying. This is where I explain the need for Web Services by telling you a few horror stories from my own career as a full-time software developer at PocketDBA Systems (and earlier).

By the time you are finished reading this section, you should be saying to yourself, "There *must* be some better way out there to build complex, Internet-driven applications." (Or possibly you'll be saying, "Boy, that Derek really isn't much of a developer is he?" But I hope not!)

### How Banner Advertisers Ruin Everything

My first horror story took place just a little earlier in the evening I sat down to write this chapter. The idea was simple enough: to adapt the stock quote Web application that I showed you in the previous chapter for use as a Web Service in this chapter. However, upon completing the code (shown later in the chapter in Listing 10-1), I was astonished to find out that it returned a price of "0.01" for any stock symbol I chose. "This recession," I thought, "has really gotten serious."

Fortunately, the Visual Basic .NET IDE now allows you to step through Web-based application code just as easily as through Windows-based code. So, I set a breakpoint on the following line:

```
inStream.Close()
```

At this point in the code, all of the data about the stock has been returned by Quote.com, and the application is just about ready to begin parsing it for the required pricing information. Once the debugger had paused execution at my breakpoint, I was able to inspect the raw text of the response for myself by copying it to the Windows Notepad application. Searching for the string "0.01" provided a fascinating, though disheartening, revelation.

Between the time when I wrote the original Web application a few weeks ago and the evening of this writing, Quote.com sold banner advertising space to some new client who apparently uses JavaScript to produce a pop-up window that offers you bill reduction services. This is all very good and well for those in need of debt reduction, but it worked a mischief on my otherwise well-designed code.

Specifically, the new JavaScript on Quote.com's page included the string literal "0.01". My code, as initially conceived, used a regular expression to find the first pattern-matching digits on either side of a decimal point. Once this new "0.01" literal was added to Quote.com's page, my code started matching to this literal, rather than the price of the stock, which was located further down the page.

 **NOTE** *For a complete description of the workaround applied to overcome this and (hopefully) limit future breakage, see the exercise at the end of this chapter.*

## How Human Nature Ruins Everything

The vacuum theory of human cognition, loosely stated, claims that the amount of work to be done will always expand to fill all time available for it. Consider the job of system administrators, for example. At the very least, they typically need only to ensure that the latest upgrades and patches are always kept installed on whatever machines they administer. However, this would not keep them occupied on a full-time basis. So, in their spare moments, they look for developers to harass.

I was working at my former employer's company and I had just built my first three-tier, Windows DNA, DCOM-based application. It was a beautiful thing to behold: an ActiveX document user interface talking to a COM+ business logic tier talking to a SQL Server database. Using this, our sales force could have access to our company's CRM system from any place in the world—instantly!

So, the time came to roll out my new creation on an internal-use-only basis. Everything went splendidly for several weeks, and I was quite proud of myself. Soon, the application was approved for use by our salespeople "in the field."

This is where it all started to go horribly wrong. In order for our salespeople to use this system on site, the company would have to open up its corporate firewall. "So," asked our system administrator, "on what ports shall I make the hole?" After a quick glance at the documentation for DCOM, I returned the answer, "All of them."

This is not a popular answer with system administrators. Leaving a production server completely exposed to the Internet is an excellent way to get hacked. Fortunately, I had seniority at my former employer's company and was able to get all of the ports opened in spite of the system administrator's objections. Unfortunately, the box was hacked several times just within the first month.

(Remember, you're supposed to be thinking to yourself, "There *must* be a better way to build complex, Internet-driven applications.")

## How Vendors Ruin Everything

After a great deal of effort, we were able to reduce the number of ports that had to remain open on the production box in order to continue using DCOM and, thus, my DCOM-based Windows DNA application. Our outside sales force began using the application directly from potential customers' sites and all was right with the world.

And then someone decided to buy a Java Application Server (JAS). I was not privy to this decision, but it had all the technological insight that developers have come to expect from management. Someone on the board knew somebody who had once gone to school with someone else and, at the end of the day, we were getting a JAS and I would be expected to make it work with our existing system.

Fortunately, I was given the opportunity to select between varieties of different JASs and took the opportunity to ask some key technical questions. "Can it work with DCOM," I asked? "Yes," the various vendors assured me. "Does it provide JDBC drivers for our database," I asked? "Absolutely," they guaranteed.

Unfortunately, two months and $50,000 later, I learned that I *should* have asked, "Can we use DCOM and your JDBC driver *simultaneously*?" Because, of course, the answer would have been, "No, you can't." In this particular case, in order to use the JDBC driver, you had to be running under Sun's JDK, which doesn't support DCOM. Alternatively, you could run under Microsoft's JDK but, in this case, you would lose the use of the required JDBC driver.

The trap I was caught in was one of conflicting standards. My application required DCOM. Sun's JDK wanted to speak RMI (the Java equivalent of DCOM—loosely). My application's components were written in COM. Our new application server only served Enterprise Java Beans (EJBs).

## The Museum of Obsolete Technology

The only thing that is worse than conflicting standards is no standards at all.

### My Fourth Beautiful System

When Visual Basic 5 was first released, I (like many other developers) couldn't wait to create my first ActiveX control. ActiveX controls at that point in time were being touted as Microsoft's answer to Java applets. The only thing was, ActiveX controls were a lot easier to create and offered a heck of a lot more flexibility than Java applets.

So, for my next application, I created a bunch of pages with ActiveX controls on them and tested them thoroughly in the privacy of my own office on Internet Explorer 4. The grand unveiling of my new application was set to kick off a company-wide meeting, and I could hardly wait.

### How Zealots Ruin Everything

Unfortunately, the computer that was set up when I first arrived for the demonstration was a Sun Microsystems workstation running the Solaris operating system. ActiveX controls, with their deep links into the Windows operating system, do not run on non-Windows computers.

> **NOTE**   *I believe that the ActiveX specification is phrased in such a way as to provide for the creation of non-Windows ActiveX controls. This is an idea that simply never caught on, though, and (in any event) it is immaterial to the discussion at hand.*

The second machine, which I was brought after a brief delay in our meeting, was an older version of Windows with only Netscape installed. Netscape was not usable as an ActiveX container at that point and, as a result, my application wouldn't work on it, either. My demonstration had to be delayed until the end of the meeting to give me time to upgrade the version of Internet Explorer on the machine.

My real troubles had only started, however. Netscape and Unix were very popular platforms at the ISP where I worked, and the advocates of these platforms made it known very quickly that they would *not* be willing to sacrifice them in order to use my application. This is the price of platform dependence.

## Meet the Web Service

If Web Services had existed when I began the projects described in the preceding sections, these horror stories never would have happened.

### What Are They?

You can think of standard Web applications as all being based on HTML-over-HTTP. The problem with this is that HTML describes how a user interface should look—not the raw data that is to be transferred. This is problematic because the user interface for a given application is far more likely to change frequently than is the underlying data. As you saw with the stock quote server, Quote.com caused my application to crash simply by adding a banner advertisement—not a good thing!

Web Services turns this situation on its head by creating a new kind of Internet application that works by transferring XML over *some standard protocol*. Requests coming into a Web Service are XML and so are the responses. By basing themselves on XML, Web Services are able to deal directly in data, and thus avoid the kinds of cosmetic issues described in the first horror story earlier.

The *some standard protocol* reference is another key strength of Web Services. Unlike traditional Web applications, Web Services are not bound to HTTP. A Web Service could operate just as well via SMTP or even FTP. In these cases, entirely new kinds of asynchronous functionality might be possible, in which a client would send a Web Service request, go about its business, and then react to a response received at some point in the future.

### Making a Clean Break with SOAP

At this point, it is important to stop thinking about Web Services strictly in comparison to the Web applications that have gone before them and to begin thinking of them in the larger context of *all* applications. In this context, Web Services represent a revolutionary solution to the great remote procedure call (RPC) standards debates of the 1990s. These debates centered around whether CORBA, DCOM, RMI, or any of a half-dozen other standards would become the dominant means of calling one application's functionalities from another across the network.

One reason why this debate was never resolved in favor of any single approach was that the technologies in question all had serious drawbacks. CORBA, for example, was much more difficult to use than DCOM. However, DCOM could only be used on Windows and, as demonstrated in my second horror story, was a firewall administrator's nightmare.

Web Services address the RPC issue wonderfully. By defining an XML-based standard for RPCs, they bring the power of distributed computing within reach of even the least powerful handhelds. The rule is this: if a device can create text (which is all that XML boils down to) and get it onto "the network" in some standard fashion (HTTP, SMTP, and so on), then it can use Web Services. The XML-based standard that Web Services use for RPC is known as SOAP, which stands for *Simple Object Access Protocol*.

## What Good Does Any of This Do?

So, how does this new Web Services approach to creating distributed systems address the issues illustrated in the horror stories earlier? It addresses them by facilitating the easy creation of distributed applications that are

- More maintainable

- Capable of communicating over virtually any Internet protocol

- Easier to keep secure

### Documenting Your Partnerships

If Quote.com made stock price information available using Web Services, then the disaster that befell me in the first of my horror stories could never have happened. In the first place, the format of the data transferred by the site's Web Service would be far less likely to change the appearance of the current Web application.

To play devil's advocate, consider the case in which the format of the data *did* change. In this event, my client could very well stop working. However, an appropriate error would have been generated that would have let me resolve the issue in short order. Instead, with the HTML-based approach, I was actually receiving false answers for quite a while before I even realized that there was a problem. If real money had been riding on the answers given by my application, there would have been serious trouble.

So, Web Services address my first issue by clearly documenting my application's relationships with its other Internet-based applications. This for the first time allows Internet-driven applications to achieve a high degree of reliability. The business benefit in this is that Internet-driven applications can now form the basis of mission-critical applications.

## Using the Transport of Your Choice

By running on virtually any Internet-standard protocol, Web Services make themselves infinitely more appealing to firewalls and the system administrators who run them. Rather than having to ask your administrator to leave a box completely open in order to use DCOM, you can simply ask for a hole on, for example, port 80 or 443—the standard ports for HTTP/HTTPS traffic. There aren't many system administrators who will object to this.

The business benefit to Web Services in this case then is increased security and ease of administration. This addresses the problems in the second horror story.

## Standardizing the Protocols

The latest version of the Java Application Server (JAS) that my company acquired in my third horror story supports Web Services. If this had been the case when I had begun my project, I could have done the following:

- Run the application under Sun's Java SDK

- Adapted my Windows application to get it to use SOAP

- Leveraged the JAS's JDBC driver to talk to the database

So, in this case, Web Services become the glue that binds disparate technologies from different vendors more tightly together. This decreases the amount of application development time that must be devoted to enterprise integration efforts. The benefit to business is decreased development costs. The benefit to developers is more time to focus on really interesting programming issues.

## Lowering the Bar

As you will see in the next chapter, Web Services can be invoked from virtually any device. To put this in the context of my fourth, and final, horror story: if Web Services had been available three years ago, I could have created the same rich functionality without the use of platform-dependent ActiveX controls.

Web Services can be invoked from Java applets running under Netscape. Web Services can be invoked from a native Unix application running under X on a Solaris workstation. Web Services can even be invoked from J2ME-powered mobile devices (as you will see in the next chapter).

Once again, the business benefit is a vast reduction in the amount of time that must be spent on enterprise integration efforts. Remember, the rule is this: *if it can generate and receive text on some network interface, then it can interact with Web Services!*

## The Downloadable Deliverables

So, all of this pie-in-the-sky talk is very interesting, but where things like this are concerned, developers have learned to be skeptical. You could be forgiven at this point for making like Jerry Maguire and saying, "Show me the code!" Here it is.

### The Microsoft Camp

The good news is that by installing Visual Studio .NET, you have already given yourself everything you need in order to create and invoke Web Services the Microsoft way. As you will see in the exercise at the end of this chapter, creating Microsoft Web Services can be as easy as choosing the right project type and adding a few public procedures to a preconstructed public class.

This technology will suffice if you want to invoke your Web Services from Visual Studio .NET as well, but what about if you want to invoke your services from other technologies? For example, what if you want to call a Web Service from a legacy application you wrote last year in Visual Basic 6 (which, of course, you never dreamed would become legacy in just one year)?

 **TIP** *As you will see in the next chapter, the SOAP Toolkit described in the next section can also be used to invoke .NET Web Services from pre-.NET Active Server Pages.*

### The SOAP Toolkit, 2.0

Microsoft produced the SOAP Toolkit for Visual Studio shortly before .NET was first announced to the public. Initially, it used an older implementation of SOAP that was commonly referred to as "SOAP on a ROPE." (In this case, ROPE was an acronym for something or another—but whatever it was, it's history now.)

With the version 2.0 release of this toolkit, the official protocol is now WSDL—the same protocol supported by .NET. The SOAP Toolkit is therefore the tool of choice for creating COM-based Windows applications (Visual Studio 4–6 or pre-.NET Active Server Pages) that will do one of the following:

• Act as a client for WSDL-based Web Services.

• Serve COM components as Web Services.

In this book, we will focus upon the former of these two alternatives. For more information on exposing COM components as Web Services, see the WSDL Generator tool included with the SOAP Toolkit.

The Soap Toolkit can be downloaded directly from the Microsoft Developers Network site at

```
http://msdn.microsoft.com/downloads
```

As of the time of writing, it is still listed as one of the top ten most popular downloads. This situation is likely to persist well into the future, as the legions of Visual Studio developers begin to wrestle with upgrading their existing applications to integrate with .NET. Table 10-1 describes the three components that are available for download.

*Table 10-1: The SOAP Toolkit Downloads*

| FILENAME | FULL NAME | REQUIRED FOR THE EXERCISES IN THIS BOOK? |
|---|---|---|
| soaptoolkit20.exe | Soap Toolkit 2.0 | Yes |
| soaptoolkit20redist.exe | Soap Toolkit 2.0 Redistributables | No |
| soaptoolkit20samples.exe | Soap Toolkit 2.0 Samples | Recommended |

**TIP**   *The Redistributables package listed in Table 10-1 is useful when distributing pre-.NET Visual Studio executables that must make use of the SOAP Toolkit's functionality.*

In order to complete the exercise at the end of this chapter, you will need to have installed at least the first file from Table 10-1, the Soap Toolkit proper. In order to install it, simply run the self-extracting executable and when prompted choose the Complete Install option.

**CAUTION**   *On Windows XP, you may receive an error to the effect that the installer isn't able to update some of the files because Windows is protecting them. Fortunately (according to the README file, at least) it is safe to ignore these errors.*

### Invoking Web Services Wirelessly

Of course, the Holy Grail of Web Services as far as this book is concerned is to be able to invoke these services wirelessly. In the next chapter, we will show you how to invoke .NET Web Services from every kind of wireless device discussed so far in this book.

### The Sun Camp

Web Services were a key topic this year at JavaOne (Sun's annual Java conference). I attended the conference and sat in on as many sessions as human endurance would permit. And, at the end of it all, the one thing that seems very clear is that Sun is playing serious "catch up" to Microsoft on this front.

Amusingly, Sun has only itself to blame for this sad state of affairs. The company chose not to participate in the early standardizations of the SOAP protocol and its successor, WSDL. Unfortunately for Sun, these standards have now become the de facto laws of the land where Web Services are concerned. So, Sun has to work fast if it wants to even stay in the game.

The main value proposition that Sun is proposing for Web Services is that, by creating them with Java, you can create systems with true end-to-end platform independence. For example, consider the J2ME devices that we have already discussed in this book. Now, imagine J2ME code running on the client, conversing with Web Services running on a Java-based server. In this architecture, you could freely mix and match combinations of hardware and OS anywhere in your system.

 **NOTE** *At the time of writing, Microsoft has recently announced that it will be partnering with Corel to make a version of .NET available on the FreeBSD operating system. This apparent move towards true platform independence for the .NET platform is completely unexpected and may undermine much of Java's value.*

The only problem is the key pieces of technology required for Java Web Services are not yet widely available. Specifically, the Java XML Messaging (JAXM) frameworks have yet to be released to the public. Without classes to support the automatic creation and transmission of complicated WSDL messages, Java will remain a second choice at best for creating Web Services.

## Exercise

In this chapter's exercise, we continue to expand and improve the stock price server. This time, you are going to convert it from a .NET Web application to a .NET Web Service. As a Web Service, it will become far less bound by the unique characteristics of its clients.

## Writing the Server

The server consists of a single Visual Basic .NET project.

### The Code

Listing 10-1 shows the code for the stock quote Web Service.

*Listing 10-1. The Stock Quote Web Service*

```
Imports System.Net
Imports System.Web.Services
Imports System.Text.RegularExpressions
```

```vb
<WebService(Namespace:="http://pocketdba.com/webservices/")> Public Class Service1

    Inherits System.Web.Services.WebService

    <WebMethod()> Public Function getQuote(ByVal symbol As String,_
    ByRef price As String) As _ Boolean

        Dim hwreq As HttpWebRequest
        Dim hwres As HttpWebResponse
        Dim inStream As System.IO.Stream
        Dim strResponse As String
        Dim rgExp As Regex
        Dim m As Match

        m = rgExp.Match(symbol, "[a-zA-Z]{4}")

        If m.Success Then

hwreq = CType(WebRequest.Create(_
"http://finance.lycos.com/home/stocks/" & _
quotes.asp?symbols=" & _
symbol), HttpWebRequest)
            hwres = CType(hwreq.GetResponse(), HttpWebResponse)
            inStream = hwres.GetResponseStream()

            Try
                Do While True
                    strResponse = strResponse & Chr(inStream.ReadByte())
                Loop
            Catch ex As Exception
            End Try

            inStream.Close()

            Dim temp As String

            m = rgExp.Match(strResponse,_
            "(?:Last Sale.*)\d+\.\d+",_
            RegexOptions.Singleline)
```

```
      If m.Success Then

          temp = m.Value()
          m = rgExp.Match(temp, "\d+\.\d+", RegexOptions.Singleline)

          If m.Success Then

              price = m.Value()
              getQuote = True
              Exit Function

          End If

      End If

   End If

   getQuote = False

End Function

End Class
```

## The Walk-Through

In order to create the stock quote Web Service using the code in Listing 10-1, follow these steps:

1.  Open a new instance of the Visual Studio .NET IDE.

2.  Select the project type option Visual Basic Projects.

3.  Select the ASP.NET Web Service template.

4.  Enter the name C10Server in the Project Name field and click OK.

5.  Click the link in the main window labeled Click here to switch to code view.

6.  Tweak the auto-generated code to look like the code shown in Listing 10-1.

When you are done entering the code, click the Run button on the toolbar. After a moment, Internet Explorer should open to a Web page like the one shown in Figure 10-1.

*Figure 10-1. .NET Web Service home page*

For every Web Service you create using .NET, you will get a home page like the one in Figure 10-1. As you can see, it will give you a list of every operation (read "function" or "subroutine") that your service is making available. Best of all, each list entry is a link to further information about the particular operation. Go ahead and click the link to getQuote to see a page like the one in Figure 10-2.

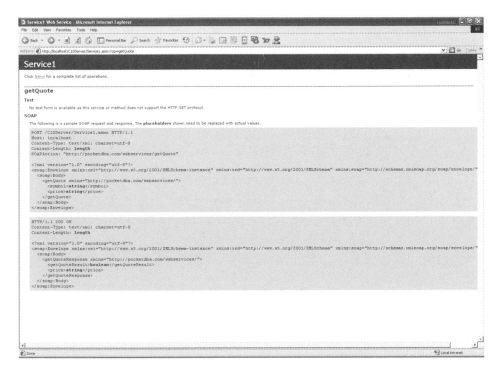

*Figure 10-2. The getQuote page*

This page is your salvation, pure and simple. By giving you a sample header and body for WSDL requests, .NET has just saved you from the tedium of figuring out the WSDL all on your own. All you have to do now to invoke a Web Service from any device that supports HTTP is substitute specific values for the placeholder variables in the samples, send the samples across the wire, and then parse the XML that gets sent back.

**NOTE** *This is exactly what we show you how to do on all of our mobile devices in the next chapter.*

For those of you who are truly gluttons for punishment, return now to the page containing the list of operations. Notice that, at the top of this page, there is a link to a complete Service description. Follow this link and you will see the sort of impenetrable nomenclature that could only possibly be a WSDL document.

Although this isn't very pleasant for humans to read, .NET's ability to provide WSDL documentation like this on-the-fly across the Internet is vital to its ability to integrate with Visual Studio and other client tools. As you will see in the next section, which describes building Web Service clients, both Visual Studio .NET and the SOAP Toolkit depend upon the ability to connect to this WSDL page in order to function properly.

Now, as a temporary experiment, close Internet Explorer and go back into the code for your new Web Service. In the line that reads

```
<WebMethod()> Public Function getQuote(ByVal symbol As String,_
ByRef price As String) As Boolean
```

change `price` into a `ByVal` variable instead, and then rerun the service. When the main service page opens in Internet Explorer, run the `getQuote` operation. Presto! You now have a test form that specifically allows you to try out your new Web Service with some sample values for its parameters.

> **NOTE**  *Of course, by changing* `price` *to a* `ByVal` *parameter, you have essentially made it impossible for the Web Service to return the price of your stock. This is why you won't see a stock price anywhere in the XML that is generated in response to your test form submissions.*

> **CAUTION**  *Make sure to change* `price` *back to* `ByRef` *before continuing, or the server won't work properly.*

The first interesting bit in the code is this line:

```
<WebService(Namespace:="http://pocketdba.com/webservices/")> Public Class Service1
    Inherits System.Web.Services.WebService
```

This is the way that you tell .NET to expose a given class as a Web Service. This way, you could potentially have multiple classes in a single ASMX file, but the only ones that will be available for Web Service access will be the ones that meet these criteria:

• Include the `<WebService>` tag

• Inherit from `Web.Services.WebService`

The namespace is just the XML namespace into which your WSDL will be placed. Although it has the form of a URL, it does not need to correspond to any "real" URL. The standard seems to be to use your company's domain name, followed by a path that suggests some kind of ordering for your company's code. For example, at PocketDBA Systems, we might have the following namespaces.

```
http://pocketdba.com/databases/oracle
http://pocketdba.com/databases/sqlserver
http://pocketdba.com/humanresources/employeecode/derek
http://pocketdba.com/humanresources/employeecode/dave
http://pocketdba.com/humanresources/benefits/pending/401k/calculations
```

The next interesting bit of code is this one:

```
<WebMethod()> Public Function getQuote(ByVal symbol As String,_
ByRef price As String) As _Boolean
```

This is just a regular function definition, with a `<WebMethod()>` tag added. This is how you tell .NET which procedures within a Web Service class are to be exposed for Web Service access. This way, you can keep some of your parameters confined to access only on the same machine as the code itself.

The final bit of code that deserves mention is the portion surrounding this line:

```
m = rgExp.Match(strResponse, "(?:Last Sale.*)\d+\.\d+", RegexOptions.Singleline)
```

This is a variation on the previous use of regular expression matching to find the most recent sale price of the target stock. This search basically says, "Find the first instance of the phrase 'Last Sale' that is followed by any number of characters, then digits, then a period, and then more digits." By adding the "Last Sale" verbiage to the search, you are able to skip over any prices that might occur earlier in the document.

## Writing the Client

Creating .NET clients for .NET Web Services is as easy as pie! Thankfully, with the release of the version 2 of the SOAP Toolkit, it is also pretty easy to create legacy Windows applications that make use of .NET Web Services.

## The Code

Listing 10-2 shows the code for the stock quote Web Service client, and Listing 10-3 shows the code for the Visual Basic 6 Web Service client.

*Listing 10-2. The Stock Quote Web Service Client*

```
Public Class Form1
    Inherits System.Windows.Forms.Form

Private Sub Button1_Click(ByVal sender As System.Object,_
ByVal e As System.EventArgs) Handles _ Button1.Click

        Dim price As String
        Dim ws As localhost.Service1 = New localhost.Service1()

        Label1.Text = ""

        If ws.getQuote(TextBox1.Text, price) Then
            Label1.Text = price
        Else
            Label1.Text = "No such stock!"
        End If

    End Sub
End Class
```

*Listing 10-3. The Visual Studio 6 Web Service Client*

```
Private Sub Command1_Click()

    Dim SoapClient As New MSSOAPLib.SoapClient
    Dim ok As Boolean
    Dim i As Integer
    Dim c As String
```

```
    If Len(Text1.Text) <> 4 Then

        GoTo DontBother

    End If

    For i = 1 To 4

        c = Mid(Text1.Text, i, 1)

        If (c < "a" Or c > "z") And (c < "A" And c > "Z") Then

            GoTo DontBother

        End If

    Next i

    Call SoapClient.mssoapinit("http://localhost/c10server/"&_
    "service1.asmx?WSDL", "Service1")

    ok = SoapClient.getQuote(Text1.Text, price)

DontBother:

    If ok Then
        MsgBox price
    Else
        MsgBox "Houston, we have a problem!"
    End If

End Sub
```

## The Walk-Through

The beauty of calling .NET Web Services from .NET applications is that you
can add references to them just as you would add references to standard
Windows components.

### Visual Studio .NET

In order to create the stock quote Web Service client using the preceding code, follow these steps:

1. Open a new instance of the Visual Studio .NET IDE.

2. Click New Project.

3. Select a project type option Visual Basic Projects.

4. Select the Windows Application template.

5. Enter the name Chapter10Client and click OK.

6. Add a textbox, a button, and a label to the default form.

7. Select Add Web Reference from the Project menu.

8. Enter the full URL for your Web Service into the Add Web Reference address bar, and then press Enter. An example of this might be

   ```
   http://localhost/C10Server/Service1.asmx
   ```

9. After pressing Enter, you should see a screen like the one in Figure 10-3. If not, you need to try a different URL.

10. Click Add Reference.

11. Double-click the button on your default form to open its code view.

12. Alter this code listing to look as much like Listing 10-2 as possible.

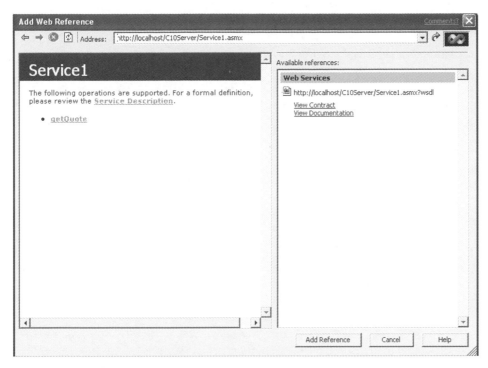

*Figure 10-3. Adding a Web reference*

At this point, you are ready to try your new Web Service! Simply run this application, enter a valid stock symbol in the textbox, and click the button. After a few moments, your price data should appear in the label control.

An interesting bit of the example code is the line that reads:

```
Dim ws As localhost.Service1 = New localhost.Service1()
```

This line could easily be mistaken for instantiation of any other Windows component, except that we know better. .NET has assigned the machine name, in this case localhost, for use as the library name. The name of the service, Service1, serves as the name of the component. Everything else is just as it would be for using a standard Windows component—.NET does an excellent job of concealing the internal workings of XML and HTTP from the application developer. It is a beautiful thing, no?

### Visual Studios 4–6

In order to create a Web Services client using a pre-.NET version of Visual Studio, you must first install the SOAP Toolkit. We described this process earlier in this chapter in the section "The Downloadable Deliverables." Please refer back to that section if you have not yet acquired and installed the SOAP Toolkit. If you have already installed the SOAP Toolkit, simply follow these instructions:

1. Locate your pre-.NET version of Visual Studio on the Windows Start menu.

2. Select the Microsoft Visual Basic option to launch the VB IDE.

3. If the New Project dialog box presents itself, choose Standard EXE and click OK.

4. If the New Project dialog box did *not* present itself, you can bring it up by choosing New Project from the File menu.

5. Choose References from the Project menu.

6. Place a check mark next to Microsoft SOAP Type Library and click OK.

7. Add a text box and a button to your project's default form.

8. Double-click your newly added button to open the Code View.

9. Make your code listing look like the code in Listing 10-3.

As you can see, the SOAP Toolkit makes it *almost* as easy to use Web Services from pre-.NET Microsoft tools as from .NET—but not quite! The relevant line of code is this one:

```
Call SoapClient.mssoapinit("http://localhost/c10server/"&_
"service1.asmx?WSDL", "Service1")
```

Unlike Visual Studio .NET, which allows you to put all of your direct URL references into the Add Web Reference section of its IDE, the SOAP Toolkit requires that you hard-code this information to some extent into your code. This line of code says, in effect, "Tell our `SoapClient` object to act as a proxy for the `Service1` Web Service, defined by WSDL at the following URL." Thankfully, after this, invoking procedures on the Web Service is as easy as it should be:

```
ok = SoapClient.getQuote(Text1.Text, price)
```

**CAUTION**   *One drawback to this approach is that you don't get the same kind of compile-time bug detection that you would get by setting a .NET Web Reference. Think about it— if Visual Studio doesn't even know what Web Service you will be connecting to until it executes the* mssoapinit *method shown in the preceding text, how can it possibly verify that you are calling valid methods and/or using valid parameters in those calls?*

If you run this application now, you should try entering both valid and invalid stock symbols into the text box. We have added some code for client-side error detection, to avoid any unnecessary calls across the Internet. Adding similar code to the .NET version is left as an exercise for you to do. (You should know enough about regular expressions at this point to be able to handle it—if not, see the exercise at the end of Chapter 8.)

**NOTE**   *Use of the SOAP Toolkit can form the first step in the (admittedly painful) process of adapting legacy Windows applications for use with .NET. For more information on the topic, see the book* Moving to VB.NET: Strategies, Concepts, and Code *by Dan Appleman.*

## Final Thoughts

At this point, you have seen how easy it is to create and call Web Services using .NET. We think you will agree it is a very exciting way to create new Internet applications. In the next chapter, we will make it even more exciting by showing you how Web Services can be invoked from virtually *any* wireless client!

*Part Four*

# Mobile .NET

# CHAPTER 11

# Mobile Web Services

## How to Invoke Web Services from Any Mobile Device

THERE IS A LOT OF CODE IN this chapter. . .a *lot* of code! The contents are the result of approximately one weekend that we spent figuring out how to use .NET Web Services from each of the devices discussed in this book. Some of them were easy (Internet Explorer and the Pocket PC). Some of them were seemingly impossible at first (Palm OS). All are presented here in a ready-to-use form, for your benefit.

## Lathering Up the Web Service

The first thing that you must do in order to get your Web Service operating with devices is to simplify its access methodology a little.

### The Code

Listing 11-1 shows the code for the simplified Web Service.

*Listing 11-1. The Simplified Web Service*

```
Imports System.Web.Services
Imports System.Web.Services.Protocols

Imports System.Net
Imports System.Text.RegularExpressions

<WebService(Namespace:="http://pocketdba.com/webservices/")> Public Class Service1
    Inherits System.Web.Services.WebService
```

```vb
<WebMethod(),SoapRpcMethod()> Public Function getQuote(ByVal_
_
symbol As String) As String

        Dim hwreq As HttpWebRequest
        Dim hwres As HttpWebResponse
        Dim inStream As System.IO.Stream
        Dim strResponse As String
        Dim rgExp As Regex
        Dim m As Match

        m = rgExp.Match(symbol, "[a-zA-Z]{4}")

        If m.Success Then

            hwreq = _
CType(WebRequest.Create("http://finance.lycos.com/"&_
"home/stocks/quotes.asp?symbols=" &_
symbol), HttpWebRequest)
            hwres = CType(hwreq.GetResponse(), HttpWebResponse)
            inStream = hwres.GetResponseStream()

            Try
                Do While True
                    strResponse = strResponse & Chr(inStream.ReadByte())
                Loop
            Catch ex As Exception
            End Try

            inStream.Close()

            Dim temp As String

            m = rgExp.Match(strResponse, "(?:Last Sale.*)\d+\.\d+", _
RegexOptions.Singleline)

            If m.Success Then

                temp = m.Value()
                m = rgExp.Match(temp, "\d+\.\d+", RegexOptions.Singleline)

                If m.Success Then
                    getQuote = m.Value()
                    Exit Function
```

```
            End If

        End If

    End If

    throw new Exception("Invalid stock symbol!")

  End Function

End Class
```

## *The Walk-Through*

Listing 11-1 should look very familiar to you. This is the same Web Service
that was created in the previous chapter. However, we have made a few modifications—as indicated by the lines printed in bold.

The first bold line tells .NET to include support in this application for Web
Service protocols beyond .NET's native WSDL implementation. The reason for
this is that some of the devices you want to serve are not capable of speaking
WSDL out of the box. In most cases, you could force them to do so by parsing
the XML yourself—but why go to that effort when you can just tell .NET to speak
their language instead?

So, the next logical question then is what language these devices speak. In
most cases, the answer to this is the simple SOAP RPC protocol. This was, in
many respects, the original SOAP implementation and in fact was used by
Microsoft's SOAP Toolkit and .NET itself while they were still in Beta 1. Devices
such as those powered by J2ME still often use this technology, as it is simpler to
implement than WSDL.

The second bold line in the Listing 11-1 has added the phrase SoapRpcMethod
to tell .NET that this function should be made available to clients still using the
SOAP RPC protocol. It is much easier to add this tag than to reprogram all of
the clients to speak a new language, wouldn't you agree?

Another change on this line is that a Boolean is no longer being returned to
indicate whether or not the symbol lookup was a success. This required passing
in an additional ByRef parameter in order to return the price data. Methods that
require ByRef parameters are much harder to test, as .NET is incapable of providing test pages for them.

The way that information about success and failure will be returned instead
is shown in the last bolded line of code. If the method succeeds, it should return

before the line is ever reached. If not, a .NET exception is thrown containing the "Invalid stock symbol!" message.

## Internet Explorer

As you might have guessed, the easiest client from which to invoke .NET Web Services is Internet Explorer.

### Choosing Your Weapon

Two unique strengths of Internet Explorer that set it apart from other Internet browsers are its support for DHTML and its advanced XML capabilities. These two strengths are combined in a piece of Microsoft technology known as the *Internet Explorer Web Services Behavior.*

The Web Services Behavior is a script-based component that you can have automatically downloaded for use with your Web pages under Internet Explorer. In order to do this, you must first download the behavior from the following site: `http://msdn.microsoft.com/Downloads/samples/Internet/behaviors/library/webservice/webservice.htc.`

---

**TIP** *Remember that wherever you store the Web Service Behavior's HTC file, it will ultimately need to be accessible to the Internet in order for the component to be downloaded. For example, a Web page that is served off of c:\inetpub\wwwroot might expect to find its associated HTC files in the same directory.*

---

### The Code

Listing 11-2 shows the code for the Internet Explorer Client.

*Listing 11-2. The Internet Explorer Client*

```
<html>

   <head>
      <title>Mobile Stock Quotes</title>
      <script language="javascript">
```

```
        function getQuote()
        {


service.useService("http://localhost/Chapter10Server/Service1.asmx?WSDL",
"Chapter10Server");
            var iCallID;
            iCallID = service.Chapter10Server.callService(handleit, "getQuote",
  symbol.value);

        }

        function handleit(result)
        {

            if(result.error)
            {
                alert("Error getting stock quote!");
            }
            else
            {
                alert(result.value);
            }

        }

    </script>
  </head>

  <body>
    <div id="service" style="behavior:url(webservice.htc)"></div>
    Stock Symbol: <input id="symbol"><br>
    <input type="button" value="Get Quote!" onclick="getQuote()">
  </body>

</html>
```

## The Walk-Through

Begin your examination of this code by skipping down towards the bottom. In particular, you should first focus on the HTML inside of the body tag. The first element is a <div> tag. You can think of <div> tags as arbitrary subdivisions of other HTML markup. They have no specific UI representation.

In this context, the <div> element exists only to provide a specific element for the Web Service behavior to latch onto. This allows you to refer to the behavior programmatically using the ID of the associated element—in this example, the service element. The bit inside the parentheses in behavior:url() tells Internet Explorer where it can locate the component on the Internet for download. Since the code hasn't provided any kind of path information, it will look at whatever location this page itself was downloaded from.

By way of comparison, look at the following piece of code:

```
behavior:url(http://msdn.microsoft.com/workshop/author/webservice/webservice.htc)
```

This line of code would tell Internet Explorer to download the behavior directly from Microsoft's own Web site. This would save you the effort of having to download the component for hosting on your own server. On the other hand, Microsoft might easily decide to move this file on their servers, which would break your page. For this reason, it is probably better to download the file and host it yourself.

When the button in this section is clicked, it triggers the getQuote function in the preceding code. The first line in the getQuote function invokes the behavior's useService method. This method takes two parameters. The first is a URL pointing to the SDL for the service that you want to use. The second parameter is the name that will be used in the remainder of the code to refer to this Web Service.

The last line of code in the getQuote function is the line that actually calls the getQuote method on the Web Service. It does this by way of the behavior's callService method. This method takes two parameters. The first parameter is the name of the function that should be called whenever the Web Service sends back its response. The second parameter is the name of the Web Service method to invoke.

*All additional parameters are passed directly to the method of the Web Service that is being invoked.* For example, if your Web Service's method took five parameters, you would expect to find five additional parameters here. This would give you a total of seven parameters for the callService method (the two required by callService plus the five for your Web Service itself).

You have to provide the name of a callback function in the method just described because the Web Service behavior executes asynchronously by default. This has the interesting benefit of allowing you to send several requests before you have received even a single response. Try this for yourself, if you like. Enter several stock symbols, clicking the button after each one. Momentarily, you will receive several message boxes in response—one for each symbol entered.

**NOTE** *Of course, you won't know which prices go with which symbols using this approach. The* iCallID *variable shown in the preceding code could potentially be used to record which symbols were associated with which service method invocations—but these associations would have to be saved into some kind of global data structure for later recall. This is left as an exercise for the reader with entirely too much time on his or her hands!*

## Pocket PC

As you will see in Chapter 16, invoking .NET Web Services from Pocket PCs using the .NET Compact Frameworks is a piece of cake! In this section, however, let's consider how we might invoke .NET Web Services from Pocket PCs without the use of the .NET Compact Frameworks.

### Choosing Your Weapon

The best non-Microsoft Web Service client software available for the Pocket PC is known, appropriately enough, as pocketSOAP. It can be downloaded directly from the Internet at http://www.pocketsoap.com.

When looking at all of the binaries that are available, you want to make sure that you download the x86 binaries that are specifically for the Pocket PC emulator. (This is assuming, of course, that you want to test on the emulator before deploying to a real Pocket PC—which is always a good idea.)

**CAUTION** *The Win32 binaries are not the same as the x86 emulator binaries—even though you could get them to install on the emulator, you won't be able to get them to work. Take my word for it—I wasted an entire Friday afternoon trying it!*

In order to install the binaries on your emulator, follow these steps:

1. Extract the files from the downloaded zip file.

2. From the Windows Start menu, select Emulation Environment for Pocket PC to start the emulator.

3. Copy all of the DLLs from the pocketSOAP distribution to the location in which the Emulation Environment opened (example: C:\Windows CE Tools\wce300\MS Pocket PC\emulation\palm300\windows).

4. For each of the DLLs copied from the pocketSOAP distribution, complete the following steps:

   a. Enter **regsvrce** in the Emulation Environment window.

   b. On the Pocket PC Emulator screen, enter **\windows\** and then the name of the DLL in the textbox (example: \windows\psoap.dll).

   c. Click OK.

## The Code

Listing 11-3 shows the code for the Pocket PC client.

*Listing 11-3. The Pocket PC Client*

```
Private Sub Command1_Click()

    Dim strRequest As String, strResponse As String
    Dim psEnvelope As PocketSOAP.CoEnvelope
    Dim psTransport As PocketSOAP.IHTTPTransportAdv

    Set psEnvelope = CreateObject("PocketSOAP.Envelope")
    Set psTransport = CreateObject("PocketSOAP.HTTPTransport")

    psEnvelope.MethodName = "getQuote"
    psEnvelope.URI = "http://pocketdba.com/webservices/"
    psEnvelope.CreateParameter "symbol", Text1.Text
    strRequest = psEnvelope.Serialize
    MsgBox strRequest

    psTransport.SOAPAction = "http://pocketdba.com/webservices/getQuote"
    psTransport.Timeout = 99999

    psTransport.Send "http://localhost/Chapter10Server/Service1.asmx", strRequest
    strResponse = psTransport.Receive

    psEnvelope.parse (strResponse)
    MsgBox psEnvelope.Parameters.Item(0).Value

End Sub
```

## The Walk-Through

To use the code shown in Listing 11-3, simply create a new Pocket PC project using eMbedded Visual Basic. Add a single command button to the default form, and then add the code shown in Listing 11-3 to this button's click event.

The first interesting bits of the code in Listing 11-3 are the object instantiations. The first object, psEnvelope, is a container for the messages that will be passed back and forth between your Pocket PC and the .NET server. The other object, psTransport, represents support for the underlying communications mechanism—in this case HTTP—by which your SOAP messages will actually travel across the airwaves and Internet.

The following lines set up the envelope appropriately for the specific .NET Web Service that is to be accessed. The MethodName property on psEnvelope is probably pretty self-explanatory; it corresponds exactly to the name of the Web Service method that is to be invoked. The URI must match the namespace of the Web Service's public class.

For each parameter required by the Web Service's function to be invoked, you must call the envelope's CreateParameter method. Pass this method the name of your Web Service function's parameter and the value you wish to send.

> **TIP** *We serialize the SOAP envelope into a simple string and display it in a message box here for instructional purposes only.*

The transport mechanism is configured in the second half of the code. SOAPAction is determined by concatenating the name of the function (getQuote) onto the namespace of the Web Service (as shown in the preceding code). The timeout is set to a particularly long value because the sample service takes a rather long time to respond.

The code concludes by sending the request envelope to the URL of the .NET Web Service and waiting for a response. The response comes back as a raw string that gets promptly stuffed into the strResponse variable. The parse method on the envelope is used to parse this returned string into a proper SOAP response. Since only a single value is being returned, it is then easy to display this value using the Items subcollection within the Parameters collection of the psEnvelope object.

## J2ME

The overall flow of this chapter is from easiest to hardest in terms of .NET interoperability. It should come as no surprise, then, to learn that our next set of devices—J2ME devices—feature less support for .NET than Pocket PCs do. Under J2ME, you have fairly strong support for XML parsing (though not quite full support). There is also some support for SOAP.

## Choosing Your Weapon

The best starting point for using .NET Web Services from J2ME is a technology called kSOAP. This is a creation of the Enhydra.org Open Source software project. You can visit the Web site for this project at http://www.enhydra.org.

To zoom straight to the bit that is of direct interest to us at this point, however, navigate to http://ksoap.enhydra.org.

From here, you can click the Downloads link to get to all of the tools that you need to access .NET Web Services from J2ME devices. The important one for your purposes is the CashConv.zip sample. This will give you a complete project that you can install into the J2ME Wireless Toolkit (downloaded earlier) and use as the basis for creating your own application.

## The Code

Listing 11-4 shows the J2ME Stock Quote client code.

*Listing 11-4. J2ME Stock Quoter Client*

```
import javax.microedition.midlet.*;
import javax.microedition.lcdui.*;
import java.io.*;
import javax.microedition.io.*;


import org.ksoap.*;
import org.kxml.*;
import org.kxml.io.*;
import org.kxml.parser.*;

public class FergieStock extends MIDlet implements CommandListener {

    static final String serviceNamespace = "http://pocketdba.com/webservices/";

    Form mainForm = new Form ("Fergie Stock");
    TextField fromField = new TextField ("Symbol :", "ALGX", 4, TextField.ANY);
    StringItem resultItem = new StringItem ("", "");
    Command getCommand = new Command ("Get", Command.SCREEN, 1);
```

```java
public FergieStock () {
  mainForm.append (fromField);
  mainForm.append (resultItem);
  mainForm.addCommand (getCommand);
  mainForm.setCommandListener (this);
}

public void startApp () {
    Display.getDisplay (this).setCurrent (mainForm);
}

public void pauseApp () {
}

public void destroyApp (boolean unconditional) {
}

public void commandAction (Command c, Displayable d) {
  try {
        // build request string

    String from = fromField.getString ();

    ByteArrayOutputStream bos = new ByteArrayOutputStream ();

      SoapObject request = new SoapObject
          (serviceNamespace, "getQuote");

    request.addProperty ("symbol", fromField.getString ());

      ClassMap classMap = new ClassMap();
    classMap.prefixMap = new PrefixMap
      (classMap.prefixMap, "tns",
      "http://pocketdba.com/webservices/");

      SoapEnvelope envelope = new SoapEnvelope (classMap);
      envelope.setBody (request);

    XmlWriter xw = new XmlWriter (new OutputStreamWriter (bos));
```

```
            envelope.write (xw);
                xw.flush ();


                byte [] data = bos.toByteArray();

        System.out.println (new String (data));

            HttpConnection connection = (HttpConnection) Connector.open
    ("http://localhost/Chapter10Server/Service1.asmx",Connector.READ_WRITE);

            connection.setRequestMethod (HttpConnection.POST);
            connection.setRequestProperty ("Content-Type", "text/xml");
            connection.setRequestProperty ("Connection", "close");
            connection.setRequestProperty
            ("Content-Length", ""+data.length);
            connection.setRequestProperty("SOAPAction",
            "\"http://pocketdba.com/webservices/getQuote\"");

        OutputStream os = connection.openOutputStream ();
            os.write (data);
            os.flush ();

        InputStream is=((StreamConnection) connection).openInputStream ();
            int buffSize=200;
            byte[] buff = new byte[buffSize];
            ByteArrayOutputStream bytebuff=new ByteArrayOutputStream(buffSize);
            // read the response
            int eof=0;
            while(eof!=-1) {
               eof=is.read(buff);
               if (eof!=-1) {
                  bytebuff.write(buff,0,eof);
               }
            }

        is.close();

            String response = new String(bytebuff.toByteArray());
            System.out.println (response);

        Reader reader = new InputStreamReader(new
            ByteArrayInputStream(bytebuff.toByteArray()));
            XmlParser parser = new XmlParser (reader);
```

```
                SoapEnvelope resultEnvelope = new SoapEnvelope ();
                resultEnvelope.parse (parser);

                resultItem.setLabel ("amount :");
                String result = (String)resultEnvelope.getResult();
                result = result.substring(0,result.indexOf("."+3);
                resultItem.setText (" "+result);

                os.close ();
                reader.close ();
                connection.close ();
             }
          catch (Exception e) {
              resultItem.setLabel ("Error:");
              resultItem.setText (e.toString ());
          }
      }
   private static byte[] extractXml(byte[] extractFrom){
      byte[] result;
      int off=0;
      boolean nonStop=true;
      for(int i=0;nonStop;i++){
       if (extra ctFrom[i]==60) {
         off=i;
         nonStop=false;
       }
      }
      result=new byte[extractFrom.length -off];
      for(int i=off;i<extractFrom.length;i++){
         result[i-off]=extractFrom[i];
      }
      return result;
   }
}
}
```

## The Walk-Through

In order to run the code shown in Listing 11-4, follow these steps:

1. Extract the CashConv sample downloaded into your
   \j2mewtk\apps directory.

2. Rename the CashConv folder to FergieStock.

3. Navigate to the \j2mewtk\apps\FergieStock\src directory.

4. Rename the CashConv.java file to FergieStock.java.

5. Change around the source code until you get what is shown in Listing 11-4, and then save it.

6. Rename the CashConv.jad file to FergieStock.jad.

7. Change FergieStock.jad's source code until you get what is shown below:

```
MIDlet-1: FergieStock, CashConv.png, FergieStock
MIDlet-Jar-Size: 40598
MIDlet-Jar-URL: FergieStock.jar
MIDlet-Name: FergieStock
MIDlet-Vendor: Sun Microsystems
MIDlet-Version: 1.0
```

8. From the Windows Start menu, choose the J2ME Wireless Toolkit program group.

9. Start up the KToolBar application.

10. Select Open Project.

11. Select FergieStock, and then select Open Project.

12. Click Build.

13  Click Run.

At this point, you should be able to enter a stock symbol and get its price sent back to you. So, how did the code accomplish this? The interesting lines are bold in the preceding code and described next.

At the top of the code appear some import lines. These tell the Java compiler to include support for XML parsing and SOAP (which were included along with the CashConv sample that you just downloaded). You can thank the guys at Enhydra for creating all of this—otherwise your job would be a whole lot harder!

The next line sets the namespace for the Web Service.

**NOTE**    *It is essential that there be a slash at the end of this namespace. Without it, you will get back a cryptic error message that will cause you to rip your hair out trying to understand. Take it from one who knows!*

When you instantiate the SoapObject, you pass it your namespace and the name of the method that you will be invoking. In this case, the addProperty method is used on this object to add the parameters that you wish to pass to your Web Service's method.

Once this object is instantiated, you use a ClassMap object to associate your service's namespace with the prefix "tns." This ClassMap is then passed to the constructor for SoapEnvelope, so that you can begin building the object that you will ultimately pass across the wire to your .NET Web Service. The setBody method on this SoapEnvelope object is passed the text of the request to flesh it out before transmission.

The connection that will ultimately perform this transmission is opened in the next line. The setRequestProperty method of the Connection object is used to set the SOAPAction.

**NOTE**    *It is essential that there not be a slash at the end of* SOAPAction. *Once again, if you have one, you will get a cryptic error message that you will not be able to figure out.*

The final three lines of interest take place after the request has been sent and a response has been received. The response has been loaded into a reader, which is then passed to the XML parser. This XML parser is used by a SoapEnvelope object to convert the raw string into XML and then ultimately into a meaningful SOAP response.

As you can see, J2ME devices give you one less level of abstraction between calling methods and dealing with raw XML than Pocket PCs do. Palm OS is at a lower level still!

## Palm OS

I hate C, and I'm not ashamed to admit it. Almost one-third of this chapter is devoted to listing just three functions from a C application that you will use to invoke a .NET Web Service across the Internet. Still, for those of you who are operating on Palm OS or similar devices (an approach very similar to this would be used on Blackberry RIM devices, for example) you can be thankful that I am the one who had to do the footwork here, rather than you!

## Choosing Your Weapon

In all fairness, a great deal of the footwork has already been done for you by the people at Palm Computing (or whatever the company will be called by the time you read this). They've built a great sample application that encompasses all of the nasty grunt work needed in order to make HTTP connections using the low-level TCP/IP interface of Palm OS. In order to get this sample, follow these steps:

1. Navigate to `http://www.palmos.com`.

2. Click Developers.

3. Under Quick Index, scroll to the Samples link and click it.

4. Click INet Library.

5. Click How to use the INetLib API.

6. Follow the link to download the Windows version of the sample code.

---

 **TIP** *Although this link may easily change, the direct URL at the time of writing is* `http://oasis.palm.com/dev/kb/samples/docs/1709/INetLow.zip`.

---

## The Code

Listing 11-5 shows the code for `MainFormInit` and Listing 11-6 shows the code for `MainFormDoCommand`. Listings 11-7 and 11-8 show the code snippets for `ResponseFormHandleEvent` declarations and `ResponseFormHandleEvent`'s `inetSockReadyEvent`, respectively.

*Listing 11-5. MainFormInit*

```
static void MainFormInit(void)
{
    // 4 Lines of code not reproduced here
       //ControlPtr    ctlP;
     // Numerous lines non reproduced here
       FrmSetFocus(frmP,
           FrmGetObjectIndex(frmP, MainPostDataStringField));


    //-------------------------------
       // Initialize the checkbox to not include the HTTP headers:
       //-----------------------------
       //ctlP = GetObjectPtr(MainIncludeHTTPHeaderCheckbox);
       //CtlSetValue( ctlP, inetInfoBlock.includeHeaders );


    // Code is the same to end of chapter
}
```

*Listing 11-6. MainFormDoCommand*

```
static Boolean MainFormDoCommand(UInt16 command)
{
    Boolean          handled   = false;
      Err              error     = 0;
      Char*            urlP      =
"http://INSERTYOURSERVERIPHERE/chapter10Server/service1.asmx/getQuote";
      Char*            dataP     = MemPtrNew (sizeof(Char) * (100));
      // Numerous lines not reproduced here

   /* case MainUseLz77Checkbox:
  //-----------------------------
      // Get the socket handle from storage:
      //-----------------------------
      error = INetInfo(&inetInfoBlock,
          "get");

   if (!error &&
      inetInfoBlock.Lz77IsPresent == false)
         {
             ctlP = GetObjectPtr(MainUseLz77Checkbox);
             CtlSetValue( ctlP, 0 );
```

```
                if (inetInfoBlock.Lz77Warned == false)
                {
                    FrmAlert(NoLz77Alert);
                    inetInfoBlock.Lz77Warned = true;
                }
            }
            handled = true;
            break; */
// Many lines skipped here
//urlFldP = GetObjectPtr(MainURLStringField);
//urlP    = (Char*) FldGetTextPtr(urlFldP);
//dataP   = (Char*) FldGetTextPtr(
    GetObjectPtr(MainPostDataStringField)); */
    StrPrintF(dataP, "symbol=%s", (Char*)
    FldGetTextPtr(GetObjectPtr(MainPostDataStringField)));
// Several lines skipped here

/* ctlP = GetObjectPtr(MainUseLz77Checkbox);
    if (CtlGetValue(ctlP))
    {
        inetInfoBlock.inetLowConvAlgorithm = ctpConvNoneLZ77;
    }
    else
    {
        inetInfoBlock.inetLowConvAlgorithm = ctpConvNone;
    } */


//-----------------------------
// Set the whether to include HTTP response headers:
//-----------------------------
//ctlP = GetObjectPtr(MainIncludeHTTPHeaderCheckbox);
//inetInfoBlock.includeHeaders = CtlGetValue(ctlP);
// Code is the same to the end
}    // End MainFormDoCommand(UInt16)
```

*Listing 11-7. ResponseFormHandleEvent Declarations Snippet*

```
INetEventType*      inetEventP     = (INetEventType*) eventP;
Boolean             handled        = false;
INetLowInfoType     inetInfoBlock;
static MemHandle    responseBufH   = 0;
Char*               responseBufP   = 0;
```

```
UInt32              bytesRead       = 0;
static UInt32       totalBytesRead = 0;
Int32               waitSecs        = 20;
Int32               timeout         = waitSecs * SysTicksPerSecond();
Boolean             reset           = true;
FormType*           frmP            = FrmGetActiveForm ();
Char*               newTitleP       = MemPtrNew(sizeof(Char) *
(MAX_FORM_TITLE_LENGTH + 1));
Err                 error           = 0;
Char*               price;
Char*               truncit;
```

*Listing 11-8. ResponseFormHandleEvent's inetSockReadyEvent Snippet*

```
case inetSockReadyEvent:
// Many lines of code skipped
responseBufP  = MemHandleLock(responseBufH);
price = (MemPtrNew (StrLen (responseBufP) + 1));
StrCopy (price, StrStr(responseBufP, "/webservices/\">"));
price = &price[15];
truncit = StrStr(price, "</string>");
truncit[0] = '\0';
StrCopy (responseBufP, price);
```

**NOTE** *The preceding code listings are all snippets rather than full code listings to avoid lengthening this book by an unnecessary 50 pages. Instead, please download the full code for this section from* http://www.MobileDotNet.com.

**CAUTION** *Don't forget to insert your server's own IP where indicated in Listing 11-6!*

## The Walk-Through

In order to turn the preceding code listings into code that can actually be run under Palm OS, you must perform quite a bit of work. Fortunately, Palm's decision to provide the INetLib.zip sample on its Web site greatly reduces your work from what it might have been!

1. Extract the INetLib.zip file downloaded earlier.

2. Double-click the INetLib.mcp icon to launch the CodeWarrior project.

3. Allow it to convert itself, if requested.

4. Launch the emulator.

5. Enable debugger.

6. Double-click INetLow.rsrc to start the Constructor.

7. Double-click Main under Forms to open the design view.

8. Click the label 1004 and change its Text property to Stock Symbol:.

9. Click 1001, 1002, and everything above 1006 and press Delete to remove these items.

10. Close the Constructor (by clicking upper-right Close button) and choose Save.

11. Choose Remove Object Code from the Project menu.

12. Alter the three procedures to match Listings 11-5, 11-6, 11-7, and 11-8.

13. Click the green Run arrow to start the program.

14. When execution pauses on the first line, click the green arrow again to proceed.

All of the code that has been altered in Listing 11-5 appears bold. It was all altered to avoid errors owing to the removal of unneeded user interface elements in Steps 6 through 10.

The code in Listing 11-6 is intended to read the symbol entered from the user interface. Once again, most of the commented out code is simply to avoid errors owing to the removal of unneeded user interface elements.

The code in Listing 11-7 contains the variable declarations needed in order to make the code in Listing 11-8 work. This is where the interesting stuff really happens—right at the end. By this point, the request has already been made using the simple POST request format supported by .NET Web Services. For more information on this, examine the test page provided by .NET for your Web Service.

When the response comes back, it will be pure XML. Palm OS devices lack XML parsing capabilities so, as far as we're concerned, this is just a big, long, nasty string. The code at the end of Listing 11-7 treats it exactly as such. It uses string manipulation functions such as StrStr and StrCopy to locate your answer amidst all of the XML nonsense, parse it out, and stuff it into a variable that is about to be displayed on the screen.

We're sure you will agree that this is, by far, the least pleasant of all possible ways to invoke .NET Web Services. The WAP and i-Mode devices that we are about to cover have even less capability than the Palm OS ones.

## WAP and i-Mode

In many ways, WAP and i-Mode phones are the least powerful of all the devices about which you have learned. Their programmability is limited to simple scripting, which denies you access to either XML parsing or network access features. This makes sending and receiving SOAP (or WSDL) content directly from the current generation of WAP and i-Mode phones virtually impossible.

## *Choosing Your Weapon*

Fortunately, however, there are a couple of Microsoft technologies that make talking to these devices much, much easier! The first of these is known as XSLISAPI, and will be discussed in this section. The other is the Mobile Internet Toolkit, which will be the focus of Chapters 12 through 14.

---

 **TIP**  *A potential third Microsoft technology for talking to devices with currently limited programmability would be the .NET Compact Frameworks, discussed in Chapters 15 and 16 of this book. Using the Cross Platform profile of the .NET Compact Frameworks, many of the vendors manufacturing these devices would be afforded the opportunity to add support for running .NET bytecode directly on their devices.*

---

XSLISAPI is what is known as an *ISAPI filter*. This means that it is a piece of code that runs in response to *every single request that comes into your IIS server and every single response that goes out from your IIS server*. Since ISAPI filters sit in between the client and server for every single IIS transaction, they have a unique opportunity to modify data as it travels in either direction. This is what XSLISAPI does.

When requests are made to IIS from mobile devices, XSLISAPI helps IIS to identify the unique markup needs of different clients. For example, if the client is a WAP phone, XSLISAPI tells IIS that this device will need WML; if the device is i-Mode, XSLISAPI will suggest cHTML.

When it comes times for a response to be sent, XSLISAPI performs an even more important function. Using simple XML files stored on the server as its working basis, XSLISAPI can translate that XML into appropriate markup for different devices using the XML Scripting Language (XSL). You can download XSLISAPI version 2.1 directly from Microsoft at http://msdn.microsoft.com/msdn-files/026/002/187/xslisapi21.exe.

Complete instructions for installing the software onto IIS are included in the download package. Follow these instructions to the letter, and you should be good to go. However, the browscap.ini file included in the distribution lacks entries capable of detecting either the UP.SDK WAP emulator or the Pixo i-Mode emulator that we have shown you in this book. Therefore, you will need to add the text shown in Listing 11-9 to the bottom of your \windows\system32\inetsrv\browscap.ini file.

*Listing 11-9. New browscap.ini Entries*

```
; OpenWave SDK Simulator v 4.1 for WML
[*OWG1*]
browser=Openwave.com simulator
target-markup=WML1.1
content-type=text/vnd.wap.wml

; PIXO Internet Microbrowser 2.1
[Pixo-Browser/2.1]
browser=Pixo Internet Microbrowser 2.1
target-markup=CHTML
content-type=text/html
```

**CAUTION** *In order to get the listings shown in the next section to operate properly, you will also need to set the process isolation for your XSLISAPI samples virtual directory to High. This is to allow the use of the SOAP Toolkit directly from Active Server Pages.*

## *The Code*

Listings 11-10 through 11-18 present the code for the example Web Services for WAP and i-Mode.

*Listing 11-10. questions.xml*

```xml
<?xml version="1.0" ?>
<?xml-stylesheet type="text/xsl" server-config="questions-config.xml"
href="questions-HTML.xsl" ?>
<questions>

  <question>
     <display>Stock symbol:</display>
     <variable>symbol</variable>
  </question>

</questions>
```

*Listing 11-11. questions-config.xml*

```xml
<?xml version="1.0" ?>

<server-styles-config>

  <device target-markup="HTML">
    <stylesheet href="questions-HTML.xsl"/>
  </device>

  <device target-markup="WML1.1">
    <stylesheet href="questions-WML11.xsl"/>
  </device>

  <device target-markup="CHTML">
```

```
                    <stylesheet href="questions-HTML.xsl"/>
            </device>

    </server-styles-config>
```

*Listing 11-12. questions-HTML.xsl*

```xml
<?xml version="1.0" ?>
<xsl:stylesheet xmlns:xsl="http://www.w3.org/TR/WD-xsl">
  <xsl:template match="/" >
    <HTML>
      <BODY>
        <form method="post" action="answer.pasp">
          <xsl:for-each select="questions/question">



              <xsl:value-of select="display"/>

            <input>
              <xsl:attribute name="name"><xsl:value-of select="variable"/>
                  </xsl:attribute>
            </input>
            <br/>
            <input type="submit" value="Get Quote"/>

          </xsl:for-each>
        </form>
      </BODY>
    </HTML>
  </xsl:template>
</xsl:stylesheet>
```

*Listing 11-13. questions-WML11.xsl*

```xml
<?xml version="1.0" ?>
<xsl:stylesheet xmlns:xsl="http://www.w3.org/TR/WD-xsl">
  <xsl:template match="/" >
    <xsl:pi name="xml">version="1.0"</xsl:pi>
    <xsl:doctype>wml PUBLIC "-//WAPFORUM//DTD WML 1.1//EN"
```

```
"http://www.wapforum.org/DTD/wml_1.1.xml"</xsl:doctype>
    <wml>
      <card>
        <p>

            <xsl:for-each select="questions/question">
              <xsl:value-of select="display"/>
              <br/>
            </xsl:for-each>

          <input name="symbol"/><br/>
          <anchor>
            <go method="post" href="answer.pasp">
              <postfield>
                <xsl:attribute name="name">symbol</xsl:attribute>
                      <xsl:attribute name="value">&var;(symbol)</xsl:attribute>
              </postfield>
            </go>
          </anchor>

        </p>
      </card>
    </wml>
  </xsl:template>
</xsl:stylesheet>
```

*Listing 11-14. answer.pasp*

```
<?xml version="1.0" ?>
<?xml-stylesheet type="text/xsl" server-config="answer-config.xml" href="answer-
IE.xsl" ?>
<answer>
<%

    Dim x

    Set x = Server.CreateObject("MSSOAP.SoapClient")
    x.ClientProperty("ServerHTTPRequest") = True
    Call x.mssoapinit("http://localhost/Chapter10Server/Service1.asmx?WSDL",
"Service1")

%>
```

```
<price><%= x.getquote (request("symbol")) %></price>

</answer>
```

*Listing 11-15. answer-config.xml*

```
<?xml version="1.0" ?>

<server-styles-config>

  <device browser="IE">
      <stylesheet href="answer-IE.xsl"/>
  </device>

  <device target-markup="CHTML">
      <stylesheet href="answer-CHTML.xsl"/>
  </device>

  <device target-markup="WML1.1">
      <stylesheet href="answer-WML11.xsl"/>
  </device>

</server-styles-config>
```

*Listing 11-16. answer-IE.xsl*

```
<?xml version="1.0" ?>
<xsl:stylesheet xmlns:xsl="http://www.w3.org/TR/WD-xsl">
  <xsl:template match="/" >
    <HTML>
      <BODY>
        <IMG SRC="http://www.pocketdba.com/images/pocketdba.gif" />

        <!-- show the file elements -->
        <xsl:for-each select="answer/price">
          <xsl:value-of select="text()"/>
          <br/>
        </xsl:for-each>
      </BODY>
    </HTML>
  </xsl:template>
</xsl:stylesheet>
```

*Listing 11-17. answer-CHTML.xsl*

```
<?xml version="1.0" ?>
<xsl:stylesheet xmlns:xsl="http://www.w3.org/TR/WD-xsl">
  <xsl:template match="/" >
    <HTML>
      <BODY>

        <xsl:for-each select="answer/price">
          <xsl:value-of select="text()"/>
          <br/>
        </xsl:for-each>
      </BODY>
    </HTML>
  </xsl:template>
</xsl:stylesheet>
```

*Listing 11-18. answer-WML.xsl*

```
<?xml version="1.0" ?>
<xsl:stylesheet xmlns:xsl="http://www.w3.org/TR/WD-xsl">
  <xsl:template match="/" >
    <xsl:pi name="xml">version="1.0"</xsl:pi>
    <xsl:doctype>wml PUBLIC "-//WAPFORUM//DTD WML 1.1//EN"
"http://www.wapforum.org/DTD/wml_1.1.xml"</xsl:doctype>
    <wml>
      <card>
        <p>
          <xsl:for-each select="answer/price">
            <xsl:value-of select="text()"/>
            <br/>
          </xsl:for-each>
        </p>
      </card>
    </wml>
  </xsl:template>
</xsl:stylesheet>
```

## *The Walk-Through*

The first thing that you need in order to get this Web Services example running on WAP and i-Mode is some page that is capable of asking both kinds of devices which stock symbol they want to look up. This function is served by the XML code in Listing 11-10. "But wait," you say, "this is pure XML. I thought that WAP phones wanted WML and i-Mode phones wanted cHTML. What gives?"

What gives is that XSLISAPI automatically applies the appropriate XSL transformations onto this XML file before transmitting it to the client. These translations will (if written properly) transform the XML into WML for WAP phones and cHTML for i-Mode phones. The XML configuration document in Listing 11-11 tells XSLISAPI which scripts to use for which kinds of devices.

The three device nodes in Listing 11-11 refer HTML clients (such as Internet Explorer) to the XSL transformation in Listing 11-12, WML clients to Listing 11-13, and cHTML clients to Listing 11-14, respectively. Each of these XSL scripts had to be handwritten for use with XSLISAPI as, unfortunately, XSLISAPI lacks the ability to translate XML into appropriate markup automatically.

If you use Listing 11-13 as a typical example, this code is really quite simple. It begins by declaring itself as an XML document—which is exactly what all XSL scripts are at heart. Next, it provides some static markup that will be a part of virtually every WML page. Fortunately, WML is itself always well-formed XML, so you needn't worry about any conflicts here.

---

 **CAUTION** *It is important to realize that everything you put into an XSL file for use with XSLISAPI must be well-formed XML. This means, for example, that even though HTML will allow you to use the paragraph element, <p>, without a closing tag, </p>, XSLISAPI will generate an error on this.*

---

The next bit of the XSL script is dynamic. It basically iterates through every question node in the base XML document (Listing 11-11) and outputs its value to the device on a line by itself. This is followed by a combination of static markup and dynamic code that is intended to create a form for submitting any of the values collected by the questions that preceded it. The listing finishes with the static WML needed to properly terminate any WML document.

Now, once the data has been gathered and submitted to the server, how do you generate a dynamic response that is device-appropriate? The answer to this is the use of PASP files. PASP files are ASP files specially designated for processing by XSLISAPI. XSLISAPI expects that the Active Server Page code in any PASP file will always generate a well-formed XML document as its output.

Listing 11-14 is a perfect example of such a file. It begins with static XML that establishes this as an XML document right from the start. The dynamic code in the middle then invokes your Web Service using the COM-based Soap Toolkit that you first encountered in the previous chapter. You use this because, as a COM-based tool, it works with Active Server Pages.

 **NOTE** *Please remember that this PASP script could be run on a machine completely different from the one(s) hosting your Web Service(s).*

Note the presence of the following line in Listing 11-14:

```
x.ClientProperty("ServerHTTPRequest") = True
```

You should add this line to any Active Server Page where you use the SOAP Toolkit. If you don't, you will get a cryptic error message that will have you pulling your hair out.

The configuration file in Listing 11-15 stipulates that the XML output by the PASP in Listing 11-14 will be transformed before transmission by the code in Listings 11-16 through 11-18. Unlike the set of XSL scripts used for the question.xml file, this batch targets Internet Explorer and cHTML clients separately. This is done primarily to demonstrate that it can be done, rather than for any practical purpose. (The only difference is that, under Internet Explorer, you will get a PocketDBA Systems icon on your display in addition to the price of your desired stock).

## Final Thoughts

If you're thinking that using XSLISAPI might be more trouble than its worth, you're not alone. For serving up dynamic markup to WAP, i-Mode, and mobile HTML clients, Microsoft now recommends its Mobile Internet Toolkit (affectionately known as the MIT) software instead. By the time the next three chapters are finished, we'll have you using the MIT just like a pro!

# CHAPTER 12

# The Mobile Internet Toolkit

## Your Mobile Applications' Salvation

So far in this book, we have shown you how to communicate effectively with most Microsoft products using Web Applications and with everything else using Web Services. This has represented an enormous improvement over pre-.NET approaches to multiplatform development, which would often have required some extremely heinous coding.

Even so, you may have been struck by the sense that things could be made even better. Starting with this chapter and continuing until the end of Chapter 14, you will learn how Microsoft's Mobile Internet Toolkit (MIT) does exactly this.

## Getting Started

Before you jump straight into coding with the MIT, you need to first understand what still isn't quite perfect with the approach we have instructed you to take up to this point and how the MIT fixes it.

### Technical Challenges in Building Multidevice Web Applications

So, what's the problem with the .NET approaches we've shown you up to this point? Writing code, maintaining state, and handling errors—that's what!

#### Too Much Coding

In the previous chapter, we showed you how to invoke .NET Web Services from virtually every kind of mobile device that is currently popular:

- Internet Explorer

- Pocket PC

- WAP (WML)

- i-Mode (cHTML)

- Palm OS

- J2ME

We were able to show you how to do these things because our job with PocketDBA Systems requires being constantly informed about developing for virtually every kind of wireless platform. And let us tell you something, you don't want this kind of responsibility!

The number of different devices on the market and approaches to developing for them seems to double just about every six months. Just as soon as you have mastered a certain skill, such as C development for Palm OS, something happens that makes that approach seem completely antiquated. If you value your peace of mind and family time anywhere near as much as we do, there has got to be a better way than having to know everything about everything.

 **NOTE** *It is also worth noting the massive labor costs involved in finding and retaining people skilled in the really obscure platforms (like the Newton, for example).*

Besides the resources consumed in having to learn about all of the different mobile platforms, there is also the time required to create custom code for each of these platforms. In Chapter 7, you created a single ASP-era application that was capable of interacting with all of the platforms previously listed. You should recall that besides making the server software approximately three times longer than it needed to be, it also required the creation of special client software for a few of the platforms.

The new Web Services version we showed you how to create in Chapters 10 and 11 has greatly improved this situation. Now you have a single, XML-based piece of server code. If you are in a position to provide strictly server software, then your job is done. You have saved time both in the learning department and in the creation of the code itself.

Unfortunately, you may also be called upon to get involved with the clients. As you saw in the previous chapter, if these clients directly support WSDL, then this task is a piece of cake. On the other hand, when the clients don't support WSDL—or when they don't even directly support XML—then you have to write additional code.

## Maintaining State

One of the worst problems associated with maintaining state on mobile devices is dealt with wonderfully by .NET right out of the box. This has to do with the fact that some devices can't support cookies, which form the basis of identifying individual client sessions in many Web-based platforms. .NET is typically smart enough to work around problems like this via URL-based session identifiers and hidden fields.

The use of hidden fields to contain session state can become problematic on small devices, however. The reason for this is that the amount of data being maintained in session state can actually become too large for the limited amount of memory in these devices to maintain.

## Handling Errors

Wireless devices present two key challenges in the area of error handling. The first of these is common to almost all mobile development platforms. If a server-based application encounters an error and returns an HTTP status code that indicates this fact, many mobile devices will display their own internal error messages rather than whatever text is returned by the server. This makes trouble-shooting bugs in wireless applications difficult sometimes, because it is impossible to see the actual error messages that are being generated.

The other problem is more specific to .NET. One of the wonderful things about .NET is that it can give very long, detailed error messages when config-ured to do so. This can, however, become a problem when mobile devices are involved.

On one hand, most devices don't have the screen size to accommodate these messages without a great deal of scrolling. On the other hand, this amount of text is enough to actually crash some of the less powerful devices by causing them to run out of memory. This is a bad thing.

## The Mobile Internet Toolkit to the Rescue!

As you might have guessed from the title of this chapter and the rather elaborate setup, it is the MIT that waves a magic wand and makes all of these issues disap-pear for us.

## The Adaptive User Interface

The MIT has what is known in the business as an *adaptive user interface*. This means that depending on the client connecting to it, MIT can alter its output accordingly. You saw minor examples of this process in action earlier in Chapter 9 with the IE Web Controls.

The MIT carries this process several steps further. Using the MIT, you can create Mobile Web Applications that can automatically serve up HTML to browser-based clients and then turn around and serve up equivalent WML to WAP-based clients or cHTML to i-Mode clients.

This is a great thing for developers for a couple of reasons. First, by using the MIT, you are saved the time and effort associated with having to port your application to every conceivable mobile platform. Instead, you just create a single, server-based application and let the MIT take care of the client details.

The other benefit is that, by using the mobile controls that form the foundation of the MIT, you can save yourself the headache of having to learn the inner workings and markup requirements of multiple client devices. As one example of this, a Command button under the MIT is a Command button whether it is being served up to an HTML, cHTML, or WAP client (you will learn more about this in the next section).

## Maintaining State in a Device-Friendly Manner

As we mentioned previously, .NET would ordinarily maintain state in hidden fields that are sent back and forth between client and server. This becomes problematic on some mobile devices because their limited RAM may not be sufficient to store all of the state data. It should also be mentioned that mobile devices have such slow connections that sending the complete session state round-trip on every request is not always such a good idea.

For this reason, the MIT stores its session state on the server. This is similar to the way in which traditional Active Server Pages stored their session state. One key difference, however, is that the MIT uses URL-based session identifiers rather than cookies. This prevents any problems with devices that don't support cookies.

A more difficult problem to overcome is the tendency of mobile devices to support (and require) the constant flipping around among multiple screens that are cached on the client. This can easily cause any state data that is stored on the server to become stale and out of sync with the current state of the client.

The MIT overcomes this obstacle by maintaining a history of session states for each session. It also generates a unique reference number for each screen that can be sent back to the server. This way, the MIT can always identify what point in the session state a given client is at and match it up with the appropriate point in the session data that is stored on the server.

Of course, as complicated as all of this sounds, the only thing you really have to remember is this: *the MIT is capable of automatically overcoming all of the most common barriers to maintaining state on wireless devices.* That's good news, eh?

### Bombing in a Device-Friendly Manner

No developer likes to see errors. On the other hand, given the choice between seeing an error that reads

```
Error encountered.
```

and seeing one that reads

```
Error encountered.
Line 148.  Variable numberOfDumbCommentsByMyBossInOneDay undefined (probably huge).
```

there is no doubt that the vast majority of developers would instantly choose the latter of these two. Well, Microsoft can't do anything for us to make our error messages wittier (or to decrease the number of dumb comments made by our bosses in a single day), but it can help to make the error message returned by our mobile devices more verbose.

The MIT preserves verbose error messages on mobile devices by returning HTTP Success error codes, even in the case of fatal errors. It does this because, on many devices, returning an HTTP error code will cause any additional text (such as the server's error message) to not be displayed. This may be what most end users prefer—but it has made debugging mobile applications in the past truly nightmarish. With the MIT, you will always get the most detailed error messages possible.

On the other hand, .NET's standard error messages are a little too lengthy for the purposes of most wireless devices. For this reason, the MIT automatically truncates the error messages it sends to mobile devices. You get enough data to know that an error has occurred and what caused it, but not enough to do a complete stack trace. If you want this level of detail, you can always avail yourself of the excellent debugging facilities of VS .NET—all of which are still available when using the MIT.

### Setting Up

Setting up to use the Mobile Internet Toolkit means getting the code, putting it on your machine, and making sure that it works.

## Acquiring the Bits

The Mobile Internet Toolkit is a separate download as of Beta 2 and is expected to remain so until after the official release of VS .NET. In order to get your hands on the bits then, simply follow this procedure:

1. Navigate to http://www.asp.net.

2. Follow the link to the ASP.NET Mobile Web SDK.

3. Click Download.

4. If you are using Internet Explorer, you may be prompted to accept a licensing agreement at this point. Do so.

5. Save the file, mobileit.exe, anywhere you like on your local disk.

 **CAUTION** *For some reason, at the time of writing, the Mobile Internet Toolkit is still listed as the ASP.NET Mobile Web SDK on this site. This is the name by which the technology shipped prior to the release of Beta 2 of Visual Studio .NET. Be aware that the link on* http://www.asp.net *is likely to change to match the Beta 2 naming standard by the time you read this.*

## Installing the Software

Installing the software comprises two steps. First, you need to run the Windows installer program to put all of the required components on your computer and make sure that they are registered properly with your operating system. Secondly, you need to run a quick test to verify that everything went properly during installation.

### Going through the Setup Wizard

To start the installation, begin by locating the mobileit.exe file that we instructed you to download in the section "Acquiring the Bits." Once you have found it, double-click it to launch the Windows installer.

The first screen is just a welcome message, so click Next. At this point, you should accept the license agreement, unless you have some reason for doing otherwise (in which case, you will be unceremoniously dumped out of the program and will not be able to use the Mobile Internet Toolkit).

You should be given two choices for installation style: Complete and Custom. Selecting Custom and clicking Next can be a good way in situations like this to find out exactly what is being installed on your computer. You can always click the Back button to return to the screen with the installation style options once you have seen what files are about to be transferred to your system.

I recommend choosing the Complete installation because it is a small installation and unlikely to have any adverse impact on a properly functioning .NET computer. Once you have made your selection and clicked Next, you should be at a point where clicking Finish will complete the Mobile Internet Toolkit's installation onto your system.

### Verifying the Results

Conventional wisdom would dictate that, once you've finished installing the Mobile Internet Toolkit, you should restart your Windows computer in order for the changes to take effect. With .NET, this isn't needed. Based upon our experiences thus far installing the MIT on more than 20 different computers, we are inclined to believe .NET's claims at this point.

So, when the MIT installer is finished, simply try launching VS .NET and seeing what happens. If the installation has worked at all, you should now be able to access a Mobile Web Application project type from your New Project dialog box, as shown in Figure 12-1.

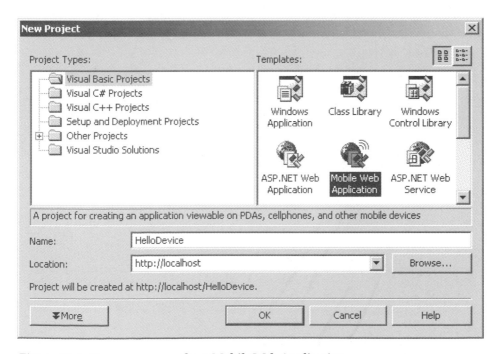

*Figure 12-1. Now you can make a Mobile Web Application.*

A more debatable part of the equation is whether or not the appropriate .NET assemblies have been registered with and accepted by the instance of Internet Information Server (IIS) running on your machine. To test this, follow these steps:

1. Choose Visual Basic Projects under Project Types in the New Project dialog box.

2. Click Mobile Web Applications under Templates.

3. Enter the name HelloDevice for your project.

4. Click OK.

5. Click the Form object in the Design pane of the IDE twice *slowly* (so that they are interpreted as two separate clicks rather than a single double-click).

6. Enter the text "Hello, Device!" into the Form object.

7. Press F5 to run your new creation.

If you get the words "Hello, Device" to appear in Internet Explorer at this point, then your system is properly set up to use the Mobile Internet Toolkit. Admittedly, this isn't a very impressive demonstration—we leave that to the exercise at the end of this chapter.

## Using the Mobile Controls

And now, it is time for you to have some real fun. If you examine the HelloDevice project that you just created in the VS .NET IDE for a moment, you will notice that a new Mobile Web Forms palette has been added to the Toolbox pane, as shown in Figure 12-2.

*Figure 12-2. The Mobile Web Forms palette*

Let's take a look at each of these in turn and discover what they can do for you. As you read about each of these controls, please bear in mind always that their primary value proposition is their ability to work equally well on any of the supported .NET client platforms. This means whenever you use one of these controls in a Mobile Web Application, you can expect it to appear correctly on any Internet Explorer (5 and better), Pocket PC, WAP, or cHTML (i-Mode) device.

## Containers

The containers are in some ways the most important of all the new mobile controls. Paradoxically, they are also the ones that receive the least amount of attention. For although they are ubiquitous in MIT usage, their usefulness is often obscured by that of the controls they serve to contain.

### MobilePage

The prime example of a container that is enormously useful but almost always ignored is the MobilePage container. The MobilePage container is, in fact, so important that it is a required part of every MIT-based page. On the other hand, it can't be found anywhere on the Mobile Web Forms palette.

So, how is this possible? To find out the answer, switch your new HelloDevice application into code view mode by right-clicking an unused portion of the application's user interface and choosing View Code from the pop-up context menu. The relevant lines of code read as follows:

```
Public Class MobileWebForm1
Inherits System.Web.UI.MobileControls.MobilePage
```

What this is telling you is that the entire class upon which this page is based is derived or inherited from the MobilePage class within the MobileControls namespace. This is a key requirement for creating Mobile Web Applications—every page must inherit from MobilePage.

The easiest way to accomplish this inheritance is simply to always use the VS .NET IDE to add new Mobile Web Forms to your Mobile Web Applications. To try this for yourself, follow these steps:

1.  Right-click HelloDevice in the Solution Explorer.

2.  Choose Add and then Add Web Form from the pop-up context menus.

3.  Click Mobile Web Form.

4.  Name your new Mobile Web Form MyOtherPage.aspx and click Open.

5.  Add the text "Changing mobile pages is usually overkill" to Form1 on your new mobile page.

We will explain the full significance of the final step shortly. For the time being, suffice it to say that each mobile page in your application will correspond to exactly one distinct URL within your application. There is some additional overhead associated with navigating between different URLs in a mobile application, so unless you have reason to do otherwise, you should always try to use multiple forms within single pages—rather than multiple pages.

**TIP** *One legitimate reason for using multiple mobile pages would be if you needed to present multiple entry points into your application to the outside world. For example, you might have one mobile page for use by novice users of your application. Another mobile page might present a more sophisticated user interface to expert users.*

## Form

To illustrate our next point, try dragging a `Panel` control to any location on your application's user interface *except the portion currently occupied by the existing Form*. Rather than getting the panel that you might have expected, you will instead get what might be termed an error control. The error reads as follows: "This control must be placed in a Form or Panel control, or within a template. Please move or delete this control."

You will get the same kind of error if you try the same thing with any of the other controls on the palette. If you apply logic to the situation, you will soon realize another fundamental rule of MIT application design: every non-Form control must ultimately be contained by a Form.

For example, you might have a Command button within a panel within another panel within yet another panel. However, at the end of the day, whichever panel is the top-level panel, we guarantee that it will be inside a Form.

**NOTE** *We're purposely putting aside the issue of templates here. Templates are a useful way to increase code reuse and improve the overall look and feel of your applications, but they are in no way essential to the topic at hand.*

Whereas pages correspond in a strict one-to-one relationship with the number of unique URLs in your mobile applications, Forms correspond in a strict one-to-one relationship with the number of unique screens in your application. When constructing a mobile application, whenever you think to yourself, "Okay, now I want to change screens," you should also think to yourself, "okay, now I want to change Forms."

Forms are changed within a page by setting the page's `ActiveForm` property. To see how this is accomplished, follow these steps:

1.  Return to the MobileWebForm1.aspx page under the VS .NET IDE in your HelloDevice application.

2.  Drag a new Form onto any unused portion of the page's user interface.

3.  Add the text "Gee, our second page!" to your new Form (which should be named Form2).

4.  Drag a `Command` control out of the palette and drop it on your original Form (which should be named Form1).

5.  Double-click the new `Command` control to open its code view.

6.  Enter the following line of code in the `click` event for the Command button, and then run your application:

```
Me.ActiveForm = Form2
```

Now, when you click the Command button, you should be taken from the screen reading "Hello, Device!" to one reading "Gee, our second page!" Notice, however, that the base URL remains the same.

## Seeing It on a Phone

Just to prove to you that these really are *mobile* controls, let's take a look at this example now within the UP.Simulator WAP emulator. With the "Hello, Device" page still visible in Internet Explorer, simply copy the URL to your clipboard, and then launch the UP.Simulator. Paste the same URL into its Go textbox. After pressing Enter, you will have one of two experiences:

- The application will work, and you will see the screen shown in Figure 12-3.

- The emulator will generate an error about not being able to interpret HTML.

*Figure 12-3. "Hello, Device" page on the UP.Simulator WAP emulator*

Now, of course, the former result described in the preceding list is the one that you desire. So why is the latter result sometimes generated? In short, we don't know. Maybe it's a bug in the emulator. Maybe it's a bug in this version (Beta 2) of the MIT. In any event, here is how we have resolved the issue when it has occurred:

1.  Choose Open Configuration from the File menu.

2.  Open the ERKO.pho configuration.

3.  Visit your new mobile application using this configuration.

4.  Use the same Open Configuration option to switch back to the OWG1.pho file—if you desire.

Strangely enough, this seems to fix the problem. As you enter both valid and invalid stock symbols, you may notice some additional minor weirdness. The rule is to always try your application a few times before you decide that it simply won't work. The good news is this weirdness seems to fade away completely on actual phones—the Mobile Internet Toolkit is a really solid bit of code of which Microsoft should really be quite proud.

## Normal Controls

The controls that I refer to as "normal" are the ones that you will spend the majority of your time coding. They fall into three broad categories: I/O, validators, and "special" controls.

### I/O Classes

Almost every modern programmer can relate instantly to the I/O classes. Virtually every modern programming platform (.NET, Java, COM, and so on) has analogs for the functionality embodied by these controls. Their purpose is simply to facilitate the transfer of information to and from the end user of a device.

#### *Label*

Labels are dead easy to understand! As a general rule, whenever you have text that you would like to display that is *not* subject to editing by the end user, it should be in a Label control. We violated this rule in our HelloDevice application in order to keep things simple by adding text directly to the Form controls. In order to see one advantage of using Label controls, try the following:

1. Erase the text "Gee, our second page!" from Form2.

2. Drag a label onto Form2.

3. Add the following line to the end of the Command button's click event:

```
Label1.Text = "It is now " & Now
```

4. Run the program and click the Command button to see the difference.

As you now understand, the use of Label controls allows you to generate dynamic output in your applications programmatically.

**TIP**   *Text that is in specific controls, rather than just in Forms, can also be better formatted by .NET adaptive user interface logic.*

### TextBox

A TextBox control is to input what a Label control is to output. By dropping a textbox on a Form control, you gain the ability to receive input from your application's end user and process it in some way. Try this: drag a TextBox control onto Form1 in your HelloDevice project. Next, change the line that currently reads

```
Label1.Text = "It is now " & Now
```

to read

```
Label1.Text = TextBox1.Text
```

This will give you the educational (though practically useless) experience of seeing how easy the MIT makes it to enter and process data from mobile devices. This will be especially instructive if you now build this project and access it from the WAP emulator, explained previously.

### *TextView*

The best use for the TextView control is for adding automatic pagination to large amounts of text that must be displayed on mobile devices with limited amounts of screen space. A good example of this would be trying to convey the Gettysburg Address to the typical WAP phone. There are at least three reasons why sending the entire thing at once would be a bad idea:

- It would require an awful lot of scrolling to see the whole thing.

- It would take a really long time to download.

- It might just consume all available memory and crash the phone.

The TextView control protects you from all of these eventualities by using its knowledge of what various devices can handle (in terms of screen and memory size) and using that to break long amounts of text up into multiple pages of more easily managed size. The control also then gives the end user (without any additional effort on your part) the ability to page back and forth through these pieces.

### *Command*

Under HTML and cHTML, Command controls appear as buttons on the user interface of the application. On WAP devices, however, they typically become mapped to one of the soft buttons on the actual hardware of the device. In instances where there are more commands on the Form than soft buttons on the device, one of the soft buttons will typically become a menu that allows the end user to choose between multiple commands.

### *Link*

Links provide a device-independent way to navigate to other URLs from within your Mobile Web Applications. To see this in action, follow these steps:

1. Drag a Link control from the Mobile Web Forms palette in your HelloDevice application to Form1.

2. Set the Link control's SoftKeyLabel property to JUMP.

3. Click the tab labeled "dropdown" inside the Link control's NavigateURL property.

4.   Choose Select URL.

5.   Choose MyOtherPage.aspx and click OK.

6.   Rebuild the application.

You should now be able to view the application under both Internet Explorer and the WAP emulator. On the WAP emulator, you should see that one of the soft buttons is labeled OK initially. If you click this, it will take you to a menu of links with just one member—this member is labeled JUMP. Click this link, and it will take you to the second page of the HelloDevice application.

### *Image*

The Image control is truly a beautiful piece of technology. In order to fully understand its proper use, however, you must first have a grasp of a concept in the MIT that we will refer to as the *Device Filter Property override*. We will discuss this concept fully in the next chapter, so we will reserve more complete coverage of the Image control for later.

For now, suffice it to say that the use of Device Filter Property overrides with the Image control allows your application to display different images for different clients. This is important because the image formats supported by one client (for example, WAP phones that require WBMP-format graphics) may not be supported by others.

### *SelectionList*

The SelectionList control provides a more sophisticated, multiple-choice approach to soliciting input from the end-user of your application. In its simplest form, it will appear as a drop-down combo list on an HTML client. On WAP devices, it interfaces nicely with the soft buttons to create a convenient, menu-based way to select a single value from a list of virtually any (reasonable) size.

To see the SelectionList control in action, follow these steps:

1.   Remove the TextBox control from Form1 on the MobileWebForm1 page of your HelloDevice application.

2.   Drag a SelectionList application from the palette onto Form1.

3.   Click the ellipses inside the new list's Items property.

4.   In the Selection1 Properties dialog box, click Create new item.

5.  Set the new item's text to "One" and its value to "Alpha".

6.  Create however many additional items you like, and then click OK.

Once you have finished this process, change the line in Command1's code that currently reads

```
Label1.Text = TextBox1.Text
```

to read

```
Label1.Text = SelectionList1.Selection.Text
```

When this is done, you may now try running the application under both Internet Explorer and the WAP emulator. Select any value from the selection list and click the button to see it echoed to you on the next screen. Now, if you change the preceding line of code to read

```
Label1.Text = SelectionList1.Selection.Value
```

and rerun the application, you will see that it is now populating the label on the second screen with the associated values in the selection list, rather than the text of the items themselves. This could be useful in instances when you wish to show the end user something understandable, for example, "pi," but use a related value in your code (in this case, 3.14. . .).

## Validator Classes

With a single exception, the Validator classes under MIT all behave exactly the same as their counterparts in the standard .NET Web Applications. As a reminder, the validators are listed here:

- RequiredFieldValidator

- CompareValidator

- RangeValidator

- RegularExpressionValidator

- CustomValidator

- ValidatorSummary

**CAUTION** *The single exception alluded to in the preceding text is the fact that the Mobile* ValidatorSummary *does not inherit from its Web Forms counterpart. For this reason, you can't access any of the properties that would ordinarily be able to affect this control's output.*

## Special Controls

The "special" controls are the ones that serve very specific purposes, and as such will probably not form a part of every mobile application that you create.

### Call

The Call control allows you to add functionality to your application that will facilitate the dialing of outbound telephone calls. Needless to say, this won't work on non-phone clients. On Internet Explorer, for example, it simply renders as the word "Call" followed by the telephone number specified by the developer. A developer can specify the number to be dialed via the Call control's aptly named PhoneNumber property.

On WAP devices, this control will typically map to one of the soft keys. Pressing the soft key will then dial the specified number. On the emulators, of course, outbound calls are not possible!

### Calendar

On HTML clients (Internet Explorer and Pocket IE), the mobile calendar is rendered rather like a less ornate version of the standard Web Application Calendar control. On cHTML (i-Mode) and WML (WAP) devices, however, the calendar is rendered as a peculiar, menu-based construction. The first menu that appears is shown in Figure 12-4 on the Pixo Internet Microbrowser.

*Figure 12-4. The mobile Calendar control*

The first option shown on the menu will allow you to select the current day (or whatever day was last entered into the Calendar control, if this isn't your first page hit). The second option allows the entry of a specific date in the format MMDDYYYY.

 **TIP**  *If you enter an invalid date here, the control will automatically correct you.*

The third option presents you with a list of months centered on the current month. The exact length of this list is based on the MIT's knowledge about the size of your client's display. Options are automatically provided for paging to both earlier and later months than those shown.

Selecting a given month takes you to a list of all the weeks within that month. Selecting a week takes you to a list of all the dates within that week.

**NOTE** *We have to admit, we think that this is a pretty slick solution to a tricky problem in multiplatform user interfaces! Contrast this to the way that Java might attempt to solve the same problem. Java would require only the client capabilities of the least powerful device supported, which in this case would be a WML phone with a three-line display. Phones with larger displays and even Internet Explorer would just have to suffer right along with the "cheap phone" owners.*

### AdRotator

AdRotator allows you to devote a portion of your Mobile Web Application's screen space to advertising. As its name implies, AdRotator can automatically rotate these ads for you to avoid showing the same ad over and over again. There's nothing in the technology of this control that can't be gleaned from the documentation based upon your understanding of the preceding material, so we won't discuss this any further.

## Data

The data-binding capabilities of the List and ObjectList controls are where the Mobile Internet Toolkit really shows its potential as an enterprise-grade application platform.

## List

The List control is similar to the SelectList control that was shown in the previous section. One noteworthy difference is that on HTML clients, this control renders by default as a full list rather than a drop-down list. This gives it a different appearance and slightly different user interface behavior.

Data binding to the List control is also particularly easy. We haven't discussed much about data so far in this book because this is really a .NET topic that deserves a book all by itself. However, if you follow the steps below, you should be pleasantly surprised by how easy it is to get some simple data binding going without knowing much about .NET data access at all.

1. Open any Mobile Web Application (create a new one if you need to, or reuse the HelloDevice example, if you still have it).

2. Hover over the Server Explorer tab in the upper-right corner of the VS .NET IDE.

3. Once the tab expands into a new palette, expand the node that ends with NETSDK.Northwind.dbo (this is a sample database that is included with VS .NET).

4. Expand the Tables node.

5. Drag the Employees table onto any unused portion of your application's user interface.

6. At this point, icons should appear on the display for both SqlConnection1 and SqlDataAdapter1. Right-click SqlDataAdapter1 and choose Configure Data Adapter from the pop-up context menu.

7. Step through the wizard presented, accepting all the defaults until you get to a SQL dialog box like the one shown in Figure 12-5.

8. Alter the SQL here to read SELECT EmployeeID, LastName, FirstName FROM Employees.

9. Step through the wizard until it finishes.

10. Right-click SqlDataAdapter1 and choose Generate Dataset from the pop-up context menu.

11. Name your dataSet MyDataSet and click OK.

12. Add a List control to a Form in your Mobile Web Application.

13. Select MyDataSet1 as the DataSource property for your List control.

14. Select Employees as the DataMember property for your List control.

15. Select LastName as the DataTextField property for your List control.

16. Select EmployeeID as the DataValueField property for your List control.

17. Make sure that the Page_Load code for your page looks like Listing 12-1.

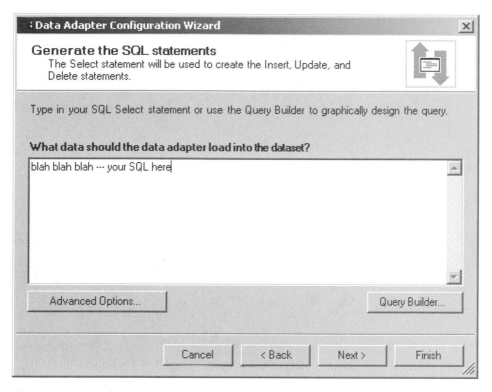

*Figure 12-5. Configuring your data adapter's SQL*

*Listing 12-1. Binding Your List to Its Data*

```
Private Sub Page_Load(ByVal sender As System.Object, ByVal e As_
System.EventArgs) Handles _ MyBase.Load
        'Put user code to initialize the page here
        SqlDataAdapter1.Fill(MyDataSet1)
        List1.DataBind()
    End Sub
```

At this point, you should be able to view your list on any of the supported devices and see the data from the Employees table in it.

## ObjectList

The ObjectList can be thought of as the "List Deluxe." It features two main enhancements over the standard List control discussed in the preceding section. The first of these is the fact that it can display more than a single column of data at a time. The second, potentially more important, of the two is that is automatically allows you to "punch down" to specific records within the list and execute arbitrary commands that you define.

As with many of the other mobile controls, actually using this on a page will make its functionality much clearer:

1. Remove the List control from the previous project.

2. Drag an ObjectList control onto the space where the List control had been.

3. Set the ObjectList control's DataSource property to MyDataSet1.

4. Set the ObjectList control's LabelField property to LastName.

5. Click the ellipses button in the ObjectList's TableFields property to get to the ObjectList1 Properties dialog box, as shown in Figure 12-6.

6. Move all of the fields from AvailableFields to SelectedFields and click OK.

7. Click the ellipses button in the control's Commands property to get the ObjectList1 Properties dialog box, as shown in Figure 12-7.

8. Use the Create New Command button to create three commands, named anything you like, with the labels "Fold", "Spindle", and "Mutilate".

9. Click OK to close the dialog box.

10. Set the ObjectList control's DataMember property to Employees.

11. Set the ObjectList control's DefaultCommand property to any of the commands you created in Step 8.

12. Change the line in your Page_Load event reads List1.DataBind() to ObjectList1.DataBind().

13. Finally, click F5 to run your application under Internet Explorer.

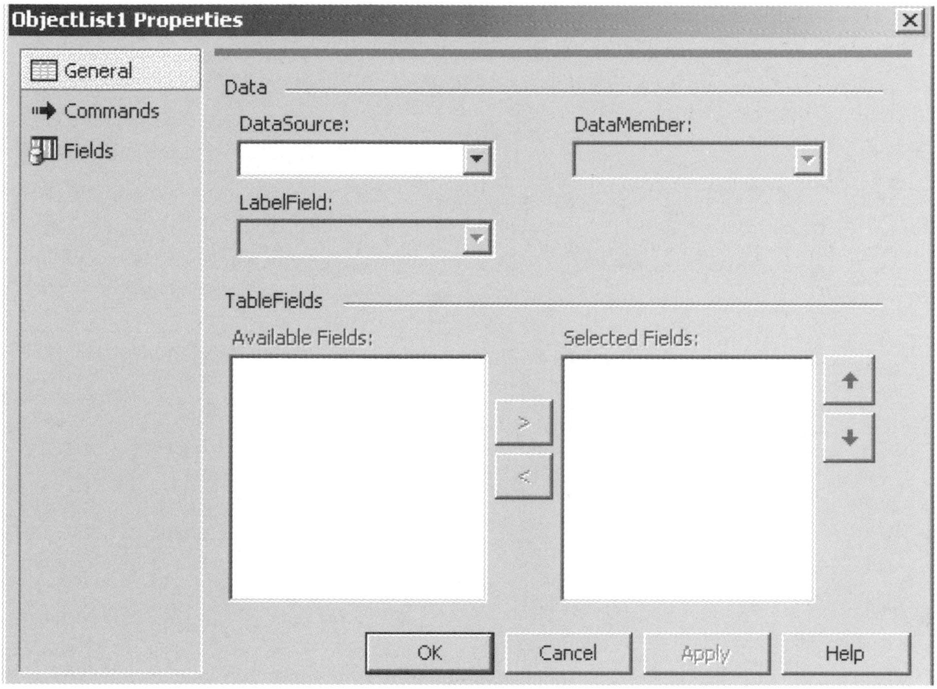

*Figure 12-6. Adding fields to the ObjectList control*

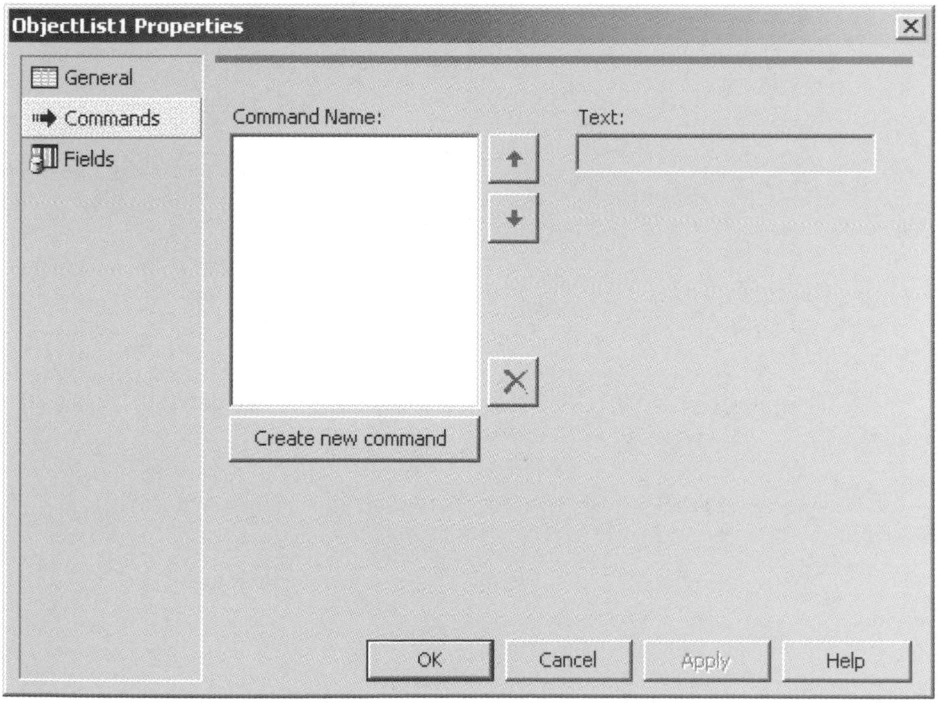

*Figure 12-7. Adding commands to the ObjectList control*

The first thing you should be struck by when looking at the `ObjectList` control in Internet Explorer is how much data is being presented. Figure 12-8 shows a sample object list. This will obviously require considerable scaling back for display on mobile devices.

| First_Name | Last_Name | ID | Status | Group_ID | |
|---|---|---|---|---|---|
| Web | Site | 1 | ACTIVE | 1 | More |
| Sample | ChannelGirl | 2 | ACTIVE | 2 | More |
| ADMIN | ACCOUNT | 3 | ACTIVE | 2 | More |
| Sample | ChannelGuy | 4 | ACTIVE | 2 | More |
| Lyle | Wells | 5 | ACTIVE | 3 | More |
| Stephanie | Taddei | 6 | ACTIVE | 5 | More |
| Kevin | Doyle | 7 | ACTIVE | 1 | More |
| Joe | Redd | 8 | ACTIVE | 1 | More |
| Paul | Lawhead | 9 | ACTIVE | 1 | More |
| Peter | Kim | 10 | ACTIVE | 4 | More |
| Maureen | Gallagher | 11 | ACTIVE | 6 | More |
| Ari | Kaplan | 12 | ACTIVE | 3 | More |
| Derek | Ferguson | 13 | ACTIVE | 7 | More |
| Rachel | Greene | 14 | ACTIVE | 3 | More |
| Margaret | LeClair | 15 | ACTIVE | 3 | More |

*Figure 12-8. Object lists can display a lot of data!*

The next thing you should notice is the presence of hyperlinks on the display. All of the hyperlinks on the left of Figure 12-8 are capable of raising `ItemCommand` events at the server for the `ObjectList` control. On one hand, this allows you to respond to something as simple as selecting one of these records.

On the other hand, if you click any of the hyperlinks labeled "More," you will be taken to a special "punch down" view for the chosen record. If you look carefully in this view, you will see hyperlinks for all of the commands that you added in the preceding procedure. Clicking any of these commands will also raise an `ItemCommand` event on the server.

**TIP** *The ability to respond to all of these different commands on the server gives you a tremendous degree of power! You may have been wondering, however, how to tell the various commands apart—since they all raise the same event on the server. This is accomplished by inspection of the special* `ObjectListCommandEventArgs` *object that is passed into the event.*

Before proceeding, you should examine your application under a WAP emulator as well. In this case, the amount of data presented at first is not nearly as detailed, as you can see in Figure 12-9.

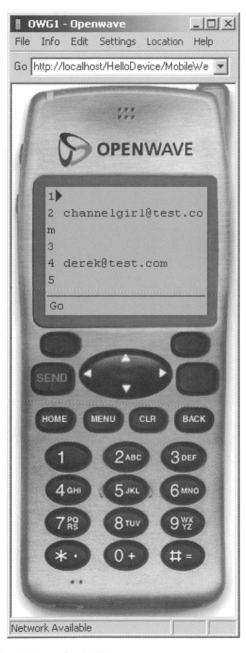

*Figure 12-9. The object list under WAP*

In this model, you must first choose a record on the basis only of that record's LabelField. After this, you may either choose to see additional details (the first option on the next menu), or execute any of the custom commands you have added to the ObjectList control.

In this exercise, you will finally come to the realization that .NET makes creating Web applications a piece of cake for any of the directly supported client devices: Internet Explorer, Pocket PC, WAP, and i-Mode.

## Writing the Server

Most of the construction for this server will take place using the drag-and-drop capabilities of the Visual Studio .NET IDE.

### The Code

Listing 12-2 shows the code for the mobile stock quote application's Command button.

*Listing 12-2. The Mobile Stock Quote Application's Command Button*

```
Private Sub Command1_Click(ByVal sender As System.Object,_
_
ByVal e As System.EventArgs) Handles Command1.Click

        Dim price As String
        Dim ws As localhost.Service1 = New localhost.Service1()

        If Page.IsValid Then

            Me.ActiveForm = Form2

            If ws.getQuote(TextBox1.Text, price) Then
                Label1.Text = price
            Else
                Label1.Text = "No such stock!"
            End If
```

```
    End If

End Sub
```

## The Walk-Through

Most of the time you spend creating Mobile Web Applications will be spent building user interfaces. The steps in this section explain how to do this for the example server in this exercise, as well as how to add the appropriate code required to make it a fully functional Mobile Web Application.

1.  Start the Visual Studio .NET IDE.

2.  Under Project Types, select Visual Basic Projects.

3.  Under Templates, select Mobile Web Application.

4.  Enter the name **Chapter12Exercise**.

5.  Under Location, choose the Web server where you have already installed the Mobile Internet Toolkit.

6.  Click OK.

7.  Drag a `TextBox`, `Command`, and `RegularExpressionValidator` control from the Mobile Web Forms tab on the toolbox to the Form1 control on the Design window.

8.  Add another Form control to the Design window, just beneath Form1.

9.  Drag a `Label` control onto your new Form, Form2.

10. Right-click References in the Solution Explorer and choose Add Web Reference from the pop-up context menu.

11. In the Address field of the Add Web Reference dialog box, enter the address for the Web Service you built in Chapters 10 and 11 and press Enter.

12. If done correctly, the Add Reference button should become available. Click this button.

13. Double-click the Command button on your UI to open its code view, and then enter the code from Listing 12-2.

14. Change the RegularExpressionValidator's properties as follows:

    - ErrorMessage = Invalid stock symbol!
    - ControlToValidate = TextBox1
    - ValidationExpression = [a-zA-Z]{4}

15. Change the Command control's Text property to Get Quote.

16. Verify that your UI now looks like Figure 12-10.

*Figure 12-10. The mobile stock quote application*

 **CAUTION**  *It is important that there always be clear paths of network accessibility between the Web server(s) running your Web applications and those hosting any Web Services upon which they might rely. In the case of the preceding application, we first constructed it on a public Web server, but had it referencing a Web Service being served up from a laptop. This worked fine while we were still in Design mode. However, when we finally tried to actually run the application, it failed immediately after hitting Get Quote. The reason for this is that the laptop is protected by a firewall that prevents access by outside machines. The public Web server was, therefore, unable to contact the Web Service running on the local machine.*

## Trying the Clients

If you are using one of the client devices that are directly supported by .NET, then you rarely (if ever) need to create a separate client application for your device. For this reason, at this point we will simply be looking at how to test the application under each of the supported client devices.

### Internet Explorer

Internet Explorer is probably the easiest of all the target client devices on which to try out the application. Simply click F5 or choose Run from Visual Studio .NET's Debug menu. You will then be presented with a screen similar to that shown in Figure 12-11. Be sure to try entering both valid and invalid stock symbols!

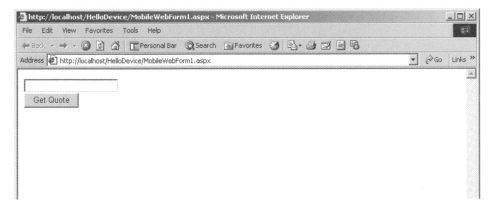

*Figure 12-11. The application under Internet Explorer*

You should also avail yourself of this opportunity to view the source that was generated by the Mobile Internet Toolkit. You can do this by choosing Source from Internet Explorer's View menu. First, examine the <form> tag and, in particular, its ACTION parameter:

```
MobileWebForm1.aspx?__ufps=631008999520208480
```

This is MIT's way of keeping track of its specific point within an ongoing conversation in a given client device. If you submit a page and look at this same bit of source code for the next page that you receive, you will notice that this number has changed.

However, if you were to click the Back button on your browser, you would be using the same number again. This is how MIT would be able to tell that you had navigated backwards, and thus be able to use the appropriate state snapshot for interpreting your actions.

Also of interest in this source code is the presence of a small amount of JavaScript. MIT has detected that you are using Internet Explorer, which it knows to be a JavaScript-enabled client and has therefore sent you some JavaScript to enhance your experience.

 **NOTE**   *Although JavaScript is present on this page, it is not being used for validation of the stock symbol. In order to guarantee platform independence, the mobile versions of the* Validator *controls perform their functions on the server rather than the client.*

## Pocket PC

Once you've gotten the application up and running under Internet Explorer, copy the URL from the address bar and start up the Pocket PC emulator. Choose Internet Explorer from the emulator's Start menu and paste the URL into the emulator's address bar to see how your page will look on the Pocket PC.

 **TIP**   *If the emulator's address bar is not immediately visible when you open up Pocket IE, it may be added to the display by choosing Address Bar from the Pocket IE's View menu.*

When the page has loaded, be sure to try both valid and invalid stock symbols before exiting the emulator.

## WAP

After you've closed your Pocket PC, try viewing the application within the UP.Simulator. (The steps for doing this were covered in the earlier in this chapter in the section "Containers.")

The first thing you should notice while looking at the initial screen is that your Get Quote button has automatically been converted into a WML do command. For this reason, it has been associated automatically with one of the so-called soft keys on the device. If you press F5 while looking at this screen, you will be able to see the complete WML for this page in the Phone Information window. A sample from one of our own sessions is shown in Listing 12-3.

*Listing 12-3. WML for the Application's First Page*

```
<wml>
  <card id="Form1">
    <onevent type="onenterforward">
      <refresh>
        <setvar name="TextBox1" value="PRSF"/>
      </refresh>
    </onevent>
    <p>
      <do type="accept" label="Get Quote">
        <go href="MobileWebForm1.aspx?Ooc=106&__ufps=blah" method="post">
          <postfield name="__VIEWSTATE" value="blah"/>
          <postfield name="__EVENTTARGET" value="Command1"/>
          <postfield name="TextBox1" value="$$(TextBox1:noesc)"/>
        </go>
      </do>
      <input name="TextBox1"/>Invalid stock symbol!<br/>
    </p>
  </card>
</wml>
```

We have replaced (hopefully judiciously) some of the longer, more cryptic identifiers in the preceding code with the word "blah." The first interesting bit of WML occurs within the onevent node. What this basically says is "Whenever this client navigates directly to this card (as opposed to from another card in the deck), make sure to refresh the TextBox1 control with the string 'PRSF'." In this case, PRSF just happens to be a stock symbol that we had looked up (and mocked as another victim of the Internet Crash) shortly before we captured this WML for review.

The next interesting bit of code occurs within the <p> tag. All of the code within this tag is roughly equivalent to the <form> tag within HTML, which is responsible for acquiring an end user's input and then submitting it to the server for further processing. However, in WML, the section that specifies what is to be submitted to the server is separate from the bit that actually gathers the user's input.

The line that will actually gather the input is at the bottom of the code:

```
<input name="TextBox1"/>Invalid stock symbol!<br/>
```

The line that will do the submitting is higher up, inside of the <do> tag. The fields that will be submitted are all denoted by postfield tags. The first two fields are roughly equivalent to hidden HTML form fields, as they have specific values that are not associated with any visible user interface controls. The final <postfield> tag, however, is a field that gets its value directly from the TextBox1 input field shown previously.

The WML for the response is shown in Listing 12-4. There isn't much interesting about it, except to note that IDs for WML cards under MIT always appear to be the same as the ID of the Form mobile control upon which they are based. Recall here that mobile control Forms always exist in an exact one-to-one relationship with visible screens of information in mobile applications.

*Listing 12-4. The WML Response*

```
<wml>
  <card id="Form2">
    <p>13.56<br/>
    </p>
  </card>
</wml>
```

## i-Mode

Trying the application under i-Mode is only slightly more involved than using it under the platforms described in the preceding sections. Follow these steps:

1. Launch the Pixo Internet Microbrowser emulator.

2. Click the right-hand soft button to open the Options menu.

3. Select Open URL using the arrow keys, and then click OK.

4. Enter the URL using the numeric keypad, and then press Enter.

5. Enter a valid or invalid stock symbol.

6. Select the Get Quote button using the arrow keys.

7. Click OK.

At this point, you should be delighted to discover that everything works just wonderfully in i-Mode, as shown in Figure 12-12.

*Figure 12-12. The application in i-Mode*

## So Where Does This Leave Us?

You have now seen how seamlessly the Mobile Internet Toolkit works with those clients that are directly supported by .NET, specifically:

- Internet Explorer

- Pocket PC

- WAP (WML)

- i-Mode (cHTML)

In the next chapter, you will see how the Mobile Internet Toolkit can be expanded to work with devices that are not directly supported by .NET.

# CHAPTER 13

# Extending the MIT

## The Chapter Where You Become a Mobile Internet Toolkit Guru

THE PREVIOUS CHAPTER SHOWED YOU how to use the controls that are available out of the box as a part of Microsoft's Mobile Internet Toolkit. But what if you want to do something that isn't directly supported by these controls? In this chapter, we will show you how.

## Leveraging Mobile Capabilities

In order to extend the Mobile Internet Toolkit, we must drill down several layers deeper into the underlying .NET code than would typically be accessed by most MIT programmers. So, get your spelunker's gear ready—we're about to go digging!

### Using Device Filters

The first, and shallowest, layer beneath the surface of the MIT that most developers see is inhabited by the .NET device filters.

### What Are They?

In the previous chapter, you saw how to build a stock quoting application using just a few of the mobile controls that are available out of the box from the MIT. The nifty thing about this project was that your application was automatically able to support the following without ever having to write code to do so:

- Internet Explorer

- Pocket PC

- WML (WAP)

- cHTML (i-Mode)

All of this was accomplished for you by code existing behind the scenes in the depths of the MIT's internal infrastructure. This code encapsulates a great deal of knowledge and expertise about the differing capabilities of different devices. It knows, for example, that most WAP clients are strictly black and white, whereas most Internet Explorer installations are color. A label that uses red text will therefore be rendered by the MIT with specific font color request in HTML, and without them in WML.

A problem arises, however, whenever the MIT's decisions about adaptation might run counter to the overall design of your application. Consider the case of an application that includes the message "Press the red button to cancel, or the green button to continue." On black-and-white devices, the MIT will ensure the accurate delivery of two monochrome buttons to the device—which will allow the application to function correctly, but make it absolutely impossible for the end user to interact with it properly.

What you really need in an instance like this is some way for the MIT to inform your application about the specific characteristics of the connecting device. Your code can then make some intelligent decisions on this basis and instruct the MIT to take more appropriate actions. In the case of black-and-white devices, for example, you might write code to deliver buttons with different *shapes* rather than colors and text that reads "Press the *square* button to cancel, and the *round* button to continue."

These are exactly the kinds of activities for which device filters were developed. The most common direct use of device filters in MIT applications occurs in conjunction with the DeviceSpecific functionality.


## Demonstrating DeviceSpecific

In the previous chapter, we promised you further explanation of the Image control than was given at that point. The reason we delayed giving a more thorough explanation in the last chapter was that in order to fully understand the Image control, you must also understand the use of DeviceSpecific MIT functionality.

This is because almost every device has a slightly different set of capabilities where images are concerned. To begin with, graphics themselves come in a bewildering assortment of formats. For this reason, it would be absolutely impossible for most devices to support all of those formats—given their considerable resource restrictions.

What happens instead is that some devices support some graphics formats, and other devices support different formats. The question is, if you want to create a multidevice application, which format do you choose to support? Fortunately, under the MIT, you don't have to make this choice.

The Image control under MIT allows the use of device filters to choose different graphics for different devices at runtime, rather than compilation time. To see this capability in action, do the following:

1. Open the Visual Studio .NET IDE.

2. Click New Project.

3. Select Mobile Web Application.

4. Name your project ImageExample and click OK.

5. Drag an Image control onto Form1.

6. Select AppliedDeviceFilters in the Image control's properties list and click the ellipses ( ... ) button.

7. Expand the Available Device Filters drop-down list, as shown in Figure 13-1.

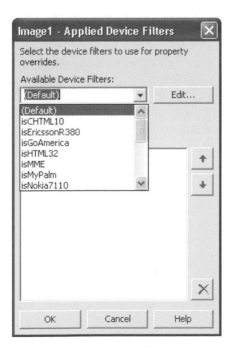

*Figure 13-1. The Applied Device Filters dialog box*

8. Select isUP4x from the drop-down list.

9. Click Add to List.

10. Repeat Steps 7 through 9 for the isPocketIE and (default) device filters also.

11. Click OK.

12. Select PropertyOverrides in the Image control's properties list and click the ellipses button.

13. Under Applied Device Filter, choose isPocketIE on the drop-down list.

14. Under Image URL, enter **http://www.eviloscar.com/images/me&duke.jpg**.

15. Under Applied Device Filter, choose (Default) on the drop-down list.

16. Under Image URL, enter **http://www.eviloscar.com/images/airview.jpg**.

17. Under Applied Device Filter, choose isUP4x on the drop-down list.

18. Using a Web browser, go to **http://www.hicon.nl/ENG/index.html**.

19. Follow the link to the Free WBMP Gallery.

20. Download any of the WBMP images here to a location on your hard disk that can be accessed by IIS.

21. Under Image URL in Visual Studio, enter the URL where the WBMP you just downloaded may be accessed on your machine via the Internet.

22. Run your project and verify that you see a picture of a house under Internet Explorer.

23. Copy the address from Internet Explorer's URL bar and start the Pocket PC emulator.

24. Launch Pocket IE and paste the address into its URL bar. Verify that you see a picture of Derek with Duke under Pocket IE.

25. Start the Openwave WAP emulator.

26. Paste the address into the Go bar and press Enter. Verify that you see the WBMP that you downloaded previously.

**TIP** *If you already have access to WBMP images at your disposal, you may elect to skip Steps 18 through 20.*

You have just witnessed a key capability of the mobile Image control. By specifying a set of device filters, you can use what are called PropertyOverrides to change the control's properties depending upon the specifics of the connecting device. The example we used was changing the Image URL property dependent upon whether the device was a Pocket PC, a particular kind of WAP phone, or something else.

**TIP**   *The specific device filters used in the preceding example were chosen for their ease of comprehension—which makes explaining their use all that much easier. However, as a general coding practice, it is usually better to use those filters that describe the specific* functionality *in which you are interested (for example,* supportsVoiceCalls*) rather than those that target specific device groups (for example,* isMyPalm*). This way, the burden of researching and maintaining the device capabilities catalogs remains with the MIT (read Microsoft), rather than yourself.*

When you connected using a regular browser, the (Default) device filter was used, and you saw the image that we associated with it—a house. When you connected using a Pocket PC, the isPocketIE device filter was used and you saw the image of Derek with Duke. And finally, when you connected with the Openwave emulator, the isUP4x device filter was invoked and you saw whatever WBMP you downloaded previously.

## The Code behind the Scenes

GUIs are easy—but for ultimate flexibility, things go better with code!

### Why Any Additional Code?

The preceding example was very good, but it revealed a limitation with the out-of-the-box MIT. Whenever we wanted to make a choice based on a device filter, we had to choose between a finite list of options with which Microsoft had already provided us. All of the filters for the base Beta 2 installation are described in Table 13-1.

*Table 13-1. MIT's Out-of-the-Box Device Filters*

| NAME | PURPOSE |
|------|---------|
| isCHTML10 | Indicates whether or not the device is an i-Mode device |
| isEricssonR380 | Indicates that the device is a specific kind of WAP phone |
| isGoAmerica | Specifies the GoAmerica browser, which is used on some BlackBerry and Palm OS devices |
| isUP3x | Specifies the device is version 3 of the UP.Simulator WAP browser |
| isWML1.1 | Indicates whether the device is any kind of modern WML device |
| prefersGIF | Indicates whether the device prefers the GIF image format |
| prefersWBMP | Specifies whether or not the device prefers the WBMP image format |
| supportsColor | Determines whether the device has a color display |
| supportsCookies | Specifies whether the device can send and receive cookies |
| supportsJavaScript | Determines whether JavaScript works on the device |
| isHTML32 | Specifies a standard Web browser |
| isMME | Specifies Microsoft's own Mobile Explorer |
| isMyPalm | Indicates the MyPalm browser, which is used on some Palm OS devices |
| isNokia7110 | Indicates a specific kind of WAP phone |
| supportsVoiceCalls | Specifies whether calls can be made from the device |

As you can see, Microsoft has done a very good job of thinking of just about every piece of information that you might want to know about a remote device's capabilities. But what if you wanted to know something different? For example, at PocketDBA Systems we often need to know whether a device connects to the Internet via a direct connection (like Pocket PCs) or a proxy connection (like Palm VIIs). How can you add support for this to the MIT?

Well, your first option would be to make this determination within the code for your own applications and completely outside the framework for the

MIT. There are a couple of reasons why this would probably not be the best choice, however.

First, any code that you put into your own applications rather than the MIT becomes code that is harder to reuse in other applications. If you are only adding sensing for a single, rarely used capability, this might not be such a downside. On the other hand, if you have some capability that you know you will want to refer to frequently from many application, why not put it into the MIT, and in so doing give yourself the ability to use it anywhere that you use the MIT?

The other reason for using the MIT's built-in extensibility mechanisms is one of supportability. This means if everyone else in the world is using the MIT to do their custom device filters, then everyone else in the world becomes a potential resource for helping you out of jams. On the other hand, if you do something that is completely off the wall and customized, to quote the theme to the movie *Ghostbusters*, "Who ya gonna call" when something breaks?

## How to Make It Happen?

The goal is to extend the MIT to automatically sense whether or not a certain device connects to the Internet via the use of a proxy, as opposed to having a direct TCP/IP-style connection. In order to make this happen, you have to do the following things:

1. Come up with a snazzy name for this capability.

2. Add this new capability to your application's web.config file.

3. Write some custom code that can actually make this determination for you.

Of all these steps, the first one is of course the easiest. We're calling the capability `requiresProxy`.

And now comes the slightly harder part—adding the capability to the web.config file. You can begin to do this by reopening (if you have closed it) the ImageExample project that you began earlier. Double-click the web.config file and verify that it opens to display a text XML document.

Now, locate the `<deviceFilters>` section within this document. Notice that each of the device filters described in Table 13-1 earlier has its own entry in the section. It stands to reason, then, that in order to add the custom `requiresProxy` filter to MIT, you must first add an entry for it to this section. Listing 13-1 shows how this section should look when you are finished (with the additional lines in bold).

*Listing 13-1. Our New DeviceFilters Node*

```
<deviceFilters>
    <!-- Markup Languages -->
    <filter name="isHTML32" compare="preferredRenderingType" argument="html32" />
    <filter name="isWML11" compare="preferredRenderingType" argument="wml11" />
    <filter name="isCHTML10" compare="preferredRenderingType" argument="chtml10" />
    <!-- Device Browsers -->
    <filter name="isGoAmerica" compare="browser" argument="Go.Web" />
    <filter name="isMME" compare="browser" argument="Microsoft Mobile Explorer" />
    <filter name="isMyPalm" compare="browser" argument="MyPalm" />
    <filter name="isPocketIE" compare="browser" argument="Pocket IE" />
    <filter name="isUP3x" compare="type" argument="Phone.com 3.x Browser" />
    <filter name="isUP4x" compare="type" argument="Phone.com 4.x Browser" />
    <!-- Specific Devices -->
    <filter name="isEricssonR380" compare="type" argument="Ericsson R380" />
    <filter name="isNokia7110" compare="type" argument="Nokia 7110" />
    <!-- Device Capabilities -->
    <filter name="prefersGIF" compare="preferredImageMIME" argument="image/gif" />
    <filter name="prefersWBMP" compare="preferredImageMIME"
            argument="image/vnd.wap.wbmp" />
    <filter name="supportsColor" compare="isColor" argument="true" />
    <filter name="supportsCookies" compare="cookies" argument="true" />
    <filter name="supportsJavaScript" compare="javascript" argument="true" />
    <filter name="supportsVoiceCalls" compare="canInitiateVoiceCall"
            argument="true" />
    <!- Custom Properties ->
    <filter name="requiresProxy"
        type="ImageExample.PocketDBA.DeviceSensor, ImageExample"
        method="determineProxyUsage" />
</deviceFilters>
```

The first bold line in the preceding code is just a comment. This example demonstrates what we at PocketDBA have elected to do with such code: we put all of our custom device filters in their own web.config section. This way, as we bring in new developers, they can immediately spot the bits of our code that are different from straight out-of-the-box MIT code.

> **NOTE** *An argument could be made that putting your custom filters in the appropriate preexisting sections would make it easier for outsiders to immediately understand their purpose and function. The decision is yours. It is unlikely to be much of an issue, either way.*

The bold lines beneath the comment tell .NET about the new custom device filter. To begin with, we tell it that our new filter is going to be known as requiresProxy via the name attribute.

The type attribute is a little misnamed as far as we're concerned. This parameter tells .NET where it can locate the custom code that will support the custom device filter. In this case, the code is telling it to look for the DeviceSensor class within the PocketDBA namespace, which in turn is within the ImageExample project and assembly.

The final attribute is method. This is the procedure within the custom code that will be called whenever you use the requiresProxy device filter.

The final step is of course the hardest. You now have to write some custom code that will sense the kind of device that is making a connection and inform the MIT as to whether or not that device requires a proxy connection. Fortunately for you, this custom code is provided in Listing 13-2.

*Listing 13-2. Supporting requiresProxy Primitively*

```
Namespace PocketDBA

    Public Class DeviceSensor

        Public Shared Function determineProxyUsage(ByVal caps As _
System.Web.Mobile.MobileCapabilities, ByVal garbage As String) As Boolean

            If caps.HasCapability("isPocketIE", "") Then
                Stop
                determineProxyUsage = False
            ElseIf caps.HasCapability("isUP4x", "") Then
                Stop
                determineProxyUsage = False
            ElseIf caps.HasCapability("isHTML32", "") Then
                Stop
                determineProxyUsage = True
            Else
                Stop
```

```
            determineProxyUsage = False
        End If

    End Function

  End Class

End Namespace
```

This code matches the entry you added earlier to the application's web.config file. The namespace is `PocketDBA`, the name of the class is `DeviceSensor`, and the method is called `determineProxyUsage`. Because this class is located in the same project as everything else, it will use the same project name and assembly name as everything else in this project—ImageExample.

 **CAUTION** *If any of these three things don't match up, you will get another one of those classic "what the heck does this mean?" error messages from .NET. In this case, the error message will indicate that it can't look up the correct type information for your class. This is .NET's way of saying that it can't locate your code, which (in this case) will mean that there is some discrepancy between the namespace/class name/method name/project name/assembly name combination in web.config and the one being used by your component.*

At this point, we have built this component directly as a part of our overall MIT example. In the real world, you could build it as part of another component project, compile it into a stand-alone assembly, and then reference that assembly from every MIT project where you wished to use this capability. This would foster the goal of increased reusability.

The code in Listing 13-2 used the `hasCapabilities` method of the `MobileCapabilities` class. Notice that the parameters being passed are all the names of other device filters. Using this technique, you can programmatically do the same kind of device-specific evaluations that you would ordinarily do using the `AppliedDeviceFilters` and `PropertyOverrides` properties of various GUI controls.

On the other hand, as you can see from the code, calling `hasCapabilities` from code is much more flexible than using `PropertyOverrides`. Using code, you can react to device differences however you like—not just by changing properties on GUI controls.

In this case, we are using existing device filters to try to glean information for our own custom device filter. We are basically saying, "If the device is an HTML 3.2–compliant browser, then say that it requires a proxy. Otherwise, say that it doesn't."

This is blatantly false, but allows us to illustrate the usage of this technology quite easily. To see the code in action, do this:

1. Right-click the ImageExample icon in Visual Studio's Solution Explorer window.

2. Choose Add, and then choose Add Class from the pop-up context menus.

3. Name your new file DeviceSensor.vb and click Open.

4. Double-click the icon for DeviceSensor.vb in Visual Studio's Solution Explorer to open its code view.

5. Make the code listing match Listing 13-2 exactly.

6. Choose Build from the VS .NET Build menu.

7. Double-click the icon for MobileWebForm1.aspx in the VS .NET Solution Explorer to open its GUI design view.

8. Select the Image1 control.

9. Select AppliedDeviceFilters in the Image control's properties list and click the ellipses button.

10. Expand the Available Device Filters drop-down list.

11. Select requiresProxy from the drop-down list.

12. Click Add to List, and then click OK.

13. Select PropertyOverrides in the Image control's properties and click the ellipses button.

14. Under Applied Device Filter, choose requiresProxy from the drop-down list.

15. Under Image URL, enter
    **http://www.pocketdba.com/images/clr_visor2.jpg**.

16. Click OK.

17. Run your new application.

Because VS .NET will automatically launch your application with Internet Explorer, you should see the IDE break on the stop line immediately below this line of code:

```
caps.HasCapability("isHTML32", "") Then
```

.NET has sensed that Internet Explorer is an HTML 3.2–compliant browser, and has therefore returned a positive value from the hasCapability method shown previously. If you select Continue from the VS .NET Debug menu, you will see that a picture of PocketDBA executing on a visor now appears in Internet Explorer. This is in response to Steps 8 through 16.

Copy the URL from Internet Explorer and use it to test your modified application in the Pocket PC and WAP emulators. In both cases, you will find that execution of your code pauses on different lines. Congratulations—you have now learned how to complete the most fundamental task in extending the MIT: adding custom device filters!

## Supporting Additional Devices

The particularly observant among you may have noticed that two devices were absent from those mentioned in the previous section: Palm OS and J2ME. You may recall from earlier discussions that neither of these devices is directly supported by .NET. In order to get them to work with you, you will need to learn even more about how .NET recognizes devices.

### The User Agent

Whenever an application connects to a Web server via HTTP, it is supposed to identify itself. By this, we do not mean that it is supposed to identify the person using the application or any details about his or her personal affairs. We simply mean that it is supposed to send a string that identifies what kind of software it is and the version of that software.

One example would be that whenever Netscape connects to a Web server, it sends a string containing the word "Mozilla" and some numbers. The word

"Mozilla" tells you it is Netscape that is making the connection and the numbers tell you exactly which version of Netscape it is.

This string is known as the *User Agent string*. It is very important to MIT. If an application doesn't properly identify itself to MIT, then the toolkit has no way of knowing what kind of device it is. Without knowing what kind of device is making the connection, there is no good way for MIT to adapt its output.

## How do You Get to It?

Fortunately, almost all major devices and applications provide a suitable User Agent string upon connecting to a Web server. By changing the determineProxyUsage function as shown in Listing 13-3, you can find out how to identify just about any device—including Palm OS and J2ME.

*Listing 13-3. The New determineProxyUsage Function*

```
Public Shared Function determineProxyUsage(ByVal caps As _
System.Web.Mobile.MobileCapabilities, _
ByVal garbage As String) As Boolean

            Dim bro As String = caps.Browser.ToString

        If caps.HasCapability("isPocketIE", "") Then
            Stop
            determineProxyUsage = False
        ElseIf caps.HasCapability("isUP4x", "") Then
            Stop
            determineProxyUsage = False
        ElseIf caps.HasCapability("isHTML32", "") Then
            Stop
            determineProxyUsage = True
        Else
            Stop
            determineProxyUsage = False
        End If


    End Function
```

The altered line is shown in bold in Listing 13-3. It will store the name of the browser, as passed in by the User Agent, in a variable called bro. Once you have added this line in your ImageExample project, you need to create clients from both of the remaining devices. Listing 13-4 shows the Web Clipping client for Palm OS. Listings 13-5 and 13-6 show the code and JAD file for the J2ME client.

*Listing 13-4. The Web Clipping MIT Client*

```
<html>

    <head>
        <title>Tell Me About Myself</title>
        <meta name="PalmComputingPlatform" content="true">
        <meta name="PalmLauncherRevision" content="1.0">
    </head>

    <body>
        <a href="http://YOURHOSTIP/ImageExample/MobileWebForm1.aspx" button>Tell
Me</a>
    </body>

</html>
```

*Listing 13-5. The J2ME MIT Client*

```
import javax.microedition.midlet.*;
import javax.microedition.lcdui.*;
import java.io.*;
import javax.microedition.io.*;

import org.kxml.*;
import org.kxml.io.*;
import org.kxml.parser.*;

public class MITStock extends MIDlet implements CommandListener {

        static final String serviceNamespace = "http://pocketdba.com/webservices/";

        Form mainForm = new Form ("Fergie Stock");
        TextField fromField = new TextField ("Symbol :", "ALGX", 4, TextField.ANY);
        StringItem resultItem = new StringItem ("", "");
        Command getCommand = new Command ("Get", Command.SCREEN, 1);
```

```
public MITStock () {
        mainForm.append (fromField);
        mainForm.append (resultItem);
        mainForm.addCommand (getCommand);
        mainForm.setCommandListener (this);
}

public void startApp () {
        Display.getDisplay (this).setCurrent (mainForm);
}

public void pauseApp () {
}

public void destroyApp (boolean unconditional) {
}

public void commandAction (Command c, Displayable d) {
        try {
            // build request string

            String from = fromField.getString ();

            HttpConnection connection = (HttpConnection) Connector.open
("http://localhost/ImageExample/MobileWebForm2.aspx",Connector.READ_WRITE);

            connection.setRequestMethod (HttpConnection.GET);
            connection.setRequestProperty ("User-Agent",
"J2ME-compliant device");

            InputStream is=((StreamConnection) connection).openInputStream ();
            int buffSize=200;
            byte[] buff = new byte[buffSize];
            ByteArrayOutputStream bytebuff=new ByteArrayOutputStream(buffSize);
            // read the response
            int eof=0;
            while(eof!=-1) {
                eof=is.read(buff);
                if (eof!=-1) {
                    bytebuff.write(buff,0,eof);
```

```
                }
            }

                is.close();

                    String response = new String(bytebuff.toByteArray());
                    System.out.println (response);

                connection.close ();
        }
        catch (Exception e) {
            resultItem.setLabel ("Error:");
            resultItem.setText (e.toString ());
            }
        }
    private static byte[] extractXml(byte[] extractFrom){
        byte[] result;
        int off=0;
    boolean nonStop=true;
    for(int i=0;nonStop;i++){
            if (extractFrom[i]==60) {
                off=i;
                nonStop=false;
            }
        }
        result=new byte[extractFrom.length -off];
        for(int i=off;i<extractFrom.length;i++){
            result[i-off]=extractFrom[i];
        }
        return result;
    }
}
```

*Listing 13-6. MITStock.jad*

```
MIDlet-1: MITStock, CashConv.png, MITStock
MIDlet-Jar-Size: 42265
MIDlet-Jar-URL: MITStock.jar
MIDlet-Name: MITStock
MIDlet-Vendor: Sun Microsystems
MIDlet-Version: 1.0
```

Once you have entered the code for Listing 13-4, use the Web Clipping Application Builder tool to assemble it into a PQA as you learned to do in Chapter 5. After this, fire up the Palm OS emulator, install the PQA, and give it a whirl.

 **NOTE** *In order for any of these examples to work, you must be running your application in Debug mode under Visual Studio .NET. This is the default execution mode for any application that is started directly from the VS .NET IDE.*

The first page will display a single button with the label "Tell Me," as shown in Figure 13-2. Click the button. At this point, results may vary depending upon which version of MIT you are using.

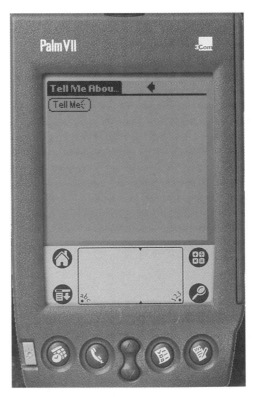

*Figure 13-2. The Web Clipping client*

**CAUTION** *There is a known issue in the Beta 2 version of MIT that causes a page that displays the message "Please click on the following link to continue" to appear occasionally when using Web Clipping. This issue may have been resolved by the final release of the toolkit. If you get this screen on your client when testing, simply click the link to continue and forget about it— you didn't do anything wrong.*

When you proceed, the VS .NET debugger will break on the stop line inside the isHTML32 section of code. Apparently, MIT is able to tell that you are using an HTML type of browser. This is surprising, considering that we have believed up to this point that the MIT features no support for Palm OS.

If the Locals window is not currently visible in the IDE, make it visible by clicking its tab. This tab will most likely be in the lower-left corner of the IDE, as shown in Figure 13-3.

| Locals | | ↕ ✕ |
|---|---|---|
| Name | Value | Type |
| ⊞ caps | {System.Web.Mobile.MobileCapabilities} | System.W |
| garbage | "" | String |
| bro | "MyPalm" | String |
| determineProxyUsage | False | Boolean |

*Figure 13-3. The Locals window*

Now, take a look at the value of your new bro variable. What does it say? MyPalm. Wow! Take a look back at Table 13-1 and what do you see? A device filter specifically called isMyPalm.

Apparently, the MIT is capable of recognizing Web Clipping Palms right out of the box. It will treat them like standard HTML 3.2–compliant browsers. This is a less-than-perfect level of support, given the many HTML 3.2 features that Web Clipping won't support and vice versa. Still, it is much better than having to code everything yourself from scratch!

In order to create a J2ME client, follow these steps:

1.  Go to the main directory for your J2ME Wireless Toolkit installation (\j2mewtk).

2.  Enter the apps subdirectory.

3. Copy the FergieStock folder created in Chapter 11 to a new folder called MITStock.

4. Enter the bin subdirectory.

5. Rename FergieStock.jad to MITStock.jad.

6. Edit the MITStock.jad file in Notepad, make it look like the code in Listing 13-6, and save it.

7. Enter the src subdirectory.

8. Rename FergieStock.java to MITStock.java.

9. Edit the MITStock.java file in Notepad, making it look like the code in Listing 13-5, and save it.

10. Open the J2ME Wireless Toolkit's KToolbar application.

11. Click Open Project.

12. Select MITStock and click Open Project.

13. Click Build and verify that no errors are generated.

14. Run ImageExample under the VS .NET debugger.

15. When the code breaks on the HTML 3.2 stop line, choose Continue from the VS .NET Debug menu.

16. In KToolbar, click Run.

17. Select MITStock in the J2MEWTK emulator.

18. Enter a stock symbol and click Get.

At this point, the VS .NET debugger will once again pause execution in the HTML 3.2 section of your code. Unlike with Web Clipping, however, the Locals window will reveal that .NET has no idea what kind of device is connecting. It refers to the browser simply as "Unknown". All unknown devices are therefore treated by .NET as HTML 3.2–compliant.

## Once You Get It, What Do You Do with It?

Having MIT think that your J2ME device is just another browser is less than acceptable. MIT can transmit HTML back to your client application, but unless you write custom code to render that HTML on your device's display, it won't do any good at all.

For this reason, it really doesn't make sense for the MIT to think that it can transmit HTML to J2ME devices at all. If anything, XML seems like a much more natural choice for transmission to these devices. As you will see in the next chapter, you can then write custom code to parse this XML and do with it as you deem appropriate.

In order to get MIT to recognize that your J2ME application is not just some HTML 3.2–compliant desktop browser, you must add an entry for it to the machine.config file. The machine.config file contains entries that uniquely identify all of the client devices with which a given .NET server is capable of interacting.

You can locate your machine's machine.config file at the following: \windows\microsoft.net\framework\v1.0.2914\config. Once you have located it, open it up in a text editor (such as Notepad) and add the code from Listing 13-7.

 **CAUTION** *Some of the specifics in the pathname in the preceding text may vary depending upon your version of Windows and your version of .NET. This is the path for a fresh installation of Windows XP running Beta 2 of Visual Studio .NET.*

*Listing 13-7. Stick This in Your machine.config*

```
<!-- J2ME Device running PocketDBA code
    Every J2ME application that connects to HTTP has the opportunity
    to set its own User Agent.  For this reason, we distinguish
    J2ME devices running PocketDBA code from devices that are
    running code beyond our control.
-->

    <case
        match="J2ME-compliant device">
        <filter>
            browser = "J2ME"
```

```
        preferredRenderingType = "xml"
        preferredRenderingMIME = "text/xml"
    </filter>
</case>
```

Listing 13-5 begins with a comment that bears clarification. If you examine the source code in Listing 13-5 carefully, you will find that one of the lines is bold. In this line, the Java code actually sets its own User Agent. The significance of this is it tells you that J2ME devices in and of themselves have no particular User Agent.

Instead, every J2ME application has the capability to set its own User Agent. This means every J2ME application in the world can potentially have a completely different User Agent, which makes it completely impossible to identify J2ME devices as a group solely on the basis of the User Agent string.

Instead, we have chosen to commit ourselves only to recognizing J2ME code that is created by PocketDBA Systems. At PocketDBA Systems, we have a standard for J2ME User Agent strings in our applications that requires them all to be the string "J2ME-compliant device". This is the string against which the match attribute in the preceding code must match.

Within the filter node in Listing 13-7, you see all of the capabilities that will be explicitly set now whenever a device is identified by this code as being a J2ME device. Specifically, its browser will be known as J2ME, and its preferred markup and rendering will be XML—not HTML 3.2!

If you rerun MITStock after adding this code to your machine.config file, you will get a piece of good news from a most unlikely source. That is to say, you will get an error. However, this error is very good news. It will indicate that the Mobile Internet Toolkit doesn't have any adapters configured to interact with this type of device.

Congratulate yourself again—you have just moved one level deeper into the intricacies of extending the Mobile Internet Toolkit. By modifying the machine.config file, you have taught .NET to recognize J2ME devices *and* you have made it realize that the MIT doesn't know how to handle this kind of device. . .yet. And this, of course, is your next challenge.

## Device Adapters

Device adapters are an essential part of extending the Mobile Internet Toolkit.

### Fundamentals

For every kind of device that is directly supported by the Mobile Internet Toolkit (HTML, i-Mode, and WAP), there is a corresponding device adapter, which is included with the base MIT distribution. It is the job of a device adapter to specify how each of the mobile controls should present itself in a way that can be understood and rendered by its device. Furthermore, the device adapter is responsible for accepting whatever input is sent back by the device and parsing it into a form that is usable by the rest of the MIT.

So, at this point, the logical question is this: what do you need to know in order to write a device adapter? Well, the first prerequisite is a thorough knowledge of the device for which you will be writing the adapter. At a minimum, you need to know all about the markup that it is capable of rendering. This will at least allow you to send output to the device.

Beyond this, however, you need to know details about the capabilities of the device's underlying communications system and its resources. For example, can the device handle cookies? If so, can the networks that provide these devices with connectivity support transmitting and receiving them, or will they be stripped out? How much memory does the device have? How big is its screen? And so on, and so forth.

Once you are an expert on a given device and have assured yourself that there is not already support for it under the MIT, then you are ready to proceed with the remainder of this chapter. In the following section, we will explain some of the more important pieces of code that every device adapter must have. We will also show you how to compile and install a device adapter, once you've written it.

 **NOTE**   *The existing device adapter code is, unfortunately, written in Microsoft's C# programming language. We say unfortunately because, up to this point, all of the other examples in this book have been written in VB .NET. For a thorough introduction to the C# programming language, please see* A Programmer's Introduction to C# *by Eric Gunnerson.*

In the next chapter, we will build enough of a J2ME adapter to allow our mobile stock quote application to finally support all five of our target devices.

## Exploring the Adapters

In this section, we will take a look at the WML device adapter that ships with the MIT.

*Important Bits of Code*

To begin with, all of the device adapter source code is located in the Adapter Source subdirectory below wherever you installed MIT on your machine. If you accepted the defaults during setup, then this subdirectory will probably be in the location \Program Files\Microsoft.NET\Mobile Internet Toolkit\Adapter Sources.

If you open this location under the Windows Explorer interface, you will see that the directory contains more than 50 different files. These files may be grouped into the following categories:

- i-Mode adapter files (those starting with "Chtml")

- HTML adapter files (those starting with "Html")

- WAP adapter files (those starting with "Wml")

- web.config-shipped adapters

- Base classes (the `ControlAdapter`, `MobileTextWriter`, and `MultiPartWriter`)

The first three on this list are the device adapters proper. They all do exactly the same thing—adapt MIT input and output—only for different devices. In this section, we will be primarily interested in the WAP adapter files. This is because the ultimate goal of the next chapter will be to produce a simplified XML device adapter for J2ME. WML is already an XML-based language, so its adapter will provide the best starting point for our efforts.

 **TIP** *For the time being, it is safe to ignore the web.config-shipped adapters and MultiPartWriter.cs files.*

Open the file named WmlLabelAdapter.cs in a standard text editor (such as Notepad). This file contains a single class, `WmlLabelAdapter`, which is descended from the `WmlControlAdapter` class. The `WmlControlAdapter` is itself descended from the `ControlAdapter` class—which illustrates an important point about all device adapter controls: they must all be descended from the `ControlAdapter` class. (This explains the purpose of the `ControlAdapter` file in the list earlier.)

The important function in the source code for `WmlLabelAdapter` is the `Render` method. The `Render` method is where every mobile control produces the markup that it will send to the client device. The code that does this for the

WmlLabelAdapter is particularly simple (as you would expect, given the simplicity of the Label control itself).

The first line:

```
RenderStyleText(writer, Style, Control.Text, true);
```

says "Send the text of this label, in whatever style is appropriate, to the device via the WmlMobileTextWriter that has been passed to me." The WmlMobileTextWriter is a class that specializes in producing output that meets the special requirements of the WML markup language. It is descended from the MobileTextWriter class, which is a class that specializes in producing output for mobile devices in general. (This explains the purpose of the MobileTextWriter class in the list earlier).

The second line:

```
writer.WriteBreak();
```

calls upon the WmlMobileTextWriter's expertise to send a line break to the client in whatever manner is appropriate for WML. For clarification, open WmlMobileTextWriter.cs in a text editor and find the WriteBreak() method. As you can tell from its single line of code:

```
Write("<br/>\r\n");
```

this is the bit of the adapter that knows essential, device-specific facts such as "Line breaks are produced in WML via the </br> markup notation." The rest of the code in WmlMobileTextWriter contains lots of similar markup-level string literals that let you know this is where the work of creating WML really gets accomplished.

### *Compiling Adapters*

Let's get a jump start on the next chapter by creating a fake J2ME adapter right now. Having this adapter will at least get rid of the errors you got the last time that you tried to connect with your J2ME application. More importantly, it will put you in a good position to create an XML-based adapter later on.

Begin by copying files as indicated in Table 13-2.

*Table 13-2. Creating a New Device Adapter by Copying These Files*

| SOURCE FILENAME | DESTINATION FILENAME |
| --- | --- |
| WmlPageAdapter.cs | XmlPageAdapter.cs |
| WmlFormAdapter.cs | XmlFormAdapter.cs |
| WmlLabelAdapter.cs | XmlLabelAdapter.cs |

Change the source code for each of your new XML device adapter files to match the code shown in Listings 13-8 through 13-10.

*Listing 13-8. XmlLabelAdapter.cs*

```
using System;
using System.IO;
using System.Web;
using System.Web.Mobile;
using System.Web.UI;
using System.Web.UI.MobileControls;
using System.Web.UI.MobileControls.Adapters;

namespace PocketDBAAdapter
{
    public class XmlLabelAdapter : WmlLabelAdapter
    {
        public static bool DeviceQualifies(HttpContext context)
        {
            String bro = context.Request.Browser.Browser.ToString();
            bool qualifies = (bro == "J2ME");
            return qualifies;
        }
    }
}
```

*Listing 13-9. XmlFormAdapter.cs*

```
using System;
using System.Collections;
using System.Collections.Specialized;
using System.Diagnostics;
```

```csharp
using System.IO;
using System.Web;
using System.Web.Mobile;
using System.Web.UI;
using System.Web.UI.MobileControls;
using System.Web.UI.MobileControls.Adapters;

namespace PocketDBAAdapter
{
    public class XmlFormAdapter : WmlFormAdapter
    {
        public static bool DeviceQualifies(HttpContext context)
        {
            String bro = context.Request.Browser.Browser.ToString();
            bool qualifies = (bro == "J2ME");
            return qualifies;
        }
    }
}
```

*Listing 13-10. XmlPageAdapter.cs*

```csharp
using System;
using System.Collections;
using System.Collections.Specialized;
using System.Diagnostics;
using System.IO;
using System.Web;
using System.Web.Mobile;
using System.Web.UI;
using System.Web.UI.MobileControls;
using System.Web.UI.MobileControls.Adapters;

namespace PocketDBAAdapter

{
    public class XmlPageAdapter : WmlPageAdapter
    {
        public static new bool DeviceQualifies(HttpContext context)
        {
            String bro = context.Request.Browser.Browser.ToString();
```

```
        bool qualifies = (bro == "J2ME");
        return qualifies;
      }
   }
}
```

Once you have changed the code as shown in Listings 13-8, 13-9, and 13-10, follow these steps to compile your new adapters:

1. Select Microsoft Visual Studio .NET 7.0 from the Windows Start Menu.

2. Open the Visual Studio.NET Tools program group.

3. Click Visual Studio .NET Command Prompt.

4. Change directories to the location of the device adapter source code.

5. Enter each of the commands shown here. If you get any errors, go back and check your code to make sure it matches Listings 13-8 through 13-10 exactly.

```
csc /target:library /out:PocketDBAAdapter.XmlLabelAdapter.dll
/r:System.Web.Mobile.dll XmlLabelAdapter.cs
csc /target:library /out:PocketDBAAdapter.XmlFormAdapter.dll
/r:System.Web.Mobile.dll XmlFormAdapter.cs
csc /target:library /out:PocketDBAAdapter.XmlPageAdapter.dll
/r:System.Web.Mobile.dll XmlPageAdapter.cs
```

**CAUTION**  *If you get an error about the System.Web.Mobile.dll file when running the three commands in the preceding text, try restarting your computer. Sometimes, the Mobile Internet Toolkit puts locks on this file that can only be removed via a reboot.*

All three of the preceding listings contain essentially the same code. The first several lines reference external namespaces containing library code that will be used in the remainder of the adapter. The first line after this declares that all of the code in this file will belong to the PocketDBAAdapter namespace. A single class is then declared, which always derives from an associated class in the WML device adapter.

Since your class derives from an existing class, the only methods you need to add are new ones and ones intended to replace methods existing in the base class. In the example, the only method you ever implement yourself is DeviceQualifies. This method will be called by .NET whenever it wants to determine whether or not the adapter is appropriate for a device connecting to it.

The test to determine this is quite simple. First, obtain a Request object from the HttpContext object that is always passed into this method. Then, get the Browser object from this Request object. Finally, get the name of the connecting browser via the Browser object's Browser property.

To clarify: there is a DeviceQualifies method in every device adapter, and .NET guarantees that an HttpContext object providing information about the connecting device will always be passed into this method. You want to know the name of the connecting browser, so you have to navigate through a series of subobjects in order to get to it.

Next, you determine whether or not this browser is named J2ME. If you recall from the additions made to the machine.config file in Listing 13-7, this is the name that will be assigned to the browser whenever a User Agent matching the string "J2ME-compliant device" is received. Whenever this happens, this method will return true (indicating that it is the appropriate adapter to use for the connecting device), otherwise it will return false (indicating that a different adapter should be used).

Finally, the csc tool used previously is the command-line C# compiler. The target switch tells the compiler to produce a library as its output, as opposed to a stand-alone executable. The r switch is similar to the classpath parameter that you may be familiar with from some Java compilers—it tells the C# compiler about other assemblies that may be referenced from the code being compiled. In this case, you have to reference System.Web.Mobile.dll in order to use any of the classes in the System.Web.Mobile namespace.

The last parameter passed into the compiler is, of course, the name of the file to be compiled.

### Installing Adapters

Once you've compiled your new device adapters, you need to install them in a mobile application in order to see them in action. The adapters you created are intended to serve up pages, forms, and labels to J2ME devices. This means that if you connect a J2ME client to a Mobile Web Form containing only these elements, you should no longer get the error about your device not being supported. Instead, you should get back WML—because you haven't yet coded the new adapters to do anything other than mimic the classes from which they inherit, which are WML adapters.

In order to install the new device adapters and try them out, follow these steps:

1. Open your ImageExample VS .NET project from earlier in this chapter.

2. Select the Image control on Form1 of your application's only page.

3. Click Delete to remove it.

4. Drag a Label control onto Form1.

5. Set the Label control's Text property to Looking good!.

6. Double-click the web.config icon in Solution Explorer.

7. Add the code from Listing 13-11 just below the </deviceFilters> line.

8. In the Solution Explorer window, click the icon for Show All Files.

9. Right-click the bin icon.

10. Choose Include in Project from the pop-up context menu.

11. Right-click the bin icon again.

12. Choose Add Existing Item from the pop-up Add context menu.

13. Navigate to the location where you built the three adapter DLLs in the previous section.

14. Choose All Files from the File Type drop-down menu.

15. Select the three DLLs and click Open.

16. Verify that the files in the Solution Explorer now match Figure 13-4.

17. Run the application.

*Listing 13-11. The web.config Addition*

```
<mobileControls allowCustomAttributes="true">
    <device name="XmlPageAdapter" inheritsFrom="WmlDeviceAdapters"
      pageAdapter="PocketDBAAdapter.XmlPageAdapter,PocketDBAAdapter.XmlPageAdapter"
    predicateClass="PocketDBAAdapter.XmlPageAdapter,PocketDBAAdapter.XmlPageAdapter"
        predicateMethod="DeviceQualifies">
      <control name="System.Web.UI.MobileControls.MobilePage"
      adapter="PocketDBAAdapter.XmlPageAdapter,PocketDBAAdapter.XmlPageAdapter" />
      <control name="System.Web.UI.MobileControls.Form"
      adapter="PocketDBAAdapter.XmlFormAdapter,PocketDBAAdapter.XmlFormAdapter" />
      <control name="System.Web.UI.MobileControls.Label"
     adapter="PocketDBAAdapter.XmlLabelAdapter,PocketDBAAdapter.XmlLabelAdapter" />
    </device>
</mobileControls>
```

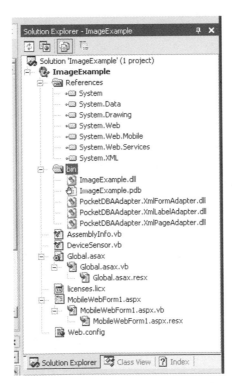

*Figure 13-4. All the right files!*

Some explanation of the preceding steps and code is appropriate at this point. The first few steps were concerned with removing the `Image` control from your application and replacing it with a `Label` control. This was necessary because you have not yet built a J2ME-compatible adapter for the `Image` control. On the other hand, you adapted the `Label` control in the previous section—so it should work fine.

The next steps were concerned with telling the application that you will be using some custom device adapters. This is accomplished via the lines that you added to the web.config file. If you plan on using any custom device adapters in a mobile application, you must have a single `mobileControls` section in your application's web.config file.

Within this `mobileControls` section, there must be one `device` section for each new kind of device that you will be supporting. In the case of our example, we are supporting one new kind of device: those that are J2ME compliant. There is, therefore, exactly one `device` section shown in Listing 13-11.

The first attribute:

```
inheritsFrom="WmlDeviceAdapters"
```

tells .NET that the device adapter is derived from the WML device adapter code. If you ever create your own device adapters that derive from one of the other adapter groups (HTML or cHTML), then you will want to make sure to change this attribute.

The `pageAdapter` attribute tells the MIT which class will be providing the top-level page rendering for these devices. This is required because in the example we have you create your own page adapter, as well. In other instances, it would not typically be used.

The `predicateClass` attribute tells .NET which class implements your new device adapter, as well as the assembly from which to load it. The class portion takes the form `Namespace.Classname`. So, in this case, you are telling .NET that your adapter is implemented by the `XmlLabelAdapter` class in the `PocketDBAAdapter` namespace. Conveniently enough, we had you name your adapter similarly: `PocketDBAAdapter.XmlLabelAdapter`—this is the portion that comes after the period in the `predicateClass` attribute's value.

Once .NET knows which class is implementing the new adapter, it needs to know something even more important: when should it use this adapter? This decision is made for .NET in the custom `DeviceQualifies` method inside the adapter classes. We therefore had you include the `predicateMethod` attribute to tell .NET to invoke this method in order to determine whether or not this adapter should be used in any given instance.

Within the node declaring the new device adapter, there are three nodes specifically for the controls that you have implemented as a part of this adapter. These are the `control` nodes and feature two attributes: `name` and `adapter`. The name attribute points at a base mobile control, which is the one that this adapter is intended to replace under the appropriate circumstances (as determined by the DeviceQualifies method.) The adapter attribute serves the same function as PredicateClass, and therefore will always have exactly the same value.

The remainder of the steps are concerned with making your compiled adapter code a part of the project. This is accomplished by adding the binary assembly files for the adapters to the project's bin folder. You would follow a similar procedure for adding almost any separately compiled .NET assembly to a Visual Studio .NET project.

## Final Thoughts

If you connect to the application that you built in the preceding sections using any of the devices we have discussed thus far (IE, Pocket PC, WAP, or i-Mode), you will see that it operates exactly as it did in the exercise at the end of the previous chapter. The one wrinkle is that you may now also connect to it using the J2ME device emulator, using the code from Listing 13-5.

When you do this, however, you may be surprised to see the data that is sent is pure WML. The reason for this is that although you have created independent J2ME adapters at this point, you have added hardly any custom code of your own. This means that the adapters will default to mimicking the behavior of the adapters from which they are derived, which (in this case) means the WML adapters.

In the next chapter, we will add custom code to the adapters to make them behave in a way that is specially suited to the needs of J2ME devices. By also showing you how to adapt the MIT stock quote application for the special needs of Web Clipping, we will finally have achieved our goal of showing you how to make .NET work equally well with all of the target devices.

# Part Five

# Mobile .NET in the Enterprise

# CHAPTER 14

# Bringing It All Together, Part Two

## Serving Up Stock Quotes to Palm OS and J2ME

IN MANY WAYS, THIS CHAPTER is the climax of our book. In previous chapters, you have learned how to invoke Web Services from virtually any mobile device. You have also learned how to access applications created using the Mobile Internet Toolkit from Internet Explorer, Pocket PCs, WAP devices, and i-Mode phones. The only thing left, which will be explained thoroughly in this chapter, is to extend the Mobile Internet Toolkit to support the remaining two clients on our list—Palm OS Web Clipping browsers and J2ME-compliant devices.

---

 **TIP** *You might have noticed that the name of this chapter suggests a certain kind of similarity to Chapter 7 earlier in this book. Indeed, our purpose in this chapter is the same as it was in that chapter: to demonstrate how stock prices may be served wirelessly to virtually any mobile device. Whereas Chapter 7 was created using legacy, pre-.NET Microsoft technologies, however, in this chapter we are using nothing but .NET!*

---

## Exercise

In this exercise, we will demonstrate how to extend the devices supported by the mobile stock quote application to include J2ME and Web Clipping devices.

### Writing the Device Adapter

In the previous chapter, you created three new device adapters for J2ME. However, these were created simply by inheriting from associated WML

adapters. The only method that was overridden was the `DeviceQualifies`
method—so that the adapters would be chosen for use with J2ME-
compliant devices.

The effects of leaving everything else unaltered can be seen by connecting to
your new ImageExample project with the J2ME-based MITStock client. After
entering your symbol and clicking Get, you will see that WML output is now generated in the J2ME Wireless Toolkit's output window, as shown in Figure 14-1.
This is because, for all intents and purposes, the J2ME adapter that you have created is identical to the WML adapters upon which it is based.

```
<?xml version='1.0'?>
<!DOCTYPE wml PUBLIC '-//WAPFORUM//DTD WML 1.1//EN' 'http://www.wapforum.org/DTD/wml_1.1.xml'><wml><head>
<meta http-equiv="Cache-Control" content="max-age=0" />
</head>


<card id="Form2">
<p>12.97<br/>
</p></card></wml>
```

*Figure 14-1. Current WML stock price output*

Our goal for the device adapter code, then, must be to alter the markup that
it produces to uniquely suit our own purposes, as shown in Listing 14-1.

*Listing 14-1. Desired XML Stock Price Output*

```
<?xml version='1.0'?>

<response id="Form1">
    <price>2.00
    </price>
</response>
```

Rather than sending generalized WML, we will strive to have it produce
an XML document that specifically addresses the goal of transmitting stock
price information.

## The Code

Listings 14-2 through 14-4 show the final XML page adapter, the final XML form
adapter, and the final XML label adapter. Listing 14-5 shows the code for the
modified mobile stock quote application.

*Listing 14-2. Final XML Page Adapter*

```
using System;
using System.Collections;
using System.Collections.Specialized;
using System.Diagnostics;
using System.IO;
using System.Web;
using System.Web.Mobile;
using System.Web.UI;
using System.Web.UI.MobileControls;
using System.Web.UI.MobileControls.Adapters;

namespace PocketDBAAdapter
{
    public class XmlPageAdapter : WmlPageAdapter
    {
        private static String _headerBegin = "<?xml version='1.0'";
        private static String _headerEncoding = " encoding ='{0}'";
        private static String _headerEnd
            = "?>\r\n";
        private IList _renderableForms;

        public static new bool DeviceQualifies(HttpContext context)
        {
            String bro = context.Request.Browser.Browser.ToString();
            bool qualifies = (bro == "J2ME");
            return qualifies;
        }

        private void RenderXmlHeader(HtmlTextWriter writer)
        {
            writer.Write(_headerBegin);
            String charset = Page.Response.Charset;
            if (charset != null && charset.Length > 0 &&
                String.Compare(charset, "utf-8", true) != 0)
            {
                writer.Write(String.Format(_headerEncoding, charset));
            }
            writer.Write(_headerEnd);
        }
```

```
        public override void Render(WmlMobileTextWriter writer)
        {
            writer.BeginResponse();
            writer.BeginFile(Page.Request.Url.ToString(), "text/xml",
Page.Response.Charset);

            RenderXmlHeader(writer);

            _renderableForms = Page.ActiveForm.GetLinkedForms(OptimumPageWeight);
            Debug.Assert(_renderableForms != null, "_renderableForms is null");

            foreach (Form form in _renderableForms)
            {
                form.RenderControl(writer);
            }

            writer.EndFile();
            writer.EndResponse();
        }
    }
}
```

*Listing 14-3. Final XML Form Adapter*

```
using System;
using System.Collections;
using System.Collections.Specialized;
using System.Diagnostics;
using System.IO;
using System.Web;
using System.Web.Mobile;
using System.Web.UI;
using System.Web.UI.MobileControls;
using System.Web.UI.MobileControls.Adapters;

namespace PocketDBAAdapter
{
    public class XmlFormAdapter : WmlFormAdapter
    {
        public static bool DeviceQualifies(HttpContext context)
        {
            String bro = context.Request.Browser.Browser.ToString();
            bool qualifies = (bro == "J2ME");
```

```
            return qualifies;
        }

    public override void Render(WmlMobileTextWriter writer)
      {
            writer.WriteLine();
            writer.WriteLine();
            writer.WriteBeginTag("response");
            if (Control.ID != null)
            {
                writer.WriteAttribute("id", Control.ClientID);
            }

            writer.Write(">");
            writer.WriteLine();
            RenderChildren(writer);
            writer.WriteEndTag("response");
        }
    }
}
```

*Listing 14-4. Final XML Label Adapter*

```
using System;
using System.IO;
using System.Web;
using System.Web.Mobile;
using System.Web.UI;
using System.Web.UI.MobileControls;
using System.Web.UI.MobileControls.Adapters;

namespace PocketDBAAdapter
{
    public class XmlLabelAdapter : WmlLabelAdapter
    {
        public static bool DeviceQualifies(HttpContext context)
        {
            String bro = context.Request.Browser.Browser.ToString();
            bool qualifies = (bro == "J2ME");
            return qualifies;
        }
```

```
    public override void Render(WmlMobileTextWriter writer)
    {
       writer.WriteBeginTag("price");
       writer.Write(">");
       writer.Write(Control.Text);
       writer.WriteEndTag("price");
    }
  }
}
```

*Listing 14-5. Modified Mobile Stock Quoter Code*

```
Private Sub Page_Load(ByVal sender As System.Object, ByVal e As _
System.EventArgs) Handles _
MyBase.Load
        'Put user code to initialize the page here
        If Request.QueryString("symbol") <> "" Then
            TextBox1.Text = Request.QueryString("symbol")
            PerformLookup()
        End If
    End Sub


    Private Sub Command1_Click(ByVal sender As System.Object, ByVal e As _
System.EventArgs) _
Handles Command1.Click


        If Page.IsValid Then


            PerformLookup()


        End If


    End Sub


    Private Sub PerformLookup()


        Dim price As String
        Dim ws As localhost.Service1 = New localhost.Service1()


        Me.ActiveForm = Form2


        If ws.getQuote(TextBox1.Text, price) Then
```

```
        Label1.Text = price
    Else
        Label1.Text = "No such stock!"
    End If

End Sub
```

## The Walk-Through

The four listings in the previous section fall into two main groups. The first three listings represent the modified device adapter listings that are needed in order to serve up pure XML to J2ME-compliant devices. The last listing, 14-5, represents the modification that must be made to the mobile stock quote application in order to support access from J2ME and Web Clipping (Palm OS) clients.

### The Device Adapters

The code that has been added to Listings 14-2, 14-3, and 14-4 appears in bold for easier identification. In all three of these files, we have overridden the base classes' Render method to produce something other than WML output. The specifics of the modifications vary slightly from one adapter to the next, however.

The bold lines at the top of Listing 14-2 declare a few constants that are used by the RenderXMLHeader method and a variable used later by the Render method. These values cannot be accessed in the base class due to their private access levels.

The RenderXMLHeader method is called by the Render method to generate the XML lines that occur at the top of every WML document produced by the MIT. In the standard implementation, the XML header would include the following:

- An XML identifier

- A WML document type declaration (DTD)

- A cache expiration header

Our customizations to RenderXMLHeader and the constants described in the previous paragraph reduce this list to just the XML identifier.

The only modification to the Render method in Listing 14-2 is to change the MIME type to text/xml in the following line:

```
writer.BeginFile(Page.Request.Url.ToString(), "text/xml", Page.Response.Charset);
```

The original code for the WML's Form adapter was quite complicated. For one thing, it had to allow for navigating between multiple pages of data on devices with varying screen sizes. For another, it had to compensate for differences in the number and styles of buttons available for navigating on different devices.

Since the J2ME client code will be 100 percent responsible for receiving, interpreting, and displaying the information returned by the adapter, we have dispensed with all of this logic in Listing 14-3. Our Render method simply generates markup for the entire Form at once and labels it with a response tag instead of WML's card tag. The RenderChildren method is called to create appropriate markup for each of the controls on the Form.

In Listing 14-4, we have put code in the Render method that simply outputs the value of our Label control inside a price tag. This differs from the code in the WmlLabelAdapter base class in that the base class code took the style (for example, bold, italic, and so on) into account. The Render method of the base class also suffixed the label with a line break—a presentation concern that is completely immaterial in a data-driven language like XML.

Once you have used the code in Listings 14-2 through 14-4 to replace the code in XmlPageAdapter.cs, XmlFormAdapter.cs, and XmlLabelAdapter.cs, respectively, you must recompile them. Use the same csc command lines described in the previous chapter.

 **CAUTION** *As of Beta 2 of Visual Studio .NET, it is still absolutely essential that you delete and add once more the assemblies containing your custom adapters to each VS .NET project where they are used after modifying their code. In order to accomplish this, simply choose the adapters in the Solution Explorer, right-click, and choose Delete from the pop-up context menu. Follow Steps 11 through 15 in the section of Chapter 13 entitled "Installing Adapters" to then add your newly modified adapters back to your project(s).*

### The Mobile Stock Quote Application—Final Version!

The Page_Load event in Listing 14-5 allows a client using the HTTP GET method to completely avoid receiving the initial stock symbol query page. If a value for the variable symbol is passed in as a part of the requested URL, execution will jump immediately to the PerformLookup routine.

On the other hand, if this variable is not provided as part of the URL, the main stock symbol entry page is rendered as usual. When the command button is clicked, however, control is passed to the PerformLookup routine for further action.

PerformLookup simply encapsulates the same interaction with the stock quoting Web Service that you have been using for the last several chapters. By removing it to a separate routine, it becomes possible to call the code from both the Page_Load and the Command1_Click events.

It is amusing to note at this point just how little code the MIT requires in order to create a Mobile Web Application that will be compatible with just about every wireless device in current existence. If you give it even a moment's reflection, you will quickly come to the conclusion that ease of use is a game that .NET wins hands down. No contest!

## Writing the Clients

We entered this chapter with the goal of supporting two additional clients: Palm OS and J2ME. In this section, we will "strike these down and complete your training" (said in our best Darth Vader impersonation).

### The Code

We made the fortunate discovery in the previous chapter that Microsoft has added some support for Web Clipping (known as the MyPalm browser) to Beta 2 of the Mobile Internet Toolkit. This has rendered our coding task for Palm OS rather trivial—simply create an appropriate client.

The gyrations required in order to support J2ME encompassed the creation of a brand new device adapter as well as a client application. The device adapter was created earlier. The client application is described in the section "J2ME" later.

#### Palm OS

Listing 14-6 shows the code for the Web Clipping client HTML.

*Listing 14-6. Web Clipping Client HTML*

```
<html>
   <head>
     <title>Mobile .NET Example</title>
        <meta name="PalmComputingPlatform" content="true">
        <meta name="PalmLauncherRevision" content="1.0">
   </head>
   <body>
```

```
          <form method="get"
action="http://YOURHOSTIP/MobileStockQuoter/MobileWebForm1.aspx">
          <input type="text" name="symbol">
          <input type="submit" value="Get Quote">
      </form>
  </body>
</html>
```

### J2ME

Listing 14-7 shows the code for the J2ME client.

*Listing 14-7. J2ME Client Code*

```java
import javax.microedition.midlet.*;
import javax.microedition.lcdui.*;
import java.io.*;
import javax.microedition.io.*;

import org.kxml.*;
import org.kxml.io.*;
import org.kxml.kdom.*;
import org.kxml.parser.*;

public class MITStock extends MIDlet implements CommandListener {

    Form mainForm = new Form ("MIT Stock");
    TextField fromField = new TextField ("Symbol :", "ALGX", 4, TextField.ANY);
    StringItem resultItem = new StringItem ("", "");
    Command getCommand = new Command ("Get", Command.SCREEN, 1);


public MITStock () {
    mainForm.append (fromField);
    mainForm.append (resultItem);
    mainForm.addCommand (getCommand);
    mainForm.setCommandListener (this);
}

    public void startApp () {
        Display.getDisplay (this).setCurrent (mainForm);
    }
```

```
public void pauseApp () {
}

public void destroyApp (boolean unconditional) {
}

public void commandAction (Command c, Displayable d) {
  try {
        // build request string

      String from = fromField.getString ();

      HttpConnection connection = (HttpConnection) Connector.open
("http://YOURHOSTIP/MobileStockQuoter/MobileWebForm1.aspx?symbol=" +
from,Connector.READ_WRITE);

              connection.setRequestMethod (HttpConnection.GET);
              connection.setRequestProperty ("User-Agent",
                 "J2ME-compliant device");
              InputStream is-((StreamConnection) connection).openInputStream ();
              int buffSize=200;
              byte[] buff = new byte[buffSize];
              ByteArrayOutputStream bytebuff=new ByteArrayOutputStream(buffSize);
              // read the response
              int eof=0;
              while(eof!=-1) {
                    eof=is.read(buff);
                    if (eof!=-1) {
                       bytebuff.write(buff,0,eof);
                    }
                 }
                 is.close();

          String response = new String(bytebuff.toByteArray());
              System.out.println (response);

          Reader reader = new InputStreamReader(new
          ByteArrayInputStream(bytebuff.toByteArray()));
              XmlParser parser = new XmlParser (reader);
               Document doc = new Document();
              doc.parse(parser);
```

```
                    Element root = doc.getRootElement();
                    Element price =
                     root.getElement(1);
                    resultItem.setLabel ("amount :");
                 resultItem.setText(price.getText());


            }
        catch (Exception e) {
            resultItem.setLabel ("Error:");
                resultItem.setText (e.toString ());
            }
        }
    }
}
```

## The Walk-Through

After much suffering, it is finally time to get some mobile stock quotes, courtesy of .NET, on our Palm OS and J2ME devices.

### Palm OS

The code in Listing 14-6 is a standard Web Clipping application. This is to say, it is simple HTML that is intended to be compiled into a PQA file using the Palm OS Web Clipping Application Builder.

The only important thing to note in the code is the use of the get method in the FORM tag. This will cause the application to transmit the value of the symbol variable as a direct part of the URL it will request from the MIT application. As a result, the Page_Load event will jump immediately to the PerformLookup routine without even rendering the initial page. This will allow us to avoid a slight issue in MIT's support for Web Clipping, as described in the previous chapter.

In order to build the Web Clipping client, follow these steps:

1. Open a standard text editor, such as Notepad.

2. Enter the code from Listing 14-6.

3. Replace the value YOURHOSTIP with the actual IP or fully qualified domain and hostname of the server running the MIT application.

4. Save your code as a file named wcstock.html.

5. Start the Web Clipping Application Builder (refer to Chapter 5 if you have forgotten how).

6. Choose Open Index from the File menu.

7. Locate wcstock.html in the Open File dialog box and double-click it.

8. Choose Build PQA from the File menu to bring up the dialog box shown in Figure 14-2.

9. Verify that the filename is wcstock.

10. Click Build.

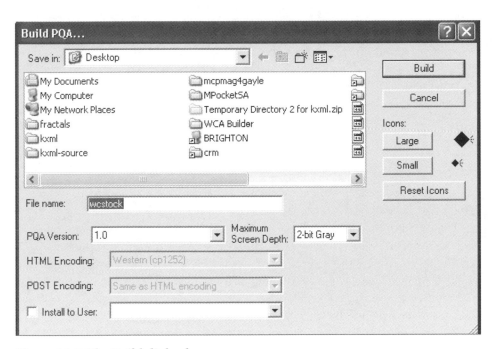

*Figure 14-2. The Build dialog box*

At this point, the dialog box will close and a file named wcstock.pqa will be created. You may close the Web Clipping Application Builder. In order to test your new Web Clipping client, follow these steps:

1. Start the Palm OS Emulator (refer to Chapter 5 if you have forgotten how).

2. Drag the wcstock.pqa file onto the Palm OS Emulator's display.

3. Refresh the emulator's display by changing to a different application group using the menu in the upper-right corner, and then changing back to All.

4. Click the wcstock icon to see the screen in Figure 14-3.

5. Enter a stock symbol on the dotted line.

6. Click Get Quote.

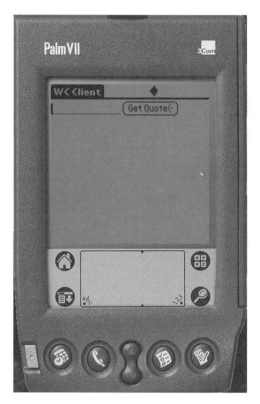

*Figure 14-3. The MIT Web Clipping client*

After a brief pause, you should get back the price of your requested stock. Congratulations—you have made MIT work with Palm OS. Five down (IE, Pocket PC, WAP, i-Mode, Palm OS), one to go!

### *J2ME*

You may already have noticed that the code in Listing 14-7 is considerably more complicated than that in Listing 14-6. Fortunately, Listing 14-7 is highly derivative of the MITStock code from the previous chapter. For this reason, we have simplified the amount to be studied by boldfacing the sections of interest.

The first bold line simply tells the Java compiler to include support for the kXML's DOM capabilities. DOM stands for Document Object Model and is one of the two main programmatic interfaces for working with XML documents (SAX—the Simple XML API—being the other). Further down in the code, DOM will allow you to navigate through the XML document returned by the MIT application to pick out the bits in which you are interested—namely, the price of the stock.

The next point of interest achieves the effect of an HTTP GET request by opening a connection to the URL of the MIT application's main page suffixed with the value of the symbol variable. We put the value of the symbol variable at the end of the URL simply by using the overloaded plus operator to concatenate the from variable's String value to the URL's constant string value.

After this a series of boldfaced lines. These are the lines that use the DOM to navigate through the document down to whatever stock price has been returned. The first line instantiates the kXML parser and passes all of the raw MIT response into it. The next two lines create a DOM document and tell kXML to populate it by parsing the raw MIT response into actual XML.

The next lines create two XML elements. The first one, root, is pointed at the root element for the entire DOM document created earlier. The second one, price, is pointed at the root element's second child. This is the node that contains the stock's price.

 **NOTE** *In this document, the* root *node is the response node. Its first child would be its own text value, which in this case would be nothing. We are interested, instead, in its second child—the* price *node. We refer to this with the numeral index 1 because the index array is 0-based.*

The final line of interest in the code uses the text value of the selected node to populate the user interface with the price of the stock. This completes the operation of retrieving a stock price from the .NET MIT application using a J2ME-compliant device. (And there was much rejoicing!)

Trying this application out for yourself is a little more complicated than simply making code changes to MITStock, recompiling, and running. The reason for this is that we have now accessed some kXML functionality (DOM) that was not included with the initial CashConv sample that you downloaded several chapters ago.

In order to recompile, build, and run this application, you must follow this procedure:

1. Download the most recent version of the complete kXML source code from `http://kxml.enhydra.org/software/downloads/current/kxml-source.zip`.

2. Unzip the source code to any location on your local disk.

3. Copy the org subdirectory from wherever you unpacked the kXML source code.

4. Navigate to \J2MEWTK\apps\MITStock\src.

5. Paste in the org subdirectory.

6. If you are asked if you still want to move or copy the folder, click Yes to All.

7. Start KToolBar.

8. Click Open Project.

9. Choose MITStock and click Open Project.

10. Click Build.

---

**CAUTION** *There may still be a bug in the kXML source code by the time you download it. If so, you will get an error message like this one when you attempt to compile: "Can't reference line before the superclass constructor has been called." In order to work around this error (a full solution is beyond the scope of this book), change the line of code in \J2MEWTK\apps\MITStock\src\org\kxml\parser\XmlParser.java that reads* `super (msg, chained, line, column);` *to instead read* `super(msg, chained, 1, 1);`*.*

---

11. Click Run.

At this point, you should be able to select the MITStock MIDlet, as shown in Figure 14-4.

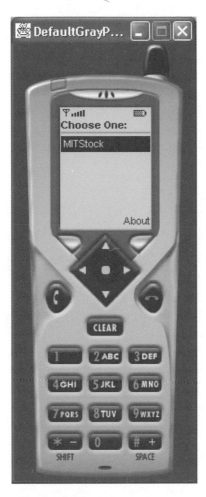

*Figure 14-4. The MIDlet selection menu*

Enter the stock symbol of your choice, and get back its current price from your MIT application. And so, at long last, you have extended the MIT to work with all of the devices discussed in this book!

## Final Thoughts

Of course, it is has not merely been our intention in the last few chapters to teach you how to accomplish the demonstrated tasks with the targeted devices. Instead, we hope that you have learned the overall principals of device characteristics and MIT extensibility well enough to do the following:

- Analyze the capabilities of virtually any device.

- Conceive strategies for avoiding the limitations of most devices.

- Customize your MIT applications based upon differences among all devices.

- Create custom device adapters for any unsupported client.

It is our intention to help spearhead the development of as many open-source MIT device adapters as possible. By sharing our device adapter code with one another, we will all benefit from the resulting increase in MIT's device compatibility. For more information, please see the Web site at the following URL: `http://www.mobiledotnet.com`.

With the next chapter, we turn our attention away from the server and begin to focus once again on the client. The .NET Compact Frameworks bring the power of .NET onto all sorts of different mobile devices, and are therefore essential to your understanding of Mobile .NET!

# CHAPTER 15

# The .NET Compact Framework

## Bringing the Power of .NET to Handhelds

WHILE FIRST RESEARCHING THE series of seminars upon which this book is based, we fell in love with .NET. For sheer ease of use and limitlessness of potential applications, we feel that there is no other programming platform in the world today that even comes close to equaling .NET. As we have become even more familiar with .NET, we have been finding programming with other technologies increasingly frustrating.

"Why can't Microsoft just port .NET to small devices," we wondered, "so we could use all of the same, great .NET tools to develop for the Pocket PC and Palm OS?" Then yesterday, we received a CD in the mail labeled "Microsoft .NET Compact Framework." Ever get the feeling that the folks up in Redmond developed some kind of secret, mind-reading technology without telling us?

## Introduction

So what exactly was on the CD, and how can you use it to create Mobile .NET applications?

### Seeing the Big Mobile .NET Picture

In order to fully understand what the .NET Compact Frameworks are, you must first understand why they exist, and specifically what void they fill within Microsoft's overall Mobile .NET strategy.

## Reviewing Your Progress

So far in this book, we have examined two kinds of Mobile .NET technologies: Mobile Web Services and Mobile Web Applications.

### Mobile Web Services

You may recall from Chapter 10 that Web Services provide you with a platform-independent way to access code libraries running on remote computers. Individual methods within these libraries may be exposed for remote invocation via industry-standard XML messages. These messages, and the responses that they generate, are typically structured according to the SOAP protocol for XML Remote Procedure Calls (RPCs).

In Chapter 11, we showed you how to use .NET Web Services from virtually any device. Table 15-1 below summarizes the devices we discussed and their level of support for .NET Web Services.

*Table 15-1. Devices and .NET Web Services*

| DEVICE NAME | WSDL? | SOAP? | XML? | HTTP? | MARKUP? |
|---|---|---|---|---|---|
| Internet Explorer | Yes | No | Yes | Yes | Yes |
| Pocket PC | No | Yes | Yes | Yes | Yes |
| J2ME | No | No | Yes | Yes | No |
| Palm OS | No | No | No | Yes | Yes |
| WAP/i-Mode | No | No | No | No | Yes |

Table 15-1 is organized from easiest to hardest in terms of getting each device to work with .NET Web Services.

The row to which particular attention should be paid is the one for Pocket PC. Were it not for Simon Fell's excellent PocketSOAP libraries, our answer for SOAP support on this device would be "No." It would then be easier to invoke a .NET Web Service from a Java Micro Edition device than from a Pocket PC. How would you feel about *that* if you were Microsoft? (Hint: this is one of the shortcomings that the .NET Compact Frameworks is meant to address.)

### Mobile Web Applications

In Chapters 12 through 14, we examined Microsoft's brilliant Mobile Internet Toolkit technology. As you might have guessed from the previous sentence, this is a particular favorite of ours. Furthermore, it should be noted that there is very little that one might want to do from a mobile device that could not be done by using the Mobile Internet Toolkit.

Still, like all markup-centric technologies, there are certain resource limitations that can have a limiting effect on their usefulness. One of the most obvious of these limited resources is bandwidth. It can be prohibitively expensive to have to send data back to the server just to respond to every minor UI event.

> **NOTE** *Moreover, consider the case of the technologist in a remote part of the world. Wireless Internet service is not available everywhere on this planet at the time of writing, so it is entirely possible to travel to areas where server-based applications using the Mobile Internet Toolkit (or any other server-based technology, for that matter) would be completely inaccessible. In these situations, the only .NET option left available would be the Mobile Device Applications you can create using the .NET Compact Frameworks.*

Another potentially even more limited resource is the number of developer hours that can be devoted to producing new device adapter code. As mentioned in the previous chapter, we would like to assist in this respect by leading some open-source device adapter initiatives at http://www.mobiledotnet.com. It would seem likely, however, that the evolution of devices will always exceed the pace at which adapters for them can be developed.

## Mobile Device Applications

There is a third kind of Mobile .NET application that we have not yet discussed. The reason is that until the arrival of the .NET Compact Frameworks, they didn't really exist as anything other than an idea on paper, the idea being that developers should be able to write .NET code for execution on devices as well as on servers.

There are a couple of wonderful possibilities that become entirely feasible once you can make this happen.

### *Leveraging Existing Skills*

The first great thing that happens when you can execute .NET code on devices is that everyone who has previously been a .NET developer suddenly becomes a device developer.

At first this might appear to be a bit of an oversimplification and/or an exaggeration. After all, devices still have peculiar limitations that need to be learned and worked around. Furthermore, the tools that support .NET on devices might require an additional degree of learning effort that not every .NET developer would feel inclined to invest.

Unfortunately for those who would like to see device development remain a black and mysterious art, Microsoft has addressed both of these issues with .NETcf. In the case of device limitations, the very nature of .NET's managed execution environment allows developers to largely (though not entirely) ignore such tricky issues as memory allocation and reclamation. After all, sorting out details like this is why we have a CLR in the first place!

Microsoft has also integrated the .NET Compact Frameworks completely and seamlessly into the existing Visual Studio architecture. This has ensured that little if any additional learning is required in order to begin immediately creating .NET applications for devices. Heck, we had our first .NETcf application running on our Pocket PC within an hour of taking the CD out of the mailbox—and we didn't even read any of the instructions until something broke!

### Supporting Multiple Platforms

The part of Microsoft's .NET Compact Frameworks initiative that you may really find surprising is its stated intention to be platform independent. Specifically, Microsoft is attempting to attract OEM licensees for this technology who manufacture non–Windows CE devices. These licensees would be encouraged to provide a special subset of the .NETcf class libraries as a part of the internal flash ROMs of their devices.

For more information on this, see the section later in this chapter entitled "The Cross-Platform Profile."

## Getting Started

To get started creating applications for devices with .NET, you need only do two things: install .NETcf and then take a quick tour of the new features it has added to Visual Studio .NET.

## Installing .NETcf

We found installing .NETcf to be extremely easy. It worked for us the first time, right out of the box. We just put the CD in the computer and ran the setup program.

**NOTE**    *The CD we received in the mail was a special Alpha-software version of .NETcf. By the time this is published, the technology will be in early Beta. By the time you read this, it may even be in its final release.*

The current plan is for the .NETcf bits to remain a freely downloadable add-on to Microsoft's Visual Studio .NET product. This means that anyone can get their hands on the bits without paying Microsoft one additional penny. On the other hand, you will have had to have already purchased Visual Studio .NET in order to derive any benefit from these bits whatsoever.

## Learning the Interface

Once the installer has finished, you should be able to launch Visual Studio .NET and take a look at the features that have been added. If you are particularly paranoid, you may reboot first—though we didn't find it to be necessary.

### Choosing Your Project Type

Immediately after starting Visual Studio .NET, you should choose to create a new project. Immediately, you will notice that options have been added to the New Project dialog box.

If you elect to create a Visual Basic project type at this point, you will see that you are able to create projects for devices now in addition to the desktop. Choose to create a Windows application for the Pocket PC platform. We will explain the significance of this choice later, in the section called "Profiles."

Name your new project Pocket Chatter and click OK.

### Selecting Your Emulator

The first thing you should notice when your new project has opened in the IDE is a new drop-down list in the upper-left corner of the screen, as shown in Figure 15-1. From this drop-down list, you can choose which device emulator you want to run your code under. For our purposes here, you should choose the Pocket PC Emulator option.

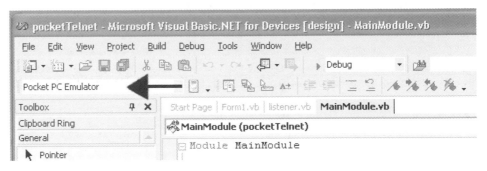

*Figure 15-1. The new emulator choices*

**TIP**  *Depending upon how far the code has progressed by the time you get your copy of .NETcf, you may notice that some of the fonts look a little off whenever you run your code in the emulator. This is not your fault—it is a minor issue with .NETcf's floating-point calculation that is currently being fixed.*

If you have a real Pocket PC device attached to your computer, it should also show up in this list. By connecting a real device to your computer and choosing it from this list, you can automatically have your code downloaded onto your device for testing whenever you run your application under the Visual Studio .NET IDE.

The most exciting thing that you should know about emulation for .NETcf is that Microsoft has completely redone its emulator for the Pocket PC. In addition, emulation for other kinds of Windows CE devices (such as the Stinger smart phones) will be made available for use with Visual Studio .NET and .NETcf.

The benefit to you, besides being able to emulate a wider range of devices, is that the new breed of emulators will run a truer implementation of the real Windows CE operating system than the current Pocket PC emulator. This means you will be able to be much more confident that your applications will work on real devices after testing them only on the emulator than you can be at present.

### Examining Your Properties

Once you have chosen to use the Pocket PC emulator, move your mouse over to the Solution Explorer window. Here, you should right-click the Pocket Chatter icon and choose Properties from the pop-up context menu. In the Properties window that pops up, notice the presence of a new option, Device Tools, under Common Properties.

If you click the Device Tools option, you should see the options shown in Figure 15-2.

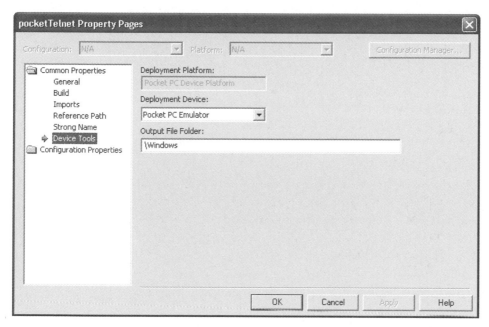

*Figure 15-2. Device tools*

The Deployment Device drop-down list is just another way to set your choice of emulator or device, as described in the previous section. The Output File Folder drop-down list is more interesting. This is the actual location on the device or emulator's file system to which the executables and other files for application will be transferred. In this case, the location will be \Windows.

If this were inappropriate for some reason, you could change it here. You should not, however, do this now—as \Windows is exactly where you want your code to go if you are following along with this example. So, just click Cancel to leave this dialog box.

### Creating Your Application

Up to this point in the book, we have explained the creation of our applications in a two-part method:

- First, draw the GUI

- Second, fill in the code

In this case, however, we would like to illustrate an important point about Visual Studio .NET that differentiates it from previous versions of Visual Studio. VS .NET creates its forms using code that is actually stored in the same file(s) as the rest of your code. This form creation code is usually stored in a collapsed portion of your code so that you don't notice it. If you observe the section of code in Listing 15-1 between the #Region and #End Region lines, however, you will see it quite clearly.

*Listing 15-1. Pocket Chatter GUI*

```
Imports System.Threading

Public Class Form1
    Inherits System.Windows.Forms.Form

#Region " Windows Form Designer generated code "

    Public Sub New()
        MyBase.New()

        'This call is required by the Windows Form Designer.
        InitializeComponent()

        'Add any initialization after the InitializeComponent() call

    End Sub

    'Form overrides dispose to clean up the component list.
    Protected Overloads Overrides Sub Dispose(ByVal disposing As Boolean)
        If disposing Then
            If Not (components Is Nothing) Then
                components.Dispose()
            End If
        End If
        MyBase.Dispose(disposing)
    End Sub
    Friend WithEvents btnStart As System.Windows.Forms.Button
    Friend WithEvents txtMessages As System.Windows.Forms.TextBox

    'Required by the Windows Form Designer
    Private components As System.ComponentModel.Container

    'NOTE: The following procedure is required by the Windows Form Designer
    'It can be modified using the Windows Form Designer.
```

```
        'Do not modify it using the code editor.
    Private Sub InitializeComponent()
        Me.btnStart = New System.Windows.Forms.Button()
        Me.txtMessages = New System.Windows.Forms.TextBox()
        Me.SuspendLayout()
        '
        'btnStart
        '
        Me.btnStart.Location = New System.Drawing.Point(8, 232)
        Me.btnStart.Name = "btnStart"
        Me.btnStart.Size = New System.Drawing.Size(216, 48)
        Me.btnStart.TabIndex = 2
        Me.btnStart.Text = "Start Listening"
        '
        'txtMessages
        '
        Me.txtMessages.Location = New System.Drawing.Point(8, 8)
        Me.txtMessages.Multiline = True
        Me.txtMessages.Name = "txtMessages"
        Me.txtMessages.ReadOnly = True
        Me.txtMessages.Size = New System.Drawing.Size(216, 216)
        Me.txtMessages.TabIndex = 0
        Me.txtMessages.Text = ""
        '
        'Form1
        '
        Me.ClientSize = New System.Drawing.Size(232, 286)
        Me.Controls.AddRange(New System.Windows.Forms.Control() {Me.btnStart, _
Me.txtMessages})
        Me.Name = "Form1"
        Me.Text = "Form1"
        Me.ResumeLayout(False)

    End Sub

#End Region

    Private Sub Form1_Load(ByVal sender As System.Object, ByVal e As _
System.EventArgs) Handles MyBase.Load

    End Sub

    Private Sub btnStart_Click(ByVal sender As System.Object, ByVal e As _
System.EventArgs) Handles btnStart.Click
```

```
        Dim lsnr As Listener = New Listener()
        lsnr.setMessageControl(txtMessages)
        Dim tsLsnr As ThreadStart = New ThreadStart(AddressOf lsnr.run)
        Dim thrLsnr As Thread = New Thread(tsLsnr)
        Dim app As Application
        thrLsnr.Start()

        btnStart.Enabled = False
    End Sub
End Class
```

To create your application, simply follow these steps:

1. In Solution Explorer, right-click the Form1.vb icon.

2. Choose View Code from the pop-up context menu.

3. In the code window, press Ctrl-A to select everything.

4. Hit the Backspace key to clear all existing code.

5. Enter the code from Listing 15-1 to replace it.

6. In Solution Explorer, right-click the Pocket Chatter icon.

7. Choose Add and then Add Class from the pop-up context menus.

8. Name your new class listener.vb and click OK.

9. Replace all of the code in this file with the code in Listing 15-2.

*Listing 15-2. Pocket Chatter Listener*

```
Imports System.Net.Sockets
Imports System.Text

Public Class Listener

    Dim txtMessages As System.Windows.Forms.TextBox

    Public Sub run()
```

```
            Dim tcpl As TcpListener = New TcpListener(1993)
            Dim enc As ASCIIEncoding = New ASCIIEncoding()
            Dim app As Application

            tcpl.Start()

            Do Until False

                Dim sckt As Socket = tcpl.AcceptSocket()
                Dim btChar(0) As Byte

                sckt.Receive(btChar, 1, 0)

                Try
                    txtMessages.Text = txtMessages.Text & Now & " - "
                    Do Until btChar(0) = 13
                        app.DoEvents()
                        txtMessages.Text = txtMessages.Text & _
enc.GetString(btChar, 0, _btChar.Length)
                        sckt.Receive(btChar, 1, 0)
                    Loop
                    txtMessages.Text = txtMessages.Text & vbCrLf & vbCrLf
                Catch Problem As Exception
                End Try

                sckt.Close()

            Loop

        End Sub

    Public Sub setMessageControl(ByVal c As System.Windows.Forms.TextBox)
        txtMessages = c
    End Sub

End Class
```

At this point, you should have your first .NETcf application!

### Testing Your Application

This application was inspired by my wife's reluctance to call me on my cell
phone for fear of running up the bill. My wireless Internet Access plan, unlike

my wireless phone plan, has an unlimited access option. I can therefore afford to leave my Pocket PC and wireless modem constantly running and connected to the Internet. (Let's imagine that battery life isn't an issue.)

So, anyhow, if I left the Pocket Chatter application running on my Pocket PC all the time, my wife could send me messages anywhere that I happened to be right from our home computer. To see this in action, start the application now by pressing F5 or choosing Start from the Debug menu.

At this point, the Pocket PC emulator should automatically launch. When you are ready to start listening to messages from my wife, click Start Listening. The button will go dark, and your Pocket PC will now be listening for connections from other computers on the Internet.

In order to simulate a message from my wife, run the following command from your Windows Run menu:

```
telnet localhost 1993
```

Shortly, you should get a completely blank Telnet window on your display. Type something, anything—but don't expect to be able to see what you are typing. There is no echo on this primitive application. When you are done, press Enter. The Telnet session will be closed by the host (the Pocket Chatter application).

If you go back to the Pocket Chatter application now, you will see that your message has been recorded, as in Figure 15-3.

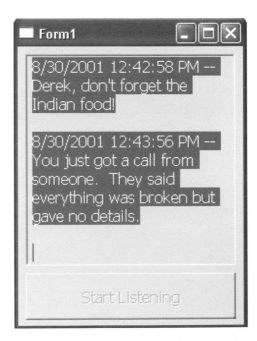

*Figure 15-3. Pocket Chatter in action*

To stop the application, first close the emulator, and then choose Stop Debugging from the Debug menu. You have now seen an Internet server running on a Pocket PC. Previously, this would have required C++ and several hundred lines of code. Why were neither of these things required in this case? It was the miracle of the .NETcf class library.

# The .NETcf Class Library

Like any .NET application, a great deal of the platform's value is conveyed to you as an application by way of the runtime's extensive class library. .NETcf's class libraries are organized around a series of profiles and vendor extensions.

## The Three Kinds of Code

There are three kinds of code involved in creating .NETcf systems: application code, device extensions, and .NETcf Profiles.

### Application Code

The code that gets created when you compile and deploy your device applications from Visual Studio .NET is the same kind of bytecode that gets generated when you are creating "regular" desktop .NET applications. This bytecode is known as MSIL, and is Microsoft's standard instruction set for programming the Common Language Runtime (CLR) virtual machine.

The general benefits of bytecode were discussed thoroughly in Chapter 8. However, there is one particular benefit that bears repeating at this point, given the peculiar nature of mobile devices. This is the fact that bytecode applications tend to be much smaller than their native counterparts.

This is extremely beneficial considering the limited storage resources of most mobile devices. .NETcf's ability to execute bytecode on devices, therefore, allows Microsoft to compete fiercely with the J2ME technologies that we have learned about previously in this book.

### Device Extensions

Device extensions are bits of .NET code that are *not* an official part of the .NETcf distribution, but are instead bits of .NET code that vendors include with the distributions to add value to their particular devices.

### Microsoft's Extensions

Microsoft is perhaps the most obvious source for device-specific extensions. When you choose to create a Pocket PC project in Visual Studio .NET, for example, you are using code contained in Microsoft's Pocket PC extensions. Similar extensions are expected from Microsoft for the Stinger phone.

The Stinger phone may present the best opportunity for explaining the existence of extensions, in fact. Imagine if Microsoft had put functionality to dial a phone in the base .NETcf class libraries. These functions would be available on any device where .NETcf was installed. The question then becomes what would happen if you called these functions on a device other than a phone.

At best, nothing would happen. At worst the device might crash or react negatively. One way or another, precious space would be taken up storing code for a part of .NETcf that would never be used. Thus, device-specific features like this are supported in extensions, rather than in the base .NETcf distributions.

### Other Extensions

As other vendors begin implementing the .NETcf in the flash ROMs of their new devices, they will also probably begin creating their own extensions. At the time of writing, no announcements about this have yet been made.

## Profiles

When we referred to the base .NETcf distributions previously, we were referring to what are known as the .NETcf Profiles. There are two of these: the Cross-Platform Profile and the Windows CE Profile. All that these do is specify particular subsets of .NET functionality that will be available in the base distributions of .NETcf for different kinds of devices.

## The Cross-Platform Profile

As we mentioned earlier, one of the most potentially shocking things about .NETcf is that Microsoft truly intends it for cross-platform use. Towards this end, Microsoft is making available a certain base package of classes that it calls the Cross-Platform Profile. The functionality embodied by the Cross-Platform Profile represents the absolute lowest common denominator of classes that need to be provided on a device in order for it to be considered .NETcf compliant.

## *What Classes Can You Use?*

Having read the preceding section, your next logical question might be, "Well, what classes are in the Cross-Platform Profile?" Delving only down to the name-space level, they are as follows:

- `System`

- `System.Collections`

- `System.Collections.Specialized`

- `System.ComponentModel`

- `System.Configuration.Assemblies`

- `System.Diagnostics`

- `System.Drawing`

- `System.Drawing.Drawing2D`

- `System.Drawing.Imaging`

- `System.Globalization`

- `System.IO`

- `System.Net`

- `System.Net.Sockets`

- `System.Reflection`

- `System.Resources`

- `System.Runtime.CompilerServices`

- `System.Runtime.CompilerServices.CSharp`

- `System.Runtime.InteropServices`

- `System.Security`

- `System.Security.Permissions`

- `System.Security.Policy`

- `System.Text`

- `System.Threading`

- `System.Windows.Forms`

- `System.Xml`

- `System.Xml.Serialization`

It is important to note that not every class within these namespaces is implemented as a part of the profile. Furthermore, on the classes that *are* implemented, not every method, property, and event is implemented. For a complete list, please see the documentation.

The important thing to take away from this is that these classes represent one of two profiles defined by .NETcf. The other profile contains all of these classes, plus a few more. What this means is whenever you are using .NETcf— whether it is this profile or the other—you can be sure that *at least* the classes in this profile are always available.

At the time of writing, Microsoft is currently negotiating with a wide range of hardware vendors to have the Cross-Platform Profile included on their devices. This would potentially allow you to run .NET code on such diverse devices as Nokia cell phones and Palm OS handhelds (if deals with those vendors were ever struck).

## What about the GUI?

The GUI capabilities of the Cross-Platform Profile are more limited in comparison to those of the Windows CE Profile.

### The Challenge

The problem with doing graphics in this profile is that it is intended for potential use on all sorts of devices: phones, set-top boxes, blenders—you name it! So, the question becomes what kind of user interface is equally well suited to a telephone and a blender.

**The Answer: the Portable Graphics Library**

The answer is this: an interface that you draw yourself, almost completely from scratch. The .NETcf Portable Graphics Library provides only graphical primitives at the time of writing, such as circles, lines, polygons, and so on. By providing simple drawing capabilities, the application developer is enabled to draw the kind of user interface that is best suited to his or her own application.

> **NOTE**   *This doesn't mean that you can't have buttons—it just means that you would have to draw the buttons yourself (as squares), and then specifically test for clicking within their bounds to be notified of button presses.*

## The Windows CE Profile

The Windows CE Profile is a superset of the Cross-Platform Profile that is intended for use with all Talisker devices. This version of Windows CE has yet to be released at the time of writing, so .NETcf is a little ahead of the technology curve here! Fortunately for us, this is also supported on Pocket PCs running Windows CE 3 and higher.

> **CAUTION**   *Another way to say this is that nothing running Windows CE prior to version 3.0 is supported. For 3.0, only Pocket PCs are supported—not handheld PCs or Palm-sized PCs.*

As mentioned, the Windows CE Profile contains all of the classes in the Cross-Platform Profile *plus* some extra classes for drawing (covered later in this chapter) and data access.

Data access is a matter that is near and dear to our hearts, so we will therefore devote the entire next chapter to covering this topic.

### What about the GUI?

Since Microsoft is the sole distributor of Windows CE, the company can be pretty sure that this profile will never be asked to run on any devices that are *too* far off the wall. For this reason, the GUI support in the Windows CE Profile consists of the vast majority of standard .NET WinForms controls with which you are probably already familiar.

These are the exact same .NET controls that you use in building Windows applications for the desktop. In fact, we used a couple of these controls (TextBox and Button) to build the Pocket Chatter application earlier in this chapter.

In order to see all of your options for yourself, open the Pocket Chatter application and go to Design Mode on Form1. If you look at the Toolbox window, you will see that almost all of the standard WinForms controls are available for your use!

Besides the controls that are included out of the box with .NET WinForms, you can also create your own .NET controls and use them with .NETcf. This includes both the "from scratch" style of controls that are drawn using graphical primitives as well as the composite user controls that are made up of several smaller .NET controls. Licensing support for these controls is also included (in case you're worried about someone stealing your controls).

### So What's Missing?

If you are a games developer, you will be saddened to hear that there is no DirectX support available in .NETcf. For everyone else, DirectX is a way of writing directly to the graphics hardware underlying most computer operating systems. This is contrary to .NET's philosophy of managed code—however, DirectX is supported on the desktop to facilitate speedy execution of graphics-intensive games.

The WinForms controls that you may have noticed absent from the Toolbox in the previous section are listed here:

- FontDialog

- Splitter

- HelpProvider

- PageSetupDialog

- PrintPreviewControl

- PrintDialog

- PrintPreviewDialog

- PrintDocument

- NotifyIcon

- RichTextBox

The reason they were absent from the Toolbox is that they are not supported on .NETcf. Most of these as you can probably tell involve printing. Due to limited storage resources, Microsoft had to make difficult decisions about what to cut—printing from devices seemed to be one of those things that consumed a lot of resources without being something that everyone seemed likely to want to do.

Some of the remaining controls on the list are ActiveX controls. Under desktop .NET, ActiveX controls could be hosted on WinForms because a large COM interoperability layer existed to make .NET and COM "play nice together." On devices, there is hardly enough room to support such interoperability. As a result, you cannot use ActiveX controls on .NETcf WinForms.

For more information on COM interoperability in general under .NETcf, read on!

## Migrating to .NETcf

By this point, you should have a pretty good idea of what .NETcf is and what you can do with it. In all likelihood, many of the things that you would like to do are things that you have already done on the desktop. In this section, we will look at which of those things will be easy to duplicate, the few that will be difficult, and even one or two things that might be absolutely impossible.

### What Languages Are Available?

At the time of writing, your language options under .NETcf are not quite the same as under .NET on the desktop. However, all .NET languages will be supported in future releases.

#### C#

In many ways, C# is the flagship language of Microsoft's .NET initiative. So, as you may have guessed, this seems to be the one language that you can be guaranteed will be available on a .NET platform. .NETcf is no exception and the support for C# here, even in the Alpha software that we are working with, is flawless.

> **TIP** *If you think you might ever be interested in migrating some of your Java code to .NET, remember that C# has the added benefit of easing this conversion. Microsoft's Java Users Migration Path (JUMP) initiative will soon translate Java source code directly into C#.*

## Arriving at Some Point in the Future

JScript .NET (JavaScript for .NET) will be available by the final release of .NETcf. Also, Microsoft will be working closely with the vendors who have created other .NET languages to ensure that these will be available for .NETcf as well.

## Visual Basic

The language that we have used most extensively in this book has been VB .NET. You will be happy to learn that VB .NET is completely available under .NETcf. However, it is important that you know a few essential differences between the desktop and device versions of this language.

### Structuring Your Application

Although you might not realize it, every VB .NET application for devices begins with a main subroutine. In order to see this for yourself, open up the Pocket Chatter application that you created earlier in this chapter under Visual Studio. In the Solution Explorer, double-click the icon for MainModule.vb.

In the code view here, you will see a single collapsed section. If you expand this section, you will see the code shown in Listing 15-3.

*Listing 15-3. The Main Module Source Code*

```
Module MainModule

#Region "The main entry point to the application."

    '--------------------------------
    'The main entry point for the application.
    '
    'The following procedure is required by the application.
    'This code is generated by the development environment.
    '
```

```
'---------------------------------
Sub Main()
    Application.Run(New Form1())
End Sub

#End Region


End Module
```

Listing 15-3 shows the main subroutine that executes when your application starts up. Since we haven't altered it in any way, it simply passes execution to a new instance of our application's main form—which is in effect the same thing as having started with that form's Load event in the first place!

The important thing to take away from this discussion is if you want to have your programs begin with main subroutines, don't add them yourself. Instead, modify the code that already exists in the MainModule file.

### *Binding Your Objects*

Under desktop VB .NET, the following code is acceptable:

```
Dim x as Object
x = new System.Text.ASCIIEncoding
```

This is known as late binding, because x was declared as a generic Object, .NET doesn't find out until runtime exactly what kind of object is going to be stored in the x variable. The opposite of this is called early binding, and would look more like this:

```
Dim x as System.Text.ASCIIEncoding
x = new System.Text.ASCIIEncoding
```

Because we have declared x as being of type System.Text.ASCIIEncoding in the preceding code, .NET knows as soon as it compiles our code what kind of object will eventually be stored in x. This is important in order to allow .NETcf to optimize its storage strategies on devices with potentially limited storage resource.

And so, for VB .NET on devices, only early binding is supported. If you have code that uses late binding, you will have to change it to explicitly declare variables as being of specific data types, rather than the catch-all data type, Object.

### *Communicating with the File System*

Under desktop-style VB .NET, the code shown in Listing 15-4 is valid.

*Listing 15-4. File Access the Old-Fashioned Way*

```
Imports Microsoft.VisualBasic.FileSystem

Public Class FileExample

    Private Sub AccessFileTheOldWay()
        FileSystem.FileOpen(1, "whatever.txt", OpenMode.Output)
        FileSystem.PrintLine(1, "this is the old way of doing things")
        FileSystem.FileClose(1)
    End Sub


End Class
```

This code is using the backwards-compatibility features built into Microsoft's .NET VB runtime (`Microsoft.VisualBasic.FileSystem`) to write to a standard text file in more-or-less the same way that the file would have been accessed under pre-.NET versions of the language. This is not possible under .NETcf.

If you look closely at the documentation that comes with .NETcf, you will quickly see why this is the case. Although the `Microsoft.VisualBasic` namespace is available under .NETcf, the `FileSystem` class within this namespace is not. This means that when you try to compile the preceding code under .NETcf, you will get error messages about the `FileSystem` class not existing.

So how do you access files under .NETcf? You have to use the streams-oriented approach that is new to .NET. If you have used other streams-oriented languages, such as C++ and Java, then this may seem quite familiar to you. Listing 15-5 shows you how to achieve the same results as in Listing 15-5—only using streams instead of old-style VB functions.

*Listing 15-5. File Access the New-Fangled Way*

```
Imports System.IO

Public Class FileExample

    Private Sub AccessFileTheOldWay()
```

```
        Dim fs As FileStream = System.IO.File.Open("whatever.txt", _
FileMode.OpenOrCreate)
        Dim enc As System.Text.ASCIIEncoding
        Dim b() As Byte

        b = enc.GetBytes("this is the new way of doing things")
        fs.Write(b, 0, b.Length)
        fs.Close()

    End Sub


End Class
```

### Using Built-In Functions

The following functions are not available under the .NETcf version of
Visual Basic:

- Shell

- GetSetting

- SetSetting

- App.Activate

### Working with COM

You may have been surprised in the earlier discussion on the Windows CE
Profile's GUI capabilities to learn that ActiveX controls cannot be hosted on
.NETcf WinForms. This is in fact merely one facet of a larger issue with .NETcf.
Stated simply, *there is no COM interoperability included in .NETcf.*

Does this mean that you can never access COM components from your
.NETcf code? Absolutely not! It just means that whereas desktop .NET provides
several layers of interoperability support to make the experience of using COM
from .NET transparent and painless, under .NETcf you will have to manage the
interactions yourself. This management needs to take place at a native code level
and will therefore vary widely from one device to another.

## Integrating with Native Code

Knowing how to integrate with native code under .NETcf is arguably more important than knowing how to do the same thing under desktop .NET. I believe this is true because under .NETcf you don't have the same interoperability layers to facilitate the easy use of COM functionality directly from .NET.

### The Way Things Were

Under desktop .NET a large library of code was specifically tasked with the job of facilitating easy use of COM functionality directly from .NET. This same batch of code worked in reverse also—allowing COM applications to call more or less transparently into existing .NET functionality.

The problem with all of this is that the code to support such transparent interchange of information between COM and .NET was quite resource intensive. To say that including it in .NETcf would have doubled the size of the final package is potentially an understatement.

Furthermore, the kind of marshaling activities that this kind of code needs to pursue can be extremely CPU intensive. On desktop machines, this is usually not even noticeable. However, such activities could easily overpower some small devices.

### The Way It Is

In order to avoid taking up too much storage space or CPU power on devices running .NETcf, Microsoft has made the decision *not* to include all of the COM interoperability layers with .NETcf. This means whenever you want to interact with the underlying operating system, you will need to code the interactions and data type conversions yourself.

#### Calling into Native DLLs

All of the .NET languages supported by .NETcf support the concept of declaring native routines stored in external DLLs for access directly from your managed code. Listing 15-6 shows an example of this under Visual Basic.

*Listing 15-6. Getting the Current Username Natively*

```
Module MainModule

#Region "The main entry point to the application.  VB.NET Development
Environment generated code."
```

```
    Declare Function GetUserName Lib "advapi32.dll" Alias _
"GetUserNameA" (ByVal lpBuffer As String, ByRef nSize As Integer) As Integer


    Sub Main()

        Dim UserName As String
        Dim Buffer As String
        Buffer = New String(CChar(" "), 25)
        GetUserName(Buffer, 25)
        UserName = Strings.Left(Buffer, InStr(Buffer, Chr(0)) - 1)
        MsgBox(UserName)

    End Sub

#End Region

End Module
```

Here, we have modified the existing main subroutine for our .NETcf application to avoid starting up the main form altogether. Instead, we declare that we will be referencing the GetUserNameA function in the native advapi32.dll library. When our application starts up, we call this native function to get the current username. The username displays in a message box before the application terminates.

 **CAUTION**   *If you try this code in a Win32 emulator, it will work because the advapi32.dll file is a part of the Win32 API. Remember, however, that the APIs under Windows CE can be quite different. This means when you move your code onto the actual devices themselves, you may have to change your function declarations drastically.*

### Calling into COM Components

In the preceding listing, we called a function in a DLL that is a built-in piece of the Windows operating system. However, there is no reason why you couldn't create your own native DLLs and call functions in these from .NETcf as well.

So what about instantiating COM components and calling their functions from .NETcf? In direct terms, the answer is you cannot access COM functionality directly from .NETcf. However, there is another way.

.NETcf code can access functions in native DLLs, as demonstrated previously. And native DLLs can access COM functionality. So if you really want to access COM from your .NETcf applications, you should wrap your COM components in standard DLLs. By means of calling functions on your DLLs, you can indirectly access whatever functionality is provided by your COM components.

This is Microsoft's official suggestion for tapping into COM from .NETcf. Not being C/C++ programmers, we honestly have no intention of ever doing this. Our strategy, which we suggest you follow as well, will be to do this:

1.  Put your targeted COM objects on a .NET server.

2.  Use the interoperability features on the server to tap into the required COM features.

3.  Expose these features as .NET Web Services.

4.  Call these Web Services directly from your .NETcf code.

This approach has several advantages. To begin with, it is much easier than messing around with the internals of COM and DLLs. Also, it allows you to centralize your business logic on the server, rather than having potentially different implementations on different devices.

Finally, .NETcf code that calls Web Services is infinitely less likely to crash than .NETcf code that calls DLLs. Calling native code directly from managed code, in many ways, undermines the reliability benefits that one is supposed to derive from managed code in the first place. One bad memory pointer pointing to the wrong place, and your entire device may crash!

So at this point, the obvious question is how to invoke .NET Web Services from .NETcf applications. Well, it couldn't get any easier, as we show you in the following exercise.

## Exercise

In this exercise, we will invoke our Mobile Stock Quote Web Service directly from the Pocket PC without the use of PocketSOAP.

## The Server

For this exercise, you may use the original Stock Quote Web Service created in Chapter 10. None of the simplifications introduced in Chapter 11 are required, as the .NET Compact Framework features full support for WSDL!

## The Client

As always, we will present you with the client in the form of some code, followed by a walk-through.

### The Code

Listing 15-7 shows the code for the .NETcf stock quote client.

*Listing 15-7. The .NETcf Stock Quote Client*

```
Public Class Form1
    Inherits System.Windows.Forms.Form

    Private Sub Button1_Click(ByVal sender As System.Object, ByVal e As _
System.EventArgs) Handles Button1.Click

        Dim price As String
        Dim ws As localhost.Service1 = New localhost.Service1()

        Label1.Text = ""

        If ws.getQuote(TextBox1.Text, price) Then
            Label1.Text = price
        Else
            Label1.Text = "No such stock!"
        End If

    End Sub
End Class
```

*The Walk-Through*

The beauty of calling .NET Web Services from .NETcf applications is that you can add references to them just as you would add references to standard Windows components. In order to create the stock quote Web Service client using the preceding code, follow these steps:

1. Open a new instance of the Visual Studio .NET IDE.

2. Click New Project.

3. Select the Visual Basic Pocket PC Projects.

4. Select the Windows Application template.

5. Enter the name Chapter15Client and click OK.

6. Add a textbox, a button, and a label to the default form.

7. Select Add Web Reference from the Project menu.

8. Enter the full URL for the Web Service you created in Chapter 10.

9. Click Add Reference.

10. Double-click the button on your default form to open its code view.

11. Alter this code listing to look as much like Listing 15-7 as possible.

At this point, you are ready to try your new Web Service! Simply run this application, enter a valid stock symbol in the textbox, and click the button. After a few moments, your price data should appear in the label control.

If you look back at Table 15-1 at this point, we think you will agree that the Pocket PC now stands head and shoulders above all of the other devices (J2ME included) in terms of the ease with which Web Services can be invoked from the device. .NETcf completely conceals the internal workings of XML and HTTP from the device application developer. This is just as good as developing for the desktop, agreed?

## Final Thoughts

In this chapter, you have gotten your first look at the .NET Compact Framework. Fortunately, because one of the driving ideas behind .NETcf is that it should be as much like the desktop .NET as possible, we were able to show you just about all of it in a very few number of pages.

The one notable absence from this discussion has been .NETcf's data-handling capabilities. In the next (and final) chapter, we will deliver Microsoft's entire mobile data strategy to you in a nutshell.

# CHAPTER 16

# Mobile Data .NET

## .NETcf, SQL Server CE, and More

IN THE PREVIOUS CHAPTER, YOU read about everything that Microsoft has given you to work with on devices in the form of the .NET Compact Frameworks. As anyone who has developed professionally for more than a few months will tell you, though, it ultimately comes down to getting at your data. And that is what this chapter is all about.

## Working with Local Data

In this section we will examine the data access parts of the .NETcf as well as Microsoft's SQL Server CE database for devices.

### ADO.NET

ADO.NET represents a revolutionary new approach to data access on Microsoft's part, as detailed in the following sections.

### Reflecting upon the Philosophical

Before .NET, the data access scheme that Microsoft was championing was known as the *Universal Data Access* approach. Under Universal Data Access, Microsoft wanted all data to be accessible via the same object-oriented APIs. It would then theoretically be possible to use the same code to sort rows in a database table as to sort messages in an e-mail application's mailbox.

The foundation for Microsoft's Universal Data Access plans was a technology known as *OLE DB*. OLE DB was the set of APIs that were supposed to make all data stores look the same to the application developer. Essentially, everything in OLE DB is represented to the developer in the form of an object. The specific mapping between "real-world" items (such as database rows or e-mail messages) and their OLE DB object counterparts was the job of a piece of code known as the OLE DB provider.

Because accessing raw OLE DB providers was deemed a bit too difficult for the majority of developers, Microsoft devised another set of objects to wrap the functionality offered by OLE DB. The objects were known as the Active Data Objects (ADO). ADO, it was thought, was simple enough for use by even the most unskilled of developers.

Two fundamental things have changed in Microsoft's data access strategy with .NET. The first of these is that Universal Data Access has gone the way of the dinosaurs. Microsoft no longer believes that all different kinds of data should be represented by the same, single set of OLE DB objects. Microsoft now argues that this robs developers of the ability to tap into the unique strengths of each data source.

In order to make this transition away from Universal Data Access complete, another change was required. With .NET, ADO has been replaced with ADO.NET.

## Delving into the Practical

ADO.NET shares an object-oriented approach to data in common with its ADO ancestors. The specific objects made available by ADO.NET, however, are quite different from those exposed by standard ADO. The most obvious difference is that because different data sources are now supposed to be accessed using different code, the specific objects associated with different data sources tend to differ from each other slightly in their naming.

The most basic object in ADO.NET is the Connection object. In Listing 16-1 below, we use a SqlConnection object to connect to the GrocerToGo database that was installed on your computer in Chapter 8 as part of the QuickStart tutorials.

*Listing 16-1. Making a Connection to SQL*

```
Imports System.Data.SqlClient

Public Class Form1
    Inherits System.Windows.Forms.Form

    Private Sub Button1_Click(ByVal sender As System.Object, ByVal e As _
System.EventArgs) Handles Button1.Click

        Dim strCnnctn As String
        Dim sqlCnnctn As SqlConnection
```

```
        strCnnctn = "Initial Catalog=GrocerToGo;"&_
"Data Source=BRIGHTON\NetSDK;" &_
"Integrated Security=SSPI;"
        sqlCnnctn = New SqlConnection(strCnnctn)
        sqlCnnctn.Open()

        ' TO DO: Use the connection

        sqlCnnctn.Close()

        End

    End Sub
End Class
```

By importing the System.Data.SqlClient namespace, we are telling .NET that we want to work with the set of ADO.NET objects that are a part of the SQL Server Managed Provider. Managed providers are the .NET replacement for OLE DB providers under Universal Data Access. All of the ADO.NET objects for working with a given data source will always be found in that data source's managed provider.

Commands encapsulate queries and instructions that are intended to be passed through a given Connection object to the database. Listing 16-2 shows some sample Command code that could easily fit in the commented TO DO area from Listing 16-1.

*Listing 16-2. Creating a SQL Command*

```
Dim strCmmnd As String
Dim sqlCmmnd As SqlCommand

strCmmnd = "select * from products"
sqlCmmnd = New SqlCommand(strCmmnd, sqlCnnctn)
```

In this code, a SQL query requesting the return of all rows and columns from the Products table in our database is associated with the sqlCnnctn Connection that was established in the previous listing. This association is accomplished via the instantiation of a new Command object called sqlCmmnd.

The final class that is a part of the SQL Server Managed Provider is System.Data.SqlDataAdapter. The purpose of a DataAdapter is to allow multiple Command objects to work together in different combinations to produce different views of the underlying data. For example, a DataAdapter might use one Command object to read data from a table and a completely different Command object to update that data.

In the case of Listing 16-3, our DataAdapter is simple. It will be used only to read data from the Products table in our database—as specified in the SQL Command object from Listing 16-2.

*Listing 16-3. A Very Simple DataAdapter*

```
Dim sqlDA As SqlDataAdapter
sqlDA = New SqlDataAdapter(sqlCmmnd)
```

The final ADO.NET object that you need to know about is the DataSet. DataSet objects are where all data ultimately resides while it is being used by a .NET application. Listing 16-4 uses the DataAdapter that we just finished building in the previous listing to populate a DataSet. This is the point at which data is finally transferred from the database into a form that our application can use!

*Listing 16-4. Data at Last!*

```
Dim sqlDS As DataSet
sqlDS = New DataSet()
sqlDA.Fill(sqlDS)
```

## Leveraging Local DataSets

DataSets are used to hold data. This capability is normally leveraged to contain data that has been transferred from a remote database server. However, on mobile devices running .NETcf, DataSets can also be used to provide structured, "persist-able" storage for application-generated data.

### The Code

Listing 16-5 shows the code for the band recorder.

*Listing 16-5. The Band Recorder*

```
Public Class Form1
    Inherits System.Windows.Forms.Form

    Dim ds As DataSet
    Dim dt As DataTable
```

```vbnet
    Dim dr As DataRow
    Dim isNew As Boolean
    Dim rn As Integer

    Private Sub Form1_Load(ByVal sender As System.Object, ByVal e As _
System.EventArgs) Handles MyBase.Load

        ds = New DataSet("Progressive Rock")

        Try

            ds.ReadXml("PR.xml")
            dt = ds.Tables("Bands")
            dr = dt.Rows(0)
            txtGuitar.Text = dr("Guitar")
            txtKeyboards.Text = dr("Keyboards")
            txtBass.Text = dr("Bass")
            txtDrums.Text = dr("Drums")
            txtVocals.Text = dr("Vocals")

        Catch problems As Exception

            dt = New DataTable("Bands")

            dt.Columns.Add("Guitar", System.Type.GetType("System.String"))
            dt.Columns.Add("Keyboards", System.Type.GetType("System.String"))
            dt.Columns.Add("Bass", System.Type.GetType("System.String"))
            dt.Columns.Add("Drums", System.Type.GetType("System.String"))
            dt.Columns.Add("Vocals", System.Type.GetType("System.String"))

            ds.Tables.Add(dt)

            dr = dt.NewRow()
            isNew = True

        End Try

        rn = 0

    End Sub

    Private Sub btnNew_Click(ByVal sender As System.Object, ByVal e As _
System.EventArgs) Handles btnNew.Click
```

```
                    saveCurrentRow()
                    dr = dt.NewRow()
                    rn = rn + 1
                    isNew = True

                    txtGuitar.Text = ""
                    txtKeyboards.Text = ""
                    txtBass.Text = ""
                    txtDrums.Text = ""
                    txtVocals.Text = ""

            End Sub

            Private Sub btnNext_Click(ByVal sender As System.Object, ByVal e As _
        System.EventArgs) Handles btnNext.Click

                Try

                        saveCurrentRow()
                        rn = rn + 1
                        dr = dt.Rows(rn)

                        txtGuitar.Text = dr("Guitar")
                        txtKeyboards.Text = dr("Keyboards")
                        txtBass.Text = dr("Bass")
                        txtDrums.Text = dr("Drums")
                        txtVocals.Text = dr("Vocals")

                Catch problem As Exception

                        rn = rn - 1

                End Try

            End Sub

            Private Sub btnPrevious_Click(ByVal sender As System.Object, ByVal e As _
        System.EventArgs) Handles btnPrevious.Click

                Try

                        saveCurrentRow()
```

```
                rn = rn - 1
                dr = dt.Rows(rn)

                txtGuitar.Text = dr("Guitar")
                txtKeyboards.Text = dr("Keyboards")
                txtBass.Text = dr("Bass")
                txtDrums.Text = dr("Drums")
                txtVocals.Text = dr("Vocals")

            Catch problem As Exception

                rn = rn + 1

            End Try

        End Sub

        Private Sub saveCurrentRow()

            dr("Guitar") = txtGuitar.Text
            dr("Keyboards") = txtKeyboards.Text
            dr("Bass") = txtBass.Text
            dr("Drums") = txtDrums.Text
            dr("Vocals") = txtVocals.Text
            Try
                dt.Rows.Add(dr)
            Catch problem As Exception
            End Try

        End Sub

        Protected Overrides Sub Finalize()
            MyBase.Finalize()
        End Sub

        Private Sub btnQuit_Click(ByVal sender As System.Object, ByVal e As _
    System.EventArgs) Handles btnQuit.Click
            saveCurrentRow()
            ds.WriteXml("PR.xml")
            Application.Exit()
        End Sub
    End Class
```

## The Walk-Through

The first things to note are the class-level declarations of DataTable and DataRow variables. DataSets contain zero or more DataTables. DataTables similarly contain zero or more DataRows. If you stop to think about it for second, this means you can think of DataSets as being kind of like miniature relational databases. This is a useful mental image considering that this is exactly what we are using a DataSet for in the preceding code.

When our main form is first loaded, a DataSet named Progressive Rock is created. Immediately thereafter, an attempt is made to read the serialized content of this DataSet from a file named PR.xml. If this file does not exist—for example, if this is the first time that the application has ever been run—an error will be raised and execution will jump to the Catch block.

Let's first consider the case where the PR.xml file *does* exist. In this case, the DataSet is populated with the contents of this file. Our DataTable variable is pointed at the Bands table within this DataSet and our DataRow variable is pointed at the first row of this table. The values in the fields of this row are used to populate the various text fields on the form.

In the case where the PR.xml file does *not* exist, an empty Bands table is created within the DataSet and our DataTable variable is pointed at it. Columns are then added to this DataTable to hold the values that will be entered into each of the text fields. The code finishes by adding a blank row to the new DataTable and signaling our application that this is a new row by setting isNew to true.

Let's skip ahead now to the btnNext_Click() and btnPrevious_Click() subroutines. These are functionally identical, except that they step in opposite directions through our DataSet. In both cases, they begin by saving the current contents of our text fields to the current DataRow via our custom saveCurrentRow subroutine. They then both attempt to progress in the DataSet in whichever direction they are designed for. If no additional rows exist in this direction, an error is raised and the code in the Catch block is invoked to return the DataRow number (rn) to its previous location.

The code in saveCurrentRow saves the text field values to our DataSet quite simply. All of the text field values are first inserted into the appropriate fields in the current DataRow. This row is then added to the DataTable. If it is already in the DataTable and hasn't been altered, the addition is silently refused. Otherwise the row is either added (if it is new) or merged (if it is an existing row that has been altered).

When the user finally clicks the Quit button, the WriteXML method of the DataSet is used to serialize the DataSet as XML. This XML is then written out to the PR.xml file immediately before the application terminates. When the application is started the next time, all of the data entered during the current session will be read back from this PR.xml file and restored for use in the application.

> **NOTE** *In the exercise at the end of this chapter, you will see how to enhance this application via the use of .NET Web Services. By transferring your DataSets back and forth via .NET Web Services, you can read and update data in desktop-based SQL Server databases.*

In order to try out the preceding code for yourself, follow these steps:

1.  Start up the Visual Studio .NET IDE.

2.  Select New Project.

3.  Create a new Visual Basic Windows application for the Pocket PC called Chapter16Example.

4.  Create a user interface on Form1 that looks like Figure 16-1.

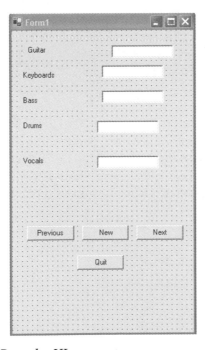

*Figure 16-1. The Band Recorder UI*

5. Make sure to name the textboxes and buttons according to the following bulleted list.

- `txtGuitar`

- `txtKeyboards`

- `txtBass`

- `txtDrums`

- `txtVocals`

- `btnPrevious`

- `btnNew`

- `btnNext`

- `btnQuit`

6. Enter Design Mode for Form1.

7. Enter the code from Listing 16-5.

8. Choose Run from the Debug menu to try out the code.

# SQL Server CE

The techniques described in the preceding section are great for managing a small amount of data that is never intended to be shared beyond a single device. In cases where the amount of data to be managed is larger, however, the power of a true relational database engine is required. SQL Server offers this power, as well as a convenient way to exchange data with desktop versions of SQL Server.

## Setting It Up

In this section, we will show you how to get SQL Server CE set up and running on your Pocket PC (or emulator, as the case may be).

### Acquiring the Software

SQL Server CE is not free software—nor is SQL Server itself. Fortunately, at the time of writing, when you install the .NET Frameworks SDK, a developers-only edition of SQL Server is included for use with the samples in that software. Before continuing with this exercise, you should follow the instructions in Chapter 8 to get the .NET Frameworks, and thus a version of SQL Server, up and running on your development machine.

 **TIP** *If for whatever reason you find that a copy of SQL Server is not installed on your machine when you install .NET, you may always download an evaluation copy from Microsoft's Web site. The URL is* `http://www.microsoft.com/sql/downloads/default.asp`.

Once you have finished this, you will need to install SQL Server CE as well. The reason for this is SQL Server CE is almost a completely different piece of code from standard SQL Server. The regular version of SQL Server would, after all, be far too big to fit on any Pocket PC (at a minimum, it requires 64MB of RAM and 100MB of free disk space).

The first step to obtaining SQL Server CE is to get ActiveSync. ActiveSync is a piece of software that facilitates so-called hot syncing between Pocket PCs and standard desktop computers. You may download a trial version of this software from `http://www.microsoft.com/mobile/PocketPC/downloads/activesync.asp`.

Simply follow the links from this page until the software has been downloaded onto your development machine.

**TIP**  *Of course, if you bought your Pocket PC from a standard retailer, chances are that you will already have all the required software available to you on a PC that came along with your purchase. Besides the required software, an additional benefit to this is the extra goodies that are often bundled by the manufacturers along with their drivers and utilities. Examples of these programs might include applications for personal finance, games, and all sorts of other diversions from your serious development efforts!*

The trial version of SQL Server CE is available at the following URL: `http://www.microsoft.com/sql/evaluation/trial/CE/download.asp`. Once again, follow the links from this page until the software has completely been downloaded onto the local hard disk on your development machine.

### Installing the Software

At this point, you have two new pieces of software on your computer that must be installed. The first of these is known as msasync.exe, the second is simply setup.exe. Run msasync.exe first.

**CAUTION**  *This software, like many other pieces of software, recommends that you close all other applications before attempting installation. We strongly advise you to heed this warning. We ignored it and were not able to successfully complete our installation until we had quit every single application.*

After the initial welcome screen, you will be given the opportunity to choose the location on your hard disk where you would like the software installed. It is a relatively small package, so just about any location should suffice. Once you have chosen the location, the installation will begin.

You will know that the installation has completed when it attempts to connect to your Pocket PC. If you own a Pocket PC, go ahead and follow the directions now for connecting it to your development PC. If not, simply cancel out of this operation. The bits of ActiveSync that you need in order to complete this exercise have already been installed.

Now, you should run the setup.exe executable that you downloaded for SQL Server CE. After the initial welcome screen, you will be prompted to choose either the Development Tools or Server Tools. Choose both and click Next.

There are three parts of the setup that will be launched one after the other at this point:

- Windows CE Data Access 3.1

- SQL Server CE Development Tools

- SQL Server CE Server Tools

 **NOTE**  *The installations for the Development Tools and Server Tools look almost identical. Don't make the mistake of thinking that the setup is caught in a loop and canceling out of it before it is finished—you need both sets of tools in order to complete this exercise!*

For all three of these packages, you will need to follow these steps:

1. Accept the licensing agreement.

2. Click Next.

3. Choose a location.

4. Click Next.

5. Click Finished.

After the final package, the Server Tools, is finished installing, you will be prompted to restart your computer. Make sure that you have saved all open documents and agree to the restart. When your computer is back up and running, you should be able to use SQL Server CE to create Pocket PC applications—at least until your trial license expires!

## Developing for SQL Server CE

A full dissertation on developing SQL Server CE applications is beyond the scope of this book. You may gain a sufficient understanding of the fundamentals, however, simply by examining one of the more interesting examples that come with the base software distribution.

### *Looking at a Sample*

The steps you completed in the previous section installed SQL Server CE on your development machine. They also automatically performed some basic configuration steps needed in order to make SQL Server CE available to the eMbedded Visual Tools that you installed in Chapter 3.

In order to access the SQL Server running on your machine from a remote Windows CE device, however, some additional manual effort is required. Specifically, you have to make a component of SQL Server CE available to IIS, which facilitates the replication of data back and forth between your device and SQL Server, as shown in Figure 16-2.

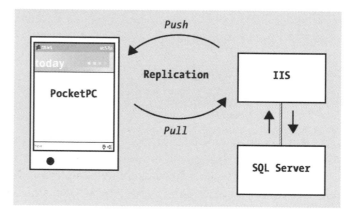

*Figure 16-2. Pocket PC to SQL Server, and back again*

Follow these steps:

1. Create a directory on your hard disk named Chapter16RDA.

2. Navigate to \Program Files\Microsoft SQL Server CE\Server.

3. Verify the existence of a file named sscesa10.dll—this is the Server Agent component. It is this component that enables replication via IIS.

4. Copy sscesa10.dll to the Chapter16RDA directory.

5. In the Chapter16RDA directory, issue the following command:

```
regsvr32 sscesa10.dll
```

6. Open the Windows Control Panel.

7. Double-click Internet Services Manager.

8. Expand the left-hand navigational tree until you find Default Web Site.

9. Right-click Default Web Site, and choose New and then Virtual Directory from the pop-up context menus.

10. Click Next.

11. Enter C16RDA as the alias, and then click Next.

12. Locate the Chapter16RDA directory using Browse, and then click Next.

13. Enabled Execute permissions *only*, and then click Next.

14. Click Finish.

At this point, you should be able to start sharing data between the Pocket PC and the instance of SQL Server running on your development box. The application that we would like you to take a look at is called SimpleRDA. RDA stands for *Remote Data Access*. This is the technology used by SQL Server CE to replicate data with server-side instances of the full SQL Server product.

What you should take away from this sample is the sense that although interacting with a SQL Server database using RDA is devastatingly simple, it is *not* intended as a 100 percent real-time affair. Instead, the proposed workflow for interacting with a server-side database is as follows:

1. Pocket PC grabs a certain amount of data off the server.

2. Applications on the Windows CE device manipulate this data offline.

3. The device reconnects to the network at some point.

4. Changes made to the data since Step 1 are uploaded back to the server.

5. Repeat Steps 1 through 4.

To try out the SimpleRDA sample, simply navigate to the \Program Files\Microsoft SQL Server CE\Samples\eVB\SimpleRDA directory. Within this directory, you should find an eMbedded Visual Basic project named evbSimpleRDA. Double-click this icon to start an instance of the eVB development environment that will load this project immediately upon opening.

Click the Debug button to start the application. We recommend running it in the "old-fashioned" eMbedded Pocket PC emulator to begin with, even if you own an actual Pocket PC. This way, you can straighten out any difficulties with IIS or your instance of SQL Server in complete isolation from any strange networking connectivity issues that your Pocket PC hardware might experience.

The first tab on the SimpleRDA application is shown in Figure 16-3. Here, you are being asked to specify the name of a database that is local to your Pocket PC. Alternatively, you can create an empty one from this same interface. Because this is your first time using SQL Server CE, you probably don't have a local database yet, so let's create one.

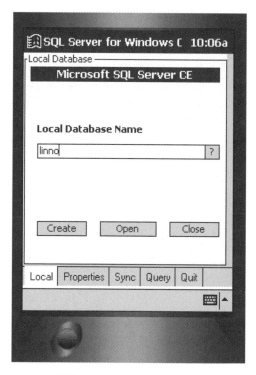

*Figure 16-3. Creating a new SQL Server CE database*

Simply type the name "linno" in the textbox, and then click Create. The application informs you that your DB has been created. Now, click Open to make this database the one that you will be working with, and you are all set to proceed to the next tab, Properties.

There are several blanks on this screen, and they can be quite misleading, so Table 16-1 gives an explanation of each.

*Table 16-1. Properties Fields Explained*

| CAPTION | MEANING | EXAMPLE |
|---|---|---|
| Internet URL | The URL that someone would have to type in his or her Web browser to access the sscesa10.dll file that you installed and configured in the previous section. | http://203.112.8.32/C16RDA/sscesa10.dll |
| DB Server | The name of the full version of SQL Server that is running on your development PC. This should be the one you installed in Chapter 8 with the "/NETSDK" suffix. | Brighton/NETSDK |
| DB Name | The name of the specific database within SQL Server to which you wish to connect. Try GrocerToGo. | GrocerToGo |
| DB UserId | The SQL Server user ID with which you want to connect. We **strongly** urge you to use "sa" first. | sa |
| DB Password | The password for the SQL Server user id chosen above. If you are using "sa" and "GrocerToGo," then leave this blank. | |

**TIP** *Using* localhost *in your Internet URL doesn't always seem to work. Try the static IP for your machine instead. If you don't know this, use the command* ipconfig *to discover it.*

And now, the moment of truth is upon you. Click the third tab, Sync, to get to the area where you will first attempt connecting to your server-side database. At the top of the screen, there is a Table Name drop-down menu. Try expanding this. If it works, congratulations—you have connected to your server-side SQL Server database. If you get an error message, return to the previous tab and fiddle with your settings until you get it right. (This is the hardest part—it took us about 15 minutes of playing around.)

The Pull and Push buttons further down on the screen indicate the two functions of database replication that are available under SQL Server CE. Typically, data is pulled to the device before it goes offline. The altered data is then pushed back to the server the next time it is connected.

To see how this works, find a table in your database (try Products) and click Pull. Due to restrictions on the kinds of tables that can be properly pulled, you may get an error on the first several tables you try. Eventually, you will find one that works. At this point, you should proceed to the next tab.

The Query tab, as shown in Figure 16-4, allows you to issue commands again the *local* copy of data that you have just pulled down from the server. Enter some text here that can be reasonably expected to alter the data on your server and click Execute. If you get a message indicating success, then you are ready to try pushing your changes back to the server.

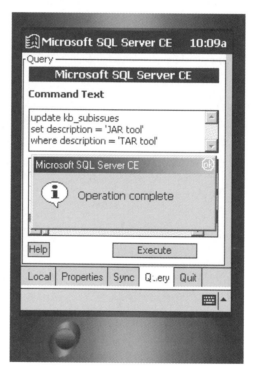

*Figure 16-4. Altering your local data*

Return to the Sync tab and click Push. At this point, the changes you made on the Query tab should be sent back up to the server. You have now seen a miniature version of how server-side data is accessed wirelessly using SQL Server CE. In a real-world application, however, the amount of time between a pull and a push of the data could easily stretch into hours, days, weeks, or even months.

### *Delving into ADOCE*

Since the initial outline for this book was written, the data objects used by the preceding SQL Server CE example have already become somewhat obsolete. As discussed earlier, ADO.NET is now the standard for accessing Microsoft databases. As detailed more later, there will shortly be a managed provider for SQL Server CE that provides ADO.NET support for .NETcf applications.

The preceding sample uses a technology known as Active Data Objects for Windows CE (ADOCE). ADOCE was a special version of Microsoft's legacy ADO technology specially adapted to work with Windows CE–powered devices. If you have not yet begun developing SQL Server CE applications and can afford to wait a bit, then we strongly advise you to wait for the availability of .NETcf's SQL Server CE Managed Provider before you begin your development.

**TIP** *For those of you who absolutely cannot afford to wait, the following article on Microsoft's MSDN Web site provides an excellent overview of developing applications for SQL Server CE using this older technology. It is called "Programming with ADOCE" and is available at the following URL:* `http://msdn.microsoft.com/library/en-us/adoce31/html/adoguide_9.asp`.

## Connecting to the Server

In the preceding examples, you saw how to manipulate data that was on the device. We also alluded to SQL Server CE's abilities to exchange this data with an instance of SQL Server running on a desktop machine. In this section, we will drill down into the details of how desktop SQL Server data can be accessed from Windows CE devices.

### SQLXML

The first way to access desktop SQL Server is via SQLXML. SQLXML is the means by which desktop SQL Server is capable of exchanging data over the Internet (wireless or otherwise) in the form of XML.

## SQL Server CE Replication

When you use SQL Server CE replication to exchange data between a SQL Server database running on your device and one running on a desktop, the details of SQLXML usage are hidden from you. Nevertheless, they are still the driving force behind all of your data exchanges.

The bit of SQL Server that conceals the details of the XML transfers from you is the sscesa10.dll component that you installed in the previous section. This component knows how to receive XML data that is sent from by SQL Server CE and convert it into specific commands to manipulate the data in your desktop SQL Server database.

This component also knows how to pull data out of SQL Server in the form of XML and feed it back to your device. The ADOCE code on your device is then capable of parsing the data out of this XML and using it to modify the data in the SQL Server CE database on your device.

## Direct Access

At this point, we are in a good position to "take a look under the hood" and see exactly what sscesa10.dll does behind the scenes to transfer data to and from a server-based SQL Server.

### Configuring the Server

In order to configure SQL Server's XML support via IIS, follow this procedure:

1.  Open the Microsoft SQL Server program group under the Windows Start menu.

2.  Select Configure SQL XML Support in IIS.

3.  Expand the left-hand navigational tree down to Default Web Site.

4.  Right-click the Default Web Site icon, and choose New and then Virtual Directory from the pop-up context menu.

5.  On the General tab, name your virtual directory Chapter16Example.

6.  Choose your IIS Web server's root directory (typically, \inetpub\wwwroot is the local path for your new virtual directory).

7.  On the Security tab, enter the user name **sa.**

8. Switch to the Data Source tab (confirming your blank password, if asked).

9. Choose the \NETSDK local SQL Server instance and the GrocerToGo database on the Data Source tab.

10. On the Settings tab choose to allow URL queries.

11. Click OK.

### Trying It Out

Under Internet Explorer, if you now navigate to the following URL: `http://localhost/Chapter16Example?SQL=select+*+from+products+for+xml+auto`, you will probably get an error on your display. This is just Internet Explorer's way of saying that the XML being returned is not formatted 100 percent acceptably for its display capabilities. Nonetheless, if you now choose Source from Internet Explorer's View menu, you will see a great deal of XML, as shown in Figure 16-5.

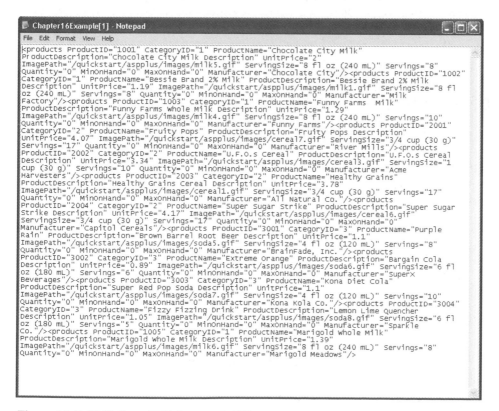

*Figure 16-5. XML from SQL Server via IIS*

You have now seen how sscesa10.dll exchanges data with desktop SQL Server over the wireless Internet.

## The Future

At this point, you have seen most of the technologies that are currently available for data access from Windows CE devices as of the time of writing. The only currently available thing that you *haven't* seen yet is discussed in the exercise at the end of this chapter. Before that, however, let's take a moment to describe two important bits of .NETcf code that will soon be making data access from devices much easier.

### The SQL Managed Provider

Microsoft has plans to port its .NET managed provider for SQL Server to the .NETcf platform. This will mean that all of the data access objects demonstrated in Listings 16-1 through 16-4 will soon be available for use right from your Windows CE–powered devices. The main benefit to this is that for the first time, Windows CE application developers will be able to have real-time access to their server-side databases.

> **TIP** *Of course, PocketDBA users have had real-time access to their databases for about a year now! Though in all fairness, our tools are geared more at administration than data access.*

The only potential negative in Microsoft's announced plans is that SQL Server will be the *only* database targeted for device-side managed providers. This means that if your data is stored in an Oracle database, for example, you will not be able to use the managed provider created by Microsoft for .NETcf.

> **TIP** *You have a few options in this case. One of which is to use the OLE DB provider on the server and access it via a Web Service (as shown in the exercise at the end of the chapter). Another alternative would be to replicate some of your data between your non-SQL Server data source and a SQL Server database that can act as a gateway for your device-based applications. The final option is to hope that your database vendor will ultimately produce its own managed provider for .NETcf.*

## The SQL CE Managed Provider

As you got a taste of earlier in this chapter, writing ADOCE code to interact with your SQL Server CE databases can be quite different from writing .NET code. Thankfully, Microsoft has plans to soon create a managed provider for SQL Server CE as well. This will hopefully allow you to interact with your SQL Server CE databases using almost exactly the same kind of .NET code that you would use to interact with the full version of SQL Server.

The only bad thing about the SQL CE Managed Provider is that as of the time of writing it is not yet available. In fact, Microsoft's schedule doesn't call for the SQL CE Managed Provider to become available until well after the release of the full SQL Server Managed Provider for .NETcf.

## .NETcf DataSets via Web Services

Skipping back now to ways in which you can currently connect to server-side data from Windows CE devices, we will demonstrate our favorite method via an end-of-chapter (end-of-book, in fact) exercise.

### Exercise

In this exercise, we will pull a `DataSet` containing our favorite progressive rock bands and their members from a SQL Server database running on our desktop. This `DataSet` will be delivered to our device via a .NET Web Method. After being modified on the device, another .NET Web Method will be used to return the modifications to our server.

## Writing the Server

The server portion of our application is represented by a .NET Web Service.

### The Code

Listing 16-6 shows the code for the Progressive Rock Web Service.

*Listing 16-6. The Progressive Rock Web Service*

```
Imports System.Web.Services
Imports System.Data.SqlClient
```

```vb
<WebService(Namespace:="http://pocketdba.com/webservices/")> Public Class Service1
    Inherits System.Web.Services.WebService

    <WebMethod()> Public Function getBands() As DataSet

        Dim strCnnctn As String
        Dim sqlCnnctn As SqlConnection

        strCnnctn = "Initial Catalog=GrocerToGo;"& _
Data Source=Brighton\NETSDK;user id=sa;"
        sqlCnnctn = New SqlConnection(strCnnctn)
        sqlCnnctn.Open()

        Dim strCmmnd As String
        Dim sqlCmmnd As SqlCommand

        strCmmnd = "select * from bands"
        sqlCmmnd = New SqlCommand(strCmmnd, sqlCnnctn)

        Dim sqlDA As SqlDataAdapter
        sqlDA = New SqlDataAdapter(sqlCmmnd)

        Dim sqlDS As DataSet
        sqlDS = New DataSet()
        sqlDA.Fill(sqlDS)

        sqlCnnctn.Close()

        getBands = sqlDS

    End Function

    <WebMethod()> Public Function updateBands(ByVal ds As DataSet) As Boolean

        Try

            Dim strCnnctn As String
            Dim sqlCnnctn As SqlConnection
```

```
            strCnnctn = "Initial Catalog=GrocerToGo;"& _
Data Source=Brighton\NETSDK;user id=sa;"
            sqlCnnctn = New SqlConnection(strCnnctn)
            sqlCnnctn.Open()

            Dim strCmmnd As String
            Dim sqlCmmnd As SqlCommand

            strCmmnd = "select * from bands"
            sqlCmmnd = New SqlCommand(strCmmnd, sqlCnnctn)

            Dim sqlDA As SqlDataAdapter
            sqlDA = New SqlDataAdapter(sqlCmmnd)

            Dim scb As SqlCommandBuilder = New SqlCommandBuilder(sqlDA)

            sqlDA.Update(ds)

            sqlCnnctn.Close()

        Catch problem As Exception

            updateBands = False
            Exit Function

        End Try

        updateBands = True

    End Function

End Class
```

## The Walk-Through

In order to use the Progressive Rock Web Service, you must first have a table in SQL Server that can hold your data. To create an appropriate table in SQL Server as well as the Progressive Rock Web Service, follow these steps:

1. Start the VS .NET IDE.

2. Click New Project.

3. Select the Visual Basic ASP.NET Web Service icon.

4. Name your Web Service ProgRock and click OK.

5. Once the Design view for your Web Service appears, expand the Server Explorer toolbar on the left of the VS .NET window.

6. Expand the nodes for Servers, your computer, SQL Servers, the database ending in \NETSDK, and the GrocerToGo database.

7. Verify that your Server Explorer looks like Figure 16-6.

8. Right-click the Tables icon beneath GrocerToGo.

9. Choose New Table.

10. Fill out the New Table design form as shown in Figure 16-7.

11. Make the ID column the primary key and the identity for this table (as shown at the bottom of Figure 16-7).

12. Close the New Table design form.

13. When prompted to name your table, name it Bands and click OK.

14. Once you have returned to Design View, click the link to enter Code View.

15. Replace all of the existing code with the code from Listing 16-6—making sure to replace both instances of the word "Brighton" with the name of your own computer!

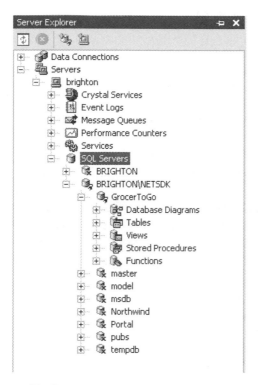

*Figure 16-6. The Server Explorer*

*Figure 16-7. The New Table design form*

Once you have entered all of the code, you should be able to run your new Web Service from the VS .NET environment to test it a bit. You can invoke the getBands Web Method from the test page provided by .NET. If you see a bunch of XML output when you do so, this means that you have done it properly.

## Writing the Client

All that we have to do to create our client is make a few, very minor modifications to the Band Recorder code from Listing 16-5.

### The Code

Listing 16-7 shows the code for retrieving data from the server, and Listing 16-8 shows the code for sending data back to the server.

*Listing 16-7. Getting the Data from the Server*

```
Private Sub Form1_Load(ByVal sender As System.Object, ByVal e As
System.EventArgs) _

Handles MyBase.Load

        Dim x As localhost.Service1 = New localhost.Service1()
        ds = x.getBands()
        dt = ds.Tables(0)


        Try


            dr = dt.Rows(0)
            txtGuitar.Text = dr("Guitar")
            txtKeyboards.Text = dr("Keyboards")
            txtBass.Text = dr("Bass")
            txtDrums.Text = dr("Drums")
            txtVocals.Text = dr("Vocals")


        Catch problems As Exception


            dr = dt.NewRow()
            isNew = True


        End Try
```

```
        rn = 0

    End Sub
```

*Listing 16-8. Sending Changes Back to the Server*

```
Private Sub btnQuit_Click(ByVal sender As System.Object, ByVal e As _
System.EventArgs) _Handles btnQuit.Click

    saveCurrentRow()

    Dim x As localhost.Service1 = New localhost.Service1()
    x.updateBands(ds.GetChanges())

End Sub
```

## The Walk-Through

As you can see from Listings 16-7 and 16-8, only two procedures in the entire application required modification. The first of these is the procedure that runs right when our application is first started: Form1_Load. The other is the procedure that runs right before our application terminates: btnQuit.

In the case of the Load procedure, it begins by instantiating an instance of the new Web Service and using its getBands method to populate the DataSet. Because our Web Method will return a DataSet regardless of whether or not there is data in the table (it will be an empty DataSet in that case), we needn't worry about not having a DataSet at the end of our efforts.

Instead, we proceed immediately to setting the DataRow variable to the first row in the DataSet. At this point, if the DataSet was empty, our attempt to access its first row will fail and the code in the Catch block will be invoked to create a new, empty row from scratch. Otherwise, the text fields will be populated with the contents of the first row.

The code in the Quit routine is devastatingly simple. As before, the current contents of the text fields are saved to the current DataRow. Then, an instance of our new Web Service is created. Finally, just the changes in our DataSet are extracted (in the form of an implicit DataSet) and passed to the GetChanges method of our Web Service.

Once you're comfortable creating Mobile .NET software, you are bound to want to share your inventions with other people. To do this, you are going to have to find someplace to host it on the Internet. To provide a suitable Web hosting environment for your software, your host must have at least two things installed:

- Visual Studio.NET

- The Mobile Internet Toolkit

Thankfully, the Web hosting service Brinkster (http://www.brinkster.com) is providing *free* hosting for sites with exactly these requirements. Better yet, the ability to upload your application to Brinkster.com is available right from within the Visual Studio.NET application. Just choose "Web Hosting" from the Visual Studio.NET start page and follow the link to Brinkster to setup your free account.

**NOTE:** *Brinkster has certain requirements about the naming of your project and some of its settings. You can get their most recent requirements off the documentation and support portions of their Web-site. If you don't follow these requirements, your Mobile Web Applications and Mobile Web Services will not work!*

## Final Thoughts

This brings us to the end of *Mobile .NET*. I hope you have found it as informative and enjoyable to read as I did to write. If you have any questions, comments, or suggestions whatsoever, please do not hesitate to contact me at derekf@speakeasy.net. Furthermore, I will be trying to maintain a site at http://www.mobiledotnet.com with all the latest news from the world of Mobile .NET—including my numerous speaking appearances. If you ever happen to be at a conference where I'm speaking, by all means make sure to stop by to say hello and let me know all about your Mobile .NET development experiences!

# APPENDIX A

# XML

## The ASCII of Tomorrow

OF ALL THE CRAZES THAT HAVE swept Internet development over the last several years, perhaps none have generated quite as much excitement as XML. Almost without doubt, none have generated anywhere near the degree of confusion. It is no overstatement to say that many of the people now championing XML as the solution to all developers' problems have absolutely no idea what they're talking about—much less why XML should really be the solution to anything.

It is our hope that, with this short appendix, we can elevate you from the realm of XML idolizers into the sphere of the truly XML knowledgeable. No short appendix can aim to make you an expert on XML, but after reading this you should at least have enough of an understanding of XML to completely understand what this technology can and cannot do to help you in your development efforts.

## About XML Document Structure

We'd like to begin with a sample of an XML document, shown in Figure A-1.

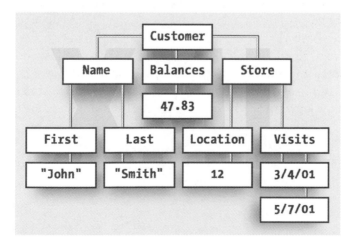

*Figure A-1. An XML document*

If you are a developer who has been casually following the development of XML over the last few years, this document may surprise you. Where are the tags? Where is the text? How would you even input a thing like this into your computer? Is this some sick kind of joke or horrible editing error on APress' part?

The reason you may be shocked is that, like most developers, you have been confused by the lax way in which the development media have reported to and educated the public regarding what XML is. The focus of XML is *not* any particular way of representing data, regardless of what you may have been lead to believe. Rather, XML is about how data may be structured for ease and efficiency of exchange between arbitrary (often automated) processes. The rules for this structure are typically embodied within the XML Infoset.

## Understanding the Infoset

The XML Infoset is the top-level Internet standard that defines what XML is at its most basic level. For this reason, understanding the Infoset is the key to understanding XML. You might think of it as being to XML what the United States Constitution is to the American legal system. There is a lot more to learn, but XML has its foundation in this critical document.

 **TIP**  *The World Wide Web Consortium (W3C) maintains the specification for the XML Infoset. If you are interested in following the development of this standard as it progresses, you may grab it directly off the Internet. Browse to* `http://www.w3.org/TR/xml-infoset`.

The Infoset tells us two important things about XML. To begin with, it tells us that XML is about data, not presentation. Secondly, it tells us that this data must be arranged in a strictly hierarchical fashion.

## It Is All about Data

Most developers nowadays have at least some passing familiarity with HTML. HTML is the markup language that allows browsers to know the exact formatting and layout of text and graphics to appear on a given Web page. This is all fine and well, except for a few problems:

- How can browsers deal with differences in hardware?

- How can pages deal with differences in browsers?

- How can automated processes deal with changes in Web pages?

As one example, imagine a situation in which a Web page has been designed to act as a form for accepting patients' medical records. On some computers with very large screens and good resolution, this form may work wonderfully. Adequate space will be available for patients to enter all of their information without any difficulty.

We can further assume that this page is being viewed by exactly the right browser—perhaps Internet Explorer—for which it was originally designed. All of the special presentation features that Internet Explorer offers are available and the full functionality of the form is therefore as it should be.

But what about cases in which these two assumptions do *not* hold true? What about computers with smaller screens—perhaps even small mobile devices? On these devices, two things will get in the way of proper page viewing. First, the screen will be too small for the patients to see all of the fields on the form. Secondly, all of the special Internet Explorer–only features will be completely lost because a different browser will be used on the mobile phone.

Even in cases where the browser and system match the page's requirements perfectly, problems can still arise. Suppose the form is being used indirectly rather than directly at some doctor's offices. At these places, information is entered into a different application, which then attempts to connect to and automatically fill out the Web page itself. Figure A-2 shows how this architecture might be arranged.

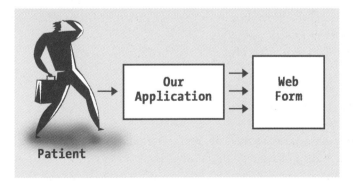

*Figure A-2. Automated Web page access*

Now, suppose that the form is changed for some reason. Using standard HTML, this would almost certainly cause the client application to break. This is true because HTML is all about *presentation*, so even the smallest changes in the look of a page require changes to their structure.

By way of contrast, XML is a data-centric markup language. The specifications on the XML Infoset say *nothing* about how data should be presented for consumption either by human beings or by automated processes. This means that regardless of the device you are using, XML documents should work as platform-independently as imaginable.

Specifically, the XML Infoset specification allows for the presence of 15 distinct kinds of data in an XML document. Some of the more common of these types of data are described in Table A-1.

*Table A-1. Data Permissible in XML Documents*

| DATA TYPE | PURPOSE |
| --- | --- |
| Document | Wrapper data type for all other elements |
| Element | In-line data corresponding to one real-world object |
| Attribute | A characteristic property of an element |
| Processing Instruction | Data for consumption by XML parsing tool only |
| Characters | Raw, unformatted low-level data—read by parsers |
| Comments | Data for consumption by human readers only |
| Document Type Declaration | A reference to DTD formatting data (see later in this appendix) |
| Entity | A reference to an external data entity |
| Notation | A macro reference to another data piece |
| CDATA | Raw, unformatted low-level data—ignored by parsers |
| Namespace Declaration | A qualification of data in a document within a specific data sphere |

## It Is Hierarchical

The structure of data under XML is strictly hierarchical. This means that every node of data is contained within some other node and may also serve as a container for additional nodes. For example, consider the data in Figure A-1.

In this figure, you can see that every customer has a name. Each name may comprise a first and last name. This is just one example of arranging data hierarchically. Similarly, if you look at the customer's stores (meaning where they have been), you will see that this winds up encompassing several nodes within nodes.

One key advantage to this kind of data organization is that it can easily be serialized for transfer across networks such as the Internet. Similar attempts at transferring data structured as tables across slow network connections have historically proven less than successful.

## How XML Is Serialized

Now that you know what kind of data can be put into XML documents, it is time to travel back into more familiar territory. Recall that in Figure A-1, we showed you an XML document that may have defied your previous understanding of how XML documents are supposed to look. The reason is that in XML, the serialization format is clearly distinguished from the data within the documents.

### It Is Similar to HTML

Although XML may be serialized in virtually any manner that developers care to code for themselves, there is in fact one officially sanctioned format that seems to be vastly more popular than any of the other formats out there—specifically, the transfer syntax described in the "XML 1.0 and Namespaces in XML" specification. Listing A-1 shows an example of an XML document using this format.

*Listing A-1. XML for My Album Collection*

```
<?xml version='1.0' ?>
<albumcollection>
    <record name='The Wake' artist='IQ'>
        <song length=8.29>Outer Limits</song>
        <song length=3.50>The Wake</song>
        <song length=6.33>The Magic Roundabout</song>
        <song length=6.22>Corners</song>
        <song length=9.10>Widow's Peak</song>
        <song length=4.00>The Thousand Days</song>
        <song length=7.27>Headlong</song>
    </record>
    <record name='Anoraknophobia' artist='Marillion'>
        <song>Between You and Me</song>
        <song>Quartz</song>
```

```
      <song>Map of the World</song>
      <song>When I Meet God</song>
      <song>The Fruit of the Wild Rose</song>
      <song>Seperated Out</song>
      <song>This is the 21st Century</song>
      <song>If My Heart Were a Ball, It Would Roll Uphill</song>
   </record>
</albumcollection>
```

If this is your first exposure to XML, you might be struck at first by its similarity to HTML. The format of the tags is certainly familiar: a less-than sign, followed by the name of tag, concluded with a greater-than sign. Beyond this, XML uses the same set of symbols for so-called closing tags, which are the same as opening tags except with a slash in front of the tag name. Finally, like HTML, parameters within tags follow this format:

```
Parametername = value
```

## But the Rules Are Stricter

One key difference in syntax between serialized XML and HTML, however, is in the strictness of the rules regarding their structure. HTML is designed to be as forgiving as possible, partly to make things easier on less technically inclined authors—HTML was envisioned as the language that would allow everyone to make their information available to the world via the Internet. Also, by being forgiving, HTML allows itself to be run on the widest variety of browsers possible, even if differences in tags understood varied greatly from one browser to the next.

XML doesn't take into consideration either of these factors to anywhere near the same extent. XML was envisioned right from the start as a protocol that would be both created and received by software, rather than human beings. For this reason, XML syntax does not need to be nearly as forgiving.

Also, unlike HTML, XML was never intended to describe things like graphics and fonts that might vary from one platform to the next. XML describes data—and data should (theoretically) be the same regardless of what platform you're on.

Some of the key rules in creating XML documents are as follows:

- An XML document must always begin with the XML version processing instruction.

- Every opening tag must have a matching closing tag.

- There must be exactly one top-level node in every XML document.

- Node names must begin with a letter or an underscore.

## Defining XML Document Structures

The rules listed in the preceding section are just the rules defined by XML for the creation of any and all XML documents. Early on in the development of XML, it became clear that authors should have the ability to define their own rules specific to their particular document types. For example, consider the variation of our previous XML example in Listing A-2.

*Listing A-2. What the Heck Does This Mean?*

```
<?xml version='1.0' ?>
<record name='The Wake' artist='IQ'>
    <albumcollection>
        <song length=8.29>Outer Limits</song>
        <song length=3.50>The Wake</song>
    </albumcollection>
</record>
```

According to the rules of XML, this is a perfectly valid document. Load it into any XML parser and it will work fine. However, it really doesn't make any sense. Because we're human beings, we can tell that it doesn't make any sense to have an album collection inside a single record. Instead, a single album collection should contain multiple records.

## The Original Solution Was the DTD

Conveying business rules like this to standard XML parsers is the purpose of a special kind of document called a Document Type Definition (DTD). DTDs allow you to specify the exact ordering and cardinality requirements of each of the nodes in your XML documents. So, for example, you could create a DTD that specifically stipulated that album collections may (or must) contain records, but never the other way around.

Similarly, DTDs can be used to define the parameters that are allowed and/or expected on various nodes. We could stipulate that every song on every record in our collection must have a length associated with it. Or, we could make that parameter completely optional.

Since DTDs are not Microsoft's preferred way of specifying XML syntax rules, we will not cover them at any length here. For more information, please consult the excellent on-line tutorial at:

```
http://www.spiderpro.com/bu/buxmlm001_dtd.html
```

## Now We Have Schemas

Microsoft's preferred way of specifying syntax rules for XML documents is through use of the XML schema. Schemas were originally designed to overcome a very simple limitation in XML and DTDs: lack of data types. For example, take a look at the following line from an XML document:

```
<vegetable name="carrot" calories=244>
```

Now, suppose that you wanted to tell someone how to create a similar line of XML. You might tell this person over the phone, "It's a vegetable node, and it takes a name parameter and a calories parameter." He or she might listen to you, and then create an XML document to send to some application that you are running that would contain this line. Unfortunately, the person might produce the line as follows:

```
<vegetable name="carrot" calories="266">
```

The problem (which is subtle) is that this person has stored calories inside of a string rather than as a numeric value. Depending on how your code to read this document operates, this either may or may not be a problem. In professional software design, however, issues like this should never be left to chance.

So, Microsoft collaborated with some other industry leaders to develop XML schemas. Unlike DTDs, XML schemas are themselves XML documents. This allows them to use the rich flexibility of XML's hierarchical data format to define both simple data types (such as integer or string) and compound data types (data types comprising multiple simple data types). For example, you might see the code from Listing A-3 in an XML document.

*Listing A-3. A Snippet from a Schema*

```
<complexType name='album' content='elementOnly' >
    <element name='producer' form='qualified' />
    <element name='band' form='unqualified' />
</complexType>
```

Using this snippet, a developer has defined a type called album. Anywhere the album data type is used in an XML document that is associated with this schema, it must contain two elements: producer and band.

## Using Programmatic Interfaces to XML

Having data in XML documents does you absolutely no good if you can't access this data in some way. As you saw in the previous section, XML was intended right from the beginning to be primarily accessed and used by automation—meaning software applications. So, as you might imagine, there are a number of tools in existence to facilitate the accessing of XML data from custom applications.

The three most popular application-level interfaces to XML data are the following:

- SAX

- DOM

- XSL

### *SAX: the Event-Based Interface*

One of the first programmatic interfaces to XML data is known as SAX. This is short for the Simple API for XML.

#### *How to Play the SAX*

What distinguishes SAX from other XML APIs is that it is event driven. In other words, SAX views the elements in an XML document as being a series of events. For example, here are some of the common events generated by SAX parsers as they interpret XML documents:

- startElement

- endElement

- startPrefixMapping

- endPrefixMapping

- characters

- ignorableWhitespace

- processingInstruction

- skippedEntity

As you can see, the names of the events generated closely correspond to the kinds of elements that are encountered. The typical code for a SAX-based application consists of three steps. First, the document is loaded into the parser. Second, the parser is told to begin processing (typically at the top, or start, of the document). Third, the parser generates events that are implemented by the application for each element as it is encountered.

## What SAX Is Good For

One of the key benefits to an event-based XML parser is that the entire document needn't be loaded into memory at any one point in time. Instead, because the parser reads the document on an element-by-element basis and generates completely discrete events as it goes, the parser can afford to only load in a small part of any document at a time.

Because of this focus on efficiency of resource usage, SAX is a natural choice for implementation on many small devices. Java, in particular, was one of the first platforms targeted by SAX. Even today, the popularity of SAX remains strong in the Java world, regardless of the progress that is made by DOM in almost every other part of the application development world.

# DOM: the Whole-Document Interface

The XML interface with which Microsoft has been most closely associated is the Document Object Model (DOM). Since DOM is also the model that was first "blessed" by the World Wide Web Consortium in the form of its acceptance as a standard, it is in many ways the most important interface to XML from a .NET perspective.

## How to DOMinate Your XML

From a Microsoft standpoint, DOM is "the one to know" in XML parsers. This is true for a few reasons:

- The DOM object model is closely related to Internet Explorer's own DHTML object model.

- Microsoft had a hand in developing the DOM standard for W3C approval.

- DOM was the first interface supported by Microsoft's own XML parser engine.

So, at this point, you are probably curious about how DOM compares to SAX in its usage and benefits. Unlike SAX, DOM is a whole-document interface to XML. This means that DOM parsers typically must load an entire XML document into memory in order to begin processing. The benefits you gain in exchange for this potentially great expense in resources is a much-improved ability to navigate arbitrarily across an XML document.

Listing A-4 shows an example of some DOM-based XML parsing code.

*Listing A-4. Creating a DOM Sales Order Document*

```
// Instantiate an instance of the Microsoft XML parse
var objXML = new ActiveXObject("Microsoft.XMLDOM");
// Load in the entire customer XML document
objXML.load("customer.xml");
// Find the top-level "order" node
var objOrder = objXML.selectSingleNode("/order");
// Look beneath this node to find the items node with a type parameter of 'sale'
var objSalesItem = objOrder.selectSingleNode("items[@type='sale']");
// Create a new element of type "total"
var objTotal = objXML.createElement("total");
// Create a new text element with the value "$32.87"
var objTotalText = objXML.createTextNode("$32.87");
// Append the new text element to the "total" element
objTotal.appendChild(objTotalText);
// Append the "total" element to the Sales Item element
objSalesItem.appendChild(objTotal);
```

You can follow what this code snippet does by reading the comments in the listing. The important thing is the way that the code is able to do searches, creations, and additions in virtually any part of the document at virtually any point in time. This kind of on-the-fly document traversal is made possible by DOM's ability to keep the entire document in memory at once.

### What DOM Is Good For

DOM is probably the best choice for all-around XML parsing. In general, DOM is considered somewhat easier for more experienced developers to pick up because it closely resembles the database manipulation models with which most of us are already familiar.

Probably, a more important thing to know about DOM is when it is an *inappropriate* choice for your applications. One case in which this would be true would be when developing for a device with limited resources. As Figure A-3 illustrates, in cases where memory is limited, SAX can make far more efficient use of a device's resources than DOM can.

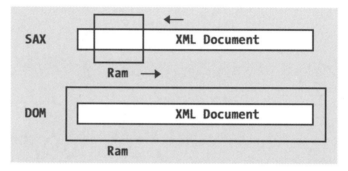

*Figure A-3. SAX vs. DOM*

In the top part of Figure A-3, the XML document is being gradually slid through a limited amount of RAM. This is the SAX approach. In the bottom part of the figure, by contrast, DOM has allocated a chunk of memory that is large enough to encompass the entire XML document at once.

Another case in which DOM would be a poor choice would be whenever the implementation of DOM for a given platform is not as complete or as reliable as the DOM implementation. This is typically the case on non–Microsoft platforms, where SAX was an earlier standard for acceptance.

## XSL: the XML-Based Interface

More often than anything else, XSL is used to translate XML into something else. This might seem rather anti-XML to you, but XML's imminent translatability is actually one of its key strengths. By representing data itself rather than any specific presentation of that data, XML makes itself the perfect intermediary between a whole host of different platforms and architectures. And XSL is the key catalyst in the process.

The key value proposition to XSL is that it constitutes a true XML-based parser for XML itself. This allows you to parse, transform, and otherwise utilize XML without having to learn rules specific to any third-party parser. The rules of XSL are the rules of XML itself. Therefore, the more you know about XML, the easier you will find it to use XSL to do your parsing for you!

One of the most important uses for XSL under .NET is in the XSLISAPI technology. Using XSLISAPI, a single XML document on the server can be translated into appropriate markup for everything from a WAP phone to a full implementation of Internet Explorer. XSLISAPI is thoroughly discussed, with examples of its usage, in Chapter 11.

# Index

# S

# Apress Titles

| ISBN | PRICE | AUTHOR | TITLE |
|---|---|---|---|
| 1-893115-01-1 | $39.95 | Appleman | Appleman's Win32 API Puzzle Book and Tutorial for Visual Basic Programmers |
| 1-893115-23-2 | $29.95 | Appleman | How Computer Programming Works |
| 1-893115-97-6 | $39.95 | Appleman | Moving to VB. NET: Strategies, Concepts, and Code |
| 1-893115-09-7 | $29.95 | Baum | Dave Baum's Definitive Guide to LEGO MINDSTORMS |
| 1-893115-84-4 | $29.95 | Baum, Gasperi, Hempel, and Villa | Extreme MINDSTORMS |
| 1-893115-82-8 | $59.95 | Ben-Gan/Moreau | Advanced Transact-SQL for SQL Server 2000 |
| 1-893115-99-2 | $39.95 | Cornell/Morrison | Programming VB .NET: A Guide for Experienced Programmers |
| 1-893115-71-2 | $39.95 | Ferguson | Mobile .NET |
| 1-893115-90-9 | $44.95 | Finsel | The Handbook for Reluctant Database Administrators |
| 1-893115-85-2 | $34.95 | Gilmore | A Programmer's Introduction to PHP 4.0 |
| 1-893115-17-8 | $59.95 | Gross | A Programmer's Introduction to Windows DNA |
| 1-893115-62-3 | $39.95 | Gunnerson | A Programmer's Introduction to C#, Second Edition |
| 1-893115-10-0 | $34.95 | Holub | Taming Java Threads |
| 1-893115-04-6 | $34.95 | Hyman/Vaddadi | Mike and Phani's Essential C++ Techniques |
| 1-893115-50-X | $34.95 | Knudsen | Wireless Java: Developing with Java 2, Micro Edition |
| 1-893115-79-8 | $49.95 | Kofler | Definitive Guide to Excel VBA |
| 1-893115-56-9 | $39.95 | Kofler | MySQL |
| 1-893115-87-9 | $39.95 | Kurata | Doing Web Development: Client-Side Techniques |
| 1-893115-75-5 | $44.95 | Kurniawan | Internet Programming with VB |
| 1-893115-19-4 | $49.95 | Macdonald | Serious ADO: Universal Data Access with Visual Basic |

| ISBN | PRICE | AUTHOR | TITLE |
| --- | --- | --- | --- |
| 1-893115-06-2 | $39.95 | Marquis/Smith | A Visual Basic 6.0 Programmer's Toolkit |
| 1-893115-22-4 | $27.95 | McCarter | David McCarter's VB Tips and Techniques |
| 1-893115-76-3 | $49.95 | Morrison | C++ For VB Programmers |
| 1-893115-80-1 | $39.95 | Newmarch | A Programmer's Guide to Jini Technology |
| 1-893115-58-5 | $49.95 | Oellermann | Architecting Web Services |
| 1-893115-81-X | $39.95 | Pike | SQL Server: Common Problems, Tested Solutions |
| 1-893115-20-8 | $34.95 | Rischpater | Wireless Web Development |
| 1-893115-93-3 | $34.95 | Rischpater | Wireless Web Development with PHP and WAP |
| 1-893115-24-0 | $49.95 | Sinclair | From Access to SQL Server |
| 1-893115-94-1 | $29.95 | Spolsky | User Interface Design for Programmers |
| 1-893115-53-4 | $39.95 | Sweeney | Visual Basic for Testers |
| 1-893115-29-1 | $44.95 | Thomsen | Database Programming with Visual Basic .NET |
| 1-893115-65-8 | $39.95 | Tiffany | Pocket PC Database Development with eMbedded Visual Basic |
| 1-893115-59-3 | $59.95 | Troelsen | C# and the .NET Platform |
| 1-893115-26-7 | | Troelsen | Visual Basic .NET and the .NET Platform |
| 1-893115-54-2 | $49.95 | Trueblood/Lovett | Data Mining and Statistical Analysis Using SQL |
| 1-893115-16-X | $49.95 | Vaughn | ADO Examples and Best Practices |
| 1-893115-83-6 | $44.95 | Wells | Code Centric: T-SQL Programming with Stored Procedures and Triggers |
| 1-893115-95-X | $49.95 | Welschenbach | Cryptography in C and C++ |
| 1-893115-05-4 | $39.95 | Williamson | Writing Cross-Browser Dynamic HTML |
| 1-893115-78-X | $49.95 | Zukowski | Definitive Guide to Swing for Java 2, Second Edition |
| 1-893115-92-5 | $49.95 | Zukowski | Java Collections |

Available at bookstores nationwide or from Springer Verlag New York, Inc. at 1-800-777-4643; fax 1-212-533-3503. Contact us for more information at sales@apress.com.

# Apress Titles Publishing SOON!

| ISBN | AUTHOR | TITLE |
|---|---|---|
| 1-893115-73-9 | Abbott | Voice Enabling Web Applications: VoiceXML and Beyond |
| 1-893115-48-8 | Bischof | The .NET Languages: A Quick Translation Reference |
| 1-893115-67-4 | Borge | Managing Enterprise Systems with the Windows Scripting Host |
| 1-893115-39-9 | Chand/Gold | A Programmer's Guide to ADO .NET in C# |
| 1-893115-47-X | Christensen | Writing Cross-Browser XHTML and CSS 2.0 |
| 1-893115-72-0 | Curtin | Building Trust: Online Security for Developers |
| 1-893115-42-9 | Foo/Lee | XML Programming Using the Microsoft XML Parser |
| 1-893115-55-0 | Frenz | Visual Basic for Scientists |
| 1-893115-36-4 | Goodwill | Apache Jakarta-Tomcat |
| 1-893115-96-8 | Jorelid | J2EE FrontEnd Technologies: A Programmer's Guide to Servlets, JavaServer Pages, and Enterprise JavaBeans |
| 1-893115-49-6 | Kilburn | Palm Programming in Basic |
| 1-893115-38-0 | Lafler | Power AOL: A Survival Guide |
| 1-893115-89-5 | Shemitz | Kylix: The Professional Developer's Guide and Reference |
| 1-893115-40-2 | Sill | An Introduction to qmail |
| 1-893115-43-7 | Stephenson | Standard VB: An Enterprise Developer's Reference for VB 6 and VB .NET |
| 1-893115-68-2 | Vaughn | ADO Examples and Best Practices, Second Edition |

Available at bookstores nationwide or from Springer Verlag New York, Inc. at 1-800-777-4643; fax 1-212-533-3503. Contact us for more information at sales@apress.com.

# Announcing *About VS.NET*—
## the *free* Apress .NET e-newsletter with great .NET news, information, code—and attitude

We guarantee that this isn't going to be your typical boring e-newsletter with just a list of URLs (though it will have them as well).

Instead, *About VS.NET* will contain contributions from a whole slate of top .NET gurus, edited by award-winning, best-selling authors Gary Cornell and Dan Appleman. Upcoming issues will feature articles on:

- Best coding practices in ADO.NET

- The hidden "gotchas" in doing thread programming in VB.NET

- Why C# is (not) a better choice than VB.NET

- What Java can learn from C# and vice versa

*About VS.NET* will cover it all!

This *free* e-newsletter will be the easiest way for you to get up-to-date .NET information delivered to your Inbox every two weeks—more often if there's breaking news!

**apress™**

*books for professionals by professionals™*

## About Apress

Apress, located in Berkeley, CA, is an innovative publishing company devoted to meeting the needs of existing and potential programming professionals. Simply put, the "A" in Apress stands for the "Author's Press™." Apress' unique author-centric approach to publishing grew from conversations between Dan Appleman and Gary Cornell, authors of best-selling, highly regarded computer books. In 1998, they set out to create a publishing company that emphasized quality above all else, a company with books that would be considered the best in their market. Dan and Gary's vision has resulted in over 30 widely acclaimed titles by some of the industry's leading software professionals.

## Do You Have What It Takes to Write for Apress?

Apress is rapidly expanding its publishing program. If you can write and refuse to compromise on the quality of your work, if you believe in doing more then rehashing existing documentation, and if you're looking for opportunities and rewards that go far beyond those offered by traditional publishing houses, we want to hear from you!

Consider these innovations that we offer all of our authors:

- **Top royalties with *no* hidden switch statements**
  Authors typically only receive half of their normal royalty rate on foreign sales. In contrast, Apress' royalty rate remains the same for both foreign and domestic sales.

- **A mechanism for authors to obtain equity in Apress**
  Unlike the software industry, where stock options are essential to motivate and retain software professionals, the publishing industry has adhered to an outdated compensation model based on royalties alone. In the spirit of most software companies, Apress reserves a significant portion of its equity for authors.

- **Serious treatment of the technical review process**
  Each Apress book has a technical reviewing team whose remuneration depends in part on the success of the book since they too receive royalties.

Moreover, through a partnership with Springer-Verlag, one of the world's major publishing houses, Apress has significant venture capital behind it. Thus, we have the resources to produce the highest quality books *and* market them aggressively.

If you fit the model of the Apress author who can write a book that gives the "professional what he or she needs to know™," then please contact one of our Editorial Directors, Gary Cornell (gary_cornell@apress.com), Dan Appleman (dan_appleman@apress.com), Karen Watterson (karen_watterson@apress.com) or Jason Gilmore (jason_gilmore@apress.com) for more information.